Desserts

Favorite Recipes® of
Home Economics Teachers

Hundreds of mouth-watering treats sure to be perfect for any occasion!

© Favorite Recipes Press/Nashville EMS MCMLXXXII
Library of Congress Cataloging in Publication Data
Main entry under title:
Desserts: hundreds of mouth-watering treats sure
  to be perfect for any occasion!
  (Favorite recipes of home economics teachers)
  Includes index.
  1. Desserts. I. Favorite Recipes Press. II. Series.
TX773.D482   1982   641.8'6   82-10343
ISBN 0-87197-141-0

Page 1, recipes on pages 86, 150, 161.
Page 2, recipe on page 57.

Dear Homemaker:

All busy homemakers know the time and concern placed on planning a meal. Still, it's the dessert that is always the show-stopper. That's why Favorite Recipes Press has brought you this new *Desserts* cookbook. It's certain to provide you with hundreds of different ideas that will steal the hearts of your family and guests.

Home Economics Teachers from around the country selected these special recipes to share with you. You'll find traditional favorites that have been in their families for generations as well as all new treats that are the talk of the country. Celebrate a special occasion with a luscious meringue or torte or delight your family with a creamy cheesecake or pudding.

I'm certain you'll find the recipes in every chapter of this new Home Economics Teachers cookbook so tempting you'll want to try them all!

Sincerely,

Mary Jane Blount

Mary Jane Blount
FAVORITE RECIPES PRESS

Board of Advisors

The editors of Favorite Recipes Press want to give special recognition to the following who graciously serve on our Home Economics Teachers' Advisory Board:

Frances Rudd
Supervisor, Home Economics Education
Arkansas Department of Education

C. Janet Latham
Supervisor, Home Economics Education
Idaho State Board of Vocational Education

Catherine A. Carter
Head Consultant, Consumer Homemaking
   Education
Illinois Division of Vocational and
   Technical Education

Barbara Gaylor
Supervisor, Home Economics Education Unit
Michigan Department of Education

Louann Heinrichs
Home Economics Teacher
Greenville High School
Greenville, Ohio

Roberta Looper
1982 President, National
   Association of Vocational Home
   Economics Teachers
Livingston, Tennessee

Phyllis Barton
Past President, National Association
   of Vocational Home Economics
   Teachers
Alexandria, Virginia

Contents

What's for Dessert?

No matter how fancy a dessert looks or tastes — if it doesn't fit the meal or occasion, your efforts are lost. Desserts must be planned carefully. If your menu is simple and informal, relying on subtlety for impact, serve a creamy, sumptuous dessert. But a rich meal with many courses cries out for a light ending, such as a fruit served with a tempting sauce, an icy sherbet, or even tiny fruit tarts.

On the other hand, if you're serving dessert by itself, the sky's the limit! That's when you want to take into consideration the time of year, the occasion, even the weather. After all, who can enjoy a slice of a seven-layer torte with whipped cream at a 10 a.m. summer social? So if the chapter on Meringues and Tortes won't do, turn to Fruit Desserts. If there's no time for last-minute preparation, consider the luscious surprises found among the Refrigerated Desserts . . . and that's only the beginning! For planning ahead, you'll find the Freezing Guide will be especially helpful.

Whatever you serve, be creative. Everyone enjoys trying something new! Here are a few of our favorite suggested recipes found in this book that will be perfect for the occasions when you want dessert to be just right.

When Boss Comes To Dinner

Red Cherry Cheesecake, page 62

Children's Parties

Twinkie Cake, page 174

Desserts For Two

Orange Fluff for Two, page 166

Bridge/Garden Club Meeting

Apple Cake with Butterscotch Pudding, page 16
Lemon Pie, a la Mode, page 203

Church Socials or Desserts For A Crowd

Frozen Fruit Cups, page 180
Peanut Butter Cake for Many, page 37

Teenage Slumber Party

Self-Filled Cupcakes, page 137
Homemade Reeses, page 123

Dinner Party

Peach Flambe with Strawberry Sauce, page 138

Showers

Peppermint Brownies, page 94
Elegant Cream Wafers, page 108

FINISHES WITH FLAIR

Top your next dessert using one of these unusual tips and make it look as good as it tastes!

- Reserve a small amount of the ingredients from the recipe itself, such as nuts or berries, and arrange, whole, over the top of your dessert . . . a show-stopper!

- Toasted slivered almonds are an elegant finish. To prepare, toast on a cookie sheet in a slow oven or brown in a small amount of butter in a medium hot skillet, stirring constantly.

- Want to save calories? Substitute slightly sweetened sour cream for whipped cream for a topping with unusually good flavor.

- For a beautifully tempting pie crust, brush with milk and sprinkle with sugar just before baking.

- Fresh fruit is a handy topper. Arrange slices of apples, bananas, or oranges in an interesting pattern to enhance the appearance of your dessert. But first, dip in a bowl of lemon, orange or grapefruit juice to keep the fruit from turning brown.

- Frosted grapes look so elegant, but are really simple to fix. Wash grapes thoroughly; dip into slightly beaten egg white; then coat with granulated sugar. Dry on waxed paper and refrigerate until needed. Arrange in clusters with real grape leaves for an easy elegant effect.

- Flowers are a beautiful cake decoration. Make sure they are fresh and not sprayed, then cut the stem to 3/4-inch. Arrange prettily on the cake before serving. NOTE: Beware of Lilies of the Valley and Star of Bethlehem which have poisonous properties. Field Daisies last well and are so bright and fresh.

- Keep a quick garnish on hand — toast chopped coconut in a 350-degree oven until lightly brown, stirring once or twice. Cool and freeze in plastic bags to use when needed. Makes a perfect garnish for coconut cream pie or tarts.

- Grate orange, lemon and lime rinds to use as a colorful garnish or flavoring. These freeze well too.

- Don't throw away stale cookies or cake. Crumble and sprinkle over ice cream or puddings for a delicious crunchy taste.

- Sweets you already have on hand are quick dessert toppers. Crush peppermint sticks or hard candy; shave chocolate bars into thin curls; cut up miniature marshmallows or dates; add a dollop of jam or whipped cream. Use your imagination!

- Finish a sponge or angel food cake with a lacey decoration. Place a paper doily on the top; sift confectioners' sugar over it; then carefully lift off the doily. Delicately beautiful!

FLAMING DESSERTS

End your meal in a blaze of glory with a delicious flambe. Fruit is delicious flaming by itself and even better served over creamy ice cream or pound cake. Flaming masterpieces are surprisingly simple if you follow these tips:

- Heat liquor first. Warmed liquor ignites more easily.

- The dessert itself should be heated too, but not smoking when liquor is added.

- Ignite at the table; don't carry a flaming dish. If, by chance, the liquor doesn't flame, don't add more. Additional flavoring will throw the other ingredients out of balance.

- Since the alcohol content vanishes completely while burning, leaving only the flavor, flaming desserts can be eaten even by people who are allergic to alcohol.

SHIPPING HOME-BAKED GOODIES

What a heartwarming surprise to receive a "Care Package" of home-baked goodies. For children away at school . . . relatives in the service . . . grandparents . . . or old friends, it's the perfect gift. But not all desserts travel well, so use these guidelines to make sure your goodies arrive as fresh and pretty as when you packed them.

TIPS TO SUCCESS

- Wrap your treats as soon as they are baked and cooled.

- Skip desserts with lots of eggs, for they change flavor and appearance quickly.

- Use a container slightly larger than the contents. Cushion with crumbled waxed paper between layers ending with waxed paper on top. Seal with strong tape. Coffee cans with plastic covers work well and, if desired, can be cheerfully decorated to highlight an occasion.

- If you send a variety of treats, be sure the heaviest is packed on the bottom.

- Wrap *cookies* individually in plastic wrap or foil, or back-to-back, Bars, rather than thin, crumbly cookies, travel best.

- Choose rich cakes to send, such as moist coffee cakes, pound cake, fruitcake, applesauce, raisin or prune cake. Don't overbake! Avoid layer cakes unless you first cut them into serving slices and wrap each slice individually.

- To ship *cupcakes,* make them into sandwiches by splitting and frosting between the layers rather than on the top.

- Wrap *candies* and *pastries individually.*

- Protect *pies* by covering with an inverted pie plate.

- Seal sauces in covered containers.

- Place your address and the recipient's address on the container; then wrap in brown paper or a cut-up grocery bag. Using waterproof ink, label the package with the mailing address and return address. Cover with clear tape for protection.

- Weigh, then call to check rates charged by the post office versus package delivery services and military delivery services. Depending on where it's going, the cost difference may surprise you.

- Look for a happy phone call or note of thanks!

FREEZING DESSERTS

How in the world can one manage to serve unexpected guests a slice of bubbly hot fruit pie . . . or have a plate full of home-baked cookies ready for children after school . . . when baking is the last thing you had time for today? Freezing is the answer! But plan ahead. Don't launch a frenzied baking spree before your family goes on vacation or on a diet. While most desserts won't spoil if stored longer than recommended, they do start to lose their flavor and texture. Remember: properly seal; then label and date every package you freeze.

DESSERT FREEZING GUIDE

	Preparing For The Freezer	Storage Time	Thawing
Cakes	*Unfrosted:* cool and wrap	3-6 months	At room temperature: quick defrost in the microwave; or in low oven for 10 minutes.
	Frosted: Freeze before wrapping to avoid sticky frosting.	2 months	Thaw in refrigerator overnight, covered loosely with plastic wrap.
Cookies	*Baked:* cool and pack in containers with waxed papers between layers.	6-12 months	In package at room temperature.
	Unbaked: pack dough in freezer containers. Not recommended for meringue-type cookies.	6 months	At room temperature until thawed. Bake as usual.
	Refrigerator: Shape dough into roll. Wrap in moisture-proof material.	6 months	Thaw slightly. Slice and bake.
Meringues	Bake. Package in rigid cartons with cardboard carton between layers.	2 weeks	Use immediately.
Nuts & Dried Fruit	Can be frozen whole, chopped or ground. Wrap in convenient quantities.	6-7 months	At room temperature or in microwave.
Pastry	Fit into pie plate. Bake, if desired. Wrap in moisture-proof material.	2 months	If baked, thaw in a 325-degree oven 8 to 10 minutes. If unbaked, bake as usual.
Pies	*Baked:* Cool. Cover with an inverted pie plate to protect crust and wrap with moisture proof material.	3 months (2 months for Chiffon pies)	Thaw in package at room temperature or cover with foil in a 300-degree oven.
	Unbaked: Treat fruit pies with ascorbic acid to prevent darkening. Do not slit top crust. Proceed as above. Not Recommended: Cream or custard pies.	6 months	Unwrap. Cut vent holes holes in top crust. Bake in a 450-degree oven for 15 minutes; then in a 375-degree oven until done.
Puddings (Fruit or Steamed)	Cool before freezing.	1 year	At room temperature or steam in double boiler.

CUTTING CAKES

The utensil you use in cutting a cake is very important. In shortening cakes, a long-bladed sharp or serrated knife will do a good job. Cakes with frosting which tend to be sticky are cut best with a knife which has been dipped in hot water. Angel food cakes require a serrated blade for ease in cutting.

There is a special way to cut each type of cake in order to get the maximum number of pieces or cuts. The following sketches show how:

Layer Cakes

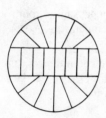

10-inch, 2-layer cake
Yield: 20 servings

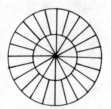

12-inch, 2-layer cake
Yield: 36 servings

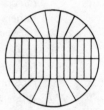

14-inch, 2-layer cake
Yield: 40 servings

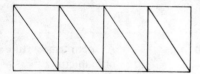

1 pound loaf cake
Yield: 8 servings

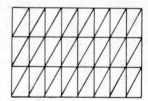

18 x 25-inch cake
Yield: 48 servings

Tier Cakes

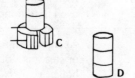

A. Cut vertically through the bottom layer at the edge of the second layer as indicated by the dotted line marked 1; then cut out wedge-shaped pieces as shown by 2.

B. When these pieces have been served, follow the same procedure with the middle layer; cut vertically through the second layer at the edge of the top layer as indicated by dotted line 3; then cut wedge-shaped pieces as shown by 4.

C. When pieces from the second layer have been served, return to the bottom layer and cut along dotted line 5; cut another row of wedge-shaped pieces as shown by 6.

D. The remaining tiers may be cut into the desired size pieces.

Cakes
and Frostings

BEST ANGEL FOOD CAKE

1 3/4 c. egg whites
1 1/4 c. sifted cake flour
1 3/4 c. sugar
1/2 tsp. salt
1 1/2 tsp. cream of tartar
1 tsp. vanilla extract
1/2 tsp. almond extract

Place .... egg whites in large mixer bowl.
Let ...... stand for 1 hour.
Sift ...... flour and 3/4 cup sugar together 4 times.
Beat ..... egg whites with salt and cream of tartar with electric mixer at high speed until soft peaks form.
Add ..... 1 cup sugar, 1/4 cup at a time, beating well after each addition.
Beat ..... until stiff peaks form.
Fold ..... in vanilla and almond extracts.
Sift ...... 1/4 cup flour mixture over egg whites, gently folding into egg whites.
Fold ..... in remaining flour mixture, 1/4 cup at a time, blending well.
Push ..... gently with rubber scraper into 10-inch tube pan.
Cut ...... thru batter twice with knife.
Spread ... batter evenly to edges of pan.
Bake ..... at 375 degrees for 35 to 40 minutes.
Invert .... pan over neck of bottle.
Cool ..... completely before removing from pan.
Yield .... 12-16 servings.

Mrs. Frances Tharpe
North Wilkes H. S., Hays, North Carolina

CHOCOLATE ANGEL FOOD CAKE

3/4 c. cake flour
1/4 c. cocoa
1 1/2 c. sugar
1 1/4 c. egg whites
1 1/2 tsp. cream of tartar
1/4 tsp. salt
1 1/2 tsp. vanilla extract

Sift ...... flour, cocoa and 1/2 cup sugar together 3 times.
Combine . next 3 ingredients in large mixing bowl.

Beat ..... until soft peaks form.
Add ..... remaining 1 cup sugar gradually, beating until stiff.
Fold ..... in flour mixture and vanilla.
Pour ..... into tube pan.
Cut ...... through with knife.
Bake ..... at 325 degrees for 1 hour.
Invert .... to cool.

Frances Woodbine
Fair Acres, Ohio

APPLE CAKE WITH BUTTERSCOTCH TOPPING

1/2 c. shortening
2 c. sugar
2 eggs
1 tsp. vanilla extract
2 c. flour
1 1/2 tsp. soda
1 tsp. each cinnamon, salt
4 c. chopped apples

Cream ... shortening and sugar together in bowl.
Add ..... eggs, 1/2 cup water and vanilla, mixing well.
Sift ...... dry ingredients together.
Stir ...... dry ingredients into creamed mixture; mix well.
Add ..... apples; mix well.
Pour ..... into 9 x 13-inch baking pan.
Bake ..... at 350 degrees for 45 minutes or until cake tests done.

Butterscotch Topping

1/2 c. packed brown sugar
1 egg
2 tbsp. butter, melted
Dash of salt
1 tsp. vanilla extract
4 oz. Cool Whip

Mix ..... brown sugar with egg in bowl, beating well.
Combine . with butter in saucepan.
Cook .... over low heat until thickened, stirring constantly.
Add ..... salt and vanilla.
Cool ..... to room temperature.
Beat ..... cooled mixture into Cool Whip in large bowl.

Pour . . . . . over cake.
Chill . . . . . until serving time.

Mrs. Richard Vaughan
Fairfield H. S., Fairfield, Illinois

APPLE CAKE WITH CARAMEL SAUCE

1/2 c. shortening
3 c. sugar
2 eggs
1/2 tsp. salt
1 tsp. each cinnamon, nutmeg
2 tsp. soda
2 c. flour
1/2 c. walnuts
4 c. diced apples
2 tsp. vanilla extract
1 c. cream
1 c. packed brown sugar
1 c. butter, melted

Cream . . . shortening and 2 cups sugar in bowl.
Add . . . . . eggs 1 at a time, beating well after each addition.
Sift . . . . . . salt, cinnamon, nutmeg, soda and flour together.
Add . . . . . to egg mixture, mixing well.
Stir . . . . . . in walnuts, apples and vanilla.
Pour . . . . . into well-greased 9 x 12-inch baking pan.
Bake . . . . . at 350 degrees for 40 minutes.
Combine . cream, 1 cup sugar, brown sugar and butter in top of double boiler.
Cook . . . . over medium heat until thickened, stirring constantly.
Serve . . . . warm over cake.
Yield . . . . 12-16 servings.

Kathleen Hammer
Cradock H. S., Portsmouth, Virginia

APPLE LOAF CAKE

3 c. flour
1 1/2 tsp. soda
1 tsp. each salt, cinnamon
2 c. sugar
1 1/4 c. oil

2 tsp. vanilla extract
3 eggs
3 c. thinly sliced apples

Sift . . . . . . flour with soda, salt and cinnamon.
Cream . . . sugar, oil and vanilla together in large bowl.
Add . . . . . eggs 1 at a time, beating well after each addition.
Add . . . . . flour mixture alternately with apples, beating well after each addition.
Pour . . . . . into 2 greased loaf pans.
Bake . . . . . at 325 degrees for 1 hour or until cake tests done.

Cheryl Vernon
Ruskin H. S., Kansas City, Missouri

DRIED APPLE CAKE

1 c. butter, softened
2 c. sugar
2 c. blackberry jam
2 1/2 c. cooked dried apples
4 c. flour
2 tsp. each allspice, nutmeg, cinnamon
3 tsp. soda
1 1-lb. box raisins
1 1/2 c. nuts
1 c. chopped dates
2 apples, sliced

Cream . . . butter and sugar in large bowl.
Add . . . . . jam and dried apples, beating well.
Sift . . . . . . together 3 cups flour, spices and soda.
Stir . . . . . . 1 cup of flour with raisins, nuts and dates in bowl, coating well.
Add . . . . . sifted dry ingredients to creamed mixture.
Stir . . . . . . in raisin mixture, blending well.
Pour . . . . . into large, greased and floured tube pan.
Bake . . . . . at 300 degrees for 1 1/2 hours.
Place . . . . pan of water in oven.
Bake . . . . . for additional 1 hour.
Store . . . . cooled cake in airtight container with sliced apples for at least 7 days before serving.
Yield . . . . 18 servings.

Mrs. Nancy Bledsoe
Fordsville H. S., Fordsville, Kentucky

FRESH PEACH COFFEECAKE

1/3 c. peach preserves
2 c. sliced peaches
1 tbsp. lemon juice
Maraschino cherries
1 1/2 c. flour
1/2 c. sugar
1 1/2 tsp. baking powder
1/2 tsp. salt
1/2 tsp. cinnamon
1/2 c. butter, softened
1 egg, slightly beaten
1/2 c. milk
1/2 tsp. vanilla extract
1/2 c. semisweet chocolate Mini Chips

Spread ... preserves in waxed paper-lined 8-inch round baking pan.
Toss ..... peaches with lemon juice in bowl.
Arrange .. on preserves with cherries.
Combine . next 5 ingredients in large bowl.
Cut ...... in butter until crumbly.
Mix ..... egg, milk and vanilla together in bowl.
Add ..... to dry ingredients, stirring until blended.
Stir ...... in chips.
Spread ... over fruit.
Bake ..... at 350 degrees for 40 to 45 minutes or until cake tests done.
Cool ..... in pan for 10 minutes.
Invert .... onto serving plate.
Remove .. waxed paper.
Serve .... warm.

Photograph for this recipe on page 35.

MINI CHIP STREUSEL COFFEECAKE

3/4 c. packed brown sugar
3/4 c. butter, softened
2 1/4 c. flour
1/4 tsp. salt
1/4 tsp. cinnamon
1 c. chopped walnuts
1 c. semisweet chocolate Mini Chips
1 c. sugar
3 eggs
1 tsp. vanilla extract
1 c. sour cream
1 tsp. baking powder
1 tsp. soda

Combine . brown sugar, 1/4 cup butter, 1/4 cup flour, salt and cinnamon in small bowl, stirring until crumbly.
Mix ..... in walnuts.
Reserve .. 1 cup streusel mixture.
Stir ...... 3/4 cup chips into remaining streusel mixture; set aside.
Cream ... 1/2 cup butter and sugar together in large bowl.
Beat ..... in eggs on low speed of electric mixer.
Stir ...... in vanilla and sour cream.
Combine . 2 cups flour, baking powder and soda.
Add ..... to batter, mixing well.
Sprinkle .. reserved 1 cup streusel mixture in greased 10-cup bundt pan.
Spread ... with 1/3 of the batter.
Sprinkle .. with 1 cup chocolate chip streusel.
Repeat ... layers, ending with batter.
Bake ..... at 350 degrees for 55 to 60 minutes.
Cool ..... in pan for 10 minutes.
Invert .... onto serving plate.
Sprinkle .. remaining 1/4 cup Mini Chips on top.

Photograph for this recipe on page 35.

APPLE LAYER CAKE

3 c. sugar
1 c. shortening
4 eggs
Flour
1 tsp. soda
1/2 tsp each salt, cloves, nutmeg
1 tsp. cinnamon
1 tsp. vanilla extract
4 green apples, finely chopped
2 c. milk
2 egg yolks
1 c. nuts

Cream ... 2 cups sugar and shortening in bowl.
Beat ..... in eggs.
Sift ...... 3 cups sifted flour with soda, salt, cloves, nutmeg and cinnamon.
Add ..... to creamed mixture, beating until smooth.
Blend .... in vanilla.

Combine . apples with 1/4 cup warm water.
Fold . . . . . into batter, mixing well.
Pour . . . . . into 3 waxed paper-lined cake pans.
Bake . . . . . at 350 degrees for 1/2 hour.
Combine . milk, 1 cup sugar, egg yolks and 3 tablespoons flour in saucepan.
Boil . . . . . until thick, stirring constantly.
Stir . . . . . . in nuts.
Spread . . . between layers of cake.

Dotty Morgan
Cartersville, Texas

SPICY APPLE BUNDT CAKE

2 c. canned applesauce
1 9-oz. package dried mincemeat
2 pkg. dry yeast
1 c. milk, scalded
2 tbsp. sugar
3 tbsp. shortening
2 tsp. salt
1 c. finely chopped nuts
7 1/2 to 8 c. sifted flour
Confectioners' sugar icing

Combine . first 2 ingredients in saucepan.
Cook . . . . until thick; set aside to cool.
Sprinkle . . yeast over 1/2 cup lukewarm water.
Let . . . . . . stand for 5 minutes.
Stir . . . . . . to blend well.
Combine . next 4 ingredients in bowl, stirring to melt shortening; cool.
Stir . . . . . . in yeast mixture and nuts.
Add . . . . . mincemeat mixture, mixing well.
Beat . . . . . in enough flour to make stiff dough.
Turn . . . . . onto floured surface.
Knead . . . until smooth and elastic.
Place . . . . in greased bowl, turning to grease surface.
Let . . . . . . rise, covered, in warm place until doubled in bulk.
Punch . . . . dough down.
Shape . . . . into long roll.
Place . . . . in well-greased tube pan.
Let . . . . . . rise until doubled in bulk.
Bake . . . . . at 350 degrees for 40 to 45 minutes or until cake tests done.
Cool . . . . . on wire rack.
Spoon . . . confectioners' sugar icing over top.

Photograph for this recipe on page 15.

DIET APPLESAUCE CAKE

1/2 c. butter, softened
1/2 c. sugar
Dry low-calorie sweetener to equal
   1 1/2 c. sugar
2 eggs
2 1/2 c. flour
1 1/2 tsp. soda
1 tsp. salt
1 1/2 c. applesauce
1/2 c. raisins
1/2 c. chopped pecans
1 tsp. vanilla extract

Cream . . . butter, sugar and low-calorie sweetener in bowl until light.
Add . . . . . eggs 1 at a time, beating well after each addition.
Sift . . . . . . dry ingredients together.
Add . . . . . to creamed mixture alternately with applesauce, stirring well after each addition.
Stir . . . . . . in remaining ingredients.
Pour . . . . . into 9 x 13-inch pan.
Bake . . . . . at 350 degrees for 40 to 45 minutes.
Cool . . . . . in pan.

Mrs. J. E. Fleming, Jr.
Marked Tree H. S., Marked Tree, Arkansas

QUICK APPLESAUCE CAKE

4 c. flour
2 c. sugar
1 tsp. each cloves, nutmeg
2 tsp. each soda, cinnamon
1/4 c. cocoa
3 c. applesauce
1 1/2 c. butter, melted
1 c. raisins
1 c. nuts

Sift . . . . . . dry ingredients together in large bowl; set aside.
Add . . . . . applesauce to butter in large bowl, mixing well.
Stir . . . . . . in dry ingredients, raisins and nuts, blending well.
Line . . . . . bottom of tube pan with waxed paper.
Pour . . . . . batter into tube pan.
Bake . . . . . at 325 degrees for 75 minutes.

Mrs. Joan R. Finch
Robert E. Lee H. S., Springfield, Virginia

AVOCADO CAKE

1/2 c. shortening
1 3/4 c. sugar
2 eggs
1/3 c. buttermilk
1 1/2 c. flour
1 tsp. soda
1/2 tsp. each salt, nutmeg, cinnamon, allspice
1 c. mashed avocado
1/2 c. raisins

Cream ... first 3 ingredients in bowl.
Add ..... buttermilk, mixing well.
Sift ...... dry ingredients together.
Blend .... into creamed mixture.
Stir ...... in avocado and raisins.
Pour ..... into greased and floured tube pan.
Bake ..... at 350 degrees for 50 minutes.

Betty Ambrose
Robert E. Lee Sr. H. S., Midland, Texas

BANANA CRUNCH CAKE

3/4 c. oats
Brown sugar
Butter, softened
Chopped nuts
1/2 tsp. cinnamon
1 c. mashed banana
2 eggs
1 tsp. vanilla extract
1 to 1 1/2 c. oats, pulverized
3/4 c. flour
1 tsp. salt
1 tsp. soda

Combine . 3/4 cup oats, 1/3 cup packed brown sugar, 2 tablespoons butter, 2 tablespoons nuts and cinnamon in bowl, mixing well.
Beat ..... 1/2 cup butter and 2/3 cup packed brown sugar in bowl until light and fluffy.
Blend .... in banana, eggs and vanilla.
Combine . 1 cup pulverized oats and remaining dry ingredients in bowl.
Add ..... to creamed mixture gradually, mixing well after each addition.
Stir ...... in 1/2 cup nuts.
Pour ..... into greased 8-inch square baking pan.

Sprinkle .. topping evenly over batter.
Bake ..... at 350 degrees for 40 to 45 minutes or until cake tests done.

Photograph for this recipe on page 104.

BANANA-APPLESAUCE SNACKING CAKE

1/2 c. shortening
1 c. sugar
2 eggs
1/2 c. mashed ripe banana
1/2 c. applesauce
1 tsp. vanilla extract
Flour
3/4 tsp. soda
1/2 tsp. salt
1/4 c. packed brown sugar
1 tsp. cinnamon
1 tbsp. melted butter
1/2 c. broken nuts

Cream ... shortening and sugar together in bowl.
Add ..... eggs 1 at a time, beating well after each addition.
Stir ...... in banana, applesauce and vanilla.
Sift ...... 1 1/2 cups flour with soda and salt.
Stir ...... into batter, mixing well.
Pour ..... into 9 x 9 x 2-inch greased baking pan.
Mix ..... 1 tablespoon flour with remaining ingredients until crumbly.
Sprinkle .. over batter.
Bake ..... at 350 degrees for 30 to 35 minutes or until cake tests done.

Delores Carriere
Irvine School, Irvine, Alberta, Canada

BANANA-WALNUT CAKE

2 1/2 c. sifted cake flour
1 1/4 tsp. baking powder
1 1/4 tsp. soda
1 tsp. salt
Sugar
2/3 c. shortening
1 1/4 c. mashed bananas
2/3 c. buttermilk
2 eggs
2/3 c. chopped black walnuts
2 egg whites

1/4 tsp. cream of tartar
1 tsp. vanilla extract

Sift . . . . . . first 4 ingredients together with 1 2/3 cups sugar in large bowl.
Add . . . . . shortening, bananas and 1/3 cup buttermilk.
Beat . . . . . for 2 minutes, mixing well.
Add . . . . . remaining buttermilk and eggs.
Beat . . . . . for 2 minutes.
Fold . . . . . in walnuts.
Pour . . . . . into 3 greased and floured 9-inch pans.
Bake . . . . . at 350 degrees for 30 minutes or until cake tests done.
Combine . egg whites, 1 1/2 cups sugar, cream of tartar and 1/3 cup water in top of double boiler.
Cook . . . . over boiling water for 7 minutes, beating constantly.
Beat . . . . . in vanilla until of spreading consistency.
Spread . . . between layers, on top and sides of cooled cake.

Dorothy Ann Garrett
Pickett County H. S., Byrdstown, Tennessee

MICROWAVE BANANA CAKE

Butter
16 pecan halves
1/2 c. chopped pecans
2 tsp. light corn syrup
1 pkg. coconut-pecan frosting mix
1 c. packed dark brown sugar
1 c. flour
2 tsp. baking powder
2 eggs, beaten
1 c. mashed bananas

Spoon . . . 1 teaspoon melted butter in 8 x 8-inch glass dish.
Arrange . . pecan halves in dish.
Sprinkle . . chopped pecans over pecan halves.
Drizzle . . . with corn syrup.
Combine . remaining dry ingredients in bowl, mixing well.
Add . . . . . 1/2 cup melted butter, eggs and bananas, blending well.
Pour . . . . . over pecans.
Microwave on High for 10 to 12 minutes, turning 1/4 turn every 4 minutes.

Cool . . . . . and invert on serving plate.
Yield . . . . 10-12 servings.

Eloise Scott
Mooreville H. S., Mooreville, Mississippi

BLUEBERRY PICNIC CAKE

3 c. flour
2 c. sugar
1 c. butter, softened
Grated rind of 1 lemon
1/2 tsp. allspice
1 tbsp. baking powder
1 tsp. salt
3 egg yolks
1 1/2 c. milk
3 egg whites, stiffly beaten
2 c. fresh blueberries, rinsed, drained

Combine . first 2 ingredients in bowl.
Cut . . . . . . in butter until crumbly.
Reserve . . 1 cup for topping.
Add . . . . . lemon rind, allspice, baking powder and salt to remaining crumbs, mixing well.
Beat . . . . . egg yolks and milk in bowl.
Stir . . . . . . into flour mixture, beating until smooth.
Fold . . . . . egg whites into batter.
Pour . . . . . into greased and floured 9 x 13-inch baking pan.
Spoon . . . blueberries on top.
Sprinkle . . with reserved crumbs.
Bake . . . . . at 350 degrees for 40 to 50 minutes or until golden brown.

Photograph for this recipe below.

BLUEBERRY CAKE

1 tsp. butter
1 1/2 c. sugar
1 tsp. cinnamon
2 eggs
1/2 tsp. salt
2 1/2 c. flour
2 tsp. baking powder
1 c. lukewarm milk
2 c. blueberries

Cream ... butter, sugar and cinnamon in bowl.
Beat ..... eggs and salt in bowl.
Add ..... to creamed mixture, blending well.
Sift ...... 2 1/4 cups flour and baking powder together.
Add ..... to creamed mixture alternately with milk, mixing well after each addition.
Combine . blueberries and 1/4 cup flour in bowl.
Fold ..... into batter.
Pour ..... into greased cake pan.
Bake ..... at 350 degrees for 30 minutes.

Mrs. Ruth Hood
A. W. Coolidge Jr. H. S., Reading, Massachusetts

CARROT CAKE

1 1/2 c. oil
2 c. sugar
4 eggs
3 c. finely grated carrots
2 tsp. soda
1 tsp. salt
2 tsp. cinnamon
2 c. flour
8 oz. cream cheese, softened
1 lb. confectioners' sugar
1 stick butter, softened
2 tsp. vanilla extract

Combine . oil and sugar in large mixer bowl.
Add ..... eggs 1 at a time, beating well with electric mixer after each addition.
Stir ...... in carrots.
Sift ...... next 4 dry ingredients together.
Blend .... into batter, mixing well.
Pour ..... into 3 greased and floured layer cake pans.
Bake ..... at 350 degrees for 35 minutes.

Combine . remaining ingredients in large bowl.
Beat ..... until smooth.
Spread ... between layers and over top and sides of cake.
Garnish .. with pecans.

Marilyn Frisbee
Cabool Middle School, Cabool, Missouri

CROWNED CARROT CAKE

1 1/2 c. packed brown sugar
3/4 c. oil
4 eggs
1 to 1 1/2 c. oats, pulverized
1 1/2 c. flour
1 tbsp. baking powder
1 tsp. each salt, allspice, cinnamon
3 c. shredded carrot
3/4 c. raisins
3/4 c. chopped nuts
3 oz. cream cheese, softened
2 tsp. lemon juice
1 c. confectioners' sugar
1 tbsp. milk

Combine . brown sugar and oil in bowl, mixing well.
Add ..... eggs 1 at a time, beating well after each addition.
Stir ...... in 1 cup pulverized oats, flour, baking powder and spices, mixing well.
Mix ..... in carrot and raisins, blending well.
Pour ..... batter into greased nut-coated 12-cup bundt pan.
Bake ..... at 350 degrees for 45 to 50 minutes or until cake tests done.
Cool ..... for 10 minutes before removing from pan.
Cool ..... completely on wire rack.
Blend .... cream cheese and juice in bowl.
Add ..... confectioners' sugar and milk gradually, beating until smooth.
Drizzle ... over cake.

Photograph for this recipe on page 104.

"KAROT" CAKE

2 c. sugar
2 tsp. soda
2 c. flour
2 1/2 tsp. cinnamon
4 eggs

2 1/2 tsp. vanilla extract
1 1/2 c. oil
3 c. grated carrots
1 c. raisins
1 c. walnuts

Combine . first 4 ingredients in bowl.
Add . . . . . eggs, vanilla and oil, mixing well.
Fold . . . . . in remaining ingredients.
Pour . . . . . into greased 9 x 13-inch baking pan.
Bake . . . . . at 350 degrees for 40 to 45 minutes or until cake tests done.

Pat Stenberg
Bingham H. S., South Jordan, Utah

WALNUT-CARROT CAKE

3 c. sifted flour
2 tsp. each baking powder, soda, cinnamon
1/2 tsp. salt
1 c. raisins
1/2 c. coarsely chopped walnuts
2 c. sugar
1 1/4 c. oil
1 tsp. vanilla extract
4 eggs
3 c. grated fresh carrots

Sift . . . . . . first 5 dry ingredients together.
Combine . raisins, walnuts and 2 tablespoons flour mixture in bowl, mixing well.
Combine . sugar, oil and vanilla in large bowl, beating well.
Add . . . . . eggs 1 at a time, beating well after each addition.
Stir . . . . . . in remaining flour mixture alternately with carrots, blending until just smooth after each addition.
Fold . . . . . in raisin mixture.
Pour . . . . . into greased tube pan.
Bake . . . . . at 350 degrees for 1 1/4 hours.
Cool . . . . . for 10 minutes.

Deborah Walsh
Oakdale Jr. H. S., Rogers, Arkansas

CHEW CAKE

4 eggs, beaten
1 box brown sugar
2 c. pecans
2 c. self-rising flour

1 tsp. vanilla extract
Confectioners' sugar

Combine . eggs and brown sugar in saucepan.
Cook . . . . until sugar melts.
Coat . . . . . pecans with small amount of flour.
Add . . . . . with remaining flour to brown sugar mixture.
Stir . . . . . . in vanilla.
Pour . . . . . into greased 9 x 13-inch baking pan.
Bake . . . . . at 300 degrees for 35 to 40 minutes.
Sprinkle . . with confectioners' sugar when cool.

Vanessa L. Robinson
Seabreeze Sr. H. S., Daytona, Florida

CHOCOLATE FRUITCAKE

1 c. butter
2 c. sugar
2 c. mashed potatoes
4 eggs
2 c. flour
1/2 c. cocoa
1 tsp. nutmeg
1/4 tsp. cloves
1 1/2 tsp. cinnamon
2 tsp. soda
1 tsp. salt
3/4 c. sour milk
1 c. mixed candied fruit
2 c. raisins
1 c. chopped nuts

Cream . . . butter and sugar in bowl.
Add . . . . . potatoes and eggs; beat until fluffy.
Mix . . . . . flour, cocoa, spices, soda and salt in bowl.
Add . . . . . dry ingredients alternately with sour milk to creamed mixture.
Stir . . . . . . in fruits and nuts.
Pour . . . . . into 2 greased 9 x 4 x 3-inch loaf pans.
Bake . . . . . at 325 degrees for 1 hour or until cake tests done.
Cool . . . . . and wrap in foil.
Ripen . . . . for several days before serving.
Yield . . . . 2 loaves.

Linda Sue James
R-4 School, Diamond, Missouri

TEATIME CHOCOLATE-RAISIN CAKE

2 1/4 c. sifted flour
1/2 tsp. each cream of tartar, soda
1 tsp. salt
1 1/4 c. sugar
2/3 c. shortening
1/2 c. milk
1 tsp. vanilla extract
1/4 tsp. almond extract
2 1-oz. squares unsweetened chocolate, melted
3 eggs
1 c. California seedless raisins, chopped
Confectioners' sugar

Sift . . . . . . first 5 dry ingredients together into bowl.
Add . . . . . shortening and milk.
Beat . . . . . for 2 minutes.
Add . . . . . flavorings and chocolate.
Beat . . . . . for 1 minute longer.
Add . . . . . eggs 1 at a time, beating well after each addition.
Stir . . . . . . in raisins.
Spoon . . . into greased and floured 9-inch tube pan.
Bake . . . . . at 350 degrees for 65 to 70 minutes.

Sift . . . . . . confectioners' sugar over warm cake.
Cool . . . . . completely before slicing.

Photograph for this recipe on this page.

CHOCOLATE FUDGE CAKE

3 1-oz. squares unsweetened chocolate
Milk
3 eggs
Sugar
1/2 c. shortening
1 tsp. vanilla extract
2 c. flour
1 tsp. soda
1/2 tsp. salt

Combine . chocolate, 1/2 cup milk, 1 egg and 2/3 cup sugar in saucepan.
Bring . . . . to a boil, stirring constantly.
Cream . . . 1 cup sugar and shortening in bowl until light.
Add . . . . . vanilla and remaining eggs, beating well.
Sift . . . . . . flour, soda and salt together.
Add . . . . . to creamed mixture alternately with 1 cup milk, beating well.
Blend . . . . in chocolate mixture.
Pour . . . . . into 2 greased 9 x 12-inch pans.
Bake . . . . . at 350 degrees for 25 to 30 minutes.
Frost . . . . with Fast Fudge Frosting.

Fast Fudge Frosting

1 lb. confectioners' sugar, sifted
1/2 c. cocoa
1/4 tsp. salt
1/3 c. butter, softened
1 tsp. vanilla extract

Combine . first 4 ingredients with 1/3 cup boiling water in bowl, blending well.
Stir . . . . . . in vanilla.

Clara J. Carroll
Des Arc H. S., Des Arc, Arkansas

CHOCOLATE FUDGE UPSIDE-DOWN CAKE

Sugar
2 tbsp. margarine

1/2 c. milk
1 c. self-rising flour
Cocoa
1/2 c. chopped pecans
1/2 c. packed brown sugar

Cream ... 3/4 cup sugar and margarine in bowl.
Stir ...... in milk, flour and 2 tablespoons cocoa.
Add ..... pecans, mixing well.
Spread ... in 9-inch square pan.
Mix ..... 1/2 cup sugar, brown sugar and 1/3 cup cocoa in bowl.
Pour ..... over batter in pan.
Add ..... 1 1/2 cups boiling water.
Bake ..... at 350 degrees for 30 to 40 minutes.
Invert .... on serving plate.
Yield .... 9-12 servings.

Mrs. Michael Sweat
West Hardin H. S., Stephensburg, Kentucky

CHOCOLATE SHEET CAKE

2 c. flour
2 c. sugar
1 tsp. soda
1/4 tsp. salt
1 stick margarine
1/2 c. shortening
4 tbsp. cocoa
1/2 c. buttermilk
2 eggs
1 tsp. vanilla extract

Sift ...... first 4 ingredients into bowl.
Melt ..... margarine and shortening with cocoa and 1 cup water in saucepan over medium heat.
Bring .... to a boil.
Stir ...... into dry ingredients.
Beat ..... in remaining ingredients.
Pour ..... into greased 10 1/2 x 15 1/2-inch baking dish.
Bake ..... at 400 degrees for 20 minutes.
Spread ... with Milnot Icing while cake is hot.

Milnot Icing

1 stick margarine
4 tbsp. cocoa
5 tbsp. Milnot

1 tsp. vanilla extract
3 to 4 c. confectioners' sugar
1 c. chopped nuts

Combine . margarine, cocoa and Milnot in saucepan.
Bring .... to a boil over medium heat, stirring constantly.
Add ..... vanilla and enough confectioners' sugar to thicken.
Stir ...... in nuts.

Dorothy Scott
Ponca City Sr. H. S., Ponca City, Oklahoma

CHOCOLATE SYRUP CAKE WITH CHOCOLATE TOPPING

1 stick margarine
1 c. sugar
4 eggs
1 c. flour
1 tsp. baking powder
Pinch of salt
1 1-lb. can chocolate syrup
1 tsp. vanilla extract

Cream ... margarine and sugar in bowl.
Add ..... eggs 1 at a time, beating well after each addition.
Combine . dry ingredients in bowl.
Add ..... alternately with chocolate syrup to creamed mixture.
Stir ...... in vanilla.
Pour ..... into greased 9 x 13-inch baking dish.
Bake ..... at 350 degrees for 25 minutes.
Pour ..... Topping over cooled cake.

Topping

1 c. sugar
1/3 c. evaporated milk
1 stick margarine
1/2 c. chocolate chips
1 c. miniature marshmallows

Bring .... first 3 ingredients to a boil in saucepan over medium heat.
Cook .... for 1 minute.
Add ..... remaining ingredients, stirring until melted.

Dorothy McLaughlin
Knox Jr. H. S., Salisbury, North Carolina

COCA-COLA CAKE

2 c. sugar
1 1/2 c. miniature marshmallows
2 c. flour
1/2 c. margarine
1/2 c. shortening
3 tbsp. cocoa
1 c. Coca-Cola
1/2 c. buttermilk
1 tsp. soda
2 eggs, well beaten

Combine . first 3 ingredients in bowl.
Blend . . . . next 4 ingredients in saucepan.
Bring . . . . to a boil over medium heat.
Pour . . . . . over dry ingredients, stirring until marshmallows melt.
Stir . . . . . . in remaining ingredients.
Pour . . . . . into greased rectangular pan.
Bake . . . . . at 350 degrees for 35 to 40 minutes or until cake tests done.
Frost . . . . with Coca-Cola Frosting.

Coca-Cola Frosting

1/2 c. margarine
3 tbsp. cocoa
6 tbsp. Coca-Cola
1 box confectioners' sugar
1 c. chopped nuts

Combine . first 3 ingredients in saucepan.
Bring . . . . to a boil over medium heat; remove from heat.
Add . . . . . confectioners' sugar, beating well.
Stir . . . . . . in nuts.

Mart Ritter
Elkins H. S., Elkins, Arkansas

FUDGE-PECAN CAKE

2 c. flour
2 c. sugar
3 sticks butter
8 tsp. cocoa
1/2 c. buttermilk
1 tsp. soda
2 tsp. cinnamon
2 eggs
Dash of salt
2 tsp. vanilla extract
1/2 c. milk
1 box confectioners' sugar, sifted
1 1/2 c. pecans

Mix . . . . . flour and sugar in large bowl.
Combine . 2 sticks butter, 4 teaspoons cocoa and 1 cup water in saucepan.
Bring . . . . to a boil.
Add . . . . . next 5 ingredients and 1 teaspoon vanilla, mixing well.
Add . . . . . hot mixture to flour mixture, blending well.
Pour . . . . . into greased and floured jelly roll pan.
Bake . . . . . at 400 degrees for 20 minutes.
Melt . . . . . 1 stick butter in saucepan.
Add . . . . . 4 teaspoons cocoa, 1 teaspoon vanilla and milk.
Bring . . . . ingredients to a boil.
Remove . . from heat.
Add . . . . . confectioners' sugar and pecans, mixing well.
Pour . . . . . over hot cake.

Kaye Derryberry
Webster Middle School, Oklahoma City, Oklahoma

HEATH CAKE

1 c. packed brown sugar
1/2 c. sugar
1 stick margarine
1 tsp. vanilla extract
2 c. sifted flour
1 tsp. soda
1 egg, beaten
1 c. buttermilk
4 Heath bars, frozen, chopped
1/2 c. chopped nuts

Combine . first 6 ingredients in bowl, mixing well.
Add . . . . . egg and buttermilk, beating well.
Pour . . . . . into greased 9 x 13-inch pan.
Sprinkle . . candy and nuts over batter.
Bake . . . . . at 350 degrees for 30 minutes.

Christine Anders
New Haven H. S., New Haven, Indiana

MISSISSIPPI MUD CAKE

2 c. sugar
4 eggs
1 1/2 c. self-rising flour
1 1/3 c. coconut
1 1/2 c. pecans
4 sticks margarine, softened
2/3 c. cocoa

2 tsp. vanilla extract
1 7-oz. jar marshmallow creme
1 lb. confectioners' sugar
1/2 c. evaporated milk

Combine . first 5 ingredients and 3 sticks margarine, 1/3 cup cocoa and 1 teaspoon vanilla in large bowl, mixing well.
Pour ..... into greased 9 x 13-inch baking pan.
Bake ..... at 350 degrees for 40 to 45 minutes or until cake tests done.
Spread ... marshmallow creme over hot cake; cool.
Mix ..... confectioners' sugar, evaporated milk, 1 stick margarine, 1/3 cup cocoa and 1 teaspoon vanilla in bowl.
Spread ... over marshmallow creme layer.
Yield .... 12 servings.

Deborah Frizzell
Fordsville Jr. H. S., Fordsville, Kentucky

MOUND CAKE

1 1/2 sticks margarine
1 c. shortening
2 1/2 c. sugar
3 eggs
3/4 c. cocoa
2 c. flour
2 tsp. baking powder
1/4 tsp. each soda, salt
1 c. buttermilk
1 c. milk
12 lg. marshmallows
2 6-oz. packages coconut
1 box confectioners' sugar
1/2 tsp. vanilla extract

Cream ... 1 stick margarine, 1/2 cup shortening and 1 1/2 cups sugar in bowl.
Beat ..... in eggs 1 at a time, beating well after each addition.
Add ..... 1/2 cup cocoa and next 4 dry ingredients alternately with buttermilk, mixing well after each addition.
Pour ..... into 3 prepared cake pans.
Boil ..... milk, 1 cup sugar, marshmallows and coconut in saucepan until marshmallows melt.
Pour ..... warm filling over cooled cake layers.

Combine . remaining 1/2 cup shortening, 1/2 stick margarine, 1/4 cup cocoa, confectioners' sugar and vanilla in bowl.
Beat ..... until smooth.
Stack .... cake layers.
Frost .... top and sides of cake.

Emily B. Fallaw
Lockhart H. S., Lockhart, South Carolina

NO EGG-NO MILK-CHOCOLATE CAKE

3 c. flour
2 c. sugar
1/2 tsp. salt
6 tbsp. cocoa
2 tsp. soda
1 c. oil
2 tsp. vinegar
2 tsp. vanilla extract

Sift ...... all dry ingredients twice into bowl.
Add ..... liquids and 2 cups water, mixing well.
Pour ..... into greased and floured 9 x 13-inch baking dish.
Bake ..... at 350 degrees for 35 minutes.

Ruby J. Dunagan
Bixby Jr. H. S., Bixby, Oklahoma

POOR MAN'S CAKE

2 1/2 c. flour
2 c. sugar
3/4 c. cocoa
1/2 tsp. each salt, cinnamon
2 tsp. each soda, baking powder
2/3 c. oil
2 tsp. vanilla extract
2 tbsp. vinegar

Combine . all dry ingredients in bowl, mixing well.
Add ..... remaining ingredients and 2 cups cold water, blending well.
Beat ..... for 2 minutes or until smooth.
Pour ..... into greased and floured 2-quart rectangular baking pan.
Shake .... pan to level batter.
Bake ..... at 350 degrees for 30 to 35 minutes or until cake tests done.

Doris Hartman
Mexia H. S., Mexia, Texas

RED VELVET CAKE

3 sticks butter, softened
2 tsp. vanilla extract
1 1/2 c. sugar
2 eggs
1 oz. red food coloring
2 tbsp. cocoa
1 tsp. salt
2 1/3 c. flour
1 c. buttermilk
1 tsp. soda
1 tsp. vinegar
8 oz. cream cheese, softened
1 lb. confectioners' sugar
1 c. chopped nuts

Cream ... 2 sticks butter and 1 teaspoon vanilla in bowl.
Add ..... sugar, 1/3 cup at a time, beating well after each addition.
Beat ..... in eggs, 1 at a time, beating well after each addition.
Stir ...... in next 3 ingredients, mixing well.
Add ..... flour, 1/3 cup at a time, alternately with buttermilk, beating well after each addition, beginning and ending with flour.
Combine . soda and vinegar.
Add ..... to batter, mixing well.
Pour ..... into 3 prepared cake pans.
Bake ..... at 350 degrees for 15 to 20 minutes or until cake tests done.
Cream ... remaining 1 stick butter and cream cheese in bowl.
Add ..... 1 teaspoon vanilla and confectioners' sugar, mixing well.
Stir ...... in nuts.
Spread ... between layers and over top and sides of cooled cake.

Mary Roddam
Clio School, Clio, Alabama

SAUERKRAUT-CHOCOLATE CAKE

2/3 c. butter
1 1/2 c. sugar
3 eggs
1 tsp. vanilla extract
1/4 tsp. salt
1/2 c. cocoa
2 1/4 c. flour
1 tsp. each baking powder, soda
2/3 c. chopped sauerkraut, rinsed, drained

Cream ... butter and sugar in bowl.
Beat ..... in eggs and vanilla.
Sift ...... dry ingredients together.
Add ..... to creamed mixture alternately with 1 cup water, beating well after each addition.
Stir ...... in sauerkraut.
Pour ..... into 2 greased and floured 8-inch cake pans.
Bake ..... at 350 degrees for 30 minutes.

Linda Finley Loman
Boonville H. S., Boonville, Missouri

TEXAS SHEET CAKE

3 sticks margarine
6 to 8 tbsp. cocoa
1 tsp. soda
1/2 tsp. salt
2 c. flour
2 c. sugar
2 eggs, beaten
1/2 c. sour cream
6 tbsp. milk
1 tsp. vanilla extract
1 box confectioners' sugar
1/2 c. nuts

Combine . 2 sticks margarine and half the cocoa with 1 cup water in saucepan.
Bring .... to a boil, stirring constantly; remove from heat.
Add ..... next 4 ingredients, mixing well.
Blend .... in eggs.
Fold ..... in sour cream.
Pour ..... into greased jelly roll pan.
Bake ..... at 350 degrees for 20 to 25 minutes.
Combine . remaining 1 stick margarine and cocoa in saucepan.
Heat ..... until melted and blended.
Add ..... remaining ingredients, mixing well.
Spread ... over hot cake.
Cool ..... until topping is firm.

Sherry Zeigler
Zane Trace H. S., Chillicothe, Ohio

TWENTY-TWO MINUTE CAKE

2 c. flour
2 c. sugar

3 1/2 tbsp. cocoa
1/2 c. shortening
1 stick margarine
1 tsp. soda
1 tsp. vanilla extract
2 eggs
1/2 c. buttermilk

Combine . flour and sugar in bowl.
Combine . cocoa, shortening, margarine and 1 cup water in saucepan.
Bring .... to a boil over medium heat.
Add ..... to flour mixture, mixing well.
Stir ...... soda, vanilla and eggs into buttermilk.
Add ..... to flour mixture, mixing well.
Pour ..... into greased 12 x 18-inch pan.
Bake ..... at 400 degrees for 20 minutes.
Pour ..... frosting over hot cake.

Cocoa Frosting

1 stick margarine
3 1/2 tbsp. cocoa
1/3 c. milk
1 lb. confectioners' sugar
1 c. nuts

Combine . first 3 ingredients in saucepan.
Bring .... to a boil.
Blend .... in confectioners' sugar.
Stir ...... in nuts.

Linda Klingstedt Sloan
Pryor Sr. H. S., Pryor, Oklahoma

WHOLE WHEAT HONEYCOMB CAKE WITH PLUM CHEESE FILLING

4 egg yolks, beaten
1 tbsp. fresh lemon juice
3/4 c. packed brown sugar
1 c. whole wheat flour, sifted
4 egg whites, stiffly beaten
1/2 c. sliced almonds
1/4 c. butter
1/4 c. honey
1 tbsp. milk
3 fresh California plums, sliced
1/4 c. fresh orange juice
1 8-oz. package cream cheese, softened, whipped

Beat ..... first 4 ingredients in bowl until well blended.

Fold ..... in egg whites.
Pour ..... into greased 9-inch cake pan.
Bake ..... at 300 degrees for 40 to 45 minutes or until cake tests done.
Cool .... inverted on wire rack, for 1 hour.
Place .... on cookie sheet.
Combine . almonds, butter, honey and milk in saucepan.
Cook .... over low heat until bubbly, stirring constantly.
Pour ..... over cake.
Broil ..... for 6 or 7 minutes or until topping is bubbly.
Cool ..... cake completely.
Split ..... into 2 layers.
Combine . plums and orange juice in small saucepan.
Bring .... to a boil over low heat.
Cook .... for 3 or 4 minutes or until plums are poached.
Drain .... and cool.
Fold ..... into cream cheese.
Spread ... over bottom cake layer.
Place .... top cake layer over filling.

Photograph for this recipe below.

COFFEE CLOUD SPONGE CAKE

Instant coffee
2 c. flour
1 tbsp. baking powder
1/2 tsp. salt
6 eggs, separated
1/2 tsp. cream of tartar
2 c. sugar
1 tsp. vanilla extract
1 c. finely ground walnuts
2 tbsp. butter, softened
2 c. confectioners' sugar
2 to 3 tbsp. milk

Dissolve .. 1 tablespoon instant coffee in 1 cup boiling water; cool.
Sift ...... flour, baking powder and salt together.
Beat ..... egg whites with cream of tartar in bowl until soft peaks form.
Add ..... 1/2 cup sugar, 2 tablespoons at a time, beating until stiff; set aside.
Add ..... 1 1/2 cups sugar and vanilla to egg yolks gradually, beating constantly.
Beat ..... with electric mixer at high speed for 4 to 5 minutes or until thick and lemon colored.
Add ..... dry ingredients to egg mixture alternately with coffee, beginning and ending with dry ingredients.
Fold ..... in walnuts.
Fold ..... batter gently into egg whites, 1/4 at a time until well blended.
Pour ..... into ungreased 10-inch tube pan.
Bake ..... at 350 degrees for 60 to 70 minutes.
Cool ..... inverted, for 1 hour or longer.
Remove .. from pan.
Blend .... butter, confectioners' sugar and 1 1/2 teaspoons instant coffee in bowl with milk to spreading consistency.
Frost .... cake with coffee icing.

Sandra Bassetto
White Cloud H. S., White Cloud, Michigan

CRANBERRY PICTURE CAKE

6 eggs
3 c. sugar
Grated rind of 2 lemons
4 c. sour cream
5 c. sifted flour
1 tbsp. baking powder
1 1/2 tsp. soda
2 14-oz. jars cranberry-orange relish
1 1/3 c. butter, softened
2 lb. confectioners' sugar
Food coloring
Pepperidge Farm cookies and crackers
Pillow mints
Fresh cranberries
Coconut, tinted green

Beat ..... eggs and sugar in large bowl until fluffy.
Add ..... lemon rind and 3 cups sour cream, beating well.
Stir ...... in dry ingredients, mixing well.
Fold ..... in 1 cup relish.
Spread ... into 2 greased and floured 10 x 15-inch pans.
Bake ..... at 350 degrees for 30 to 35 minutes or until cake tests done.
Cool ..... on cake racks.
Spread ... remaining relish between layers.
Beat ..... butter and 1 cup sour cream in large bowl.
Add ..... confectioners' sugar gradually, beating until of spreading consistency; color as desired.
Spread ... over top and sides of cake.
Decorate . with cookies, crackers, candies, cranberries and coconut.

Christmas or Friendship Wreath

Pour Cranberry Picture Cake batter into 2 greased and floured 8-cup ring molds. Bake at 350 degrees for 30 to 35 minutes. Unmold; cool. Cut each ring into 2 layers. Spread remaining relish between layers. Tint frosting green. Spread over cakes. Press coconut into frosting. Decorate as illustrated with cranberries, candies and cookies. Decorate cookies with icing.

Photograph for this recipe on page 103.

CORN BREAD CAKE

4 eggs
1 c. sugar
1 c. packed light brown sugar
1 c. oil
1 c. chopped pecans

1 tsp. vanilla extract
1 1/2 c. self-rising flour
1 1/2 c. confectioners' sugar
2 tbsp. milk

Combine . first 7 ingredients in bowl, mixing well.
Pour . . . . . into greased 9 x 13-inch baking pan.
Bake . . . . . at 350 degrees for 35 to 40 minutes.
Blend . . . . remaining ingredients in bowl.
Spread . . . over warm cake. Cake is named for its texture.
Yield . . . . 16 servings.

Brenda L. Little
Farmville Central H. S., Farmville, North Carolina

FIG CAKE

1 1/2 sticks margarine, softened
2 c. sugar
4 eggs
1 tsp. vanilla extract
3 c. flour
1 tsp. cinnamon
1 1/2 tsp. allspice
Dash of salt
1 tsp. soda
2 c. chopped pecans
1 c. buttermilk
1 pt. fig preserves, chopped

Cream . . . margarine and sugar in bowl until fluffy.
Add . . . . . eggs 1 at a time, beating well after each addition.
Stir . . . . . . in vanilla.
Sift . . . . . . flour with dry ingredients.
Combine . a small amount of dry mixture with pecans.
Add . . . . . remaining flour mixture to batter alternately with buttermilk, stirring well after each addition.
Stir . . . . . . in figs and pecans.
Pour . . . . . into greased and floured 10-inch tube pan.
Bake . . . . . at 325 degrees for 1 hour.
Reduce . . . temperature to 300 degrees.
Bake . . . . . for 15 minutes longer.

Nancy Krumnow
Santa Fe H. S., Alta Loma, Texas

FIVE-FLAVOR CAKE

2 sticks butter
1/2 c. shortening
3 c. sugar
5 eggs, well beaten
3 c. flour
1/2 tsp. baking powder
1 c. milk
1 tsp. each coconut, rum, butter, lemon, vanilla extracts

Cream . . . first 3 ingredients together in bowl until light and fluffy.
Add . . . . . eggs, mixing well.
Combine . flour and baking powder.
Add . . . . . to creamed mixture alternately with milk, beating well after each addition.
Stir . . . . . . in flavorings.
Spoon . . . into greased 10-inch bundt pan.
Bake . . . . . at 325 degrees for 1 1/2 hours or until cake tests done.

Wanda A. Gerard
Superior Sr. H. S., Superior, Wisconsin

DARK FRUITCAKE

3 c. packed brown sugar
1 c. butter, softened
4 eggs, beaten
1 lb. dark raisins
1/2 lb. citron
1 c. chunk pineapple
1/2 c. maraschino cherries
3 1/2 c. flour
1 tsp. soda
1 tsp. salt
1 tbsp. cinnamon
1 c. buttermilk

Cream . . . sugar and butter in bowl.
Add . . . . . eggs, beating well.
Coat . . . . . fruits with 1/2 cup flour.
Sift . . . . . . remaining flour with soda, salt and cinnamon.
Add . . . . . to batter alternately with buttermilk, mixing well after each addition.
Stir . . . . . . in fruits.
Pour . . . . . into greased and floured pan.
Bake . . . . . at 300 degrees for 1 1/2 hours.

Kristine Bown
American Fork H. S., American Fork, Utah

NUTRITIOUS FRUITCAKE

5 eggs, slightly beaten
3/4 c. honey
1/2 c. oil
3 tbsp. grated orange rind
2 c. whole wheat flour
1/2 c. sesame seed
1 1/2 c. raisins
1/2 c. hulled sunflower seeds
1 1/2 c. chopped pecans
1 c. slivered almonds
1 c. finely chopped dried figs
1 c. quartered pitted dates
1/2 c. chopped dried apples
1/2 c. quartered dried apricots

Combine . first 5 ingredients in bowl, mixing well.
Stir . . . . . . in remaining ingredients.
Pour . . . . . into greased loaf pan.
Bake . . . . . at 300 degrees for 1 hour and 20 minutes.

Linda Jaramillo
Los Lunas H. S., Los Lunas, New Mexico

FRUIT COCKTAIL CAKE

2 eggs
1 1/2 c. packed brown sugar
1 can fruit cocktail with juice
2 c. flour
1/2 tsp. salt
2 1/2 tsp. baking powder
1 stick butter
1 c. sugar
1/2 c. pecans
1/2 c. evaporated milk
1 c. coconut

Combine . first 2 ingredients in large bowl, mixing well.
Add . . . . . fruit cocktail, blending well.
Stir . . . . . . in flour, salt and baking powder.
Pour . . . . . into greased sheet cake pan.
Bake . . . . . at 300 degrees for 45 minutes.
Mix . . . . . last 5 ingredients in saucepan.
Boil . . . . . for 2 minutes over medium heat, stirring constantly.
Pour . . . . . over warm cake.
Yield . . . . 24 servings.

Deborah Crume
Haines City Sr. H. S., Haines City, Florida

ANGOSTURA WALNUT CAKE

5 egg yolks
Sugar
1/4 c. fine dry bread crumbs
Angostura aromatic bitters
1 c. finely ground walnuts
5 egg whites, stiffly beaten
Juice of 1/2 lemon

Beat . . . . . egg yolks and 6 tablespoons sugar in bowl until thick.
Stir . . . . . . in bread crumbs, 1 teaspoon bitters and walnuts.
Fold . . . . . in egg whites.
Pour . . . . . into greased and floured 8-inch bundt pan.
Bake . . . . . at 350 degrees for 1 hour.
Cool . . . . . unmolded, on wire rack.
Combine . 1 1/2 cups sugar, 1/2 cup water, lemon juice and 2 tablespoons bitters in saucepan.
Bring . . . . to a boil over high heat.
Boil . . . . . for 2 minutes.
Spoon . . . hot syrup slowly over cake until syrup is absorbed.

Photograph for this recipe above.

HILLBILLY CAKE

1 c. sugar
Margarine
1/2 c. nuts
1/2 tsp. each salt, cloves, allspice
1 tsp. cinnamon
1 c. raisins
2 c. flour
1 tsp. soda
1 c. coconut flakes
2 tbsp. milk
5 tbsp. brown sugar

Combine . sugar, 1/2 cup margarine, nuts, salt, spices and raisins in saucepan with 1 cup water.
Bring . . . . to a boil; cool.
Beat . . . . . in flour and soda.
Pour . . . . . into 9 x 9-inch pan.
Bake . . . . . at 375 degrees for 25 minutes.
Combine . coconut, milk, brown sugar and 2 tablespoons margarine in bowl, mixing well.
Spread . . . over cake.
Brown . . . lightly under broiler.
Yield . . . . 12 servings.

Georgia Lahmeyer
Owensville H. S., Owensville, Missouri

HONEY-WALNUT CAKE

1 c. sifted flour
2 tsp. (heaping) baking powder
1/2 tsp. salt
1/2 tsp. cinnamon
1/2 tsp. cloves
6 eggs, separated
3 c. sugar
1 lb. walnuts, finely chopped
2 c. honey

Sift . . . . . . first 5 ingredients together.
Beat . . . . . egg whites in bowl until soft peaks form.
Add . . . . . 1 cup sugar gradually, beating until stiff.
Fold . . . . . in beaten egg yolks.
Blend . . . . in flour mixture and walnuts.
Spread . . . in 9 x 13-inch baking pan.
Bake . . . . . at 350 degrees for 35 minutes.
Boil . . . . . remaining 2 cups sugar and 5 1/2 cups water in saucepan for 10 minutes.

Stir . . . . . . in honey.
Pour . . . . . cooled syrup over hot cake.
Yield . . . . 24 servings.

Hazel C. Tassis
Imperial Unified H. S., Imperial, California

SPICY WALNUT-HONEY CAKE

1/2 c. shortening
1/2 c. sugar
1 egg
2 1/2 c. sifted flour
1 1/2 tsp. soda
1 tsp. salt
1/2 tsp. cinnamon
1/4 tsp. cloves
1 c. honey
1 1/2 c. California walnuts, chopped
2 tbsp. melted butter

Cream . . . first 3 ingredients in bowl.
Sift . . . . . . next 5 dry ingredients together.
Add . . . . . to creamed mixture with 3/4 cup honey, mixing until smooth.
Stir . . . . . . in 3/4 cup walnuts.
Mix . . . . . in 1 cup hot water quickly.
Pour . . . . . into greased 9-inch square pan.
Bake . . . . . at 325 degrees for 35 to 40 minutes or until cake tests done.
Combine . butter with remaining 1/4 cup honey and 3/4 cup walnuts in bowl.
Spoon . . . over hot cake.
Broil . . . . . 8 inches from heat source until bubbly.

Photograph for this recipe below.

LEMON-PECAN CAKE

1 lb. butter
1 lb. brown sugar
6 eggs, separated
4 c. flour
1 tsp. baking powder
3 tbsp. lemon extract
1 lb. pecans, chopped
1/2 lb. candied cherries, chopped
1/2 lb. candied pineapple, chopped

Cream ... butter and sugar in large mixing bowl.
Add ..... egg yolks 1 at a time, beating well after each addition.
Sift ...... 2 cups flour and baking powder together.
Add ..... to butter mixture alternately with lemon extract, beating well after each addition.
Dredge ... pecans and fruit with remaining flour in large bowl.
Pour ..... batter over fruit mixture.
Beat ..... egg whites until stiff.
Fold ..... egg whites into batter.
Let ...... stand overnight in bowl covered with foil and damp cloth.
Pour ..... into greased and floured 10-inch tube pan.
Bake ..... at 275 degrees for 2 hours.
Cool ..... in pan before serving.

Pauline Shields
Webster Middle School, Oklahoma City, Oklahoma

NORWEGIAN KING'S CAKE

2 c. almond paste
2 egg whites, slightly beaten
1 3/4 c. confectioners' sugar
1/2 tsp. vinegar
1 egg white

Blend .... almond paste and beaten egg whites in bowl.
Mix ..... in 3/4 cup confectioners' sugar until well blended.
Chill ..... for several hours.
Roll ..... out 1/2 inch thick on lightly floured surface.
Fit ...... into kranse kake molds or cut into progressively smaller circles.
Place .... on baking sheet.
Bake ..... at 350 degrees for 10 to 15 minutes or until lightly browned.
Cool ..... on wire rack.
Blend .... 1 cup confectioners' sugar and vinegar with egg white.
Stack .... circles together to make cone shape, securing with a small amount of frosting between layers.
Top ..... with a crown.

Ruth Larson
Hickman H. S., Columbia, Missouri

OATMEAL CAKE

1 c. old-fashioned oatmeal
1/2 c. shortening
1 c. sugar
1 3/4 c. packed brown sugar
2 eggs
1 1/3 c. flour
1/2 tsp. salt
1 tsp. each soda, cinnamon
3/4 stick butter
1 tbsp. milk
1 can coconut
1 c. chopped nuts

Combine . oatmeal and 1 1/4 cups boiling water in bowl; set aside.
Cream ... shortening, sugar and 1 cup brown sugar in bowl.
Add ..... eggs, mixing well.
Sift ...... next 4 dry ingredients together.
Add ..... to creamed mixture, blending well.
Stir ...... in oatmeal.
Pour ..... into greased and floured 9 x 13-inch baking pan.
Bake ..... at 350 degrees for 30 to 35 minutes.
Boil ..... remaining 3/4 cup brown sugar, butter and milk in saucepan for 1 minute.
Stir ...... in coconut and nuts.
Spread ... over hot cake.
Broil ..... until bubbly, watching closely.

Kathleen Ann McConkie
Southwest Jr. H. S., Hot Springs, Arkansas

Recipes on page 18.

GLAZED ORANGE CAKE

2 c. sifted cake flour
2 1/2 tsp. baking powder
1/4 tsp. each soda, salt
1/2 c. butter, softened
2 c. sugar
1/2 c. chopped walnuts
1 tbsp. grated orange rind
2 eggs
3/4 c. sour cream
1/2 c. strained orange juice

Sift . . . . . . flour, baking powder, soda and salt together.
Cream . . . butter and 1 cup sugar until light and fluffy in large bowl.
Add . . . . . walnuts and orange rind, mixing well.
Add . . . . . eggs 1 at a time, beating well after each addition.
Add . . . . . dry ingredients and sour cream alternately, stirring until smooth.
Pour . . . . . into greased 9-inch square baking pan.
Bake . . . . . at 375 degrees for 40 minutes or until cake tests done.
Mix . . . . . 1 cup sugar and orange juice in small saucepan.
Boil . . . . . for 5 minutes over medium heat, stirring constantly.
Pour . . . . . over top of cake.

Miss Martha Atlas
South Panola H. S., Batesville, Mississippi

PEANUT BUTTER CAKE FOR MANY

1 1/4 c. butter
1 1/4 c. peanut butter
5 c. sugar
6 eggs
7 1/2 c. sifted flour
5 tsp. soda
4 1/2 tsp. baking powder
5 c. buttermilk
2 tbsp. vanilla extract

Cream . . . butter, peanut butter and sugar in mixing bowl until well blended.
Add . . . . . eggs 1 at a time, beating well after each addition.

Recipes on pages 93, 94, 95.

Combine . dry ingredients in bowl.
Add . . . . . dry ingredients alternately with buttermilk to creamed mixture, beating well after each addition.
Add . . . . . vanilla; mix well.
Pour . . . . . into 4 greased and floured 9 x 13-inch cake pans.
Bake . . . . . at 350 degrees for 30 to 35 minutes.
Cool . . . . . on wire racks.

Peanut Butter Icing

1 lb. butter
1 lb. peanut butter
2 lb. confectioners' sugar
2 tbsp. vanilla extract
1 1/2 to 2 c. pineapple juice

Combine . all ingredients, adding enough pineapple juice to make easy spreading consistency.
Mix . . . . . until well blended and smooth.
Ice . . . . . . cooled cakes.

Lorna Hinson
Floyd Johnson Voc. Center, York, South Carolina

PERSIMMON SPICE CAKE

3 c. sugar
1 c. oil
4 eggs, beaten
2 c. persimmon puree
3 1/2 c. flour
2 tsp. each soda, salt
1 tsp. each baking powder, nutmeg, allspice, cinnamon
1/2 tsp. cloves
2/3 c. milk
1 c. nuts

Combine . first 4 ingredients in bowl, mixing well.
Sift . . . . . . dry ingredients together.
Add . . . . . to sugar mixture alternately with milk, beating well after each addition.
Fold . . . . . in nuts.
Pour . . . . . into 2 greased and floured loaf pans.
Bake . . . . . at 350 degrees for 1 to 1 1/2 hours or until cake tests done.

Donna Chappell
Eastern Guilford H. S., Gibsonville, North Carolina

PINA COLADA CAKE

2 3/4 c. cake flour
3/4 tsp. salt
3 1/2 tsp. baking powder
1/2 c. shortening
1 tsp. rum flavoring
1 c. sugar
3 eggs
1/2 c. milk
1 c. coconut milk
3/4 c. crushed pineapple, drained

Sift ...... first 3 ingredients together.
Cream ... shortening, rum flavoring and sugar in large bowl until light and fluffy.
Add ..... eggs 1 at a time, beating well after each addition.
Add ..... dry ingredients alternately with milk and coconut milk, beating well after each addition.
Stir ...... in crushed pineapple, mixing well.
Pour ..... batter into greased 9 x 13-inch baking pan.
Swirl .... knife through batter.
Bake ..... at 350 degrees for 30 minutes or until cake tests done.

Wendy Russell
Ohio University, Athens, Ohio

AUNT HELEN'S GRAPEFRUIT PUDDING CAKE

1 tbsp. butter
2/3 c. sugar
2 eggs, separated
1 tbsp. potato starch
1/4 c. Florida frozen concentrated grapefruit juice, thawed
1 c. milk

Cream ... butter and sugar together in bowl.
Add ..... egg yolks 1 at a time, beating well after each addition.
Blend .... in potato starch.
Mix ..... in juice and milk.
Fold ..... softly beaten egg whites into pudding mixture.
Turn ..... into greased 1-quart baking dish in pan of hot water.
Bake ..... at 350 degrees for 45 to 50 minutes; cool.
Chill ..... until serving time.

Serve .... with Grapefruit Sauce.
Yield .... 4-6 servings.

Grapefruit Sauce

3/4 c. sugar
3 tsp. potato starch
1/2 c. Florida frozen concentrated grapefruit juice, thawed

Blend .... sugar and potato starch in medium saucepan.
Add ..... juice and 1/2 cup water, blending well.
Cook .... over medium heat until sauce thickens, stirring constantly.
Bring .... to a boil; cool.
Serve .... over pudding cake.
Yield .... 1 1/3 cups.

Photograph for this recipe on cover.

NOTHING CAKE

2 sticks butter
3 c. sugar
2 eggs
2 c. flour, sifted
1 tsp. soda
1/4 tsp. salt
1 lg. can crushed pineapple
1 sm. can evaporated milk
1 c. coconut
1 c. chopped pecans
1 c. chopped cherries

Cream ... 1 stick butter and 2 cups sugar in bowl.
Add ..... eggs 1 at a time, blending well after each addition.
Stir ...... in next 4 ingredients, mixing well.
Pour ..... into greased 9 x 13-inch pan.
Bake ..... at 350 degrees for 30 to 35 minutes.
Blend .... remaining 1 cup sugar, 1 stick butter and evaporated milk in saucepan.
Cook .... over medium heat for 10 minutes or until thick.
Add ..... coconut, pecans and cherries.
Pour ..... over cake.
Yield .... 15 servings.

Marcia Johnson
Prescott H. S., Prescott, Arkansas

DIANA'S PINEAPPLE CAKE

2 eggs, well beaten
1   20-oz. can crushed pineapple
2 c. flour
1 c. sugar
1 c. packed brown sugar
2 tsp. soda
1   3-oz. package cream cheese, softened
1/4 c. butter, softened
1 tsp. vanilla extract
2 c. confectioners' sugar

Combine . eggs with next 5 ingredients in large bowl, stirring well.
Pour . . . . . into 9 x 13-inch baking pan.
Bake . . . . . at 350 degrees for 45 minutes or until cake tests done.
Beat . . . . . cream cheese, butter and vanilla together in bowl until light.
Add . . . . . confectioners' sugar gradually.
Beat . . . . . until of spreading consistency.
Spread . . . over top and sides of cooled cake.

Diana Burchhardt
Princess Anne Jr. H. S., Virginia Beach, Virginia

POPPY SEED CAKE

1/2 c. poppy seed
2 tsp. vanilla extract
2 1/2 c. milk
3/4 c. butter, softened
2 1/4 c. sugar
2 c. flour
2 tsp. baking powder
3/4 tsp. salt
4 egg whites, stiffly beaten
4 egg yolks
2 tbsp. cornstarch
1/2 c. pecans
1 recipe creamy white frosting

Combine . poppy seed, 1 teaspoon vanilla and 1 cup milk in small bowl, mixing well.
Chill . . . . . overnight.
Cream . . . butter and 1 1/2 cups sugar together in bowl.
Sift . . . . . . flour, baking powder and 1/2 teaspoon salt together.
Add . . . . . to creamed mixture alternately with poppy seed mixture, blending well after each addition.
Fold . . . . . in egg whites.
Pour . . . . . into 2 greased and floured 8-inch cake pans.
Bake . . . . . at 350 degrees for 30 minutes.
Combine . remaining 3/4 cup sugar, 1 1/2 cups milk, 1/4 teaspoon salt, egg yolks and cornstarch in saucepan, mixing well.
Cook . . . . for 5 minutes, stirring constantly.
Add . . . . . nuts and 1 teaspoon vanilla; cool.
Spread . . . between layers, reserving enough to decorate top.
Frost . . . . with creamy white frosting.
Top . . . . . with remaining pecan filling.
Yield . . . . 10-12 servings.

Lois T. Webster
Central H. S., Muncie, Indiana

BRANDIED POUND CAKE

2 sticks margarine, softened
3 c. sugar
6 egg yolks
1/2 tsp. rum extract
1 tsp. orange extract
1/4 tsp. almond extract
1/2 tsp. lemon extract
1 tsp. vanilla extract
1 tsp. butter flavoring
3 c. flour
1/4 tsp. soda
1/2 tsp. salt
1 c. sour cream
1/4 c. apricot Brandy

Cream . . . margarine and sugar in large mixer bowl.
Add . . . . . egg yolks 1 at a time, beating well after each addition.
Add . . . . . flavorings.
Sift . . . . . . dry ingredients together.
Add . . . . . to creamed mixture alternately with sour cream and Brandy.
Pour . . . . . into greased tube pan.
Bake . . . . . at 325 degrees for 1 hour and 10 minutes.
Yield . . . . 20-24 servings.

Janet Apple
Jackson, Tennessee

APPLE POUND CAKE

3 c. flour
1 tsp. each soda, salt
1/2 tsp. each cinnamon, nutmeg
1 1/2 c. corn oil
2 c. sugar
3 eggs
2 tsp. vanilla extract
2 c. finely chopped pared apple
1 c. chopped pecans
1/2 c. raisins
1/2 c. applejack
1/2 c. apple juice
1/4 c. packed brown sugar
2 tbsp. butter

Combine . first 5 dry ingredients in bowl.
Beat . . . . . oil, sugar, eggs and vanilla in bowl with electric mixer at medium speed until well mixed.
Add . . . . . flour gradually, beating until smooth.
Fold . . . . . in apple, pecans and raisins.
Pour . . . . . into greased and floured 10-inch tube pan.
Bake . . . . . at 325 degrees for 1 1/4 hours or until cake tests done.
Cool . . . . . on wire rack for 10 minutes before removing from pan.
Combine . remaining ingredients in saucepan.
Boil . . . . . until sugar dissolves, stirring constantly.

Prick . . . . top of cake with fork.
Spoon . . . syrup over cake.
Store . . . . cooled cake in airtight container.

Photograph for this recipe on this page.

BUTTER POUND CAKE

2 sticks butter, softened
1/2 c. shortening
3 c. sugar
6 eggs
3 c. cake flour
1 tsp. baking powder
1/2 tsp. salt
1 c. milk
2 tsp. vanilla extract

Cream . . . butter and shortening together in bowl.
Blend . . . . in sugar, mixing well.
Add . . . . . eggs 1 at a time, beating well after each addition.
Sift . . . . . . dry ingredients together.
Add . . . . . to creamed mixture alternately with milk, beating well after each addition.
Stir . . . . . . in vanilla.
Pour . . . . . into greased and floured tube pan.
Bake . . . . . at 350 degrees for 1 hour and 20 minutes.

Yvonne Hardy
Putnam County Middle School, Eatonton, Georgia

COCONUT POUND CAKE

2 sticks margarine, softened
1/2 c. shortening
1/4 tsp. salt
3 c. sugar
6 eggs
3 c. sifted cake flour
1/2 c. milk
1/2 tsp. each almond, coconut, butter extracts
1 can flaked coconut

Cream . . . margarine, shortening, salt and sugar in bowl.
Add . . . . . eggs 1 at a time, beating well after each addition.
Beat . . . . . in flour alternately with milk, beating well after each addition.
Stir . . . . . . in flavorings and coconut.

Pour . . . . . into greased and floured tube pan.
Place . . . . in cold oven.
Turn . . . . . heat to 350 degrees.
Bake . . . . . for 1 1/4 hours.

Dana Ray Owens
Schleicher County H. S., Eldorado, Texas

TENNESSEE COCONUT POUND CAKE

1 1/2 c. shortening
2 1/2 c. sugar
5 eggs
3 c. flour
1 tsp. baking powder
1/4 tsp. salt
1 c. milk
2 tsp. coconut flavoring
1 can flaked coconut

Cream . . . shortening and sugar together in bowl.
Add . . . . . eggs 1 at a time, beating well after each addition.
Beat . . . . . with electric mixer at high speed for 10 minutes.
Sift . . . . . . next 3 dry ingredients together.
Add . . . . . to creamed mixture alternately with milk, beating well after each addition.
Stir . . . . . . in flavoring and coconut.
Pour . . . . . into greased and floured tube pan.
Place . . . . in cold oven.
Turn . . . . . heat to 350 degrees.
Bake . . . . . for 1 hour and 25 minutes.

Shirley Barnes
Rockwood H. S., Rockwood, Tennessee

MILLION DOLLAR POUND CAKE

1 lb. butter, softened
3 c. sugar
6 eggs, beaten
1/2 tsp. each vanilla, almond, lemon extracts
3/4 c. milk
4 c. flour

Cream . . . butter and sugar in large bowl until light and fluffy.
Add . . . . . eggs, beating well.
Mix . . . . . extracts with milk.
Add . . . . . milk and flour alternately to creamed mixture, beating well after each addition.

Pour . . . . . into greased and floured 10-inch tube pan.
Bake . . . . . at 300 degrees for 2 hours.
Cool . . . . . completely before inverting on serving dish.

Mary Grace Ramey
Central H. S., Englewood, Tennessee

MISS PEARL'S POUND CAKE

1/2 lb. butter, softened
1/2 c. shortening
3 c. sugar
3 c. flour, fluffed
1/2 tsp. each baking powder, salt
6 lg. eggs
1 c. milk
1 tsp. vanilla extract
2 tsp. lemon extract
Several drops of yellow food coloring

Cream . . . first 3 ingredients in bowl.
Sift . . . . . . dry ingredients together.
Add . . . . . a small amount to creamed mixture, mixing well.
Add . . . . . eggs 1 at a time, beating well after each addition.
Add . . . . . remaining flour mixture alternately with milk, beating well after each addition, beginning and ending with flour.
Stir . . . . . . in flavorings and food coloring.
Pour . . . . . into greased and floured tube pan.
Bake . . . . . at 325 degrees for 1 1/4 hours.

Lemon Frosting

2 1/3 c. sifted confectioners' sugar
1/4 tsp. salt
1 lg. egg
1/4 c. sugar
1/2 c. shortening
1 tsp. lemon flavoring

Combine . confectioners' sugar, salt and egg in bowl, mixing well.
Boil . . . . . 2 tablespoons water and sugar together in saucepan for 1 minute.
Pour . . . . . into egg mixture.
Add . . . . . shortening and flavoring, beating well.
Spread . . . on cooled cake.

Marthanne Limehouse
St. Andrew's Parish H. S.
Charleston, South Carolina

PINEAPPLE-PECAN POUND CAKE

2 1/2 c. sifted flour
1 3/4 c. sugar
1/2 tsp. each salt, baking powder
Grated lemon rind
Vanilla extract
Lemon extract
1 c. butter, softened
1 c. sour cream
3 eggs
1 20-oz. can crushed pineapple in
   heavy syrup
1/2 c. chopped pecans
1 c. confectioners' sugar

Combine . first 4 ingredients in large mixer bowl.
Add ..... 1 1/2 teaspoons lemon rind, 1/2 teaspoon each vanilla and lemon extracts, butter, sour cream and eggs.
Beat ..... with electric mixer at low speed until ingredients are combined.
Beat ..... at high speed for 3 1/2 minutes, scraping bowl often.
Drain .... pineapple, reserving syrup.
Fold ..... pineapple and pecans into batter, mixing well.
Pour ..... into greased and floured tube pan.
Bake ..... at 325 degrees for 1 hour or until golden.
Cool ..... for 10 minutes.
Combine . confectioners' sugar, 1/2 teaspoon lemon rind, 1/8 teaspoon lemon extract and enough reserved syrup to make glaze of pouring consistency.
Pour ..... over warm cake.

Pat Foley
Tempe Union H. S., Tempe, Arizona

SOUR CREAM POUND CAKE

2 3/4 c. sugar
1 c. butter, softened
6 eggs
3 c. sifted flour
1/2 tsp. each salt, soda
1 c. sour cream
1/2 tsp. each lemon, orange, vanilla extracts

Cream ... sugar and butter in bowl until light and fluffy.

Add ..... eggs 1 at a time, beating well after each addition.
Sift ...... dry ingredients together.
Add ..... to creamed mixture alternately with sour cream, beating well after each addition.
Stir ...... in flavorings, mixing well.
Pour ..... into greased and floured 10-inch tube pan.
Bake ..... at 325 degrees for 1 1/2 hours.
Cool ..... for 15 minutes in pan.
Sprinkle .. with confectioners' sugar.

Linda S. Riddick
Woodrow Wilson H. S., Portsmouth, Virginia

SUN-DROP POUND CAKE

3 c. sugar
2 sticks margarine, softened
1/2 c. shortening
5 eggs
3 c. flour
1 tsp. vanilla extract
1 tsp. lemon extract
6 oz. Sun-Drop

Cream ... first 3 ingredients in bowl.
Add ..... eggs, beating well.
Beat ..... in flour and flavorings.
Stir ...... in Sun-Drop.
Pour ..... into greased and floured tube pan.
Bake ..... at 325 degrees for 1 1/4 hours.
Drizzle ... with favorite glaze.

Vivian C. Pike
Bunker Hill H. S., Claremont, North Carolina

AMANDA'S PRUNE CAKE

1 c. oil
2 c. sugar
1 c. cooked prunes
3 eggs
2 c. flour
2 tbsp. cocoa
1 tsp. each allspice, cloves, cinnamon, salt
1 tsp. soda
1 c. sour milk
1 c. chopped pecans

Combine . oil and sugar in bowl, mixing well.
Stir ...... in prunes.

Add ..... eggs 1 at a time, beating well after each addition.
Sift ...... flour, cocoa, spices and salt together.
Stir ...... soda into milk.
Add ..... flour mixture to batter alternately with milk, mixing well after each addition.
Stir ...... in pecans.
Pour ..... into 2 greased and floured loaf pans.
Bake ..... at 300 degrees for 1 hour.

Amanda Goodson
Cedar Hill H. S., Cedar Hill, Texas

EASY PRUNE CAKE

2 c. oil
2 c. sugar
4 eggs
4 jars baby food prunes
3 1/2 c. flour
4 tsp. baking powder
2 tsp. soda
1 tsp. salt
2 tsp. cinnamon
2/3 tsp. ground cloves
1 c. chopped pecans

Combine . all ingredients in bowl in order listed, mixing well.
Pour ..... into 3 greased and floured loaf pans.
Bake ..... at 350 degrees for 40 minutes or until cakes test done.

Cream Cheese Icing

1 box confectioners' sugar
1 8-oz. package cream cheese, softened
1 stick margarine, softened
1 tsp. vanilla extract

Combine . all ingredients in bowl, blending well.
Spread ... over tops and sides of cakes.

Cheryl Yates
Dobson H. S., Mesa, Arizona

CAROL'S PUMPKIN CAKE

3 c. sifted flour
2 tsp. each baking powder, soda

1 tsp. salt
3 1/2 tsp. cinnamon
4 eggs
2 c. sugar
1 1/2 c. oil
1 can pumpkin
1 c. walnuts
1 c. maraschino cherries

Sift ...... dry ingredients together.
Beat ..... eggs in bowl with electric mixer at high speed.
Add ..... sugar, beating until thick.
Add ..... oil gradually, beating constantly.
Blend .... in dry ingredients alternately with pumpkin, beating well after each addition.
Fold ..... in walnuts and cherries.
Pour ..... into tube pan.
Bake ..... at 350 degrees for 1 hour and 5 minutes.

Carol V. Seirup
West Rocks Middle School, Norwalk, Connecticut

PUMPKIN BUNDT CAKE

2 c. sugar
1 1/2 c. oil
4 eggs
2 c. canned pumpkin
3 c. flour
2 tsp. baking powder
2 tsp. soda
3 tsp. cinnamon
1 tsp. each salt, ginger
Nuts (opt.)
Raisins (opt.)

Beat ..... first 3 ingredients in bowl until well blended.
Add ..... pumpkin, mixing well.
Sift ...... dry ingredients together.
Stir ...... into pumpkin mixture, blending well.
Fold ..... in nuts and raisins.
Pour ..... into well-greased bundt pan.
Bake ..... at 325 degrees for 1 hour.
Top ..... with confectioners' sugar glaze.

Karen Ferre
American Fork Jr. H. S., American Fork, Utah

PUMPKIN SHEET CAKE

2 tsp. soda
2 c. sugar
1 c. oil
4 eggs, well beaten
2 c. flour
2 tsp. cinnamon
1 tsp. baking powder
3/4 tsp. salt
1 c. pumpkin

Dissolve .. soda in a small amount of water.
Combine . with sugar and oil in bowl.
Add ..... eggs, mixing well.
Sift ...... dry ingredients together.
Blend .... into egg mixture.
Stir ...... in pumpkin.
Pour ..... into well-greased 11 x 17-inch pan.
Bake ..... at 350 degrees for 20 minutes.
Frost .... with cream cheese frosting.

Colleen Liebhart
Meadville R-IV Schools, Meadville, Missouri

SEVEN-UP CAKE

1   8-oz. container whipped margarine
1/2 c. shortening
3 c. sugar
5 eggs
3 1/2 c. flour
1 tsp. vanilla extract
1 1/2 tsp. lemon flavoring
1   7-oz. bottle 7-Up

Cream ... margarine, shortening and sugar in bowl.
Beat ..... in eggs.
Add ..... flour gradually, beating well.
Stir ...... in flavorings.
Add ..... 7-Up slowly, stirring to mix.
Pour ..... into large greased and floured tube pan.
Bake ..... at 325 degrees for 1 hour and 20 minutes.

Katherine Irvin Bentley
West Wilkes H. S., Millers Creek, North Carolina

SOUR CREAM CAKE

1 c. butter, softened
2 1/4 c. sugar
2 eggs
1/2 tsp. vanilla extract
1 c. sour cream
2 c. sifted flour
1 tsp. baking powder
1/4 tsp. salt
1 tsp. cinnamon
1/2 c. chopped pecans

Beat ..... butter in bowl until creamy.
Add ..... 2 cups sugar gradually, beating until smooth.
Beat ..... in eggs 1 at a time, beating well after each addition.
Fold .... in vanilla and sour cream.
Sift ...... flour, baking powder and salt together.
Stir ...... into creamed mixture, blending well.
Combine . remaining 1/4 cup sugar with cinnamon and pecans in bowl.
Pour ..... 1/3 of the batter into greased and floured bundt pan.
Sprinkle .. with 3/4 of the pecan mixture.
Top ..... with remaining batter.
Sprinkle .. with remaining pecans.
Bake ..... at 350 degrees for 1 hour.
Cool ..... for 10 to 15 minutes in pan.

Janet L. Dameron
Lincoln County R. I. Silex, Silex, Missouri

STRAWBERRY-RHUBARB CAKE

2 c. strawberries
2 c. chopped rhubarb
1 1/2 tbsp. lemon juice
2 1/3 c. sugar
1/4 c. cornstarch
3 c. Rice Chex cereal, crushed
2 1/2 c. flour
1 tbsp. baking powder
1 tsp. salt
1 1/4 c. butter
1 1/4 c. milk
2 eggs, slightly beaten
1/2 tsp. almond extract

Combine . first 2 ingredients in medium saucepan.
Cook .... covered, over low heat for 10 minutes, stirring occasionally.
Stir ...... in lemon juice.
Combine . 2/3 cup sugar and cornstarch in small bowl.

Add . . . . . to fruit mixture.
Cook . . . . for 8 minutes or until thickened, stirring constantly.
Cool . . . . . to room temperature.
Combine . crushed cereal, 2 cups flour, 1 cup sugar, baking powder and salt in large bowl.
Cut . . . . . . in 1 cup butter until crumbly.
Beat . . . . . milk, eggs and almond extract together in bowl.
Add . . . . . to cereal mixture, mixing well.
Pour . . . . . into greased 9 x 13-inch baking pan, reserving 1 cup.
Drop . . . . fruit mixture by spoonfuls on batter, spreading gently.
Spoon . . . reserved batter in small mounds over fruit.
Mix . . . . . 1/2 cup flour and 2/3 cup sugar in bowl.
Cut . . . . . . in 1/4 cup butter until crumbly.
Sprinkle . . over fruit.
Bake . . . . . at 350 degrees for 1 hour or until golden brown.
Yield . . . . 12 servings.

Ethelyn Oros
Keene H. S., Keene, New Hampshire

ZUCCHINI CAKE

2 c. sugar
3 eggs, beaten
1 c. oil
1 tsp. vanilla extract
3 c. flour
1/2 tsp. salt
1 tsp. each soda, baking powder, ginger, cloves, cinnamon
1/2 c. each nuts, raisins
3 c. shredded zucchini

Combine . first 4 ingredients in bowl, mixing well.
Sift . . . . . . dry ingredients together.
Add . . . . . to egg mixture, mixing well.
Fold . . . . . in nuts, raisins and zucchini.
Pour . . . . . into 2 greased 5 x 8-inch loaf pans.
Bake . . . . . at 325 degrees for 1 1/4 hours.
Dust . . . . . cooled cakes with confectioners' sugar.

Marie T. Butler
Palmyra-Macedon H. S., Palmyra, New York

DOUBLE PEACH UPSIDE-DOWN CAKE

2 tbsp. butter
1 c. packed light brown sugar
1 29-oz. can cling peach slices, drained
1/4 tsp. nutmeg
1 pkg. burnt sugar cake mix
1 c. whipping cream
2 tbsp. confectioners' sugar
Several drops of almond extract

Melt . . . . . 1 tablespoon butter in each of two 9-inch layer pans.
Spread . . . butter over bottoms and sides of pans.
Sprinkle . . each pan with 1/2 cup brown sugar.
Arrange . . peaches in pinwheel pattern over top.
Sprinkle . . with nutmeg.
Prepare . . . cake mix using package directions.
Spoon . . . over sliced peaches.
Bake . . . . . at 350 degrees for 40 to 45 minutes or until cake tests done.
Cool . . . . . on wire racks.
Turn . . . . . 1 layer out, peach side up, onto serving plate.
Whip . . . . cream with remaining ingredients in bowl until stiff.
Spread . . . over peaches.
Top . . . . . with remaining layer.
Chill . . . . . for 1 hour.
Yield . . . . 12 servings.

Photograph for this recipe above.

AMAZING DUMP CAKE

1 can apple pie filling
1 lg. can crushed pineapple
1 box yellow cake mix
1/4 lb. margarine, cut up
1/2 c. chopped nuts

Layer .... ingredients in order listed in greased 9 x 13-inch baking dish.
Bake ..... at 325 degrees for 1 hour.
Yield .... 12 servings.

Marjorie Grantham
Dolan Middle School, Stamford, Connecticut

CRUNCHY APRICOT CAKE

1 can apricot pie filling
1 sm. package white cake mix
1 egg
1/2 c. flaked coconut
1/2 c. chopped pecans
1/2 c. butter, melted

Spread ... pie filling in bottom of 9 x 9-inch baking dish.
Combine . next 2 ingredients with 1/3 cup water in mixing bowl.
Beat ..... with electric mixer at medium speed for 4 minutes.
Pour ..... over pie filling.
Sprinkle .. with coconut and pecans.
Drizzle ... butter over top.
Bake ..... at 350 degrees for 40 minutes.
Yield .... 9-12 servings.

Sandra J. Lau
Lockport Sr. H. S., Lockport, New York

BANANA-APRICOT CAKE

1 pkg. yellow cake mix
4 eggs
3/4 c. oil
1 box banana instant pudding mix
1/4 tsp. each cinnamon, nutmeg
1 1/4 c. apricot nectar
3 bananas, mashed
1 stick margarine, softened
1 box confectioners' sugar
4 oz. cream cheese, softened

Combine . first 6 ingredients and 3/4 cup apricot nectar in mixing bowl.
Beat ..... for 3 minutes.
Fold ..... in bananas.

Pour ..... into prepared tube pan.
Bake ..... at 350 degrees until cake tests done.
Combine . 1/2 cup apricot nectar with remaining ingredients in bowl.
Beat ..... until fluffy.
Frost .... cooled cake.

Pam Eastup
Northwest H. S., Justin, Texas

BANANA BRUNCH CAKE

1 pkg. coconut-pecan frosting mix
1 c. oats
5 tbsp. margarine, melted
1 c. sour cream
4 eggs
3 lg. bananas, mashed
1 pkg. yellow cake mix
1 tsp. vanilla extract

Combine . frosting mix, oats and margarine until crumbly.
Mix ..... sour cream, eggs and bananas in large mixer bowl until smooth.
Add ..... cake mix and vanilla.
Beat ..... for 2 minutes.
Pour ..... 1/3 of the batter into greased and floured 10-inch tube pan.
Sprinkle .. with 1/3 of the oat mixture.
Repeat ... layers, ending with oat mixture.
Bake ..... in 350-degree oven for 1 hour.
Cool ..... in pan for 15 minutes.

Mrs. Patricia Donahoo
Webster County H. S., Dixon, Kentucky

CHERRY-NUT-RUM CAKE

1 pkg. yellow cake mix
1 sm. package instant vanilla pudding mix
4 eggs
1/2 c. oil
2/3 c. rum
1/2 c. butter
1 c. packed light brown sugar
1 c. maraschino cherries
1 c. chopped nuts

Combine . first 4 ingredients with 1/2 cup water and 1/2 cup rum in bowl, beating well.
Melt ..... butter in bundt pan.
Add ..... brown sugar.
Sprinkle .. with cherries and nuts.

Pour . . . . . in batter.
Bake . . . . . at 325 degrees for 45 to 60 minutes or until cake tests done.
Cool . . . . . for 5 minutes before inverting on plate.
Drizzle . . . remaining rum over top.

Evelyn B. Willey
Gates County H. S., Gatesville, North Carolina

CHOCOLATE-RUM CAKE

1 18 1/2-oz. box chocolate cake mix
1 pkg. chocolate instant pudding mix
4 eggs
1/2 c. dark rum
1/2 c. oil
1/2 c. slivered almonds
Chocolate curls
Chocolate-Rum Filling

Combine . all ingredients except almonds, chocolate curls and filling in mixer bowl with 1/4 cup cold water.
Mix . . . . . with electric mixer at medium speed for 2 minutes.
Stir . . . . . . in almonds.
Pour . . . . . into 2 greased and floured 9-inch cake pans.
Bake . . . . . at 350 degrees for 30 minutes.
Cool . . . . . for 10 minutes in pan.
Remove . . and cool on cake rack.
Split . . . . . each layer into halves.
Spread . . . each layer with rum filling.
Garnish . . with chocolate curls.
Chill . . . . . until used.

Chocolate-Rum Filling

1 1/2 c. cold milk
1/4 c. dark rum
1 pkg. chocolate instant pudding mix
1 env. whipped topping mix

Combine . all ingredients in deep narrow mixer bowl.
Beat . . . . . with electric mixer at high speed for 4 minutes until light and fluffy.

Micki Jeffery
Center Jr. H. S., Kansas City, Missouri

EASY RED VELVET CAKE

1 box white cake mix
1 box instant chocolate pudding mix

2 c. milk
2 eggs
1 sm. bottle red food coloring
1/4 c. oil
1 tsp. soda
1 tbsp. vinegar
1 stick butter, softened
1 8-oz. package cream cheese, softened
1 box confectioners' sugar
1 tsp. vanilla extract

Combine . first 6 ingredients in bowl in order given, mixing well.
Dissolve . . soda in vinegar.
Add . . . . . to batter, mixing well.
Pour . . . . . into 3 prepared round cake pans.
Bake . . . . . at 350 degrees for 18 to 20 minutes or until cake tests done.
Cream . . . butter and cream cheese in bowl until fluffy.
Add . . . . . confectioners' sugar gradually, beating until smooth and creamy.
Stir . . . . . . in vanilla.
Spread . . . between layers and over top and side of cooled cake.

Becky Raney
Central Heights H. S., Nacogdoches, Texas

HONEY BUN CAKE

1 pkg. yellow cake mix
1 c. sour cream
4 eggs
1/3 c. oil
1 c. packed brown sugar
3 tsp. cinnamon
2 c. confectioners' sugar
3 to 4 tbsp. milk

Combine . first 4 ingredients in bowl, mixing well.
Pour . . . . . into greased and floured 9 x 13-inch baking pan.
Mix . . . . . brown sugar and cinnamon in bowl.
Sprinkle . . over batter.
Swirl . . . . batter with knife.
Bake . . . . . using cake mix directions.
Combine . remaining ingredients in small bowl.
Drizzle . . . over warm cake.

Audrey S. Williams
Walhalla Sr. H. S., Walhalla, South Carolina

KAHLUA CAKE

1 pkg. golden butter cake mix
4 eggs
1 c. sour cream
1   3 3/4-oz. package vanilla instant
   pudding mix
3/4 c. Wesson oil
1 tsp. vanilla extract
1 c. packed brown sugar
1/3 c. Kahlua
3/4 c. chopped pecans

Place ..... cake mix in large bowl.
Add ...... eggs 1 at a time, beating well after each addition.
Mix ...... in next 4 ingredients, blending well.
Stir ...... brown sugar, Kahlua and pecans into half the batter.
Pour ...... half the pecan batter into greased bundt pan.
Spoon ... in plain batter.
Top ...... with remaining pecan batter.
Swirl .... with knife to marbleize.
Bake ..... at 350 degrees for 1 to 1 1/4 hours or until cake tests done.

Frances B. Bishop
Denton Sr. H. S., Denton, Texas

SUMMER LEMON CAKE

1   3-oz. box lemon gelatin
4 eggs
3/4 c. oil
Salt
1 pkg. yellow cake mix
2 c. confectioners' sugar
1/2 c. fresh lemon juice

Prepare ... gelatin according to package directions using 1 cup boiling water.
Combine . next 2 ingredients and dash of salt in large bowl, mixing well.
Stir ...... in gelatin.
Add ...... cake mix and beat for 2 minutes.
Pour ...... into a greased 9 x 13-inch baking pan.
Bake ..... at 350 degrees for 30 to 45 minutes or until cake tests done.
Remove .. from oven and pierce with fork every 2 inches.
Mix ...... confectioners' sugar and lemon juice in bowl until smooth.

Pour ..... over warm cake.
Let ...... stand 1 day before serving.
Yield .... 12-16 servings.

Cynthia A. Cirelli
Lincoln H. S., Ellwood City, Pennsylvania

APRICOT-GLAZED GRAHAM CAKE

1/2 c. flour
1 tsp. baking powder
1/2 tsp. soda
1/4 tsp. salt
1 1/2 c. graham cracker crumbs
Butter, softened
1/2 c. sugar
1 1/4 c. packed brown sugar
2 eggs
1 tsp. vanilla extract
1   8-oz. cup yogurt
1 c. walnuts, chopped
1 tbsp. cornstarch
1/2 c. apricot juice
1/4 c. apricot preserves
1   16-oz. can apricot halves, drained, sliced

Combine . first 5 ingredients in small bowl, mixing well.
Cream ... 1/2 cup butter, sugar and 1 cup brown sugar in large bowl.
Beat ..... in eggs and vanilla until fluffy.
Add ...... dry ingredients to creamed mixture alternately with yogurt, mixing to blend after each addition.
Stir ...... in nuts.
Pour ...... into greased 12-cup glass bundt pan.
Microwave on High for 12 to 14 minutes, rotating 1/4 turn every 3 minutes.
Let ...... stand for 10 minutes.
Combine . 1/4 cup brown sugar and cornstarch in glass casserole.
Stir ...... in juice and preserves.
Microwave on High for 4 to 5 minutes, or until thick, stirring after 2 minutes.
Stir ...... in 2 tablespoons butter until melted.
Arrange .. sliced apricots on top of cake.
Spoon ... glaze over hot cake.

Photograph for this recipe on opposite page.

MICROWAVE GERMAN CHOCOLATE MYSTERY CAKE

1 pkg. German chocolate pudding cake mix
1 c. sour cream
3 eggs
1/3 c. milk
1/4 c. margarine
1 pkg. coconut-pecan frosting mix

Combine . first 3 ingredients with 1 cup water in bowl, mixing well.
Combine . milk and margarine in glass bowl.
Microwave on High for 1 minute.
Blend . . . . in frosting mix.
Pour . . . . . cake batter into lightly greased glass tube pan.
Spoon . . . frosting into ring over batter. Do not allow frosting to touch sides of pan.
Microwave on Simmer for 10 minutes.
Microwave on High for 6 minutes.
Let stand . for 5 minutes.
Cool . . . . . for 10 minutes or longer before turning out on plate.

Joyce Cole
Bell County H. S., Pineville, Kentucky

MICROWAVE LEMON BUNDT CAKE

1 pkg. lemon supreme cake mix
1 pkg. instant lemon pudding mix
2 tbsp. oil
4 lg. eggs
1 6-oz. can frozen lemonade, thawed
1 c. confectioners' sugar

Combine . first 4 ingredients with 3/4 cup water in bowl, mixing well.
Pour . . . . . into microwave bundt pan.
Let stand . for 15 minutes.
Microwave on Medium for 12 to 14 minutes or until completely risen, turning 1/4 turn every 4 minutes.
Microwave on High for 1 to 2 minutes or until cake tests done.
Let stand . for 5 to 10 minutes.
Turn . . . . . out onto plate.
Combine . lemonade and confectioners' sugar in glass bowl, blending well.
Microwave on High for 2 minutes or until heated through.
Pour . . . . . over hot cake.

Lucinda B. Helton
Conway Jr. H. S., Orlando, Florida

MICROWAVE PISTACHIO CAKE

1 c. finely chopped pecans
3/4 c. sugar
2 tbsp. cinnamon
1 pkg. yellow cake mix
1 sm. package instant pistachio pudding mix
4 eggs
1 c. sour cream
3/4 c. orange juice
1/4 c. oil
1 tsp. vanilla extract

Combine . pecans, sugar and cinnamon in small bowl, mixing well.
Sprinkle . . 1/3 of the mixture into generously greased glass bundt pan.
Combine . remaining ingredients in large bowl, beating well.
Alternate . layers of batter and cinnamon mixture in bundt pan.
Swirl . . . . batter with fork.
Microwave on High for 10 to 12 minutes or until cake tests done, rotating once.
Let stand . for 10 minutes.

Mary Jane Laing
Canutillo Jr. H. S., Canutillo, Texas

MOUNTAIN-HIGH CAKE

1 box orange cake mix
1 c. shortening
1 box coconut cream pie filling
4 eggs
1 12-oz. bottle Mountain Dew
1 c. sugar
1 tbsp. flour
1 20-oz. can crushed pineapple
3 tbsp. butter
1 c. grated coconut

Combine . first 5 ingredients in bowl, mixing
well.
Pour . . . . . into three 9-inch cake pans.
Bake . . . . . at 350 degrees for 30 minutes.
Cool . . . . . cake layers on wire rack.
Combine . remaining ingredients in saucepan.
Bring . . . . to a boil.
Boil . . . . . until mixture thickens.
Cool . . . . . slightly.
Spread . . . between layers and on top of cake.
Chill . . . . . until serving time.

Mrs. Euzelia M. Vollbracht
Burns Sr. H. S., Lawndale, North Carolina

NEOPOLITAN CAKE

1 8-oz. package cream cheese, softened
4 eggs
1 env. Dream Whip
1 white cake mix
Milk
2 tsp. vanilla extract
3/4 c. powdered strawberry drink mix
3/4 c. powdered chocolate drink mix
4 tbsp. margarine, melted
1 box confectioners' sugar, sifted

Place . . . . cream cheese in bowl.
Add . . . . . eggs 1 at a time, beating well after
each addition.
Combine . Dream Whip and cake mix in bowl.
Add . . . . . cheese mixture alternately with 3/4
cup milk and vanilla, beating well
after each addition.
Divide . . . batter into thirds.
Add . . . . . strawberry mix to one portion.
Pour . . . . . into prepared cake pan.
Cover . . . . with one portion batter.
Add . . . . . chocolate mix to remaining batter.
Pour . . . . . on top.

Bake . . . . . at 350 degrees for 45 minutes.
Combine . remaining ingredients with 7 table-
spoons milk in bowl, mixing well.
Pour . . . . . over warm cake.
Cool . . . . . before serving.

Mary Grace Ramey
Central H. S., Englewood, Tennessee

EASY ORANGE CAKE

1 box butter cake mix
3/4 c. oil
4 eggs
1 can mandarin oranges
1 box instant vanilla pudding mix
1 15-oz. can crushed pineapple
1 9-oz. container Cool Whip

Combine . first 4 ingredients in large bowl,
mixing well.
Pour . . . . . into 3 greased and floured cake
pans.
Bake . . . . . at 350 degrees for 30 minutes.
Stir . . . . . . pudding mix together with
pineapple.
Fold . . . . . in Cool Whip.
Spread . . . between layers, over top and sides
of cooled cake.
Chill . . . . . until serving time.
Garnish . . with sliced orange.
Yield . . . . 15 servings.

Alma Lee Hicks
Murphysboro H. S., Murphysboro, Illinois

STRAWBERRY SHORTCUT CAKE

1 c. miniature marshmallows
2 c. frozen strawberries, thawed
1 pkg. strawberry gelatin
1 pkg. strawberry cake mix
3 eggs
1/3 c. oil
Whipped cream

Sprinkle . . marshmallows over bottom of
greased 9 x 13-inch baking pan.
Combine . strawberries and gelatin in bowl,
mixing well.
Mix . . . . . next 3 ingredients and 3/4 cup
water in large mixing bowl.
Beat . . . . . with electric mixer at high speed
for 2 minutes.
Pour . . . . . batter over marshmallows.
Spoon . . . strawberry mixture over batter.

Bake . . . . . at 350 degrees for 40 minutes or until cake tests done.
Cool . . . . . completely and invert.
Top . . . . . with whipped cream before serving.

Ilene F. Olson
Rush City H. S., Rush City, Minnesota

SUGAR-CREAM CAKE

1 box yellow cake mix with pudding
1 stick melted butter
4 eggs
1 box confectioners' sugar
1 8-oz. package cream cheese, softened

Combine . cake mix, butter and 2 eggs in bowl, mixing well.
Press . . . . . into bottom of 9 x 13-inch pan.
Mix . . . . . remaining ingredients and eggs in bowl.
Pour . . . . . over crust.
Bake . . . . . at 350 degrees for 25 to 30 minutes or until cake tests done.

Jan McAninch
Wes-Del H. S., Gaston, Indiana

BLACK BOTTOM CUPCAKES

1 8-oz. package cream cheese, softened
1 egg
Sugar
Salt
1 6-oz. package chocolate chips
1 c. chopped pecans
1 1/2 c. flour
1/4 c. cocoa
1 tsp. soda
1/3 c. oil
1 tsp. vinegar
1 tsp. vanilla extract
Confectioners' sugar

Combine . cream cheese, egg, 1/3 cup sugar and 1 teaspoon salt in bowl, mixing well.
Add . . . . . chocolate chips and pecans.
Mix . . . . . 1 cup sugar, 1/2 teaspoon salt and remaining ingredients except confectioners' sugar in bowl with 1 cup water.
Place . . . . paper liners in muffin tin cups.
Fill . . . . . . each 1/3 full of chocolate batter.

Drop . . . . 1 spoonful of cream cheese mixture on top.
Bake . . . . . at 350 degrees for 20 minutes.
Sprinkle . . with confectioners' sugar.
Yield . . . . 24 cupcakes.

Barbara J. King
Grandview East Jr. H. S., Grandview, Missouri

SELF-FILLED CUPCAKES

1/3 c. sugar
1 8-oz. package cream cheese, softened
1 egg
1 6-oz. package semisweet chocolate chips
1 18 1/2-oz. package chocolate cake mix

Cream . . . sugar and cream cheese together in mixer bowl.
Beat . . . . . in egg.
Stir . . . . . . in chocolate chips.
Prepare . . . cake mix using package directions.
Fill . . . . . . paper-lined muffin cups 2/3 full.
Drop . . . . one rounded teaspoonful of the cheese mixture into each cupcake.
Bake . . . . . according to package directions.
Yield . . . . 30 cupcakes.

Carol Harding
Florence H. S., Florence, Texas

TRULY DIFFERENT CUPCAKES

4 sq. semisweet chocolate
1 c. margarine
3 tbsp. vanilla extract
1 1/2 c. chopped pecans
1 3/4 c. sugar
1 c. flour
4 eggs

Melt . . . . . chocolate squares and margarine in saucepan over low heat.
Stir . . . . . . in vanilla and pecans; remove from heat.
Combine . sugar, flour and eggs in bowl, stirring lightly.
Stir . . . . . . into chocolate mixture with wooden spoon, mixing lightly.
Fill . . . . . . lined muffin cups 1/2 full.
Bake . . . . . at 350 degrees for 30 to 35 minutes.
Yield . . . . 18 cupcakes.

Linsae Snider
Robert E. Lee H. S., Baytown, Texas

CHOCOLATE-CHERRY LOG

2/3 c. sifted cake flour
3/4 tsp. baking powder
1/4 tsp. salt
1/3 c. unsweetened cocoa
6 eggs
1 1/4 c. sugar
3 tsp. vanilla extract
Confectioners' sugar
2 c. heavy cream
1 8-oz. jar red maraschino cherries,
*   drained, chopped*

Sift . . . . . . first 4 ingredients together twice.
Beat . . . . . eggs in large bowl.
Add . . . . . 1 cup and 2 tablespoons sugar and 1 1/2 teaspoons vanilla, beating until thick.
Fold . . . . . dry ingredients into creamed mixture 1/3 at a time.
Line . . . . . greased 10 x 15-inch baking pan with waxed paper.
Grease . . . waxed paper.
Pour . . . . . in batter.

Bake . . . . . at 350 degrees for 20 minutes.
Cool . . . . . for 5 minutes.
Invert . . . . onto towel sprinkled with confectioners' sugar.
Trim . . . . . edges.
Roll . . . . . cake in towel.
Cool . . . . . for 30 minutes.
Whip . . . . 1 cup cream with 1 tablespoon sugar and 3/4 teaspoon vanilla in bowl until stiff.
Fold . . . . . in cherries.
Unroll . . . cake, removing towel.
Spread . . . with cherry mixture.
Reroll . . . . cake.
Chill . . . . . for 2 hours or longer.
Place . . . . seam side down on serving plate.
Whip . . . . remaining 1 cup cream, with 1 tablespoon sugar and 3/4 teaspoon vanilla in bowl until stiff.
Spread . . . over cake roll.
Garnish . . with stemmed cherries and chocolate curls.
Chill . . . . . until serving time.

Photograph for this recipe above.

MARY'S CAKE ROLL

3 eggs
Sugar
2 tsp. vanilla extract
1 c. flour
1/2 tsp. baking powder
1/4 tsp. salt
1 c. milk
3 tbsp. flour
1 c. butter

Beat . . . . . eggs in bowl until light.
Add . . . . . 1 cup sugar gradually, beating well.
Blend . . . . in 1/3 cup water and 1 teaspoon vanilla.
Add . . . . . flour, baking powder and salt, mixing well.
Pour . . . . . onto waxed paper-lined jelly roll pan.
Bake . . . . . at 350 degrees for 10 minutes or until cake tests done.
Remove . . from pan onto dish towel.
Roll . . . . . in towel and cool on wire rack.
Combine . milk and flour in saucepan.
Cook . . . . over medium heat, stirring constantly, until thick.
Add . . . . . 1 cup sugar, 1 teaspoon vanilla and butter, beating until smooth.
Unroll . . . cake and spread with filling.
Roll . . . . . cake and slice.

Mary M. Glasser
Mapleton H. S., Ashland, Ohio

LINDA'S CHOCOLATE ROLL

1/4 c. cake flour
1/2 tsp. salt
1 c. confectioners' sugar
3 tbsp. cocoa
5 egg yolks, beaten
1 tsp. vanilla extract
5 egg whites, stiffly beaten
Cool Whip

Sift . . . . . . first 4 ingredients together in bowl.
Add . . . . . egg yolks and vanilla, mixing well.
Fold . . . . . in egg whites.
Pour . . . . . into greased and floured jelly roll pan.
Bake . . . . . at 350 degrees for 15 minutes.
Cool . . . . . slightly and turn out on towel.
Roll . . . . . in towel and cool on wire rack.
Unroll . . . cake and spread with Cool Whip.

Roll . . . . . cake carefully.
Store . . . . in refrigerator.
Yield . . . . 10 servings.

Linda Valentine
University H. S., Greeley, Colorado

CHOCOLATE-PEPPERMINT CAKE ROLL

3/4 c. sifted cake flour
1/4 c. cocoa
1/2 tsp. baking powder
1/2 tsp. salt
4 eggs
3/4 c. sugar
1 tsp. vanilla extract
Confectioners' sugar
1 tsp. unflavored gelatin
1 c. whipping cream, whipped
1/3 c. finely crushed peppermint candy

Sift . . . . . . first 4 ingredients together.
Beat . . . . . eggs in bowl with electric mixer at high speed until thick and light.
Add . . . . . sugar gradually, beating well after each addition.
Stir . . . . . . in vanilla and 1 tablespoon water.
Fold . . . . . in flour mixture gradually, blending well.
Spread . . . in greased and floured, waxed paper-lined 10 x 15-inch jelly roll pan.
Bake . . . . . at 375 degrees for 8 to 10 minutes or until cake tests done.
Invert . . . . on towel sprinkled with confectioners' sugar.
Peel . . . . . off waxed paper.
Roll . . . . . cake and towel as for jelly roll.
Cool . . . . . for 20 minutes.
Soften . . . gelatin in 1/4 cup water in saucepan.
Cook . . . . over low heat until gelatin dissolves.
Cool . . . . . to room temperature.
Fold . . . . . into whipped cream.
Add . . . . . crushed candy.
Chill . . . . . covered, for 5 to 10 minutes.
Unroll . . . cake, removing towel.
Spread . . . with filling and reroll.
Chill . . . . . covered, for 1 hour or longer.
Sprinkle . . with confectioners' sugar.

Mary Jo Conatser
Bristol, Virginia

CHOCOLATE-STRAWBERRY ROLL

3/4 c. flour
1/4 c. cocoa
1 tsp. baking powder
1/4 tsp. salt
3 eggs, well beaten
1 c. sugar
1 tsp. vanilla extract
Confectioners' sugar
Strawberry ice cream, softened

Sift . . . . . . first 4 ingredients together.
Combine . eggs and sugar in bowl, mixing well.
Add . . . . . vanilla and 1/3 cup water.
Add . . . . . flour mixture gradually, blending well.
Pour . . . . . into greased foil-lined jelly roll pan.
Bake . . . . . at 375 degrees for 12 minutes or until cake tests done.
Remove . . to towel sprinkled with confectioners' sugar.
Roll . . . . . cake in towel and cool on wire rack.
Unroll . . . and spread with ice cream.
Roll . . . . . cake carefully.
Sprinkle . . with confectioners' sugar.
Store . . . . in freezer.
Yield . . . . 10 servings.

Terry Naylor
West Jordan H. S., West Jordan, Utah

EASY CHOCOLATE ROLL

1 /4 c. butter
1 c. chopped pecans
1 1/3 c. coconut
1   15-oz. can sweetened condensed milk
3 eggs
1 c. sugar
1/3 c. cocoa
2/3 c. flour
1/4 tsp. each salt, soda
1 tsp. vanilla extract
Confectioners' sugar

Line . . . . . jelly roll pan with foil.
Melt . . . . . butter in pan.
Sprinkle . . with pecans and coconut.
Drizzle . . . with condensed milk.
Beat . . . . . eggs in bowl with electric mixer at high speed until fluffy.
Add . . . . . sugar gradually, beating constantly.

Beat . . . . . for 2 minutes longer.
Add . . . . . remaining ingredients except confectioners' sugar and 1/3 cup water, blending at low speed for 1 minute.
Pour . . . . . evenly over pecans and coconut.
Bake . . . . . at 375 degrees for 20 minutes or until cake tests done.
Sprinkle . . cake with confectioners' sugar.
Cover . . . . with towel and cookie sheet.
Invert . . . . cake.
Remove . . pan and foil.
Roll . . . . . as for jelly roll.
Yield . . . . 10-12 slices.

Linda M. Frank
Dublin H. S., Dublin, Texas

PENNSYLVANIA NUT ROLLS

Milk
Sugar
4 eggs
1 tsp. vanilla extract
1 pkg. dry yeast
5 c. flour
1 c. butter, melted
1 tsp. salt
1 lb. ground pecans
1/2 c. butter, softened
1 egg yolk, beaten

Heat . . . . . 1 cup milk in saucepan over medium heat.
Add . . . . . 3/4 cup sugar, 3 eggs and vanilla.
Dissolve . . yeast in 1 cup warm water.
Add . . . . . to milk mixture.
Add . . . . . a small amount flour, stirring until smooth.
Stir . . . . . . in melted butter, salt and remaining flour.
Knead . . . until smooth.
Cover . . . . dough and let rise in warm place until doubled in size.
Combine . pecans, softened butter, 1 1/4 cups sugar, 1 egg and 2/3 cup milk, mixing well.
Divide . . . dough into 8 portions.
Roll . . . . . into 1/4-inch thick squares on floured surface.
Spread . . . each with pecan mixture.
Roll . . . . . jelly roll fashion.
Brush . . . . with egg yolk.

Place .... in shallow pan.
Bake ..... at 350 degrees for 45 minutes.

Nancy Buffington
Marshall County H. S., Benton, Kentucky

PUMPKIN CAKE ROLL

3 eggs
1 c. sugar
2/3 c. pumpkin
1 tsp. lemon juice
3/4 c. flour
1 tsp. baking powder
2 tsp. cinnamon
1 tsp. ginger
1/2 tsp. each nutmeg, salt
1 c. finely chopped walnuts
Confectioners' sugar
2 3-oz. packages cream cheese, softened
4 tbsp. margarine, softened
1/2 tsp. vanilla extract

Beat ..... eggs and sugar in mixer bowl with electric mixer on high for 5 minutes.
Stir ...... in pumpkin and lemon juice.
Sift ...... flour, baking powder, spices and salt together.
Fold ..... into batter.
Spread ... in greased and floured 10 x 15-inch pan.
Top ..... with nuts.
Bake ..... at 375 degrees for 15 minutes.
Remove .. to towel sprinkled with confectioners' sugar.
Roll ..... cake in towel and cool on wire rack.
Combine . 1 cup confectioners' sugar, cream cheese, margarine and vanilla in bowl, beating until smooth.
Unroll ... cake and spread with filling.
Roll ..... cake carefully.
Store .... in refrigerator.
Yield .... 12-16 servings.

Beverley Clear Goodman
Smyth County Vocational School, Marion, Virginia

CREAMY ALMOND TOPPING

1/4 c. flour
1/4 c. sugar

1/4 c. cold milk
1 c. hot milk
Butter
1/2 c. confectioners' sugar
2 tsp. vanilla extract
1/2 c. slivered almonds

Combine . first 3 ingredients in bowl, mixing well.
Stir ...... into hot milk in saucepan.
Cook .... for 5 minutes or until thick, stirring constantly.
Cool ..... to lukewarm.
Cream ... 1/2 cup butter, confectioners' sugar and vanilla in bowl.
Stir ...... into cooked mixture.
Brown ... almonds in 1 tablespoon butter in skillet.
Fold ..... into cooked mixture.
Chill ..... until of spreading consistency.

Arlene Nettles
Huntsville, Alabama

AMBROSIA CAKE FILLING

1 can flaked coconut
1 lg. can crushed pineapple
Juice of 2 oranges
Juice of 2 lemons
4 tbsp. cornstarch
1 1/2 c. sugar

Combine . all ingredients in saucepan, mixing well.
Cook .... over medium heat until thick, stirring constantly.
Yield .... frosting for 3-layer cake.

Catherine G. Ward
G. P. Babb Jr. H. S., Forest Park, Georgia

ANY-FLAVOR DECORATOR'S FROSTING

1/2 c. shortening
1 box confectioners' sugar
1/2 to 1 tsp. vanilla extract

Combine . all ingredients and 1/4 cup hot water in mixing bowl.
Beat ..... with electric mixer at low speed until just blended.

Mabel Buxton
Sherryville, Alabama

CREAMY CARAMEL ICING

2 c. packed light brown sugar
1 tbsp. light corn syrup
1/2 c. milk
Shortening
2 1/2 c. sifted confectioners' sugar
4 tbsp. hot milk
1 tsp. vanilla extract

Combine . first 3 ingredients and 1 tablespoon shortening in saucepan.
Cook .... to soft-ball stage or 235 degrees on candy thermometer.
Combine . 1/3 cup shortening with remaining ingredients in bowl, beating until smooth.
Pour ..... cooked syrup over vanilla mixture, beating until creamy.
Yield .... Icing for 2 nine-inch layers.

Ann Moore
Jackson County H. S., Gainesboro, Tennessee

CHOCOLATE BUTTER CREAM FROSTING

1 c. butter, softened
2 lb. confectioners' sugar
1/2 c. cocoa
1 tsp. vanilla extract

Combine . all ingredients in bowl.
Beat ..... for 10 minutes until light and fluffy.
Yield .... frosting for 2-3 cakes.

Janelle L. Jones
Spearfish Schools, Spearfish, South Dakota

HEATH BAR FROSTING

4 tbsp. cocoa
1 c. confectioners' sugar
1 pt. whipping cream
6 Heath bars, frozen, crushed
1 angel food cake

Blend .... cocoa, confectioners' sugar and whipping cream in bowl.
Let ...... stand for 6 hours.
Whip .... as for whipped cream.
Fold ..... in candy.
Cut ...... angel food cake into 3 layers.
Frost .... between layers and top of cake.

Carol Jacobsen
Hoffman Estates H. S., Hoffman Estates, Illinois

CREAM CHEESE FROSTING

2 3-oz. packages cream cheese, softened
3 tbsp. light cream
1 tbsp. grated orange rind
1/4 c. confectioners' sugar

Combine . all ingredients in mixer bowl.
Cream ... until smooth.
Serve .... with unfrosted cake.
Yield .... 1 1/4 cups.

Margaret Polkabla
Memorial H. S., Campbell, Ohio

CREAMY WHITE ICING

3 tbsp. flour
1 c. milk
1/2 c. butter
1/2 c. shortening
1 c. sugar
1 tsp. vanilla extract

Blend .... flour and milk in saucepan.
Cook .... over medium heat until thick, stirring constantly.
Cool ..... covered, to prevent film from forming.
Cream ... butter, shortening, sugar and vanilla in bowl.
Add ..... flour mixture, beating constantly.
Beat ..... for 5 minutes longer or until consistency of fluffy whipped cream.
Yield .... 2 cups.

Susan M. Davis
Northside H. S., Warner Robins, Georgia

EASY BIRTHDAY FROSTING

2 egg whites, stiffly beaten
1 box confectioners' sugar
1/2 c. shortening
1/2 tsp. almond extract
Pinch of salt
Milk

Combine . first 3 ingredients in bowl, beating well.
Add ..... remaining ingredients except milk, beating well.
Add ..... a small amount of milk for desired consistency, if necessary.
Yield .... frosting for 1 sheet cake.

Brenda Long
Smiths Station H. S., Smiths, Alabama

ORANGE CREAM FROSTING

3 tbsp. butter, softened
1 3-oz. package cream cheese, softened
Dash of salt
1/4 c. frozen orange juice, thawed
4 1/2 c. sifted confectioners' sugar

Cream ... butter, cream cheese, salt and orange juice in bowl until light and fluffy.
Add ..... sugar gradually, blending well after each addition.
Beat ..... until of spreading consistency.
Yield .... frosting for two 8-inch layers.

Mary Beth Cowden
Westdale, Arizona

PEANUT BUTTER FROSTING

1 c. milk
2 c. sugar
1 c. peanut butter
1 tsp. vanilla extract

Combine . milk and sugar in saucepan.
Cook .... at a rolling boil for 15 minutes.
Remove .. from heat.
Stir ...... in peanut butter and vanilla.
Beat ..... until of desired consistency.
Yield .... frosting for 9 x 13-inch cake.

Gail Helms
Enterprise H. S., Enterprise, Alabama

PEPPERMINT DECORATOR'S ICING

1 1/3 c. shortening
2 tsp. peppermint flavoring
Dash of salt
2 lb. confectioners' sugar

Combine . shortening, flavoring and salt in bowl, mixing well.
Blend .... in 1 pound confectioners' sugar and 1/4 cup water until smooth.
Stir ...... in remaining confectioners' sugar and 1/4 cup water until creamy. Do not overbeat.
Tint ..... as desired with paste food colors.
Yield .... 6 cups.

Sandra Salas DeBord
Spring Oaks Jr. H. S., Houston, Texas

PROFESSIONAL BAKER'S ICING

1/2 c. shortening
1 lb. confectioners' sugar
2 egg whites
3 drops of butter extract
1 tsp. almond extract
Dash of salt

Cream ... shortening and half the confectioners' sugar in bowl.
Blend .... in egg whites, flavorings and salt.
Beat ..... in remaining confectioners' sugar to spreading consistency.
Yield .... icing for 2 layers.

Brenda Broaddus
Berea Community School, Berea, Kentucky

SWISS CHOCOLATE SAUCE

1 can sweetened condensed milk
1/4 c. butter
Pinch of salt
1 6-oz. package chocolate chips
1 tsp. vanilla extract

Combine . sweetened condensed milk and butter in saucepan.
Bring .... to a boil over medium heat, stirring constantly.
Boil ..... for 1 minute.
Remove .. from heat.
Stir ...... in chocolate chips, vanilla and 1/4 cup hot water, mixing well.

Janet Miller
Strong Vincent H. S., Erie, Pennsylvania

OLD-FASHIONED LEMON CURD

1 egg, beaten
2 egg yolks, beaten
2 tsp. grated lemon peel
6 tbsp. lemon juice
3/4 c. sugar
1/4 c. butter
Dash of salt

Combine . all ingredients in saucepan, blending well.
Cook .... over low heat for 5 to 8 minutes or until mixture thickens, stirring constantly.
Serve .... hot or cold over fruit, cake, etc.

Photograph for this recipe on page 2.

OLE TIME FAVORITE CARAMEL SAUCE

1 can sweetened condensed milk
1/4 c. milk
1 c. whipping cream, whipped
1/2 c. chopped nuts
1/2 c. chopped maraschino cherries

Boil ..... unopened sweetened condensed milk submerged in water for 2 1/2 to 3 hours.
Cool ..... completely.
Combine . condensed milk and milk in bowl.
Fold ..... in whipped cream, nuts and cherries.
Serve .... over angel food cake.

Rebecca W. Harrell
Franklin-Simpson Middle School, Franklin, Kentucky

CITRUS TOPPING

2 tbsp. flour
1/2 c. sugar
Pinch of salt
Juice and grated rind of 1/2 lemon
Juice and grated rind of 1 orange
1 tbsp. butter
1/2 pt. whipping cream, whipped

Combine . first 3 ingredients in saucepan.
Add ..... juices, grated rinds and butter.
Cook .... over medium heat until thick.
Chill ..... in refrigerator.
Fold ..... chilled mixture into whipped cream.
Serve .... on unfrosted cake.

Eunice Grand
Grovesville, California

FRUIT TOPPING

1   11-oz. can mandarin oranges
1   29-oz. can sliced peaches
3 tbsp. tapioca
1/2 c. sugar
Dash of salt
1 6-oz. can frozen orange juice concentrate
1 10-oz. box frozen strawberries, thawed
2 bananas, sliced

Drain .... oranges and peaches, reserving juice.

Combine . reserved fruit juices and enough water to measure 2 1/2 cups.
Add ..... 1 cup juice to tapioca, sugar and salt in saucepan.
Let ...... stand for 5 minutes.
Cook .... over medium heat until thick and clear, stirring frequently.
Add ..... remaining liquid, mixing well.
Combine . orange juice concentrate, strawberries, mandarin oranges and peaches in large bowl.
Stir ...... in tapioca mixture.
Add ..... bananas just before serving.
Serve .... over pound cake.

Bonnie Roelofs
Evangelical Christian School, Cordova, Tennessee

WHIPPED BANANA TOPPING

1 egg white
1/3 c. sugar
Juice of 1 lemon
1 lg. ripe banana, sliced

Beat ..... egg white in bowl until foamy.
Add ..... sugar and lemon juice gradually, beating until stiff.
Beat ..... in banana until well blended.
Serve .... on hot gingerbread.

Nancy Dunn
Roanoke, Virginia

FLUFFY LEMON SAUCE

1 c. sugar
5 tbsp. cake flour
1 egg, slightly beaten
1/3 c. lemon juice
2 tsp. butter
1 tsp. grated lemon rind
1/2 pt. whipping cream, whipped

Combine . first 4 ingredients in top of double boiler.
Add ..... 2/3 cup cold water and butter, mixing well.
Cook .... over boiling water for 10 minutes or until thick.
Chill ..... in refrigerator.
Fold ..... in lemon rind and whipped cream.

Barbara Metcalf
Martinsville, Ohio

Cheesecakes
and Puddings

APRICOT CHEESECAKE

1   30-oz. can apricot halves
1 1/2 tsp. unflavored gelatin
1   3-oz. package cream cheese, softened
1/4 c. sugar
1   6-oz. can evaporated milk, chilled
2 tbsp. lemon juice
1 recipe graham cracker crust
Red food coloring

Drain .... apricots, reserving 1/4 cup syrup
and 6 apricot halves.
Chop .... remaining apricots.
Soften ... gelatin in reserved syrup in double
boiler pan.
Heat ..... over hot water until gelatin
dissolves.
Beat ..... cream cheese in bowl until creamy.
Add ..... sugar and gelatin gradually, beating
well.
Whip .... chilled milk in bowl until fluffy.
Add ..... lemon juice, beating until stiff.
Blend .... into gelatin mixture.
Fold ..... in apricots.
Pat ...... graham cracker crust into 9-inch
cake pan.
Pour ..... apricot mixture over top.
Brush .... reserved apricots with food
coloring.
Arrange .. on top of cheesecake.
Chill ..... until firm.
Garnish .. with mint.

Sara Norton
Reidsville, Maryland

BANANA CHEESECAKE SUPREME

1 c. graham cracker crumbs
Sugar
3 tbsp. butter, melted
2 env. unflavored gelatin
2 egg yolks
1/2 c. milk
Lemon juice
1 tsp. grated lemon rind
3 c. cottage cheese
3 egg whites, stiffly beaten
5 med. bananas, divided
1 c. heavy cream, whipped
1 tsp. cornstarch

Combine . 3/4 cup graham cracker crumbs and
2 tablespoons sugar.

Blend .... in butter.
Press ..... evenly on bottom of 9-inch spring-
form pan.
Chill ..... until firm.
Combine . gelatin and 1/2 cup sugar in me-
dium saucepan.
Beat ..... egg yolks and milk in bowl.
Stir ...... into gelatin mixture.
Cook .... over low heat for 5 minutes until
gelatin dissolves, stirring constantly.
Stir ...... in 2 teaspoons lemon juice and
rind.
Beat ..... cottage cheese in bowl with electric
mixer at high speed for 4 to 5 min-
utes or until smooth.
Add ..... gelatin mixture gradually, beating
well.
Chill ..... until partially set.
Fold ..... in egg whites.
Stir ...... in 2 diced bananas.
Blend .... in whipped cream.
Pour ..... into prepared pan.
Chill ..... for 3 hours or until firm.
Remove .. side of pan.
Press ..... remaining crumbs around side.
Combine . 1/3 cup lemon juice with 1/2 cup
sugar in saucepan.
Cook .... over low heat until dissolved.
Mix ..... cornstarch with 1/4 cup cold water.
Stir ...... into lemon juice.
Cook .... until thick, stirring constantly.
Slice ..... remaining 3 bananas.
Dip ...... into lemon glaze.
Arrange .. in rings around cheesecake, starting
at outer edge.
Chill ..... for 30 minutes.
Yield .... 12 servings.

Photograph for this recipe on page 59.

BLENDER CHEESECAKE

1 2/3 c. graham cracker crumbs
1/2 c. butter, melted
1   3-oz. package lemon gelatin
2 tbsp. lemon juice
2 c. cottage cheese
1   10-oz. package Cool Whip

Combine . graham cracker crumbs and butter
in bowl, mixing well.
Press ..... into 7 x 11-inch serving dish.

Pour . . . . . 1/2 cup boiling water into blender container.
Add . . . . . gelatin; process until dissolved.
Add . . . . . lemon juice and cottage cheese, 1 cup at a time.
Process . . . on high until smooth.
Pour . . . . . into large mixer bowl.
Add . . . . . Cool Whip.
Beat . . . . . with electric mixer at medium speed until smooth.
Pour . . . . . over graham cracker crust.
Chill . . . . . in refrigerator until set.
Yield . . . . 10-12 servings.

Arlene Maisel
Highland Park H. S., Highland Park, New Jersey

BLUEBERRY CHEESECAKE

1/2 c. butter, softened
1 12-oz. package Zwieback, crushed
1/2 c. super-fine sugar
1 tbsp. grated lemon rind
5 8-oz. packages cream cheese, softened
1 3/4 c. sugar
3 tbsp. flour
1 1/2 tsp. grated orange rind
1/2 tsp. vanilla extract
5 eggs
2 egg yolks
1/4 c. whipping cream
1 c. fresh blueberries, rinsed, drained

Combine . butter, crumbs, super-fine sugar and 1 1/2 teaspoons rind in bowl, mixing well.
Press . . . . over bottom and side of buttered springform pan.
Combine . next 5 ingredients and 1 1/2 teaspoons lemon rind in bowl.
Beat . . . . . until smooth and fluffy.
Add . . . . . eggs and egg yolks 1 at a time, beating well after each addition.
Stir . . . . . . in cream.
Spoon . . . into prepared pan.
Bake . . . . . at 300 degrees for 1 hour.
Turn . . . . . off oven, leaving cake for 1 hour longer.
Cool . . . . . to room temperature.
Chill . . . . . overnight.
Arrange . . blueberries over top.
Yield . . . . 16 servings.

Photograph for this recipe on this page.

CLAUDIA'S CHEESECAKE

1 1/2 c. graham cracker crumbs
2 c. sugar
1 stick butter, melted
2 8-oz. packages cream cheese, softened
1 pt. sour cream
1 lb. ricotta cheese
3 eggs
3 tbsp. cornstarch
2 tsp. vanilla extract
1 tsp. lemon juice
1 can cherry pie filling

Combine . crumbs, 1/2 cup sugar and half the melted butter in bowl, mixing well.
Press . . . . . into bottom of 10-inch springform pan.
Beat . . . . . next 4 ingredients and 1 1/2 cups sugar in bowl with electric mixer at low speed.
Add . . . . . cornstarch, vanilla, lemon juice and remaining butter.
Beat . . . . . at high speed until smooth.
Pour . . . . . into crust.
Bake . . . . . at 350 degrees for 1 hour.
Turn . . . . . off oven, leaving cheesecake for 2 hours longer.
Top . . . . . with pie filling.

Claudia Triolo
Dayton Avenue School, Manorville, New York

EASY CHERRY CHEESECAKE

1 8-oz. package cream cheese, softened
1/8 tsp. salt
2 eggs
1 tbsp. lemon juice
Sugar
Vanilla extract
1 9-in. baked graham cracker crust
1 c. sour cream
1 can cherry pie filling

Combine . first 4 ingredients in blender container with 1/2 cup sugar and 1/2 teaspoon vanilla.
Process . . . until smooth.
Pour . . . . . into cooled graham cracker crust.
Bake . . . . . at 325 degrees for 25 minutes.
Combine . sour cream, 2 tablespoons sugar and 1 tablespoon vanilla, mixing well.
Spread . . . sour cream mixture over cream cheese mixture.
Bake . . . . . for 5 minutes longer.
Chill . . . . . in refrigerator.
Spoon . . . on cherry pie filling.
Yield . . . . 6-8 servings.

Patricia M. Fritz
Bayshore H. S., Bradenton, Florida

RED CHERRY CHEESECAKE

Flour
Sugar
Grated lemon rind
Vanilla extract
3 egg yolks
1/4 c. butter, softened
5 8-oz. packages cream cheese, softened
1 1/2 tsp. grated orange rind
5 eggs
1/4 c. heavy cream
1 1-lb. can sour red water-packed cherries
1 tbsp. cornstarch
1 tbsp. lemon juice
2 drops of red food coloring

Combine . 1 cup sifted flour, 1/4 cup sugar and 1 teaspoon lemon rind in bowl.
Add . . . . . 1/2 teaspoon vanilla, 1 egg yolk and butter, mixing well.
Shape . . . . into ball; wrap in waxed paper.
Chill . . . . . for 1 hour.
Press . . . . . 1/3 of the dough on bottom of separated springform pan.

Bake . . . . . at 400 degrees for 8 to 10 minutes.
Assemble . springform pan.
Press . . . . . remaining 2/3 of the dough 3/4 of way up side.
Chill . . . . . in refrigerator.
Combine . cream cheese, 1 3/4 cups sugar, 3 tablespoons flour and 1 1/2 teaspoons each lemon and orange rind, blending well.
Mix . . . . . in 1/4 teaspoon vanilla, 2 egg yolks and whole eggs 1 at a time, beating well after each addition.
Add . . . . . cream, beating just until mixed.
Pour . . . . . mixture into springform pan.
Bake . . . . . at 500 degrees for 10 minutes.
Reduce . . . temperature to 250 degrees.
Bake . . . . . for 1 hour longer.
Cool . . . . . in pan on wire rack.
Drain . . . . cherries, reserving 1/2 cup liquid.
Blend . . . . reserved liquid, 1/2 cup sugar and cornstarch in small saucepan until smooth.
Bring . . . . to a boil.
Cook . . . . for 1 minute, stirring constantly. Cool.
Add . . . . . lemon juice, cherries and food coloring, mixing well.
Spoon . . . over cheesecake.
Chill . . . . . for 3 hours or longer.
Yield . . . . 16-20 servings.

Celia Eldridge
Mabank H. S., Mabank, Texas

BITTERSWEET CHOCOLATE CHEESECAKE

1 1/4 c. graham cracker crumbs
2 tbsp. sugar
1/4 c. margarine, melted
1/2 c. chopped peanuts
2 8-oz. packages cream cheese, softened
1 can sweetened condensed milk
1 tsp. almond extract
1 6-oz. package chocolate chips, melted

Combine . first 4 ingredients in bowl, mixing well.
Press . . . . . into baking dish.
Bake . . . . . at 350 degrees for 10 minutes.
Beat . . . . . together next 3 ingredients in bowl.
Pour . . . . . melted chocolate into pie crust.
Cover . . . . with cream cheese mixture.

Swirl .... with knife to marbleize.
Chill ..... in refrigerator.
Yield .... 8 slices.

Linda J. Dobbins
Indian River H. S., Chesapeake, Virginia

CHEESECAKE FREEZE

1 c. graham cracker crumbs
Sugar
3 tbsp. butter, melted
2 8-oz. packages cream cheese, softened
2 eggs, separated
2 tbsp. frozen orange juice concentrate,
thawed
2 c. heavy cream, whipped
1 c. chopped M & M plain chocolate
candies, frozen

Combine . crumbs, 3 tablespoons sugar and butter in bowl, mixing well.
Press ..... into 9-inch springform pan.
Bake ..... at 350 degrees for 10 minutes; cool.
Beat ..... cream cheese, 1 cup sugar, egg yolks and juice in bowl with electric mixer at medium speed until smooth.
Fold ..... stiffly beaten egg whites and whipped cream into cream cheese mixture.
Stir ...... in candies.
Spoon ... over crust.
Freeze ... until firm.
Thaw .... for 10 minutes before serving.
Cut ...... into wedges.

Photograph for this recipe on page 70.

ALMOND CHEESECAKE

2 c. fine vanilla wafer crumbs
1/2 c. butter, melted
1/4 c. finely chopped blanched almonds
Sugar
2 8-oz. packages cream cheese, softened
4 eggs
1 tsp. grated lemon rind
1 tsp. vanilla extract
1/4 tsp. almond extract
2 tbsp. flour
1/2 tsp. salt
1 tbsp. cornstarch

1 10-oz. package frozen sliced peaches
in syrup, thawed
1/4 c. toasted slivered almonds

Combine . first 3 ingredients and 1/3 cup sugar in bowl, mixing well.
Press ..... over bottom and 1 3/4 inches up side of buttered 9-inch springform pan.
Chill ..... until firm.
Beat ..... cream cheese in bowl until smooth.
Add ..... eggs 1 at a time, beating well after each addition.
Beat ..... in lemon rind, vanilla and almond extract.
Combine . flour, salt and 1/2 cup sugar.
Blend .... into cheese mixture.
Pour ..... into prepared pan.
Bake ..... at 350 degrees for 35 to 40 minutes or until firm.
Chill ..... in refrigerator.
Mix ..... cornstarch and 2 tablespoons sugar in saucepan.
Drain .... peaches, reserving syrup.
Stir ...... syrup into sugar mixture.
Cook .... until thick and clear, stirring constantly.
Add ..... peaches.
Cook .... until heated.
Spoon ... over cheesecake.
Sprinkle .. with almonds.
Chill ..... for 2 to 4 hours.

Photograph for this recipe below.

CHOCOLATE CHEESECAKE

1 pkg. chocolate wafers
1/2 tsp. cinnamon
Butter, melted
3/4 c. sugar
3 eggs
18 oz. cream cheese, softened
12 oz. semisweet chocolate, melted
1 tsp. vanilla extract
1 1/2 tbsp. cocoa
2 1/4 c. sour cream

Process ... wafers in blender to make very fine crumbs.
Mix ..... crumbs, cinnamon and 1/2 cup butter in bowl.
Press ..... firmly into bottom and side of 9-inch springform pan.
Beat ..... sugar with eggs in mixer bowl until light and fluffy.
Beat ..... cream cheese until light in large bowl.
Add ..... egg mixture gradually, blending well.
Add ..... chocolate, vanilla, cocoa and sour cream, beating constantly.
Stir ...... in 3 tablespoons melted butter, mixing well.
Pour ..... into chilled crust.
Bake ..... at 350 degrees for 1 hour.
Turn ..... oven off and open door.
Leave .... cheesecake in oven for 1 hour longer.
Chill ..... overnight.

Nancy A. Blue
Mount Vernon H. S., Mount Vernon, Washington

CHOCOLATE CREAM CHEESECAKE

1 1/4 c. self-rising flour
1 stick butter, softened
1 c. chopped nuts
1 c. confectioners' sugar
1 8-oz. package cream cheese, softened
1 9-oz. carton Cool Whip
2 sm. packages instant chocolate pudding mix
3 c. milk

Combine . first 3 ingredients in bowl, mixing well.
Press ..... into 9 x 13-inch baking dish.
Bake ..... at 375 degrees for 20 minutes.

Combine . confectioners' sugar, cream cheese and half the Cool Whip in bowl, mixing well.
Spread ... mixture on cooled crust.
Mix ..... instant pudding and milk using package directions.
Spread ... over cream cheese mixture.
Chill ..... until set.
Top ..... with remaining Cool Whip.
Sprinkle .. with chopped nuts and shaved chocolate.
Chill ..... until served.

Brenda Doss
Haines City Jr. H. S., Haines City, Florida

CHOCOLATE FUDGE CHEESECAKE

1 1/3 c. chocolate pieces
1/4 c. margarine, melted
1 c. crushed chocolate wafers
3 8-oz. packages cream cheese, softened
1 c. sugar
2 eggs
1 c. sour cream
1 tsp. vanilla extract

Combine . 1/4 cup water and chocolate pieces in saucepan.
Cook .... over low heat until chocolate melts, stirring constantly.
Combine . margarine and crushed wafers in bowl, mixing well.
Press ..... into bottom of 9-inch springform pan.
Beat ..... cream cheese, sugar and eggs in mixer bowl until well blended.
Stir ...... in chocolate mixture, mixing well.
Add ..... remaining ingredients, blending well.
Pour ..... into wafer crust.
Bake ..... at 350 degrees for 55 to 60 minutes; center will be soft.

Mrs. Mary Agnes Mosher
Chantilly H. S., Chantilly, Virginia

CHOCOLATE MARBLE CHEESECAKE

2 lb. cream cheese, softened
1 tsp. vanilla extract
1/4 tsp. almond extract
1 3/4 c. sugar
4 eggs

2 oz. unsweetened chocolate, melted, cooled
1/3 c. graham cracker crumbs
1 lg. milk chocolate bar

Combine . first 4 ingredients in bowl, beating well.
Add . . . . . eggs 1 at a time, beating well after each addition.
Blend . . . . 1/3 of the batter with chocolate in small bowl.
Drop . . . . tablespoons of white batter alternately with teaspoons of dark batter into deep greased 8-inch round baking pan.
Place . . . . in hot water on low rack of oven.
Bake . . . . . at 350 degrees for 90 minutes.
Cool . . . . . on wire rack.
Invert . . . . onto serving plate.
Sprinkle . . with graham cracker crumbs.
Chill . . . . . for 5 to 6 hours.
Decorate . with curls from chocolate bar.

Jan Tuchscherer
Durango Sr. H. S., Durango, Colorado

CHOCOLATE SWIRL CHEESECAKE

1 6-oz. package semisweet chocolate pieces
Sugar
1 1/4 c. graham cracker crumbs
1/4 c. butter, melted
2 8-oz. packages cream cheese, softened
1/2 c. sour cream
1 tsp. vanilla extract
4 eggs

Melt . . . . . chocolate pieces and 1/2 cup sugar in double boiler.
Combine . graham cracker crumbs, 2 tablespoons sugar and butter in bowl, mixing well.
Press . . . . . into bottom and 1/2 inch up side of 9-inch springform pan.
Beat . . . . . cream cheese, 3/4 cup sugar, sour cream and vanilla in bowl until smooth.
Add . . . . . eggs 1 at a time, beating well after each addition.
Divide . . . batter in half.
Stir . . . . . . chocolate mixture into half the batter.
Pour . . . . . into crumb-lined pan.
Cover . . . . with plain batter.
Swirl . . . . batter with knife to marbleize.

COLOR-CODED CHEESECAKE

3 8-oz. packages cream cheese, softened
Sugar
4 tsp. vanilla extract
1 3-oz. package Jell-O
4 pkg. Dream Whip
2 c. milk
30 graham crackers, crushed
1/4 lb. butter, softened

Combine . cream cheese, 1 1/3 cups sugar and
2 teaspoons vanilla in bowl; mix
well.
Dissolve .. Jell-O in 1 cup hot water in bowl;
cool.
Prepare ... Dream Whip according to package
directions, using milk and 2 tea-
spoons vanilla.
Fold ..... into cream cheese mixture.
Add ..... Jell-O, mixing well.
Combine . crumbs, butter and 1/2 cup sugar in
bowl.
Pat ...... into 11 x 13-inch pan, reserving a
small amount for topping.
Pour ..... cream cheese mixture over crust.
Top ..... with reserved crumbs.
Chill ..... overnight.

Lyle Ann Miller
Bear River H. S., Tremonton, Utah

CREAMY BAKED CHEESECAKE

1/4 c. margarine, melted
1 c. graham cracker crumbs
1/4 c. sugar
2 8-oz. packages cream cheese, softened
1 14-oz. can sweetened condensed milk
3 eggs
1/4 tsp. salt
1/4 c. lemon juice
1 8-oz. container sour cream

Combine . first 3 ingredients in bowl, mixing
well.
Press ..... into buttered 9-inch springform
pan.
Beat ..... cream cheese in mixer bowl until
fluffy.
Add ..... condensed milk, eggs, salt and
lemon juice, beating until smooth.
Pour ..... mixture over crust.

Bake ..... at 300 degrees for 50 minutes or
until cake tests done.
Cool ..... to room temperature.
Spread ... sour cream over cheesecake.
Chill ..... in refrigerator.

Pat N. Park
Pierce County H. S., Blackshear, Georgia

EASY CHEESECAKE

32 oz. cream cheese, softened
5 eggs
1 1/2 c. sugar
2 tsp. lemon juice
2 tsp. vanilla extract
1 1/2 pt. sour cream

Beat ..... cream cheese in bowl until creamy.
Add ..... eggs 1 at a time, mixing well after
each addition.
Stir ...... 1 cup sugar, 1 teaspoon lemon juice
and 1/2 teaspoon vanilla into
mixture.
Pour ..... into buttered springform pan.
Bake ..... at 300 degrees for 1 hour.
Combine . sour cream with remaining sugar,
lemon juice and vanilla in bowl.
Pour ..... on top of hot cheesecake.
Bake ..... for 5 additional minutes.
Chill ..... in refrigerator until cold.
Yield .... 12-16 servings.

Katrina W. Ross
South Mecklenburg H. S., Pineville, North Carolina

GERMAN CHEESECAKE

18 Zwieback, crumbled
1 tsp. cinnamon
1 1/2 c. sugar
4 tbsp. butter
1 1/2 lg. packages cream cheese, softened
1 tbsp. flour
1 tbsp. cornstarch
5 egg yolks, well beaten
1 pt. sour cream
1 tsp. vanilla extract
5 egg whites, stiffly beaten

Combine . first 2 ingredients with 1/2 cup
sugar in bowl.
Cut ...... in butter until crumbly.
Reserve .. 1/4 of crumbs for topping.
Press ..... remaining crumbs into 9-inch
springform pan.

Bake . . . . . at 350 degrees for 10 minutes.
Combine . next 3 ingredients with 1 cup sugar in bowl, mixing well.
Add . . . . . egg yolks.
Stir . . . . . . in sour cream and vanilla.
Fold . . . . . in egg whites.
Pour . . . . . over baked crust.
Sprinkle . . with reserved crumbs.
Bake . . . . . at 375 degrees for 1 hour.
Turn . . . . . oven off, leaving cheesecake for 10 minutes longer.
Top . . . . . with fruit.

Audrey Starkey
Keene H. S., Keene, New Hampshire

GLAMOUR CHEESECAKE

1 1/2 c. quick-cooking oats
1/2 c. finely chopped nuts
1/2 c. packed brown sugar
1/3 c. butter, melted
2 8 oz. packages cream cheese, softened
Sugar
1 tbsp. lemon juice
3 eggs
2 c. sour cream
1 to 2 tsp. vanilla extract

Combine . first 4 ingredients in bowl, mixing well.
Press . . . . . firmly onto bottom and side of 9-inch springform pan.
Bake . . . . . at 350 degrees for 18 minutes or until golden brown.
Combine . cream cheese, 1/2 cup sugar and lemon juice in bowl, beating well.
Add . . . . . eggs 1 at a time, beating well after each addition.
Blend . . . . in 1 cup sour cream.
Pour . . . . . into cooled crust.
Bake . . . . . at 350 degrees for 50 minutes.
Combine . 1 cup sour cream, 2 tablespoons sugar and vanilla in bowl, mixing well.
Spread . . . over cheesecake.
Bake . . . . . for 10 minutes longer.
Chill . . . . . for several hours.
Garnish . . with fruit.

Photograph for this recipe on page 104.

ORANGE CHEESECAKE

1/4 tsp. salt
2 egg yolks, well beaten

1 6-oz. can frozen orange juice
1 c. sugar
2 env. unflavored gelatin
2 c. cottage cheese, strained
2 egg whites
1 c. whipped cream
1 c. vanilla wafer crumbs
2 tbsp. butter, melted

Combine . first 3 ingredients with 3/4 cup sugar in saucepan.
Cook . . . . over medium heat until thick, stirring constantly.
Add . . . . . gelatin; set aside to cool.
Add . . . . . cottage cheese, mixing well.
Chill . . . . . until partially congealed.
Beat . . . . . egg whites in bowl until soft peaks form.
Add . . . . . 1/4 cup sugar gradually, beating until stiff.
Fold . . . . . whipped cream and egg white mixture into chilled mixture.
Pour . . . . . into buttered serving dish.
Mix . . . . . vanilla wafer crumbs with butter in bowl.
Sprinkle . . crumbs over cheesecake.
Chill . . . . . for 3 hours.
Yield . . . . 12 servings.

Stella Heath
John Marshall H. S., Oklahoma City, Oklahoma

LOW-CALORIE PINEAPPLE CHEESECAKE

2 env. unflavored gelatin
2 c. crushed pineapple
1 1/3 c. powdered milk
2 or 3 pkg. artificial sweetener
1 tbsp. lemon juice
1 tsp. vanilla extract
1 tbsp. butter extract

Dissolve . . gelatin in 1/2 cup boiling water in bowl.
Combine . gelatin and remaining ingredients in blender container.
Process . . . until well blended.
Pour . . . . . into 8 x 8-inch dish.
Chill . . . . . for 1 hour.
Yield . . . . 4 servings.

Marie Heltzel
Union County H. S., Lake Butler, Florida

COTTAGE CHEESE-PINEAPPLE CHEESECAKE

2 env. unflavored gelatin
1/8 tsp. salt
Sugar
2 eggs, separated
1 c. milk
1 tbsp. lemon juice
1 tsp. grated lemon rind
1 tsp. vanilla extract
2 tbsp. melted butter
1/2 c. graham cracker crumbs
1/4 tsp. each cinnamon, nutmeg
3 c. creamed cottage cheese
1 c. heavy cream, whipped
1 c. crushed pineapple

Combine . gelatin, salt and 3/4 cup sugar in double boiler pan.
Beat ..... egg yolks and milk together in bowl.
Stir ...... into gelatin mixture.
Cook .... over boiling water for 5 minutes or until gelatin dissolves, stirring constantly.
Remove .. from heat.
Stir ...... in lemon juice, rind and vanilla.
Chill ..... until partially set.
Mix ..... butter, 1 tablespoon sugar, cracker crumbs, cinnamon and nutmeg in bowl.
Beat ..... cottage cheese in bowl with electric mixer at high speed for 3 minutes.
Stir ...... into gelatin mixture.
Beat ..... egg whites in bowl until stiff.
Add ..... 1/4 cup sugar, beating well.
Fold ..... into gelatin mixture.
Blend .... in whipped cream.
Stir ...... in pineapple.
Pour ..... into 8-inch springform pan.
Sprinkle .. with crumb mixture.
Chill ..... until firm.

Holly Leepak
Lincoln, Nebraska

LOW-CAL PINEAPPLE CHEESECAKE

4 pkg. Sweet 'N' Low
2 pkg. unflavored gelatin
1/2 tsp. pineapple extract
1/2 tsp. butter flavoring
1 tsp. butternut flavoring
1 tsp. vanilla extract
3 tbsp. lemon juice
1 c. crushed pineapple
1 1/3 c. plain Alba
Cinnamon

Place .... first 2 ingredients and 1 cup boiling water in blender container.
Blend .... for 4 to 5 seconds.
Add ..... next 5 ingredients.
Process ... for 4 seconds.
Drain .... pineapple, reserving 4 tablespoons juice.
Add ..... Alba, pineapple and remaining pineapple juice, blending until smooth.
Pour ..... into Pam-sprayed 9-inch round pan.
Sprinkle .. with cinnamon and reserved juice.
Chill ..... until set.

Cheryl A. Smith
Forest Park Jr. H. S., Forest Park, Georgia

SALLY'S FAMOUS PINEAPPLE CHEESECAKE

1/4 stick butter, melted
14 graham crackers, crushed
2 8-oz. packages cream cheese, softened
2 eggs
1/8 tsp. salt
Sugar
2 tsp. vanilla extract
2 c. drained pineapple
1 pt. sour cream

Combine . first 2 ingredients in bowl, mixing well.
Press ..... into buttered baking dish.
Combine . next 3 ingredients with 1/2 cup sugar and 1 teaspoon vanilla in bowl, mixing well.
Stir ...... in pineapple.
Bake ..... at 375 degrees for 20 minutes.
Cool ..... for 1 hour.
Combine . sour cream, 3 tablespoons sugar and remaining vanilla in bowl, mixing well.
Spread ... over cooled cheesecake.
Bake ..... at 375 degrees for 5 minutes.

Sally Mace Gallagher
Capuchino H. S., San Bruno, California

Recipe on page 83.

RASPBERRY-GLAZED CHEESECAKE

11 graham crackers, crushed
Sugar
1/4 c. melted butter
3 eggs, beaten
1/2 tsp. vanilla extract
8 oz. cream cheese, softened
1 pkg. frozen raspberries, thawed
2 tbsp. cornstarch

Combine . crumbs, 1/2 cup sugar and butter in bowl.
Press . . . . . into 9-inch square pan.
Mix . . . . . eggs, vanilla, cream cheese and 1/2 cup sugar in bowl, beating until smooth.
Pour . . . . . over prepared crust.
Bake . . . . . at 375 degrees for 15 minutes.
Drain . . . . raspberries, reserving juice.
Combine . reserved juice, cornstarch and 2 tablespoons sugar in saucepan.
Cook . . . . until thick, stirring constantly.
Stir . . . . . . in raspberries.
Spread . . . cooled glaze over cooled cheesecake.
Let . . . . . . stand for 4 to 5 hours.

Eunice Smith
Ashville, North Carolina

RASPBERRY CHEESECAKE DESSERT

2 c. flour
1/2 c. packed brown sugar
1/2 c. chopped nuts
2 sticks margarine
2 pkg. Dream Whip
1 c. milk
1 tsp. vanilla extract
8 oz. cream cheese, softened
1 c. confectioners' sugar
Black raspberry pie filling

Combine . first 4 ingredients in bowl, mixing until crumbly.
Spread . . . on cookie sheet.
Bake . . . . . at 325 degrees for 15 minutes.
Crumble . . and cool.
Mix . . . . . Dream Whip, milk and vanilla using package directions.
Add . . . . . cream cheese and confectioners' sugar, mixing well.

Recipe on page 63.

Sprinkle . . 2/3 of the crumbled nut mixture in bottom of 9 x 13-inch serving dish.
Top . . . . . with cream cheese mixture.
Spread . . . on pie filling.
Sprinkle . . with remaining crumbs.
Chill . . . . . in refrigerator.

Carol Winter
Millcreek Jr. H. S., Bountiful, Utah

SHORTCUT STRAWBERRY-LEMON CHEESECAKE

1 1/2 c. graham cracker crumbs
3 tbsp. sugar
1/4 c. margarine, melted
1 pkg. fluffy white frosting mix
1 8-oz. package cream cheese, softened
1 1/2 c. sour cream
1 tbsp. grated lemon rind
1 10-oz. package frozen strawberries, thawed

Combine . crumbs, sugar and margarine in bowl, mixing well.
Press . . . . . into 9 x 9-inch baking pan.
Prepare . . . frosting mix using package directions.
Beat . . . . . cream cheese, sour cream and lemon rind in bowl until smooth.
Fold . . . . . in frosting.
Pour . . . . . over crust.
Bake . . . . . at 300 degrees for 45 minutes.
Chill . . . . . in refrigerator.
Top . . . . . with strawberries.

Nita De Grand
Nacogdoches H. S., Nacogdoches, Texas

MINI CHEESCAKES

2 lg. packages cream cheese, softened
3/4 c. sugar
2 eggs, slightly beaten
1 tsp. vanilla extract
12 vanilla wafers
2 can cherry pie filling

Combine . first 4 ingredients in bowl, mixing well.
Place . . . . wafers in lined muffin cups.
Pour . . . . . cheese mixture over wafers.
Bake . . . . . at 375 degrees for 20 minutes.
Top . . . . . cooled cheesecakes with pie filling.

Diane Norbury
Holton Public Schools, Holton, Michigan

MICROWAVE CHEESECAKE

2 c. graham cracker crumbs
1/2 c. butter, melted
1/2 tsp. cinnamon
Sugar
3 8-oz. packages cream cheese, softened
5 eggs
2 tsp. vanilla extract
2 1/2 c. sour cream

Combine . first 3 ingredients and 1/2 cup sugar in 9 x 13-inch glass baking dish, mixing well and spreading over bottom of dish.
Microwave on High for 2 minutes.
Beat ..... cream cheese in bowl until smooth.
Add ..... eggs 1 at a time, beating well after each addition.
Stir ...... in 1/2 teaspoon vanilla and 1 cup sugar.
Pour ..... into crust.
Microwave on Medium for 15 minutes, turning every 4 minutes.
Combine . sour cream with 1/3 cup sugar and 1 1/2 teaspoons vanilla in bowl, blending well.
Pour ..... over cheesecake.
Microwave on High for 1 1/4 minutes.
Chill .... before serving.
Yield .... 8-10 servings.

K. Alicia Hampton
Pewitt H. S., Omaha, Texas

MICROWAVE CHERRY CHEESECAKE CUPS

1 8-oz. package cream cheese, softened
1/3 c. sugar
1 egg
1 tbsp. lemon juice
1/2 tsp. vanilla extract
6 vanilla wafers
1 can cherry pie filling

Beat ..... cream cheese in bowl until fluffy.
Add ..... sugar, egg, lemon juice and vanilla, beating well.
Line ..... muffin cups with cupcake papers.
Place .... 1 vanilla wafer in each cup.
Fill ...... cups 2/3 full with cheesecake mixture.
Microwave on Medium for 4 1/2 minutes or until almost set, turning once.
Top ..... with pie filling.
Chill .... in refrigerator until serving time.
Yield .... 6 servings.

Deb Sundem
Sandhills Public School, Dunning, Nebraska

MICROWAVE CHOCOLATE-ALMOND CHEESECAKE

1 2 graham crackers, crushed
1/3 c. slivered almonds
1/4 c. butter, melted
Sugar
2 8-oz. packages cream cheese, softened
2 eggs
1 tsp. almond extract
1/3 c. semisweet chocolate chips
1 c. sour cream
1/2 tsp. vanilla extract

Combine . first 3 ingredients with 2 tablespoons sugar in bowl, mixing well.
Press ..... into bottom and side of 8-inch round glass baking dish.
Microwave on High for 2 to 3 minutes.
Combine . cream cheese, 2/3 cup sugar, eggs and almond extract in blender container.
Process ... until smooth.
Pour ..... 2/3 of the mixture into crust.
Microwave chocolate chips on High for 1 1/2 to 2 minutes until glossy.
Blend .... with remaining cream cheese mixture.
Pour ..... over mixture in crust.
Microwave on Medium for 14 to 16 minutes or until center is set, rotating twice.
Blend .... sour cream, 2 tablespoons sugar and vanilla.
Spoon ... over cheesecake.
Microwave on High for 1 1/2 to 2 minutes.
Chill ..... for 6 hours or longer.

Mrs. L. Adams
St. Clair Public School, St. Clair, Minnesota

ARIZONA PUDDING

2 eggs
1 c. packed dark brown sugar
1/2 c. flour
2 tsp. baking powder

1/2 tsp. salt
2 tsp. vanilla extract
1/2 c. walnuts
1 c. chopped peeled apples

Beat ..... eggs and brown sugar together in large bowl until creamy.
Sift ...... dry ingredients together.
Add ..... to egg mixture, mixing well.
Mix ..... in vanilla, walnuts and apples, blending well.
Pour ..... into greased 9-inch pie plate.
Bake ..... at 350 degrees for 35 minutes.
Cut ...... into wedges.
Serve .... warm with ice cream.
Yield .... 6-8 servings.

Joy L. Manson
Miami H. S., Miami, Arizona

BREAD PUDDING

2 c. milk
4 eggs
1/2 c. sugar
1/4 tsp. salt
1 tsp. vanilla extract
5 slices dry white bread, cubed
1/2 tsp. nutmeg

Combine . first 5 ingredients in large mixer bowl.
Beat ..... until well blended.
Fold ..... in bread cubes.
Pour ..... into 9-inch square baking pan.
Sprinkle .. with nutmeg.
Bake ..... at 350 degrees for 35 to 40 minutes.
Yield .... 9 servings.

Peggy Sumner
Bishop Ward H. S., Kansas City, Kansas

COCONUT BREAD PUDDING

1 1/4 c. sugar
6 slices day-old bread
1 c. flaked coconut
3 eggs
1/4 tsp. salt
2 c. scalded milk
1 1/2 tsp. vanilla extract

Heat ..... 3/4 cup sugar in heavy saucepan over low heat until melted, stirring frequently.
Pour ..... in 1/2 cup hot water.

Cook .... until smooth and thick.
Pour ..... into 9 x 5-inch loaf pan, coating bottom and sides well.
Chill ..... until firm.
Remove .. crusts from bread.
Place .... layer of bread over hardened syrup in pan.
Top ..... with 1/2 cup coconut.
Add ..... remaining bread slices and 1/2 cup coconut.
Combine . 1/2 cup sugar, eggs and salt in bowl.
Stir ...... in scalded milk and vanilla.
Pour ..... over bread mixture.
Place .... in pan of hot water.
Bake ..... at 325 degrees for 1 hour or until pudding tests done.
Yield .... 6-8 servings.

Ruth Finefield
Albuquerque, New Mexico

BUTTERSCOTCH BATTER PUDDING

1 1/2 c. packed dark brown sugar
Flour
3/4 tsp. salt
2 tbsp. butter
2 tbsp. melted margarine
1 tsp. vanilla extract
1 tsp. baking powder
1/2 c. milk
1/2 c. chopped nuts

Blend .... 1 cup brown sugar, 1 tablespoon flour, 1/4 teaspoon salt and 2 tablespoons butter with 2 cups boiling water in bowl.
Pour ..... into 6 x 10-inch baking dish.
Combine . margarine, 1/2 cup brown sugar and vanilla in bowl, mixing well.
Sift ...... 1 cup flour, baking powder and 1/2 teaspoon salt together.
Add ..... alternately with milk to sugar mixture, beating well after each addition.
Stir ...... in nuts.
Spoon ... batter over sauce mixture.
Bake ..... at 350 degrees for 40 to 45 minutes.
Serve .... with whipped cream.
Yield .... 6-8 servings.

Jewell Blevins
Carl Junction H. S., Carl Junction, Missouri

LEMON PUDDING

2 tbsp. butter, softened
1 c. sugar
3 eggs, separated
Juice and rind of 1 lemon
2 tbsp. flour
1 c. milk

Cream ... butter and sugar together in bowl.
Add ..... egg yolks with lemon juice and rind.
Blend .... in flour and milk.
Beat ..... egg whites until stiff.
Fold ..... into milk mixture.
Pour ..... into casserole in pan of water.
Bake ..... at 350 degrees for 45 minutes.
Yield .... 4 servings.

Mona B. Peterson
Orem H. S., Orem, Utah

PASSOVER CHEESE PUDDING

3 c. cottage cheese
2 tsp. grated orange rind
1 c. Florida orange juice
1/2 c. sugar
3 tbsp. butter, melted
5 tsp. potato starch
4 eggs, separated
4 Florida oranges, peeled, sectioned
1 c. sour cream

Combine . first 6 ingredients with 4 egg yolks in medium bowl, mixing well.
Fold ..... stiffly beaten egg whites into cottage cheese mixture.
Pour ..... into greased 8 x 12-inch baking dish.
Bake ..... at 300 degrees for 1 hour.
Turn ..... off oven, leaving pudding in closed oven until cool.
Chill ..... until serving time.
Garnish .. pudding with rows of orange sections.
Spread ... Orange Glaze over sections.
Spoon ... sour cream between rows.
Yield .... 6-8 servings.

Orange Glaze

1 tbsp. sugar
1 tsp. potato starch
1/2 c. Florida orange juice

Combine . sugar and potato starch in small saucepan.
Stir ...... in orange juice, blending well.
Cook .... over low heat until mixture thickens, stirring constantly.

Photograph for this recipe on cover.

PEACHES AND CREAM DESSERT

1 1/2 c. sifted flour
1/2 tsp. salt
1/2 c. butter, softened
1 29-oz. can sliced peaches
1/2 c. sugar
1/2 tsp. cinnamon
1 egg, slightly beaten
1 c. evaporated milk

Combine . flour and salt in bowl.
Cut ...... in butter until crumbly.
Press ..... into bottom of 8-inch baking pan.
Drain .... peaches, reserving 1/2 cup syrup.
Arrange .. peaches over crust.
Sprinkle .. with sugar and cinnamon.
Bake ..... at 375 degrees for 20 minutes.
Blend .... egg with milk and reserved peach syrup.
Pour ..... over peaches.
Bake ..... at 350 degrees for 30 minutes or until custard is firm around edges and slightly soft in center.
Serve .... warm or cold.

Joni Sturm
Muenster Public School, Muenster, Texas

PUMPKIN COTTAGE PUDDING

1/3 c. shortening
1/2 c. sugar
2 eggs
1 c. canned pumpkin
1/2 c. light molasses
1 tbsp. grated orange rind
1 2/3 c. sifted flour
1 tsp. each, salt, soda
1/2 tsp. baking powder
1 tsp. cinnamon
1/2 tsp. each cloves, nutmeg
1/4 tsp. ginger
1/3 c. orange juice
1/2 c. chopped walnuts

2 3-oz. packages cream cheese, softened
2 tbsp. milk

Cream ... shortening and sugar in bowl.
Add ..... eggs 1 at a time, beating well after each addition.
Stir ...... in next 3 ingredients, mixing well.
Sift ...... dry ingredients together.
Add ..... to creamed mixture alternately with orange juice, mixing well after each addition.
Stir ...... in walnuts.
Pour ..... into greased and waxed paper-lined 9-inch square cake pan.
Bake ..... at 350 degrees for 30 to 35 minutes.
Beat ..... cream cheese and milk in bowl until smooth.
Serve .... pudding with cream cheese and orange slices.

Cora Ann Ferrara
Smithsburg H. S., Smithsburg, Maryland

WALNUT SPOON PUDDING

1/4 c. soft butter
2/3 c. packed brown sugar
1 egg, beaten
1/4 tsp. cinnamon
1/8 tsp. each cloves, nutmeg
3/4 c. sifted flour
1/4 tsp. soda
Salt
1 c. soft dried figs, chopped
1 c. California walnuts, chopped
2 egg yolks, beaten
1 c. sifted confectioners' sugar
3 to 4 tbsp. Bourbon
1 c. whipping cream, whipped

Cream ... first 3 ingredients with spices in bowl until fluffy.
Sift ...... in flour, soda and 1/2 teaspoon salt, mixing well.
Stir ...... in figs and walnuts.
Pour ..... into buttered 8-inch square pan.
Bake ..... at 350 degrees for 20 to 25 minutes.
Beat ..... egg yolks, confectioners' sugar and pinch of salt until thick and lemon colored.
Stir ...... in Bourbon.
Fold ..... in whipping cream.

Chill ..... until serving time.
Serve .... pudding warm with chilled sauce.

Photograph for this recipe on page 6.

BAKED APRICOT CUSTARDS

1 30-oz. can apricot halves, drained
3 eggs
1/4 c. sugar
Dash of salt
1/2 tsp. vanilla extract
2 c. milk
1/2 c. apricot syrup
1 1/2 tsp. butter
3 to 4 tbsp. apricot liqueur

Place .... apricots in six 6-ounce custard cups, reserving 6 halves.
Beat ..... next 4 ingredients in bowl.
Add ..... milk, mixing well.
Pour ..... into custard cups.
Place .... cups in pan filled with hot water.
Bake ..... at 350 degrees until custard tests done.
Boil ..... syrup in saucepan until reduced to 1/3 cup.
Add ..... reserved apricots, butter and liqueur.
Heat ..... to boiling point.
Spoon ... 1 apricot and sauce over each cooled custard.
Chill ..... until serving time.

Photograph for this recipe below.

YOGURT PUDDING PARFAITS

1/3 c. butter
1/3 c. chunky peanut butter
2 1/2 c. oats
1/3 c. packed brown sugar
1 c. yogurt
1 c. milk
1   3 3/4-oz. package vanilla instant
*   pudding mix*
Food coloring (opt.)

Melt . . . . . first 2 ingredients in saucepan over low heat, stirring occasionally.
Add . . . . . oats and brown sugar, mixing well.
Spread . . . evenly in 10 x 15-inch pan.
Bake . . . . . at 350 degrees for 15 to 18 minutes or until golden brown, stirring occasionally.
Set . . . . . . aside to cool.
Combine . remaining ingredients in mixer bowl.
Beat . . . . . with electric mixer at low speed for 2 minutes.
Alternate . layers of pudding mixture and oats mixture in dessert dishes.
Chill . . . . . for 3 to 4 hours.
Yield . . . . 4 servings.

Photograph for this recipe on page 104.

BURNT CREAM CUSTARD

1 pt. whipping cream
4 egg yolks
Sugar
1 tbsp. vanilla extract

Scald . . . . cream over low heat in saucepan until bubbles form around edge.
Beat . . . . . egg yolks and 1/2 cup sugar together until thick and lemon colored.
Add . . . . . cream to egg yolks gradually, beating constantly.
Stir . . . . . . in vanilla.
Pour . . . . . into six 6-ounce baking cups.
Place . . . . cups in pan containing 1/2 inch water.
Bake . . . . . at 350 degrees for 45 minutes or until custard is set.
Remove . . from water and chill.
Sprinkle . . each custard cup with 2 teaspoons sugar.

Broil . . . . . until topping is medium brown.
Chill . . . . . before serving.

Nancy A. Gearhart
Westwood H. S., Mesa, Arizona

MICROWAVE BOILED CUSTARD

3 eggs
1/4 tsp. nutmeg
1 1/2 c. sugar
3 c. milk, scalded
1 tsp. vanilla extract

Beat . . . . . eggs in glass bowl until frothy.
Blend . . . . in nutmeg and sugar.
Add . . . . . milk gradually, mixing until smooth.
Microwave on Medium for 12 minutes, stirring every 2 minutes. Do not boil.
Stir . . . . . . in vanilla.
Chill . . . . . in refrigerator.
Yield . . . . 6-8 servings.

Anita Stubblefield
Rivercrest H. S., Bogata, Texas

SPANISH CREAM CUSTARD

1 c. milk
3 tbsp. sugar
Pinch of salt
1 egg yolk, slightly beaten
1 tbsp. unflavored gelatin
1/4 c. cold milk
1 tsp. vanilla extract
1 egg white, beaten stiffly
1/3 c. macaroon crumbs
1/3 c. toasted coconut

Combine . milk, sugar and salt in top of double boiler.
Bring . . . . to boiling point over medium heat.
Stir . . . . . . a small amount of hot mixture into egg yolk.
Stir . . . . . . egg yolk into hot mixture.
Dissolve . . gelatin in 1/4 cup cold milk.
Blend . . . . into custard, stirring well.
Add . . . . . vanilla and cool.
Fold . . . . . egg white, crumbs and coconut into custard.
Pour . . . . . into mold.
Chill . . . . . until firm.
Yield . . . . six 1/2-cup servings.

Alma Van Beek
Western Christian H. S., Hull, Iowa

Meringues
and Tortes

CHERRY MELBA MERINGUES

4 egg whites
1/2 tsp. vanilla extract
1/4 tsp. salt
1/4 tsp. cream of tartar
1 1/3 c. sugar
8 fresh peach halves, chilled
1 qt. vanilla ice cream
Cherry Melba Sauce

Combine . first 4 ingredients in large mixer bowl.
Beat . . . . . with electric mixer at high speed until soft peaks form.
Add . . . . . sugar very gradually, beating until stiff.
Spread . . . meringue 1/4 inch thick into 3 1/2-inch circles on foil-lined cookie sheet.
Add . . . . . additional meringue to build up sides.
Bake . . . . . at 250 degrees for 45 minutes.
Turn . . . . . oven off, leaving meringue for 30 minutes longer.
Place . . . . peach half in each meringue shell.
Top . . . . . with scoops of ice cream.
Spoon . . . Cherry Melba Sauce over top.

Cherry Melba Sauce

1 8-oz. jar maraschino cherries
1 tbsp. cornstarch
1/2 c. currant jelly
4 tsp. lemon juice
1/4 tsp. grated lemon rind

Puree . . . . cherries in blender.
Blend . . . . cornstarch with 1 tablespoon cold water in saucepan.
Add . . . . . cherries and remaining ingredients.
Cook . . . . over medium heat until thick and clear, stirring constantly.
Chill . . . . . in refrigerator.

Photograph for this recipe on page 77.

CHOCOLATE ANGEL PIE

2 egg whites
1/8 tsp. salt
1/8 tsp. cream of tartar
1/2 c. sugar
1/2 c. finely chopped nuts

1 1/2 tsp. vanilla extract
1 pkg. German's chocolate
1 c. cream, whipped

Beat . . . . . egg whites, salt and cream of tartar in bowl until foamy.
Add . . . . . sugar gradually, beating until stiff.
Fold . . . . . in nuts and 1/2 teaspoon vanilla.
Spread . . . in greased 8-inch pie pan.
Bake . . . . . at 275 degrees for 50 to 55 minutes.
Melt . . . . . chocolate in 3 tablespoons water in saucepan over low heat.
Fold . . . . . cream and 1 teaspoon vanilla into cooled chocolate.
Pour . . . . . into cooled meringue shell.
Chill . . . . . until set.

Sybil B. Murphy
Northwood H. S., Pittsboro, North Carolina

CHOCOLATE DREAM PIE

2 egg whites
Pinch of cream of tartar
1 tsp. vanilla extract
1/2 c. sugar
1 6-oz. package chocolate chips, melted
1 c. whipping cream, whipped
Chopped nuts (opt.)
Coconut (opt.)

Beat . . . . . egg whites with cream of tartar in bowl until foamy.
Stir . . . . . . in vanilla.
Add . . . . . sugar gradually, beating until stiff.
Spread . . . in 10-inch greased pie pan.
Bake . . . . . at 275 degrees for 45 minutes.
Fold . . . . . melted chocolate into whipped cream.
Pour . . . . . into cooled meringue shell.
Garnish . . with chopped nuts and coconut.
Chill . . . . . for 4 hours or longer.

Joan Stenger
Norwalk H. S., Norwalk, Connecticut

CHOCOLATE MERINGUE

2 egg whites
1/4 tsp. salt
1/2 tsp. vinegar
3/4 c. sugar
1/2 tsp. cinnamon

1 6-oz. package semisweet chocolate
   pieces, melted
2 egg yolks, beaten
1 c. heavy cream

Beat . . . . . egg whites, salt and vinegar in bowl
              until soft peaks form.
Add . . . . . 1/2 cup sugar and 1/4 teaspoon cin-
              namon gradually, beating until stiff.
Spread . . . into 8-inch circle 1/2 inch thick
              with 3/4-inch thick rim on cookie
              sheet.
Bake . . . . . at 275 degrees for 1 hour.
Turn . . . . . off oven leaving meringue to dry in
              closed oven for 2 hours.
Spread . . . 2 tablespoons melted chocolate
              over bottom of meringue shell.
Beat . . . . . egg yolks and 1/4 cup water into
              remaining chocolate.
Chill . . . . . until thick.
Blend . . . . cream with 1/4 cup sugar and 1/4
              teaspoon cinnamon in bowl.
Whip . . . . until stiff.
Spread . . . half the whipped cream over choco-
              late in shell.
Fold . . . . . remaining whipped cream into
              remaining chocolate mixture.
Spread . . . over top.
Chill . . . . . for several hours.
Garnish . . with additional whipped cream and
              pecans.

Beth Howland
Groton, Connecticut

CHOCOLATE MOUSSE CAKE

12 egg whites
Cream of tartar
3/4 c. sugar
1 3/4 c. confectioners' sugar
1/3 c. cocoa
3 c. heavy cream, chilled
1 1/2 tsp. vanilla extract
13 oz. semisweet chocolate, melted

Beat . . . . . 5 egg whites and pinch of cream of
              tartar in large bowl until soft peaks
              form.
Add . . . . . sugar gradually, beating until stiff.
Sift . . . . . . confectioners' sugar and cocoa
              together.
Fold . . . . . into beaten egg whites.

Spread . . . into three 8-inch squares on
             parchment-lined cookie sheet.
Bake . . . . . at 300 degrees for 1 hour.
Cool . . . . . on wire racks.
Beat . . . . . cream and vanilla in bowl until
             stiff.
Combine . 7 egg whites and 1/4 teaspoon
             cream of tartar in bowl, beating
             until stiff peaks form.
Fold . . . . . chocolate into egg whites.
Blend . . . . in whipped cream.
Spread . . . 1/3 of the chocolate mousse over
             each of 2 meringues.
Stack . . . . to assemble, topping with remain-
             ing meringue.
Force . . . . remaining mousse through pastry
             bag fitted with decorative tip to
             decorate top layer.
Chill . . . . . loosely covered, for 4 hours or
             longer.

Nancy Van Ogtrop
Chantilly H. S., Chantilly, Virginia

FORGOTTEN DESSERT

5 egg whites
1/4 tsp. salt
1/2 tsp. cream of tartar
1 c. sugar
1 tsp. vanilla extract
1/2 pt. whipping cream
1 tbsp. confectioners' sugar
Fruit

Beat . . . . . egg whites and salt in bowl until
             frothy.
Add . . . . . cream of tartar, beating until stiff.
Beat . . . . . in sugar very gradually.
Add . . . . . vanilla.
Beat . . . . . for 15 minutes.
Pour . . . . . into greased 9 x 9-inch pan.
Place . . . . in preheated 450-degree oven.
Turn . . . . . off heat.
Leave . . . . meringue in closed oven overnight.
Combine . next 2 ingredients in bowl, beating
             until stiff.
Spread . . . over meringue.
Chill . . . . until serving time.
Top . . . . . with fruit.

Jane Markham
Spring Oaks Jr. H. S., Houston, Texas

LEMON ANGEL PIE

4 egg whites
1 1/4 c. sugar
Salt
1/4 tsp. cream of tartar
4 egg yolks
1 tbsp. grated lemon rind
3 tbsp. lemon juice
1 c. heavy cream, whipped

Combine . egg whites, 3/4 cup sugar, 1/4 tea-
spoon salt and cream of tartar in
bowl.
Beat . . . . . until stiff peaks form.
Spread . . . in buttered 9-inch pie plate.
Place . . . . in preheated 450-degree oven; turn
oven off.
Let . . . . . . stand in closed oven for 5 hours or
longer.
Beat . . . . . egg yolks in double boiler until
thick.
Add . . . . . 1/2 cup sugar, dash of salt, lemon
rind and juice, beating constantly.
Cook . . . . for 5 minutes or until thick, stirring
constantly.
Spread . . . half the whipped cream in shell.
Spoon . . . on cooled filling.
Top . . . . . with remaining whipped cream.
Chill . . . . . for 5 hours or longer.

Tamara Dobson
Pierre, South Dakota

STRAWBERRY ANGEL MERINGUE PIE

6 egg whites
1/2 tsp. cream of tartar
2 c. sugar
1 c. whipping cream, whipped
1 to 2 tbsp. confectioners' sugar
1 pt. fresh strawberries, sliced

Beat . . . . . egg whites and cream of tartar in
bowl until frothy.
Add . . . . . sugar gradually, beating until stiff.
Spread . . . into 12-inch circle on baking sheet
lined with parchment, building up
side to form rim.
Bake . . . . . at 270 degrees for 1 hour.
Turn . . . . . off oven, leaving meringue until
oven has cooled.
Beat . . . . . cream and confectioners' sugar in
bowl until stiff.

Fold . . . . . in strawberries.
Spread . . . over cooled meringue.
Chill . . . . . before serving.

Eleanor P. Hamme
Lake Gibson Jr. H. S., Lakeland, Florida

ANGEL PECAN PIE

3 egg whites, stiffly beaten
1 c. sugar
1/4 tsp. baking powder
1 tsp. vanilla extract
12 graham crackers, crushed
1 c. chopped pecans
1/2 pt. sweetened whipping cream, whipped

Combine . all ingredients except whipped
cream in large bowl in order given,
blending well.
Spread . . . in greased pie pan.
Bake . . . . . at 350 degrees for 25 minutes.
Top . . . . . cooled crust with whipped cream.
Chill . . . . . for 2 to 3 hours.

Carolyn F. Chipman
Alta H. S., Sandy, Utah

BLUEBERRY DELIGHT PIE

6 egg whites
1 tsp. cream of tartar
2 c. sugar
2 c. crushed saltine crackers
2 c. chopped nuts
12 oz. Cool Whip
1 can blueberry pie filling

Beat . . . . . egg whites and cream of tartar to-
gether in bowl until soft peaks
form.
Add . . . . . sugar gradually, beating until stiff.
Fold . . . . . in crackers and nuts.
Spread . . . batter 1/2 inch thick in 9 x 12-inch
baking dish.
Bake . . . . . at 325 degrees for 25 minutes or
until very lightly browned.
Spread . . . cooled crust with Cool Whip.
Chill . . . . . for several hours.
Top . . . . . with pie filling.

Joan W. Harmon
Bleckley County H. S., Cochran, Georgia

FRENCH CHERRY PIE

3 egg whites, stiffly beaten
1 c. sugar

1 tsp. vinegar
1 tsp. baking powder
1/2 c. chopped pecans
2 tsp. vanilla extract
12 soda crackers, crushed
1 3-oz. package cream cheese, softened
1/2 c. confectioners' sugar
1 c. whipping cream, whipped
1 can cherry pie filling

Combine . first 5 ingredients and 1 teaspoon vanilla in large bowl, mixing gently.
Fold . . . . . in crackers.
Pour . . . . . into well-greased baking dish.
Bake . . . . . at 350 degrees for 20 minutes.
Cream . . . next 2 ingredients and 1 teaspoon vanilla together in bowl.
Stir . . . . . . in whipped cream.
Pour . . . . . over cooled crust.
Spread . . . pie filling over top.
Chill . . . . . until serving time.
Yield . . . . 12 servings.

Cathy James
Crescent H. S., Crescent, Oklahoma

CHERRY-WALNUT MERINGUE

6 egg whites
3/4 tsp. cream of tartar
2 c. sugar
2 tsp. vanilla extract
2 c. crushed saltine crackers
3/4 c. chopped walnuts
2 pkg. Dream Whip
1 can cherry pie filling

Beat . . . . . egg whites with cream of tartar in large bowl until soft peaks form.
Add . . . . . sugar and vanilla gradually, beating until stiff.
Fold . . . . . in crackers and walnuts.
Spread . . . evenly in greased 9 x 13-inch baking pan.
Bake . . . . . at 350 for 25 minutes.
Prepare . . . Dream Whip using package directions.
Spread . . . over cooled torte.
Top . . . . . with pie filling.
Chill . . . . . for 4 hours before serving.

Jo Anne M. Stringer
Liberty H. S., Youngstown, Ohio

CHOCO-COCONUT PIE

3 egg whites, stiffly beaten
1/3 tsp. cream of tartar
1 1/4 c. sugar
1 1/2 tsp. vanilla extract
1 c. chopped nuts
18 soda crackers, crushed
1/2 pt. whipping cream
2 tbsp. cocoa
1 can shredded coconut

Combine . stiffly beaten egg whites and cream of tartar in bowl.
Add . . . . . 1 cup sugar gradually, beating until very stiff.
Fold . . . . . in 1 teaspoon vanilla, nuts and crumbs.
Spread . . . in greased pie plate.
Bake . . . . . at 325 degrees for 35 minutes.
Combine . whipping cream, 1/4 cup sugar and cocoa in bowl, blending well.
Chill . . . . . for 1 hour or longer.
Beat . . . . . until stiff, adding 1/2 teaspoon vanilla.
Spread . . . over cooled crust.
Sprinkle . . with coconut.
Chill . . . . . for several hours.

Rene Kaufman
Swanton, Nebraska

COCONUT CRUNCH PIE

4 egg whites
1/8 tsp. salt
1 tsp. vanilla extract
1 c. sugar
1 c. graham cracker crumbs
1/2 c. chopped moist coconut
1/2 c. chopped walnuts
1 pt. butter-brickle ice cream

Beat . . . . . egg whites with salt and vanilla until soft peaks form.
Add . . . . . sugar gradually, beating until stiff.
Combine . next 3 ingredients.
Fold . . . . . into stiffly beaten egg whites.
Spread . . . in greased 9-inch pie plate.
Bake . . . . . at 350 degrees for 30 minutes.
Serve . . . . hot or cold with ice cream.

Nancy Crawford
Phoenix, Arizona

CRUNCHY MERINGUE CASSEROLE

3 egg whites
1 c. sugar
23 Ritz crackers, finely crushed
1 c. chopped pecans
1 tsp. vanilla extract
3 tbsp. instant chocolate drink powder
1 c. whipping cream, whipped

Beat . . . . . egg whites until soft peaks form.
Add . . . . . sugar gradually, beating until stiff.
Fold . . . . . in cracker crumbs, pecans and vanilla.
Pour . . . . . into buttered casserole.
Bake . . . . . at 350 degrees for 30 minutes.
Beat . . . . . chocolate powder into whipped cream.
Top . . . . . cooled meringue with chocolate whipped cream.

Jean Roswell
Calhoun, Iowa

DATE MERINGUE DELIGHT

1 c. sugar
1 tsp. vanilla extract
3 egg whites, stiffly beaten
10 soda crackers, finely crushed
1 tsp. baking powder
1 c. chopped walnuts
1 c. chopped dates
1 pt. whipping cream, whipped

Fold . . . . . sugar and vanilla into stiffly beaten egg whites.
Combine . cracker crumbs and baking powder.
Fold . . . . . into meringue with walnuts and dates.
Spread . . . in greased 8-inch square pan.
Bake . . . . . at 325 degrees for 30 minutes.
Top . . . . . cooled meringue with whipped cream.
Chill . . . . . for several hours.

Cecile O'Roarke
Kalamazoo, Michigan

MACAROON TORTE

2/3 c. finely crushed saltine crackers
1 c. sugar
1/2 c. chopped English walnuts
1/2 c. chopped dates
1 tsp. baking powder
3 egg whites, stiffly beaten
1 tsp. almond extract

Combine . first 5 ingredients in bowl, mixing well.
Fold . . . . . in egg whites and almond extract.
Pour . . . . . into well-greased 9-inch pie pan.
Bake . . . . . at 350 degrees for 25 minutes or until lightly browned.
Serve . . . . with whipped cream.

Melba Sue Hanks
Preble Shawnee H. S., Camden, Ohio

RANCH-STYLE PEACH PIE

3 egg whites
1 c. sugar
1/3 c. crushed soda crackers
1/2 c. finely chopped pecans
1/4 tsp. baking powder
1/4 tsp. vanilla extract
1   1-lb. can peach halves, drained, thinly sliced
1   8-oz. carton whipped topping

Beat . . . . . egg whites in bowl until soft peaks form.
Add . . . . . sugar very gradually, beating until stiff.
Fold . . . . in next 4 ingredients.
Spread . . . over bottom and side of greased 9-inch pie pan.
Bake . . . . . at 325 degrees for 30 minutes.
Reserve . . several peach slices for garnish.
Alternate . layers of whipped topping and peaches on cooled crust, ending with topping.
Chill . . . . . until serving time.
Garnish . . with peach slices.

Judy Meek
Marshall Jr. H. S., Wichita, Kansas

MRS. ROGERS' COMPANY COMING PIE

3 egg whites
1/4 tsp. cream of tartar
1 c. chopped pecans
1 c. sugar
18 saltine crackers, crushed
1 sm. jar pineapple preserves
1/2 pt. whipping cream, whipped
1 c. coconut

Beat . . . . . egg whites and cream of tartar in bowl until stiff peaks form.
Fold . . . . . in pecans and sugar gradually.

Stir . . . . . . in crackers gently.
Spoon . . . into greased pie pan, shaping to form shell.
Bake . . . . . at 325 degrees for 25 minutes.
Press . . . . . cooled meringue down into shape of pie pan.
Fold . . . . . preserves into whipped cream.
Spoon . . . into shell.
Sprinkle . . with coconut.
Chill . . . . . for several hours.

Wanda Clark
Crystal Springs H. S., Crystal Springs, Mississippi

STRAWBERRY MERINGUE PIE

3 egg whites
1 tsp. baking powder
1 c. sugar
11 saltine crackers, finely crushed
1/2 c. chopped pecans
1 pt. fresh strawberries, sliced
Sweetened whipped cream

Beat . . . . . egg whites and baking powder together until frothy.
Add . . . . . sugar gradually, beating until stiff.
Fold . . . . . in crackers and pecans.
Spread . . . in buttered 9-inch pie pan.
Bake . . . . . at 325 degrees for 30 minutes.
Fill . . . . . . cooled crust with strawberries.
Top . . . . . with whipped cream.
Serve . . . . immediately.

Anne F. Farris
Soldan H. S., St. Louis, Missouri

SUNNY CRACKER-NUT PIE

20 crackers, finely crushed
1 1/4 tsp. baking powder
4 egg whites
1 1/3 c. sugar
1 tsp. vanilla extract
1 c. pecans
1 c. heavy cream, whipped
Strawberries

Combine . crackers and baking powder, mixing well.
Beat . . . . . egg whites until soft peaks form.
Add . . . . . sugar gradually, beating until stiff.
Fold . . . . . in vanilla, pecans and crumb mixture, mixing well.
Pour . . . . . into buttered 9-inch pie pan.
Bake . . . . . at 350 degrees for 30 minutes or until golden brown.

Top . . . . . with whipped cream and strawberries.

Linda J. Bland
Luverne H. S., Luverne, Alabama

RASPBERRY MOUSSE IN MERINGUE SHELLS

5 egg whites
1/4 tsp. cream of tartar
1 1/4 c. sugar
1 tsp. vanilla extract
2 env. unflavored gelatin
1 12-oz. jar red raspberry preserves
1 tbsp. lemon juice
2 egg whites, stiffly beaten
1/2 pt. heavy cream, whipped
1 sq. semisweet chocolate, shaved into curls

Beat . . . . . egg whites and cream of tartar with electric mixer at high speed until foamy.
Add . . . . . sugar, 2 tablespoons at a time, and vanilla, beating until stiff.
Spread . . . half the meringue into ten 3-inch circles, using 2 greased cookie sheets.
Make . . . . 3/4-inch high sides around meringue circles with remaining meringue in fluted shell-shaped design, using Wear-Ever Super Shooter.
Bake . . . . . at 250 degrees for 1 to 1 1/4 hours or until shells are crisp and dry.
Turn . . . . . off oven, leaving meringues in closed oven for 1 hour longer.
Cool . . . . . on cookie sheet.
Soften . . . gelatin in 1/2 cup water in saucepan.
Stir . . . . . . preserves with wire whisk in large bowl until smooth.
Heat . . . . . gelatin over low heat until dissolved; add lemon juice.
Stir . . . . . . into preserves.
Chill . . . . . until partially set, stirring occasionally.
Fold . . . . . 2 stiffly beaten egg whites and whipped cream into raspberry mixture.
Chill . . . . . for several hours until firm.
Spoon . . . raspberry mousse into shells.
Garnish . . with chocolate curls.
Yield . . . . 10 servings.

Photograph for this recipe on page 69.

APRICOT LINZER TORTE

1 c. diced dried California apricots
1 8-oz. can crushed pineapple in
  unsweetened juice
Sugar
1/2 c. butter, softened
1 egg
1/2 tsp. grated lemon rind
1/4 tsp. cinnamon
3/4 c. flour
3/4 c. ground toasted blanched almonds
Confectioners' sugar
Red glace cherries (opt.)

Combine . apricots, pineapple and juice, 2/3
            cup sugar and 1/2 cup water in
            saucepan.
Simmer .. covered, for 15 minutes, stirring
            occasionally, until thick.
Cream ... butter and 1/4 cup sugar in bowl
            until light and fluffy.
Beat ..... in egg.
Stir ...... in next 4 ingredients, mixing well.
Chill ..... for 1 hour.
Reserve .. 1/5 of the pastry in refrigerator.
Press ..... remaining pastry over bottom and 1
            inch up side of 9-inch springform
            pan.
Spoon ... in cooled apricot filling.
Bake ..... at 350 degrees for 35 to 40 minutes
            or until pastry is browned.
Remove .. rim of pan.
Cool ..... torte completely.
Roll ..... out remaining pastry on lightly
            floured surface.
Cut ...... out nine 1-inch stars with cookie
            cutter.
Place .... on cookie sheet.
Bake ..... at 350 degrees for 3 minutes.
Cover .... center of torte with foil circle.
Sprinkle .. torte and stars with confectioners'
            sugar.
Remove .. foil, placing stars in center.
Garnish .. with glace cherry quarters.

Photograph for this recipe on page 4.

EASY ALMOND TORTE

7/8 c. flour, sifted
2 tsp. baking powder
1/4 tsp. salt
1/3 c. butter, softened
1 1/2 c. sugar
4 eggs, separated
1 tsp. vanilla extract
1/4 c. milk
1/2 c. blanched almond halves

Sift ...... first 3 ingredients together.
Cream ... butter and 1/2 cup sugar together
            in bowl.
Beat ..... in egg yolks and vanilla.
Add ..... sifted dry ingredients alternately
            with milk, beating well after each
            addition.
Pour ..... into 2 loose bottom layer cake
            pans.
Beat ..... egg whites until soft peaks form.
Add ..... 1 cup sugar gradually, beating until
            stiff.
Spread ... meringue over batter to within 1
            inch of pan sides.
Arrange .. almonds on edge in meringue.
Bake ..... at 350 degrees for 35 minutes.
Remove .. cooled layers from pan.
Serve .... with whipped cream, fresh berries
            or ice cream between layers.

Charlene Woodson
San Jose, California

APPLE-PECAN TORTE

4 eggs
3 c. sugar
8 tbsp. flour
5 tsp. baking powder
1/2 tsp. salt
2 c. chopped tart cooking apples
2 c. chopped pecans
2 tsp. vanilla extract
Whipped cream

Beat ..... eggs in large bowl until lemon
            colored.
Add ..... remaining ingredients except
            whipped cream in order listed, beat-
            ing well.
Pour ..... into 2 greased 8 x 12-inch baking
            pans.
Bake ..... at 325 degrees for 45 minutes or
            until brown and crusty.
Spread ... whipped cream between layers and
            over top.

Myra Hawkinson
Olean, New York

AUSTRIAN DATE TORTE

2 eggs, separated
3/4 c. corn syrup
1/3 c. pastry flour
1/2 tsp. salt
3/4 tsp. baking powder
1 c. chopped dates
1/3 c. chopped nuts
1/2 tsp. grated orange rind
1/4 c. sugar
3/4 c. dry bread crumbs

Beat ..... egg yolks and syrup in bowl until smooth.
Sift ...... flour, salt and baking powder together.
Add ..... dates, nuts, orange rind and sifted dry ingredients to syrup mixture, mixing well.
Beat ..... egg whites until soft peaks form.
Add ..... sugar gradually, beating until stiff.
Fold ..... 1/3 of the meringue into batter.
Stir ...... in crumbs.
Fold ..... in remaining meringue.
Spread ... in greased 8-inch square pan.
Bake ..... at 375 degrees for 25 minutes or until set.
Cool ..... slightly before cutting into squares.
Serve .... with whipped topping.

E. Klassen
Georges P. Vanier School, Donnelly, Alberta, Canada

CHOCOLATE CHIP-DATE TORTE

1 c. finely chopped dates
1 tsp. soda
1 c. butter
1/4 c. cocoa
1 c. sugar
2 eggs
1 tsp. vanilla extract
1 3/4 c. sifted flour
1/2 tsp. salt
1 c. finely chopped nuts
1 6-oz. package semisweet chocolate chips

Combine . dates, soda and 1 cup boiling water in small bowl, mixing well.
Cream ... butter, cocoa and sugar in bowl until fluffy.
Beat ..... in eggs and vanilla.

Add ..... flour and salt alternately with cooled date mixture, beating well after each addition.
Pour ..... into greased and floured 9 x 13-inch baking dish.
Sprinkle .. with nuts and chocolate chips.
Bake ..... at 350 degrees for 40 to 45 minutes.

Sally Montgomery
Amarillo, Texas

CHOCOLATE DESSERT TORTE

1/2 c. butter, softened
2 c. confectioners' sugar
4 egg yolks
4 egg whites, stiffly beaten
1 6-oz. package semisweet chocolate pieces, melted
1 c. chopped walnuts
1 tsp. vanilla extract
1 sponge cake

Cream ... butter and confectioners' sugar in bowl.
Add ..... egg yolks 1 at a time, beating well after each addition.
Fold ..... in egg whites.
Stir ...... in melted chocolate.
Add ..... walnuts and vanilla, mixing well.
Cut ...... sponge cake into thin slices.
Spread ... chocolate mixture between layers and on top of cake.

Georgia Busch
Northfield H. S., Wabash, Indiana

CHOCOLATE TORTE

1 oblong pound cake
1 6-oz. package chocolate chips, melted
1 tsp. (heaping) instant coffee
1 c. sour cream
1/2 c. chopped pecans

Cut ...... cake lengthwise into 6 layers.
Mix ..... chocolate and coffee together.
Add ..... sour cream and pecans to slightly cooled chocolate mixture, blending well.
Spread ... between layers and on top of cake.
Chill ..... in refrigerator.
Slice ..... and top with whipped cream and cherry.

Louise B. Howell
Stewart County H. S., Dover, Tennessee

ELEGANT HOLIDAY TORTE

1/2 c. sifted flour
1/2 c. sifted cocoa
1 tsp. baking powder
4 eggs
1 1/4 c. sugar
2 tsp. vanilla extract
Confectioners' sugar
4 tbsp. cornstarch
1/4 tsp. salt
2 1/2 c. milk
3 egg yolks, beaten
4 to 5 bananas, thinly sliced
1 c. heavy cream, whipped

Sift . . . . . . first 3 ingredients together into bowl.
Beat . . . . . eggs in large bowl until foamy.
Add . . . . . 3/4 cup sugar gradually, beating constantly until thick.
Add . . . . . 1 teaspoon vanilla.
Fold . . . . . into flour mixture, blending until smooth.
Pour . . . . . batter into lightly greased waxed paper-lined 10 x 15-inch pan.
Bake . . . . . at 375 degrees for 12 minutes or until cake tests done.
Invert . . . . onto towel dusted with sifted confectioners' sugar.
Cool . . . . . on wire rack.
Combine . 1/2 cup sugar, cornstarch and salt in double boiler.
Stir . . . . . . in milk gradually, blending well.
Cook . . . . over boiling water until thick, stirring constantly.
Cook . . . . covered, for 10 minutes.
Stir . . . . . . a small amount of hot mixture into egg yolks; stir egg yolks into hot mixture.
Cook . . . . for 2 minutes longer, stirring constantly.
Remove . . from heat; add 1 teaspoon vanilla.
Cool . . . . . without stirring.
Cut . . . . . . cake into four 4 x 10-inch layers.
Alternate . layers of cake, cream filling, bananas and cream filling until all ingredients are used, ending with cake.
Frost . . . . top and sides with whipped cream.
Garnish . . with banana slices, chocolate curls and pistachio nuts.

Photograph for this recipe on page 1.

FIG MERINGUE TORTE

3 egg whites
1 c. sugar
1/8 tsp. salt
1 tsp. baking powder
3/4 c. chopped walnuts
1 1/2 c. ground California dried figs
20 Ritz crackers, finely crushed
1/2 tsp. vanilla extract

Beat . . . . . egg whites in bowl until stiff peaks form.
Add . . . . . sugar gradually, beating until stiff.
Combine . remaining ingredients in bowl.
Fold . . . . . into meringue.
Spoon . . . into buttered 8-inch springform pan.
Bake . . . . . at 350 degrees for 20 to 25 minutes.
Yield . . . . 6 servings.

Photograph for this recipe above.

HEAVENLY CHOCOLATE TORTE

1 c. butter, softened
4 1/2 c. sugar
4 eggs
Flour
1/4 tsp. salt
2 tbsp. cocoa
2 tsp. soda
2 c. buttermilk
3 tbsp. vanilla extract
1 c. evaporated milk
1 c. coconut
1 c. chopped pecans

Cream ... butter and 2 1/2 cups sugar in bowl until fluffy.

Add ..... 2 eggs 1 at a time, beating well after each addition.

Sift ...... 3 cups flour, salt, cocoa and soda together.

Add ..... sifted dry ingredients to creamed mixture alternately with buttermilk, beating well after each addition.

Stir ...... in 2 tablespoons vanilla.

Pour ..... into 4 greased and floured layer pans.

Bake ..... at 350 degrees for 25 minutes or until cake tests done.

Combine . 2 tablespoons flour with 2 cups sugar in saucepan.

Beat ..... 2 eggs with evaporated milk.

Blend .... into sugar mixture.

Cook .... over low heat until thick, stirring constantly.

Stir ...... in coconut, pecans and 1 tablespoon vanilla.

Spread ... cooled filling between layers and over top.

Shirley Lenahan
College Station, Texas

COCONUT TORTE

2 9-oz. packages frozen coconut, thawed
12 oz. sour cream
2 c. sugar
1 pkg. butter cake mix
1 9-oz. container Cool Whip

Combine . coconut, sour cream and sugar in bowl, mixing well.

Chill ..... in refrigerator overnight.

Prepare ... cake mix using package directions.

Pour ..... into 2 prepared layer cake pans.

Bake ..... using package directions.

Split ..... layers in half.

Combine . 1 cup coconut mixture with Cool Whip in bowl.

Spread ... remaining coconut mixture between layers.

Frost .... top and sides with Cool Whip mixture.

Place .... in airtight container.

Chill ..... for 4 days before serving.

Carolyn Hix
Community H. S., Unionville, Tennessee

STRAWBERRY-ALMOND PANCAKE TORTE

1 1/2 c. sifted flour
3 tbsp. sugar
2 tsp. baking powder
3/4 tsp. salt
1 egg, beaten
1 1/3 c. milk
3 tbsp. melted shortening
1/2 tsp. almond extract
1 2-oz. package whipped topping mix
1 pt. whole fresh strawberries, sliced

Sift ...... first 4 ingredients together in bowl.

Blend .... egg, milk, shortening and almond extract in small bowl.

Add ..... to flour mixture, mixing until smooth.

Pour ..... by 2/3 cupfuls onto preheated griddle.

Spread ... to 8-inch diameter circles.

Bake ..... until small bubbles appear; turn.

Bake ..... until golden brown.

Cool ..... on wire racks.

Prepare ... topping mix using package directions.

Fold ..... in strawberries.

Spread ... 1/4 of the strawberry mixture over 1 pancake.

Repeat ... layers until all ingredients are used, ending with strawberry mixture.

Chill ..... until serving time.

Yield .... 6-8 servings.

Photograph for this recipe above.

FRESH FRUIT TORTE

1   10 3/4-oz. pound cake
1 c. ricotta cheese
1/4 c. confectioners' sugar
1 tsp. vanilla extract
1 lg. banana, thickly sliced
Lemon juice
1 1/2 c. sliced fresh strawberries

Slice ..... cake into 3 layers.
Beat ..... ricotta, sugar and vanilla in bowl.
Coat ..... banana slices with lemon juice.
Arrange .. bananas on bottom cake layer.
Spread ... 1/3 of the cheese mixture on top.
Top ..... with half the strawberries.
Repeat ... layers, ending with top cake layer.
Frost .... with remaining cheese mixture.
Garnish .. with additional sliced bananas and strawberries.
Chill ..... for 1 hour.
Yield .... 6-8 servings.

Sue Ellen Green
Elizabeth Forward H. S., Elizabeth, Pennsylvania

RUMANIAN TORTE

Sugar
5 egg yolks
1 1/2 tsp. soda
1 tbsp. lemon juice
Flour, sifted
5 egg whites, stiffly beaten
3/4 c. milk
1 1/4 sticks unsalted butter, softened

Caramelize 4 tablespoons sugar in heavy saucepan.
Add ..... 1/2 cup water, mixing well.
Combine . egg yolks, 10 tablespoons sugar, soda, lemon juice and 1 tablespoon water in bowl, beating until thick.
Stir ...... in half the caramelized sugar.
Sift ...... in 10 tablespoons flour, beating well.
Fold ..... into egg whites.
Pour ..... into waxed paper-lined jelly roll pan.
Bake ..... at 400 degrees for 25 minutes.
Combine . milk, 3 tablespoons flour and 2 tablespoons sugar in saucepan.

Cook .... until very thick, stirring constantly.
Cream ... butter and 5 tablespoons sugar together until well blended.
Add ..... remaining caramelized sugar, beating well.
Beat ..... in cooled flour mixture.
Cut ...... cake into layers.
Spread ... filling between layers and over top of torte.

Helen R. Kelley
Lockhart Jr. H. S., Orlando, Florida

STRAWBERRY CROWN TORTE

1 pkg. white cake mix
2 egg yolks
1 1/2 tsp. almond flavoring
4 egg whites
1/4 tsp. cream of tartar
1 c. sugar
1/2 tsp. nutmeg
Few drops of red food coloring
2 c. heavy cream, whipped
1 qt. strawberries, cut in half

Prepare ... cake mix according to package directions substituting 2 egg yolks for egg whites and adding 1 teaspoon almond flavoring.
Pour ..... into 3 waxed paper-lined 9-inch layer pans.
Chill ..... in refrigerator.
Beat ..... egg whites with cream of tartar until frothy.
Add ..... sugar gradually, beating until stiff.
Fold ..... in nutmeg.
Spread ... evenly over layers.
Bake ..... at 325 degrees for 40 minutes.
Cool ..... slightly before removing from pans.
Add ..... food coloring and 1/2 teaspoon almond flavoring to whipped cream, mixing well.
Layer .... cake, whipped cream and a few strawberries alternately ending with strawberries.
Frost .... sides with remaining whipped cream.
Mound ... remaining strawberries in center of top.

Verna Carlson
Watchita, Oklahoma

Cookies

APPLE BARS

1 3/4 c. sugar
3 eggs
1 c. oil
1 tsp. vanilla extract
2 c. flour
1 tsp. each salt, soda, cinnamon
2 c. apples, sliced
1 c. chopped nuts
Confectioners' sugar

Blend .... first 4 ingredients together in large mixing bowl.
Sift ...... dry ingredients together.
Add ..... to sugar mixture, mixing well.
Fold ..... in apples and nuts.
Pour ..... into greased 9 x 13-inch baking pan.
Bake ..... at 375 degrees for 45 to 50 minutes.
Sprinkle .. with confectioners' sugar when cool.
Cut ...... into 2-inch bars.

Susan Levi
Buckeye West H. S., Mt. Pleasant, Ohio

APPLE PIE BARS

Flour
1 tsp. salt
1 c. shortening
1 egg, separated
2/3 c. milk
6 or 7 fresh apples, sliced
Sugar
1 1/2 tsp. cinnamon
1 tbsp. lemon juice

Combine . 3 cups flour and salt in bowl.
Cut ...... in shortening.
Beat ..... egg yolk and milk in bowl.
Add ..... to flour mixture, blending well.
Roll ..... out 1/2 of the dough.
Place .... on 11 x 15-inch cookie sheet.
Combine . apples, 1 1/3 cups sugar, 4 table-spoons flour, 1 teaspoon cinnamon and lemon juice in bowl, mixing well.
Spread ... on crust on cookie sheet.
Roll ..... out remaining dough.
Place .... over apple filling, sealing edges.
Beat ..... egg white until soft peaks form.

Add ..... 2 tablespoons sugar gradually, beating until stiff.
Fold ..... in 1/2 teaspoon cinnamon.
Spread ... over crust.
Bake ..... at 350 degrees for 45 minutes.
Cut ...... into bars.
Yield .... 24 to 30 bars.

Phyllis Pope
Medford Jr. H. S., Medford, Wisconsin

APPLESAUCE-RAISIN BARS

1 c. flour
2/3 c. packed brown sugar
1 tsp. soda
1/2 tsp. salt
1 tsp. pumpkin pie spice
1/4 c. shortening
1 c. applesauce
1 egg
1/2 c. raisins
3 tbsp. butter
1 1/2 c. confectioners' sugar
1 tsp. vanilla extract
1 tbsp. milk

Combine . first 9 ingredients in large mixing bowl, stirring well.
Spread ... in greased 9 x 13-inch baking pan.
Bake ..... at 350 degrees for 25 minutes.
Heat ..... butter in saucepan over medium heat until light brown.
Remove .. from heat.
Blend .... in remaining ingredients until of spreading consistency.
Spread ... on cooled cake.
Yield .... 32 bars.

Theresa Fox
Campbell Memorial H. S., Campbell, Ohio

BUTTERSCOTCH BARS

1/2 c. margarine
1 c. graham cracker crumbs
1 c. chopped nuts
1 sm. package butterscotch chips
1 c. coconut
1 c. sweetened condensed milk

Melt ..... margarine in 9-inch square baking pan.
Coat ..... sides of pan with melted butter.

Layer .... remaining ingredients in pan in order listed.
Bake ..... at 350 degrees for 25 to 30 minutes.
Cut ...... into bars.

Helen Webster
Newcomerstown H. S., Newcomerstown, Ohio

CARAMEL-COCONUT SQUARES

1/2 c. butter
1/2 c. sifted confectioners' sugar
1 c. flour
1 14-oz. can sweetened condensed milk
1 6-oz. package butterscotch pieces
1 3 1/2-oz. can flaked coconut
1 tsp. vanilla extract

Cream ... butter and sugar in bowl until light and fluffy.
Add ..... flour and mix well.
Press ..... into 9 x 9-inch baking pan.
Bake ..... at 350 degrees for 12 minutes.
Combine . remaining ingredients and pour over cake layer.
Bake ..... 25 minutes longer or until golden brown around edges.
Yield .... 36 bars.

Nan S. Griffith
Clark H. S., Plano, Texas

CHEESECAKE DATE BARS

1 11-oz. package coconut cookies, finely crushed
1/2 c. melted butter
1 1/2 c. sugar
1/2 c. finely chopped dates
2 tbsp. flour
3 8-oz. packages cream cheese, softened
4 eggs
1/8 tsp. lemon extract
1/2 tsp. salt

Combine . first 2 ingredients with 1/2 cup sugar in bowl, mixing well.
Set ...... aside 1/2 cup mixture.
Press ..... remaining mixture onto cookie sheet.
Bake ..... at 325 degrees for 10 minutes.
Mix ..... dates with flour. Set aside.
Combine . remaining ingredients with 1 cup sugar in bowl, mixing until smooth.

Add ..... date mixture, blending well.
Pour ..... over crust, spreading to cover.
Sprinkle .. reserved crumb mixture over top.
Bake ..... at 325 degrees for 30 minutes. Cool.
Cut ...... into bars.
Yield .... 4 dozen.

Janice Dye
Waynesville Sr. H. S., Waynesville, Missouri

PEANUT BUTTERSCOTCH SQUARES

1/2 c. peanut oil
1 c. packed dark brown sugar
1 egg
1 tsp. vanilla extract
2 c. sifted flour
1/4 tsp. baking powder
Milk
1/2 c. chopped salted peanuts
1 c. sifted confectioners' sugar
1/4 tsp. lemon extract

Combine . first 4 ingredients in mixing bowl, blending well.
Sift ...... flour and baking powder together.
Stir ...... into brown sugar mixture.
Add ..... 2 to 3 tablespoons milk, stirring to make stiff dough.
Stir ...... in peanuts.
Pack ..... dough into 9 x 9-inch baking pan.
Bake ..... at 350 degrees for 25 to 30 minutes or until edges are lightly browned.
Combine . remaining ingredients with 2 to 3 tablespoons milk to make thin glaze.
Pour ..... over hot cookie layer.
Yield .... 3 dozen cookies.

Photograph for this recipe below.

CHERRY FRUIT SWIRLS

1 1/2 c. sugar
1/2 c. margarine, softened
1/2 c. shortening
1 1/2 tsp. baking powder
4 eggs
1 tsp. each vanilla, almond extracts
3 c. flour
1 can cherry pie filling
3/4 c. confectioners' sugar
Milk

Combine . first 5 ingredients with flavorings in large mixer bowl.
Beat . . . . . for 3 minutes at high speed.
Stir . . . . . . in flour.
Spread . . . 2/3 of the batter on a cookie sheet with sides.
Spread . . . pie filling over batter.
Bake . . . . . at 350 degrees for 45 minutes.
Blend . . . . confectioners' sugar with small amount of milk for glaze.
Drizzle . . . over warm cake.
Yield . . . . 18 squares.

Nancy Finck
Brattleboro Union H. S., Brattleboro, Vermont

CHOCOLATE PIXIES

1/2 c. butter
4 oz. unsweetened chocolate
4 eggs
2 c. sugar
3 c. flour
2 tsp. baking powder
1/2 tsp. salt
1/2 c. chopped walnuts
Confectioners' sugar

Melt . . . . . butter and chocolate over low heat in heavy saucepan.
Beat . . . . . eggs and sugar in bowl.
Add . . . . . chocolate mixture gradually, mixing well.
Sift . . . . . . flour, baking powder and salt together.
Add . . . . . to chocolate mixture gradually, blending well.
Stir . . . . . . in walnuts.
Chill . . . . . for 30 minutes or longer.
Shape . . . . into 1-inch balls.
Roll . . . . . in confectioners' sugar.

Place . . . . on baking sheets.
Bake . . . . . at 300 degrees for 15 to 18 minutes.
Cool . . . . . on wire racks.
Yield . . . . 7 dozen.

Photograph for this recipe on page 8.

BLONDE BROWNIES

2 c. packed brown sugar
2/3 c. margarine, melted
2 eggs
1 tsp. vanilla extract
2 c. flour
1 c. chopped pecans (opt.)
1 tsp. salt
1 tsp. baking powder
1/4 tsp. soda
1 c. chocolate chips

Combine . sugar and margarine in bowl.
Add . . . . . eggs and vanilla, mixing well.
Stir . . . . . . in flour, pecans, salt, baking powder and soda, blending well.
Pour . . . . . into greased and floured 9 x 13-inch baking pan.
Sprinkle . . with chocolate chips.
Bake . . . . . at 350 degrees for 25 minutes.
Yield . . . . 15 servings.

Mrs. Edith Carter
Hamlin H. S., Hamlin, Texas

BOYLE COUNTY CHEERLEADERS BROWNIES

4 sq. unsweetened chocolate
2/3 c. margarine
4 eggs
2 c. sugar
1 1/4 c. flour
1 tsp. baking powder
1 tsp. salt
1 c. chopped nuts
1 tsp. vanilla extract

Melt . . . . . chocolate and margarine in saucepan over low heat.
Add . . . . . eggs to sugar in bowl 1 at a time, beating well after each addition.
Stir . . . . . . in chocolate mixture.
Sift . . . . . . flour, baking powder and salt together.

Add . . . . . to chocolate mixture, mixing well.
Stir . . . . . . in last 2 ingredients.
Spread . . . in greased 9 x 13-inch baking pan.
Bake . . . . . at 350 degrees for 30 minutes or until brownies pull away from sides of pan.

Marianne Kirby
Boyle County H. S., Danville, Kentucky

BUTTERMILK BROWNIES

2 c. sugar
2 c. flour
4 tbsp. cocoa
1/4 tsp. salt
1/2 c. oil
1/2 c. margarine
2 eggs, beaten
1/2 c. buttermilk
1 tsp. soda
1 tsp. vanilla extract

Sift . . . . . . dry ingredients together into large bowl.
Combine . 1 cup water, oil and margarine in saucepan.
Bring . . . . to a boil over medium heat.
Cool . . . . . for several minutes.
Pour . . . . . over dry ingredients, beating well.
Add . . . . . remaining ingredients, mixing well.
Pour . . . . . into greased jelly roll pan.
Bake . . . . . at 350 degrees for 20 minutes.
Frost . . . . with favorite chocolate icing.
Yield . . . . 24 squares.

Debbie Hart
Emerson Jr. H. S., Enid, Oklahoma

DOUBLE CHOCOLATE BROWNIES

1/2 c. butter
3/4 c. sugar
1 egg
1/2 c. sour cream
1 tsp. vanilla extract
1 c. flour
1/4 c. cocoa
1/4 tsp. soda
1/4 tsp. salt
1 c. semisweet chocolate Mini Chips
Easy Brownie Frosting

Cream . . . first 3 ingredients in bowl until fluffy.

Add . . . . . sour cream and vanilla, beating well.
Combine . dry ingredients in bowl.
Blend . . . . into creamed mixture.
Stir . . . . . . in chips.
Spread . . . in greased 9-inch square baking dish.
Bake . . . . . at 350 degrees for 30 to 35 minutes or until brownie tests nearly done.
Frost . . . . with Easy Brownie Frosting when cool.
Sprinkle . . with additional chips and nuts.

Easy Brownie Frosting

3 tbsp. butter, softened
3 tbsp. cocoa
1/2 tsp. vanilla extract
1 1/4 c. confectioners' sugar
2 tbsp. milk

Cream . . . butter and cocoa in small mixer bowl.
Add . . . . . vanilla and confectioners' sugar.
Beat . . . . . in milk until mixture is of spreading consistency.

Photograph for this recipe on page 36.

FOXY BROWNIES

1/3 c. butter
1 1/2 sq. unsweetened chocolate
1 c. sugar
2 eggs, well beaten
2/3 c. flour
1/2 tsp. baking powder
1/4 tsp. salt
3/4 c. broken pecans
1 tsp. vanilla extract

Melt . . . . . butter and chocolate together in saucepan over low heat.
Add . . . . . sugar to eggs gradually.
Blend . . . . in chocolate mixture.
Sift . . . . . . flour with baking powder and salt.
Stir . . . . . . into batter.
Add . . . . . pecans and vanilla, mixing well.
Pour . . . . . into greased 8 x 8-inch baking pan.
Bake . . . . . at 350 degrees for 25 minutes.
Cool . . . . . slightly and cut into squares.
Yield . . . . 2 dozen.

Tyran Lee Fox
Austin Jr. H. S., San Juan, Texas

FUDGE-NUT BROWNIES

2 sticks margarine
2 c. sugar
4 eggs
2 tsp. vanilla extract
2 c. flour
1/2 c. cocoa
Nuts

Cream ... first 2 ingredients together in large mixer bowl until light and fluffy.
Beat ..... in eggs and vanilla.
Mix ..... flour and cocoa in small bowl.
Add ..... to creamed mixture.
Fold ..... in nuts.
Pour ..... into jelly roll pan.
Bake ..... at 350 degrees for 20 minutes.
Yield .... 40 squares.

Naomi Austin
Gainesville H. S., Gainesville, Texas

MINI CHIP BROWNIES

1/2 c. butter, melted
1 c. packed light brown sugar
1 egg
1 tsp. vanilla extract
1 c. flour
1/2 tsp. salt
1 c. semisweet chocolate Mini Chips

Combine . first 2 ingredients in mixer bowl, mixing well; cool.
Beat ..... in egg and vanilla until fluffy.
Add ..... flour and salt.
Beat ..... until just blended.
Stir ...... in chips.
Spoon ... into greased 9-inch square baking dish.
Bake ..... at 350 degrees for 25 to 30 minutes or until brownies nearly test done.
Yield .... 16 brownies.

Photograph for this recipe on page 36.

NANCY'S BROWNIES

2 sq. unsweetened chocolate
1/3 c. shortening
3/4 c. flour
1/2 tsp. baking powder
1/2 tsp. salt
2 eggs

1 c. sugar
1 tsp. vanilla extract
1/2 c. broken nuts

Melt ..... chocolate and shortening together in saucepan over low heat.
Sift ...... flour, baking powder and salt together in bowl.
Beat ..... eggs and sugar together in bowl.
Add ..... chocolate mixture, beating well.
Blend .... in flour mixture and vanilla.
Add ..... nuts, mixing well.
Bake ..... at 350 degrees for 30 minutes.
Yield .... 18 bars.

Nancy Ann Forbear
Oakridge Sr. H. S., Muskegon, Michigan

PEPPERMINT BROWNIES

3 sq. chocolate
Margarine
2 eggs
1 c. sugar
1 tsp. vanilla extract
1/2 c. flour
1/2 c. pecans
1 c. confectioners' sugar
1 tbsp. milk
3/4 tsp. peppermint flavoring
Few drops of green food coloring

Melt ..... 2 squares chocolate and 1/2 cup margarine in saucepan over medium heat.
Combine . with next 5 ingredients in bowl, mixing well.
Pour ..... into greased 8 x 8-inch baking pan.
Bake ..... at 300 degrees for 25 minutes; cool.
Mix ..... next 4 ingredients together until smooth.
Spread ... over baked layer; set aside.
Melt ..... 1 square chocolate and 1 tablespoon margarine together in saucepan.
Pour ..... over peppermint layer; cool.
Cut ...... into 1-inch squares.

Eugenia Wilson
Heritage H. S., Maryville, Tennessee

QUICK AND EASY BROWNIES

Margarine
Sugar

4 eggs
1 c. flour
1 16-oz. can chocolate syrup
6 tbsp. milk
2/3 c. chocolate chips

Cream ... 1 stick softened margarine and 1 cup sugar in bowl until smooth.
Add ..... eggs, flour and chocolate syrup.
Mix ..... until well blended.
Pour ..... into greased and floured 9 x 13-inch baking pan.
Bake ..... at 350 degrees for 20 minutes.
Combine . 6 tablespoons margarine, milk and 1 1/3 cups sugar in saucepan.
Boil ..... for 1 minute over medium heat.
Stir ...... in chocolate chips.
Beat ..... until of spreading consistency.
Spread ... frosting over brownies.

Murriel Riedesel
Wauconda H. S., Wauconda, Illinois

ROYAL FUDGE BROWNIES

1/2 c. butter
3 oz. unsweetened chocolate
2 c. sugar
3 eggs
1 tbsp. Creme de Menthe
1/8 tsp. salt
1 1/2 c. flour
1 c. chopped walnuts
1 c. chopped candied cherries

Melt ..... butter and chocolate together in saucepan.
Pour ..... into large mixing bowl.
Add ..... sugar gradually, mixing well.
Beat ..... in eggs 1 at a time, beating well after each addition.
Stir ...... in Creme de Menthe and salt.
Add ..... flour gradually, blending well.
Fold ..... in walnuts and cherries.
Pour ..... into buttered 9-inch square baking pan.
Bake ..... at 350 degrees for 35 to 40 minutes or until brownies test done.
Yield .... 3 dozen.

Photograph for this recipe on page 8.

SAUCEPAN BROWNIES

1/2 c. sugar
2 tbsp. butter

1 1/3 c. semisweet chocolate Mini Chips
2 eggs
2/3 c. flour
1/4 tsp. soda
1/4 tsp. salt
1 tsp. vanilla extract
3/4 c. chopped nuts (opt.)

Combine . sugar, butter and 2 tablespoons water in saucepan.
Bring .... to a boil over medium heat, stirring occasionally.
Stir ...... in chips until melted.
Add ..... eggs, mixing well.
Mix ..... flour, soda and salt in bowl.
Stir ...... into chocolate mixture.
Fold ..... in vanilla and nuts.
Pour ..... into greased 9-inch square baking dish.
Bake ..... at 325 degrees for 25 to 30 minutes or until brownie tests nearly done.
Sprinkle .. with confectioners' sugar when cool.

Photograph for this recipe on page 36.

ZUCCHINI BROWNIES

1/2 c. margarine
2 sq. unsweetened chocolate
1 1/2 c. sifted flour
1/4 tsp. baking powder
1/2 tsp. salt
2 eggs, beaten
1 c. sugar
2 tsp. vanilla extract
2 c. grated zucchini
1/2 c. nuts, chopped
Confectioners' sugar

Melt ..... margarine and chocolate together in saucepan.
Sift ...... flour, baking powder and salt together in bowl.
Cream ... eggs and sugar in large bowl.
Add ..... vanilla, chocolate mixture and zucchini, mixing well.
Mix ..... in dry ingredients and nuts.
Pour ..... into greased 8-inch square pan.
Bake ..... at 375 degrees for 30 to 35 minutes.
Sprinkle .. with confectioners' sugar.

Patricia L. Baird
Aurora Hills Middle School, Aurora, Colorado

CHOC-CO-NUT SQUARES

1 can sweetened condensed milk
1 1/4 c. graham cracker crumbs
1 6-oz. package chocolate chips
1 tsp. baking powder
1 tsp. vanilla extract
Dash of salt
1/4 c. each chopped nuts, coconut

Mix .....all ingredients in order given in large bowl, stirring well.
Pour .....into greased 8 x 8-inch baking pan.
Bake .....at 325 degrees for 25 minutes.
Cool .....before removing from pan.
Yield ....sixteen 2-inch squares.

Mrs. Martha Copeland
Brownsboro H. S., Brownsboro, Texas

KRISPY BARS

1 c. sugar
1 c. light corn syrup
1 tbsp. butter
1 18-oz. jar peanut butter
6 c. Rice Krispies
1 6-oz. package chocolate chips
1 6-oz. package butterscotch chips

Combine .sugar, corn syrup and butter in saucepan.
Bring ....to a boil.
Stir ......in peanut butter, blending well.
Add .....Rice Krispies, stirring to mix well.
Press .....into greased 9 x 13-inch baking pan.
Melt .....remaining ingredients together in saucepan over low heat.
Spread ...over peanut butter mixture.
Cut ......in bars.
Yield ....5 dozen

Thelma Koupal
Tyndall-Tabor H. S., Tyndall, South Dakota

K-BARS

1 c. sugar
1 c. light corn syrup
1 c. chunky peanut butter
5 c. Special K cereal
6 oz. chocolate chips
6 oz. butterscotch chips

Combine .sugar and syrup in saucepan.
Cook ....over low heat until sugar dissolves.
Stir ......in peanut butter and cereal.
Pour .....into greased 9 x 11-inch pan.
Mix .....last 2 ingredients in saucepan.
Melt .....over low heat.
Spread ...over cookies and cool.
Yield ....15 bars.

Vanessa M. Napier
I. C. Norcom H. S., Portsmouth, Virginia

HELLO DOLLIES

1/2 c. melted butter
1 c. graham cracker crumbs
1 sm. package chocolate chips
1 sm. package butterscotch chips
1 c. chopped pecans
1 can flaked coconut
1 can sweetened condensed milk

Combine .butter and crumbs in bowl, mixing well.
Press .....into baking dish.
Layer ....next four ingredients.
Drizzle ...milk over top.
Bake .....at 350 degrees for 30 minutes or until brown.
Yield ....12 squares.

Barbara J. Kiker
Anson Jr. H. S., Wadesboro, North Carolina

NO-BAKE DATE BARS

1 lb. pitted dates, chopped
1 1/2 c. unsweetened shredded coconut
1/2 c. butter
1/4 c. honey
2 1/2 c. rolled oats
2/3 c. chopped nuts
1 tsp. vanilla extract

Combine .first 4 ingredients and 1/2 cup water in saucepan.
Cook ....over medium heat for 3 to 4 minutes until thick and blended, stirring frequently.
Add .....remaining ingredients, blending well.
Spread ...into buttered 9 x 13-inch pan.
Chill .....for 2 hours.
Cut ......into bars.
Store ....in refrigerator in airtight container.

Grace Hemingway
North Jr. H. S., Joplin, Missouri

KARIDOPETA

2 c. Bisquick
1 c. ground walnuts
1 c. oil
1 c. milk
3 eggs
1 tsp. cinnamon
1 1/2 tsp. baking powder
1/2 tsp. soda
2 c. sugar
2 tbsp. ground orange rind

Combine . first 8 ingredients with 1 cup sugar and 1 teaspoon orange rind in bowl.
Beat . . . . . until smooth.
Pour . . . . . into prepared 10 x 15-inch baking pan.
Bake . . . . . at 350 degrees for 40 minutes or until cake tests done.
Combine . 1 cup sugar, 1 teaspoon orange rind and 1 cup water in saucepan.
Boil . . . . . for 10 minutes.
Pour . . . . . over cooled cake.
Cut . . . . . . diagonally into diamond-shaped pieces.
Yield . . . . 40 pieces.

Mary Kampros Graham
East H. S., Salt Lake City, Utah.

OATMEAL CARAMELITAS

1   14-oz. package caramels
1/2 c. evaporated milk
2 c. flour
2 c. quick-cooking oats
1 1/2 c. packed brown sugar
1 tsp. soda
1/2 tsp. salt
1 c. margarine, melted
1   6-oz. package semisweet chocolate pieces
1 c. chopped pecans

Combine . caramels and milk in heavy saucepan.
Melt . . . . . over low heat; cool slightly.
Combine . next 6 ingredients in large mixing bowl.
Press . . . . . half of crumb mixture in bottom of greased 9 x 13-inch baking pan.
Bake . . . . . at 350 degrees for 10 minutes.
Remove . . from oven.
Sprinkle . . with chocolate pieces and pecans.

Spread . . . carefully with caramel mixture.
Sprinkle . . remaining crumb mixture on top.
Chill . . . . . and cut into bars.
Yield . . . . 32 bars.

Frances Tharpe
North Wilkes H. S., Hays, North Carolina

OATMEAL SQUARES

1 /2 c. margarine, softened
1 c. sugar
2 eggs
3/4 c. flour
1 tsp. cinnamon
1/4 tsp. baking powder
1 tsp. vanilla extract
3/4 c. regular oats

Cream . . . margarine and sugar in mixer bowl.
Add . . . . . eggs, mixing well.
Stir . . . . . . in dry ingredients.
Blend . . . . in vanilla and oats.
Spread . . . in greased 9-inch square baking pan.
Bake . . . . . at 350 degrees for 25 minutes.
Remove . . from pan while warm.
Cut . . . . . . into squares.
Yield . . . . 24 squares.

Jane Salisbury
Mt. Dora Middle School, Mt. Dora, Florida

ICED PEANUT BUTTER BARS

1/2 c. chunky peanut butter
1/2 c. butter
1 1/2 c. sugar
2 eggs
1 tsp. vanilla extract
1 c. self-rising flour
Chocolate icing

Melt . . . . . peanut butter and butter in top of double boiler over hot water.
Combine . butter mixture with remaining ingredients except icing in bowl, mixing well.
Pour . . . . . into greased 9 x 13-inch pan.
Bake . . . . . at 350 degrees for 25 to 30 minutes.
Top . . . . . cooled cookies with chocolate icing.
Cut . . . . . . into squares.

Katherine E. Fulmer
Cross Keys H. S., Atlanta, Georgia

MICROWAVE PECAN BARS

1/2 c. butter, melted
1 lb. light brown sugar
2 eggs, beaten
2 tsp. vanilla extract
2 c. chopped pecans
1 1/2 c. pancake mix
Confectioners' sugar

Combine . first 4 ingredients in bowl, mixing well.
Blend .... in pecans and pancake mix.
Pour ..... into greased 8 x 12-inch glass baking dish.
Microwave on High for 8 to 10 minutes, rotating dish every 3 minutes. Center will appear soft.
Cut ...... into bars when thoroughly cooled and set.
Roll ..... in confectioners' sugar.
Yield .... 40 bars.

Bonnie L. Stover
Leto H. S., Tampa, Florida

PECAN PIE BARS

1 1/2 c. flour
2 tbsp. packed brown sugar
Butter
2 eggs
1/2 c. chopped pecans
1 tsp. vanilla extract
1/4 tsp. salt

Combine . flour and brown sugar in bowl.
Cut ...... in 1/2 cup butter until crumbly.
Pat ...... into 7 x 11-inch baking pan.
Mix ..... eggs, pecans, vanilla, salt and 2 tablespoons melted butter in bowl.
Pour ..... over crust.
Bake ..... at 350 degrees for 25 minutes.
Yield .... 32 bars.

Madge D. Tapp
Webster County H. S., Dixon, Kentucky

PINEAPPLE SQUARES

1 30-oz. can crushed pineapple
Sugar
1/4 c. cornstarch
1 c. shortening
2 eggs
1/2 c. sour milk
4 c. flour
1 tsp. each salt, baking powder
1/2 tsp. soda
Condensed milk
Coconut

Combine . pineapple, 1 cup sugar and cornstarch in saucepan.
Cook .... until thick, stirring constantly.
Cream ... shortening and 1 cup sugar together in large bowl.
Add ..... eggs 1 at a time, beating well after each addition.
Add ..... sour milk and mix.
Mix ..... flour, salt, baking powder and soda with 1 cup sugar.
Add ..... to shortening mixture.
Roll ..... a little less than half the mixture between 2 layers of waxed paper to fit 11 x 17-inch jelly roll pan.
Press ..... remaining dough in bottom of jelly roll pan.
Spread ... filling over dough.
Top ..... with rolled pastry.
Brush .... with condensed milk.
Sprinkle .. with sugar and coconut.
Bake ..... at 375 degrees for 30 minutes or until golden brown.
Yield .... 4 dozen 2-inch squares.

Anna Mary Gembarosky
Girard H. S., Girard, Ohio

PUMPKIN BARS

4 eggs, beaten
1 c. oil
2 c. sugar
1 15-oz. can pumpkin
2 c. flour
2 tsp. baking powder
1 tsp. soda
2 tsp. cinnamon
1/2 tsp. each ginger, cloves, nutmeg, salt
1 6-oz. package cream cheese, softened
1/2 c. margarine, softened
1/2 tsp. vanilla extract
1 tbsp. milk
4 c. confectioners' sugar

Combine . first 4 ingredients in bowl, mixing well.
Sift ...... dry ingredients together.
Add ..... to pumpkin mixture, blending well.
Pour ..... into greased sheet cake pan.

Bake . . . . . at 350 degrees for 25 to 30 minutes.
Combine . remaining ingredients in bowl, beating to spreading consistency.
Spread . . . over cooled cake.
Cut . . . . . . into bars.

Linda Finley Loman
Boonville H. S., Boonville, Missouri

WALNUT TREASURE BARS

1/2 c. shortening
1 c. packed brown sugar
1 egg
Milk
Sherry
1 2/3 c. sifted flour
3/4 tsp. salt
1/2 tsp. each baking powder, soda, cinnamon
4 tsp. instant coffee powder
1 c. California walnuts, coarsely chopped
1 c. semisweet chocolate morsels
2 1/4 c. sifted confectioners' sugar
1 1/2 tbsp. butter, softened

Cream . . . first 3 ingredients in bowl.
Add . . . . . 1/4 cup milk and 1/4 cup Sherry, mixing well.
Sift . . . . . . next 5 dry ingredients and 3 teaspoons coffee together.
Add . . . . . to creamed mixture, blending well.
Stir . . . . . . in walnuts and chocolate morsels.
Spread . . . in 10 x 15-inch baking pan.
Bake . . . . . at 375 degrees for 20 minutes.
Cool . . . . . in pan.
Combine . confectioners' sugar, butter, 2 tablespoons Sherry, 1 tablespoon milk and 1 teaspoon instant coffee in bowl, mixing well.
Spread . . . over cookie layer.
Cut . . . . . . into bars.
Decorate . tops with additional walnuts and chocolate morsels.
Yield . . . . 36 bars.

Photograph for this recipe on this page.

PUMPKIN PIE SQUARES

1 c. sifted flour
1/2 c. quick-cooking oats
1 c. packed brown sugar
Butter

2 c. canned pumpkin
1 13 1/2-oz. can evaporated milk
2 eggs
3/4 c. sugar
1/2 tsp. salt
1 tsp. cinnamon
1/2 tsp. ginger
1/4 tsp. cloves
1/2 c. chopped pecans

Combine . flour, oats, 1/2 cup brown sugar and 1/2 cup butter in bowl.
Mix . . . . . with electric mixer at low speed until crumbly.
Press . . . . . into 9 x 13-inch baking pan.
Bake . . . . . at 350 degrees for 15 minutes.
Combine . next 8 ingredients in bowl, beating well.
Pour . . . . . over crust.
Bake . . . . . for 20 minutes longer.
Combine . pecans, remaining 1/2 cup brown sugar and 2 tablespoons butter in bowl.
Sprinkle . . over pumpkin mixure.
Bake . . . . . for 15 to 20 minutes longer or until filling tests done.
Cool . . . . . in pan.
Cut . . . . . . into 2-inch squares.
Yield . . . . 2 dozen.

Janice T. Campbell
Boyle County H. S., Danville, Kentucky

RASPBERRY BARS

1 3/4 c. flour
1 tsp. baking powder
Butter
2 eggs
1 tbsp. milk
1 c. raspberry jam
1 c. sugar
2 c. coconut
1 tsp. vanilla extract

Combine . flour and baking powder in mixing bowl.
Cut . . . . . . in 1/2 cup butter until crumbly.
Add . . . . . 1 slightly beaten egg and milk to make soft dough.
Press . . . . . into greased 8 x 12-inch baking pan.
Spread . . . with jam.
Combine . 3 tablespoons soft butter, sugar, 1 beaten egg, coconut and vanilla in bowl.
Mix . . . . . until of spreading consistency.
Spread . . . over jam.
Bake . . . . . at 350 degrees for 30 to 35 minutes.
Cut . . . . . . into squares when cool.

Nan Sulser
Chapel Hill H. S., Tyler, Texas

RHUBARB BARS

3 tbsp. cornstarch
3 c. rhubarb, cut up
1 1/2 c. sugar
1 tsp. vanilla extract
1 1/2 c. oatmeal
1 1/2 c. flour
1 c. packed brown sugar
1/2 tsp. soda
1 c. shortening
1/2 c. chopped nuts

Dissolve . . cornstarch in 1/4 cup cold water in saucepan.
Add . . . . . rhubarb, sugar and vanilla.
Cook . . . . over medium heat until thick, stirring occasionally.
Combine . remaining ingredients in bowl, mixing until crumbly.
Pat . . . . . . 3/4 of flour mixture into 9 x 13-inch baking pan.

Top . . . . . with rhubarb mixture.
Sprinkle . . with remaining crumbs.
Bake . . . . . at 375 degrees for 30 minutes.

Rita Poncelet
Irene H. S., Irene, South Dakota

SALTED NUT BARS

1 1/2 c. flour
3/4 c. brown sugar
Butter, softened
1   13-oz. can mixed nuts
6 oz. butterscotch chips
1/2 c. light corn syrup

Cream . . . together first 2 ingredients and 1/2 cup butter in mixer bowl.
Press . . . . . into 9 x 13-inch baking pan.
Bake . . . . . at 350 degrees for 10 minutes.
Cover . . . . baked crust with mixed nuts.
Combine . remaining ingredients and 1 tablespoon water in saucepan.
Cook . . . . over low heat until melted, stirring often.
Pour . . . . . over nuts.
Bake . . . . . for 10 minutes longer.
Cut . . . . . . into bars when cool.
Yield . . . . 30 bars.

Sara Clift
Cornersville H. S., Cornersville, Tennessee

SNOWBARS

1/2 c. butter, softened
Flour
1 c. sugar
2 eggs
1/4 tsp. baking powder
3 tbsp. lemon juice
Confectioners' sugar

Combine . butter, 1/3 cup flour and 1/4 cup sugar in mixer bowl.
Beat . . . . . with electric mixer on low speed for 1 minute.
Pat . . . . . . into 8-inch square baking dish.
Bake . . . . . at 350 degrees for 15 to 20 minutes or until edges are browned.
Mix . . . . . eggs, 3/4 cup sugar, 2 tablespoons flour, baking powder and lemon juice together in bowl.
Pour . . . . . over partially baked crust.
Bake . . . . . for 18 to 20 minutes longer or until cookies test done.

Sprinkle .. with confectioners' sugar.
Cool ..... and cut into bars.
Yield .... 16 bars.

Glynda Hooper
Marlow H. S., Marlow, Oklahoma

TRAPPERS

1 stick margarine, melted
1 box yellow cake mix
5 eggs
1 c. pecans
1 box confectioners' sugar
1 8-oz. package cream cheese, softened

Combine . margarine, cake mix, 1 beaten egg and pecans in bowl, mixing well.
Pat ...... into 9 x 13-inch pan.
Beat ..... confectioners' sugar, 4 eggs and cream cheese in bowl.
Pour ..... over cake mix, spreading evenly.
Bake ..... at 350 degrees for 1 hour.
Cut ...... into small squares.
Yield .... 2 dozen.

Jenell R. Griffith
A. E. Beach H. S., Savannah, Georgia

YUMMY COOKIES

1/3 c. shortening
1 c. sugar
1 1/2 c. flour
2 eggs
1 tsp. baking powder
1 tsp. vanilla extract
1/2 tsp. salt
2 egg whites
1 c. packed brown sugar
1/2 c. chopped nuts

Combine . first 7 ingredients in bowl, mixing well.
Spread ... in 9-inch square baking dish.
Beat ..... egg whites until soft peaks form.
Add ..... brown sugar gradually, beating until stiff.
Fold ..... in nuts.
Spread ... over dough.
Bake ..... at 325 degrees for 30 minutes.
Cut ...... into 2-inch squares.
Yield .... 12 squares.

Linda Traynor
Pittsford Mendon H. S., Pittsford, New York

APRICOT SWIRL COOKIES

4 oz. dried California apricots, chopped
1 c. packed light brown sugar
1/4 c. finely chopped walnuts, toasted
1/2 c. butter, softened
1/2 c. sugar
1 egg
1 3/4 c. flour
1/2 tsp. each soda, salt
1/2 tsp. vanilla extract
1 sq. unsweetened chocolate, melted

Bring .... apricots and 3/4 cup water to a boil in medium saucepan.
Simmer .. covered, over low heat for 20 minutes or until tender.
Stir ...... in 1/2 cup brown sugar, mixing well; cool.
Fold ..... in walnuts.
Cream ... butter, 1/2 cup brown sugar, sugar and egg in bowl.
Stir ...... in next 4 ingredients, mixing well.
Add ..... melted chocolate to half the dough.
Chill ..... wrapped, for several hours.
Roll ..... out chocolate dough to 8 x 12-inch rectangle between floured waxed paper.
Spread ... half the filling to within 1/2 inch of edges.
Roll ..... as for jelly roll.
Repeat ... with remaining dough.
Chill ..... wrapped, for several hours.
Slice ..... 1/4-inch thick.
Place .... on greased cookie sheet.
Bake ..... at 400 degrees for 8 to 10 minutes or until light brown.
Yield .... 8 dozen.

Photograph for this recipe above.

APRICOT-CHEESE COOKIES

1 1/2 c. margarine
1 1/2 c. sugar
1   8-oz. package cream cheese, softened
2 eggs
2 tbsp. lemon juice
2 tsp. grated lemon rind
4 1/2 c. flour
1 1/2 tsp. baking powder
Apricot preserves
Confectioners' sugar

Combine . first 3 ingredients in mixer bowl, mixing well.
Blend .... in eggs, lemon juice and rind.
Add ..... dry ingredients, mixing well.
Chill ..... in refrigerator.
Shape .... tablespoonfuls of dough into balls.
Place .... on cookie sheet.
Flatten ... slightly, indenting center.
Fill ...... centers with 1 teaspoon preserves.
Bake ..... at 350 degrees for 15 minutes.
Sprinkle .. cooled cookies with confectioners' sugar.
Yield .... 7 dozen.

Carol Jacobsen
Hoffman Estates H. S., Hoffman Estates, Illinois

COOKIE ARTISTS

1 c. sugar
1/2 c. margarine, softened
1 egg
1 tsp. vanilla extract
2 c. flour
1 tsp. baking powder
1 c. sifted confectioners' sugar
Food colorings
M & M plain chocolate candies

Cream ... sugar and margarine in bowl until light and fluffy.
Blend .... in egg and vanilla.
Mix ..... flour and baking powder together.
Add ..... to creamed mixture, blending well.
Shape .... half the dough into balls using 2 tablespoons dough for each.
Place .... on cookie sheet.
Flatten ... with glass dipped in sugar to 3-inch circle.
Insert .... wooden stick into each as for lollipop.

Shape .... remaining dough into cookie people, using 1 tablespoon dough for body and 1 teaspoon dough for each leg and arm.
Assemble . on cookie sheet.
Flatten ... to 1/4-inch thick with glass dipped in sugar.
Bake ..... at 375 degrees for 8 to 10 minutes or until edges are light brown.
Combine . confectioners' sugar and 4 teaspoons water in bowl, mixing well.
Divide ... into small cups, coloring as desired.
Apply .... glaze to cookies to resemble eyes, hair and clothes.
Secure ... chocolate candies with additional glaze in desired patterns.
Yield .... 12 large cookies.

Photograph for this recipe on page 89.

BIG BOY CHOCOLATE CHIP COOKIES

1 1/2 c. sugar
1 c. shortening
1/2 c. butter, softened
1 c. packed brown sugar
4 eggs
1 tbsp. vanilla extract
1 tsp. lemon juice
2 tsp. soda
1 tsp. each salt, cinnamon
1/2 c. rolled oats
3 c. sifted flour
2 c. chopped pecans
2   12-oz. packages semisweet chocolate chips

Combine . first 4 ingredients together in large bowl, mixing until creamy.
Add ..... eggs 1 at a time, beating well after each addition.
Stir ...... in vanilla and lemon juice.
Combine . next 5 dry ingredients in bowl.
Add ..... to creamed mixture, stirring well.
Stir ...... in nuts and chocolate chips.
Drop .... by 1/4 cupfuls 3 inches apart on greased baking sheet.
Bake ..... at 350 degrees for 16 to 18 minutes or until golden brown.

Tanya Cook
R. L. Turner H. S., Carrollton, Texas

Recipes on page 30.

NATURAL CHOCOLATE CHIP COOKIES

1 c. butter, softened
2 eggs
3/4 c. molasses
1/2 c. honey
1 1/2 tsp. vanilla extract
1/3 c. wheat germ
1 1/4 c. whole wheat flour
3/4 tsp. each salt, soda
4 c. rolled oats
1 c. chunky peanut butter
1   12-oz. package chocolate chips

Combine . first 5 ingredients in large mixing bowl, mixing until smooth.
Add . . . . . dry ingredients except oats, stirring well.
Fold . . . . . in oats.
Add . . . . . peanut butter and chocolate chips.
Drop . . . . by teaspoonfuls onto greased baking sheets.
Bake . . . . . at 325 degrees for 10 minutes or until lightly brown.
Yield . . . . 6-7 dozen.

Candis Schey
Northeast Jr. H. S., Longmont, Colorado

CHOCOLATE DROPS

2 c. sugar
4 tsp. cocoa
1/2 c. milk
1/4 c. margarine, melted
1/2 c. smooth peanut butter
3 c. oats
1/2 tsp. vanilla extract (opt.)

Combine . sugar and cocoa in heavy 2-quart saucepan.
Add . . . . . milk and margarine, mixing well.
Bring . . . . to a boil over medium heat.
Boil . . . . . for 3 minutes.
Remove . . from heat.
Stir . . . . . . in peanut butter until just melted.
Add . . . . . oats and vanilla, mixing well.
Drop . . . . by teaspoonfuls onto waxed paper to cool.

Laura Shuyler
Groveland H. S., Groveland, Florida

Recipes on pages 20, 22, 67, 76.

CHOCOLATE KRINKLES

1/2 c. shortening
1 2/3 c. sugar
2 tsp. vanilla extract
2 eggs
2 sq. unsweetened chocolate, melted
2 c. sifted flour
2 tsp. baking powder
1/2 tsp. salt
1/3 c. milk
Confectioners' sugar

Cream . . . shortening, sugar and vanilla in bowl.
Beat . . . . . in eggs and chocolate.
Sift . . . . . . dry ingredients together.
Add . . . . . milk and dry ingredients to creamed mixture alternately, beating well after each addition.
Chill . . . . . for 3 hours.
Shape . . . . dough into 1-inch balls.
Roll . . . . . in confectioners' sugar.
Place . . . . on greased cookie sheets.
Bake . . . . . at 350 degrees for 15 minutes.
Yield . . . . 48 cookies.

Mary C. Martinez
Central Lafourche H. S., Mathews, Louisiana

CHOCOLATE-OATMEAL COOKIES

1 c. shortening
1 c. packed brown sugar
1 c. sugar
2 eggs
1 1/2 c. flour
1/2 tsp. soda
1 tsp. salt
1 tsp. vanilla extract
3 c. quick oats
1 c. chocolate chips
1 c. butterscotch chips

Beat . . . . . shortening and sugars together in bowl.
Add . . . . . eggs, beating until creamy.
Blend . . . . in flour, soda, salt and vanilla.
Stir . . . . . . in oats and chips, mixing well.
Drop . . . . by teaspoonfuls onto cookie sheet.
Bake . . . . . at 350 degrees for 5 to 8 minutes.
Yield . . . . 5 dozen.

Mary Walker
Washougal H. S., Washougal, Washington

GIANT CHOCOLATE PIZZA COOKIE

1 c. sifted flour
1/2 tsp. baking powder
1/2 tsp. salt
1/8 tsp. soda
1/2 c. nuts
1/3 c. butter, melted
1 c. packed brown sugar
1 egg
1 tsp. vanilla extract
1 c. chocolate chips
3/4 c. confectioners' sugar

Combine . first 4 ingredients in bowl, mixing well.
Stir . . . . . . in nuts.
Combine . butter and brown sugar in bowl, mixing well.
Blend . . . . in egg and vanilla.
Stir . . . . . . in flour mixture.
Spread . . . into 12-inch pizza pan.
Sprinkle . . with chocolate chips.
Bake . . . . . at 350 degrees for 20 to 25 minutes.
Blend . . . . a small amount of water with confectioners' sugar in bowl to make glaze.
Drizzle . . . over cookie.

Katherine Cooper
St. Paul H. S., St. Paul, Arkansas

STUFFED DATE DROPS

1/2 lb. pitted dates
1/2 c. walnut quarters
Butter
1/3 c. packed light brown sugar
1 egg
3/4 c. flour
1/4 tsp. each baking powder, soda, nutmeg
1/8 tsp. salt
1/4 c. sour cream
1 1/4 c. confectioners' sugar
1/4 tsp. vanilla extract

Stuff . . . . each date with walnut quarter.
Cream . . . 2 tablespoons butter and sugar in bowl.
Beat . . . . . in egg.
Sift . . . . . . next 5 dry ingredients together.
Add . . . . . to creamed mixture alternately with sour cream, mixing well after each addition.
Fold . . . . . in stuffed dates.
Drop . . . . onto baking sheet, allowing 1 date per cookie.
Bake . . . . . at 400 degrees for 8 to 10 minutes.
Cool . . . . . on wire rack.
Heat . . . . . 1/4 cup butter in saucepan over medium heat until light amber.
Remove . . from heat.
Add . . . . . confectioners' sugar, vanilla and 1 to 2 tablespoons water to make of spreading consistency.
Beat . . . . . until smooth.
Frost . . . . cookies.
Yield . . . . 3 dozen.

Photograph for this recipe on page 8.

WALNUT ROCKY ROAD DROPS

3/4 c. butter
2/3 c. packed brown sugar
2 tsp. vanilla extract
1 egg, beaten
1 c. semisweet chocolate morsels
1/2 c. chopped California walnuts
1 1/2 c. sifted flour
1/2 tsp. soda
1 tsp. salt
1 tsp. instant coffee powder
2/3 c. milk
12 to 14 marshmallows, cut into thirds
36 to 40 California walnut halves
2 1/2 c. sifted confectioners' sugar

Cream . . . 1/2 cup softened butter, brown sugar and 1 teaspoon vanilla in bowl.
Beat . . . . . in egg.
Melt . . . . . 1/2 cup chocolate morsels in saucepan.
Stir . . . . . . melted chocolate and walnuts into creamed mixture.
Sift . . . . . . next 4 dry ingredients together.
Add . . . . . flour mixture and 1/3 cup milk to creamed mixture, blending well.
Drop . . . . by rounded teaspoonfuls onto greased cookie sheets.
Bake . . . . . at 350 degrees for 10 minutes.
Top . . . . . hot cookies with marshmallow slices.
Bake . . . . . for 1 minute longer.
Press . . . . . walnut half on top of each.
Cool . . . . . on wire rack.

Combine . 1/4 cup butter, 1/3 cup milk and 1/2 cup chocolate morsels in double boiler pan.
Cook .... over hot water until melted and smooth, stirring occasionally.
Add ..... 1 teaspoon vanilla.
Beat ..... in confectioners' sugar.
Place .... cookies on waxed paper.
Spoon ... warm icing over tops.

Photograph for this recipe on this page.

DISHPAN COOKIES

2 c. packed brown sugar
2 c. sugar
2 c. oil
4 eggs
1 tbsp. soda
1/2 tsp. baking powder
1 tsp. salt
4 c. flour
1 1/2 c. oatmeal
2 c. flaked coconut
4 c. corn flakes
1 6-oz. package chocolate chips
1 6-oz. package butterscotch chips

Combine . all ingredients in order given in very large bowl, mixing well.
Drop .... by spoonfuls onto cookie sheet.
Bake ..... at 3 2 5 degrees for 10 to 12 minutes.
Yield .... 14 dozen.

Glenda Nemecek
Purcell H. S., Purcell, Oklahoma

HAUSFREUNDE

3 eggs
1 1/4 c. sugar
1/2 c. chopped walnuts
1/2 c. chocolate bits
3/4 c. raisins
1/2 tsp. baking powder
3 c. flour
1 egg yolk, beaten

Beat ..... eggs and sugar in bowl until pale and thick.
Add ..... next 4 ingredients and 1 cup flour, mixing well.
Stir ...... in remaining 2 cups flour.
Shape .... into 3 loaves 3 inches wide by 1/2 inch thick on greased baking sheets.

Brush .... with egg yolk.
Bake ..... at 350 degrees for 35 minutes.
Cut ...... into 1-inch slices while warm.

Helen Babb Boots
Lakeland Village-Medical Lake School District
Cheney, Washington

TURTLE COOKIES

1 c. sugar
1 1/2 c. flour
6 3/4 tbsp. cocoa
1/2 tsp. salt
3 eggs, beaten
Margarine, melted
2 3/4 tsp. vanilla extract
1 1/2 c. confectioners' sugar
1 1/2 tbsp. peanut butter

Combine . first 5 ingredients, 3/4 cup margarine and 1 1/2 teaspoons vanilla in large mixing bowl, stirring well.
Preheat ... waffle iron on moderate setting.
Drop .... batter by teaspoonfuls onto waffle iron.
Bake ..... for 55 to 60 seconds.
Combine . confectioners' sugar, 2 tablespoons margarine, 1 1/4 teaspoons vanilla, peanut butter and 1 to 2 tablespoons hot water in bowl, mixing to spreading consistency.
Frost .... cookies.
Yield .... 70-80 cookies.

Diane Kaczmarek
Canon City Jr. H. S., Canon City, Colorado

CORNMEAL COOKIES

3/4 c. margarine, softened
3/4 c. sugar
1 egg
1 1/2 c. flour
1 tsp. baking powder
1/4 tsp. salt
1/2 c. cornmeal
1/2 tsp. nutmeg
1 tsp. vanilla
1/2 c. raisins (opt.)

Combine . margarine and sugar in large bowl, mixing well.
Add ..... egg and beat well.
Add ..... remaining ingredients, mixing well.
Drop .... by teaspoonfuls onto greased baking sheet.
Bake ..... at 350 degrees for 12 minutes or until lightly browned on top.
Yield .... 3 dozen.

Mrs. Shirley J. Dickey
Justin F. Kimball H. S., Dallas, Texas

ELEGANT CREAM WAFERS

1 1/4 c. butter, softened
1/3 c. whipping cream
2 c. flour
Sugar
3/4 c. sifted confectioners' sugar
1 egg yolk
1 tsp. vanilla extract
Food coloring (opt.)

Combine . 1 cup butter, whipping cream and flour in large bowl, mixing thoroughly.
Chill ..... for 1 hour.
Roll ..... dough to 1/8-inch thickness on floured surface.
Cut ...... into 1 to 1 1/2-inch rounds.
Sprinkle .. waxed paper heavily with sugar.
Dip ...... rounds in the sugar.
Place .... on baking sheet.
Prick .... in 4 places with fork.
Bake ..... at 375 degrees for 7 to 9 minutes or until slightly puffy.
Blend .... 1/4 cup butter with confectioners' sugar, egg yolk, vanilla and food coloring until of spreading consistency.

Join ..... 2 cookies with filling.
Yield .... 5 dozen 1 1/2-inch cookies.

Claretta Joy Beckmeyer
Snohomish H. S., Snohomish, Washington

DREAM COOKIES

1 c. butter, softened
1 c. sugar
1 tsp. vanilla extract
1 tsp. baking powder
2 c. flour

Cream ... butter and sugar together in bowl until light and fluffy.
Add ..... vanilla.
Blend .... in dry ingredients, mixing well.
Shape .... into small balls; flatten.
Place .... on cookie sheet.
Bake ..... at 400 degrees for 15 minutes.
Yield .... 6 dozen.

Helen M. Heggins
Athens H. S., Athens, Texas

GINGERSNAPS

3/4 c. shortening
1 c. packed brown sugar
1/4 c. molasses
1 egg
2 1/4 c. sifted flour
2 tsp. soda
1/2 tsp. salt
1 tsp. each ground ginger, cinnamon
1/2 tsp. ground cloves
Sugar

Combine . first 4 ingredients in large mixer bowl.
Cream ... until light and fluffy.
Sift ...... together dry ingredients except sugar.
Stir ...... into molasses mixture.
Shape .... into balls using 1 tablespoon of mixture for each one.
Roll ..... in sugar.
Place .... on greased cookie sheet 2 inches apart.
Bake ..... at 375 degrees for 12 minutes.
Yield .... 2 1/2 dozen.

Dianna Roller
Mountain Home Sr. H. S., Mountain Home, Arkansas

GREEK COOKIES

1 lb. margarine, softened
1 c. sugar
3 egg yolks
1 1/2 tsp. baking powder
4 1/2 c. cake flour
Confectioners' sugar

Cream ... margarine and sugar together in bowl.
Add ..... egg yolks, beating well.
Combine . baking powder and flour in bowl.
Add ..... to egg mixture 1/2 cup at a time, mixing well.
Shape .... dough into large balls.
Place .... on cookie sheets.
Bake ..... at 375 degrees for 10 to 12 minutes or until browned on bottom.
Sprinkle .. cooled cookies with confectioners' sugar.
Yield .... 60-65 cookies.

Sister Mary George Wilson, S. B. S.
St. Michael H. S., St. Michaels, Arizona

HONEY COOKIES

1/4 c. honey
1 stick margarine, softened
1 egg
Sugar
2 c. flour
1 tsp. each soda, nutmeg

Combine . first 3 ingredients with 1 cup sugar in large mixing bowl, stirring well.
Sift ...... last 3 ingredients together.
Add ..... to sugar mixture, blending well.
Chill ..... dough in refrigerator.
Shape .... into small balls.
Place .... on greased cookie sheet.
Flatten ... with bottom of glass dipped in sugar.
Bake ..... at 350 degrees for 10 minutes.
Yield .... 4 dozen.

Frances Stewart
Congress Jr. H. S., Denton, Texas

HONEY PUFFS

1/3 c. butter
Rind of 1 lemon
2 c. flour
1 tsp. salt
8 eggs
5 c. olive oil
1 1/2 c. honey
Cinnamon

Boil ..... 2 cups water, butter and lemon rind together in large saucepan for 2 minutes.
Remove .. from heat, removing lemon rind.
Add ..... flour and salt, stirring vigorously.
Cook .... over medium heat for 5 minutes or until mixture forms ball, stirring constantly.
Cool ..... to lukewarm.
Add ..... 1 egg at a time, beating well after each addition.
Drop .... by teaspoonfuls into very hot olive oil in skillet.
Cook .... for 8 to 10 minutes or until golden brown.
Drain .... on absorbent paper.
Dilute .... honey with a small amount of water in bowl.
Pour ..... over Honey Puffs.
Sprinkle .. with cinnamon.
Serve .... immediately.
Yield .... 55 Honey Puffs.

Hazel C. Tassis
Imperial Unified H. S., Imperial, California

MOLASSES COOKIES

3/4 c. shortening
1 egg
1/4 c. molasses
Sugar
2 c. flour
2 tsp. soda
1/2 tsp. salt
1 tbsp. ginger
1 tsp. cinnamon

Combine . first 3 ingredients with 1 cup sugar in bowl, mixing well.
Blend .... in remaining ingredients.
Shape .... into small balls; roll in additional sugar.
Place .... on cookie sheets.
Bake ..... at 350 degrees for 10 minutes or until lightly browned.
Yield .... 3-4 dozen.

Patricia A. Giles
Chidester H. S., Chidester, Arkansas

NUTMEG LOGS

1 1/3 c. butter, softened
4 tsp. vanilla extract
3/4 c. sugar
1 egg, beaten
3 c. sifted flour
Nutmeg
1/4 tsp. salt
2 c. confectioners' sugar
2 tbsp. light cream

Cream ... 1 cup butter and 2 teaspoons vanilla together in bowl.
Beat ..... in sugar gradually.
Blend .... in egg.
Sift ...... flour, 1 teaspoon nutmeg and salt together.
Add ..... to creamed mixture, mixing well.
Shape .... dough into 1/2-inch rolls on sugared surface.
Cut ...... into 2 to 3-inch lengths.
Place .... on greased cookie sheets.
Bake ..... at 350 degrees for 12 to 15 minutes; cool.
Cream ... remaining 1/3 cup butter and 2 teaspoons vanilla together in bowl.
Blend .... in confectioners' sugar and cream.
Spread ... frosting on top and sides of cookies.
Mark .... with tines of fork to resemble bark.
Sprinkle .. with additional nutmeg.
Yield .... 5-6 dozen.

Betty Ambrose
Robert E. Lee Sr. H. S., Midland, Texas

DAD'S FAVORITE OATMEAL COOKIES

1 c. butter, softened
1 c. sugar
1 c. packed brown sugar
2 eggs
1 tsp. vanilla extract
1 1/2 c. quick-cooking oatmeal
2 c. flour
1 tsp. soda
1/2 tsp. salt
1 c. chocolate chips (opt.)

Cream ... together butter and sugars in large bowl until light and fluffy.
Add ..... eggs and vanilla, beating well.

Stir ...... oatmeal into creamed mixture.
Sift ...... flour, soda and salt together.
Add ..... to mixture, stirring well.
Stir ...... in chocolate chips.
Drop .... by teaspoonfuls onto greased cookie sheet.
Bake ..... at 375 degrees for 7 minutes or until light brown.
Yield .... 6 dozen.

Mary Krans
Altoona H. S., Altoona, Wisconsin

FLYING SAUCERS

1/2 lb. butter, softened
1 1/3 c. packed brown sugar
3/4 c. sugar
2 eggs
2/3 c. molasses
1/4 c. milk
1 1/2 tsp. soda
1/2 tsp. salt
1 tsp. cinnamon
1 tsp. allspice
4 c. flour
2/3 c. raisins
3 3/4 c. oats

Cream ... butter and sugars together in bowl.
Add ..... eggs and molasses, mixing well.
Blend .... in milk, soda, salt and spices.
Mix ..... in flour, raisins and oats.
Drop .... by tablespoonfuls, onto cookie sheet, 6 per sheet; flatten.
Bake ..... at 350 degrees for 10 minutes.
Yield .... 2-3 dozen 5-inch cookies.

Donna Rychlik
Caldwell H. S., Caldwell, Texas

MISSOURI COOKIES

1 stick margarine
1/2 c. milk
2 c. sugar
3 tbsp. cocoa
1/2 c. peanut butter
1 tsp. vanilla extract
3 c. oatmeal

Combine . margarine, milk, sugar and cocoa in saucepan, mixing well.
Boil ..... for 1 minute, stirring constantly.
Remove .. from heat.

Stir . . . . . . in peanut butter, vanilla and
oatmeal.
Drop . . . . by teaspoonfuls onto waxed paper.
Cool . . . . . for 1 hour until firm.
Yield . . . . 3 dozen.

Patricia Huntington
Ipswich H. S., Ipswich, Massachusetts

OATMEAL CRISPS

3/4 c. shortening
3/4 c. packed brown sugar
3/4 c. sugar
1 egg
1 tsp. vanilla extract
1 1/4 c. sifted flour
1 tsp. salt
1/2 tsp. soda
2 1/2 c. oats

Combine . first 5 ingredients with 1/4 cup
water in bowl.
Sift . . . . . . flour, salt and soda together.
Add . . . . . to creamed mixture; mix well.
Stir . . . . . . in oats.
Drop . . . . by teaspoonfuls onto greased
cookie sheets.
Bake . . . . . at 350 degrees for 12 to 15
minutes.
Yield . . . . 4 dozen.

Carolyn Grams
Hooks H. S., Hooks, Texas

OLD-FASHIONED TEACAKES

1 c. butter, softened
2 c. sugar
2 eggs, beaten
5 c. flour
1 tsp. baking powder
1 tsp. nutmeg
1 tsp. soda
1/3 c. milk
Orange juice

Cream . . . butter and sugar together in bowl.
Add . . . . . eggs, beating well.
Sift . . . . . . flour, baking powder and nutmeg
together.
Dissolve . . soda in milk.
Add . . . . . to creamed mixture alternately
with dry ingredients, beating well
after each addition.
Stir . . . . . . in enough orange juice to make soft

Roll . . . . . out dough on floured surface to
desired thickness.
Cut . . . . . . into desired shapes.
Place . . . . on greased cookie sheets.
Bake . . . . . at 350 degrees for 15 to 20
minutes.
Store . . . . in airtight container.

Barbara Thomas
Big Sandy H. S., Big Sandy, Texas

QUICK AND EASY PEANUT BUTTER COOKIES

1 c. peanut butter
1 c. sugar
1 egg
1 tsp. vanilla extract

Blend . . . . all ingredients together in bowl.
Drop . . . . by teaspoonfuls onto greased bak-
ing sheet.
Bake . . . . . at 350 degrees for 10 minutes.
Yield . . . . 2 dozen.

Sandra C. Owen
St. Charles Jr. H. S., Lebanon, Kentucky

PEANUT REFRIGERATOR COOKIES

1 lb. butter, softened
1 c. sugar
1 c. packed brown sugar
4 eggs, beaten
1 tsp. soda
5 1/2 c. flour
1 tsp. salt
1 lb. crushed peanuts
1 tsp. vanilla extract

Cream . . . butter and sugars together in bowl.
Add . . . . . eggs, blending well.
Dissolve . . soda in 1 tablespoon warm water.
Blend . . . . into creamed mixture.
Beat . . . . . in flour and salt gradually.
Stir . . . . . . in peanuts and vanilla.
Shape . . . . into roll.
Wrap . . . . in foil.
Chill . . . . . overnight.
Cut . . . . . . into 1/8-inch slices.
Place . . . . on cookie sheet.
Bake . . . . . at 400 degrees for 8 minutes or un-
til light brown.
Yield . . . . 10-12 dozen.

Patricia Zuanich
Mariner H. S., Everett, Washington

PECAN PIE COOKIES

2 eggs
1 c. packed brown sugar
1/2 c. melted margarine
1 c. flour
1 c. chopped pecans

Combine . all ingredients in bowl, mixing lightly.
Pour . . . . . into greased muffin cups.
Bake . . . . . at 350 degrees for 20 to 25 minutes.
Yield . . . . 12 large or 36 small cookies.

Mrs. Judy Ender
Stamford H. S., Stamford, Texas

PHOENIKIA

1/2 c. oil
1/2 c. melted butter
1/2 c. orange juice
1 1/2 c. sugar
1 egg yolk
2 tbsp. shortening
1 3/4 tsp. baking powder
Pinch of soda
5 to 6 c. flour
Walnut halves
3 tbsp. honey
Chopped walnuts

Combine . first 3 ingredients with 1/2 cup sugar in bowl.
Beat . . . . . with electric mixer at high speed until well blended.
Add . . . . . egg yolk and shortening.
Beat . . . . . until thick and creamy.
Stir . . . . . . in baking powder, soda and enough flour to make a soft dough.
Roll . . . . . dough into balls.
Flatten . . . with hand.
Place . . . . walnut half in center.
Roll . . . . . to enclose walnut, sealing edges.
Place . . . . on ungreased cookie sheet.
Bake . . . . . at 350 degrees for 30 minutes.
Cool . . . . . to lukewarm.
Combine . 1 cup sugar, 1 1/2 cups water and honey in saucepan.
Boil . . . . . for 15 minutes.
Dip . . . . . . cookies in syrup.
Sprinkle . . with chopped walnuts.

Joanne Adamakos
Elon St. Jr. H. S., Nashua, New Hampshire

REFRIGERATOR COOKIES

1/4 c. butter, softened
1/4 c. shortening
1 c. packed brown sugar
1 egg
1/2 tsp. vanilla extract
1 3/4 c. flour
1/2 tsp. soda
1/4 tsp. salt

Cream . . . butter and shortening together in bowl.
Add . . . . . sugar, egg and vanilla, blending thoroughly.
Blend . . . . flour, soda and salt together in bowl.
Stir . . . . . . into creamed mixture, mixing well.
Form . . . . into rolls 2 1/2 inches in diameter.
Wrap . . . . in waxed paper.
Chill . . . . . until firm.
Cut . . . . . . dough into 1/8-inch slices.
Place . . . . on baking sheets.
Bake . . . . . at 400 degrees for 8 to 10 minutes.

Dorothy M. Ham
Brantley County H. S., Nahunta, Georgia

SPICY RAISIN COOKIES

1 1/2 c. flour
1/2 tsp. each soda, salt
1/2 c. sugar
1/2 c. packed brown sugar
1/2 c. margarine, softened
1 egg
1 tsp. each lemon extract, cinnamon
3/4 c. raisins

Combine . flour with soda and salt in bowl.
Cream . . . sugars, margarine and egg in large bowl.
Add . . . . . lemon extract, cinnamon and flour mixture; mix well.
Stir . . . . . . in raisins.
Drop . . . . by teaspoonfuls 2 inches apart on cookie sheet.
Bake . . . . . at 375 degrees for 8 minutes or until brown.
Cool . . . . . slightly before removing from cookie sheet.
Yield . . . . 36 cookies.

Debbie R. Boney
W. E. Waters Jr. H. S., Portsmouth, Virginia

SAND TARTS

1 c. margarine, softened
6 tbsp. sugar
2 c. flour
1/2 c. chopped nuts

Cream ... margarine and sugar in mixing bowl until light and fluffy.
Add ..... flour, 1 teaspoon water and nuts, mixing well.
Roll ..... into small balls.
Place .... on baking sheet.
Bake ..... at 350 degrees for 10 minutes.
Yield .... 5 dozen.

Lee Griffin
Booneville H. S., Booneville, Mississippi

GREAT-GRANDMA'S SUGAR COOKIES

1 egg
1 c. shortening
2 c. sugar
1 c. sour milk
1 tsp. soda
1 tsp. nutmeg
1 tsp. salt
4 c. flour

Cream ... egg, shortening and sugar together in bowl.
Combine . sour milk and soda in bowl.
Add ..... alternately with dry ingredients to creamed mixture, mixing well after each addition.
Roll ..... out dough on floured surface, adding additional flour if necessary.
Cut ...... into desired shapes.
Bake ..... at 375 degrees for 10 minutes or until browned.
Yield .... 5 dozen.

Anne E. Shadwick
Seneca H. S., Seneca, Missouri

SILVER DOLLAR FUNNEL CAKES

1 1/3 c. unsifted flour
1/4 tsp. salt
1/2 tsp. soda
2 tbsp. sugar
3/4 tsp. baking powder
1 egg, beaten
2/3 c. milk
Oil for deep frying
Confectioners' sugar

Sift ...... all dry ingredients together into bowl.
Combine . egg and milk in bowl, mixing well.
Add ..... to dry ingredients, beating until smooth.
Stir ...... in additional milk if necessary.
Heat ..... 1 inch oil in 6 to 8-inch heavy saucepan until very hot.
Fill ...... funnel with 1/3 cup batter, holding finger over bottom of funnel.
Drop .... batter into oil in spiral motion.
Fry ...... until golden, turning once.
Drain .... on paper towels.
Sprinkle .. with confectioners' sugar.
Yield .... 6 large funnel cakes.

Deanna Hardesty
Tuttle Public Schools, Tuttle, Oklahoma

SUGARLESS SPICE COOKIES

1 c. raisins
1/3 c. margarine, softened
2 tsp. cinnamon
1/2 tsp. nutmeg
2 eggs
1 tsp. soda
1/2 tsp. salt
2 tbsp. liquid sweetener
2 c. flour
1 tsp. baking powder

Combine . first 4 ingredients with 1 1/4 cups water in saucepan.
Bring .... to a boil.
Beat ..... eggs into cooled raisin mixture 1 at a time, beating well after each addition.
Dissolve .. soda, salt and sweetener in 2 tablespoons water in small bowl.
Add ..... to raisin mixture alternately with flour and baking powder, mixing will after each addition.
Drop .... by spoonfuls onto lightly greased cookie sheet.
Bake ..... at 350 degrees for 8 to 10 minutes.
Store .... in refrigerator or freezer.
Yield .... 5 dozen cookies.

Kathleene James
St. James H. S., St. James, Missouri

CHEWY SUGAR COOKIES

1 c. packed brown sugar
1 c. shortening
2 eggs
Sugar
2 tsp. vanilla extract
3 1/2 c. flour
3/4 tsp. salt
2 tsp. each cream of tartar, soda

Cream . . . first 3 ingredients and 1 cup sugar in bowl.
Add . . . . . vanilla, mixing well.
Sift . . . . . . dry ingredients together.
Add . . . . . to creamed mixture gradually, beating well.
Shape . . . . into 1-inch balls.
Roll . . . . . in sugar.
Place . . . . on cookie sheet.
Bake . . . . . at 350 degrees for 10 to 12 minutes.

Willene Walsh
Union City School, Union City, Oklahoma

MEXICAN SUGAR COOKIES

2 c. lard, softened
1 c. sugar
2 tsp. aniseed
2 egg yolks, beaten
6 c. sifted flour
3 tsp. baking powder
1 tsp. salt
1/2 c. orange juice
Cinnamon-sugar

Cream . . . lard and sugar together in large mixer bowl until light and fluffy.
Add . . . . . aniseed and egg yolks, mixing well.
Sift . . . . . . flour, baking powder and salt together.
Add . . . . . to creamed mixture alternately with orange juice, beating well after each addition.
Knead . . . dough until well mixed.
Roll . . . . . out 1/3 inch thick.
Cut . . . . . . with cookie cutter.
Sprinkle . . with cinnamon-sugar.
Bake . . . . . at 350 degrees for 8 to 10 minutes or until golden brown.
Yield . . . . 3 1/2 dozen cookies.

Linda Jaramillo
Los Lunas H. S., Los Lunas, New Mexico

WHOLE WHEAT SUGAR COOKIES

1 c. sugar
1 tsp. baking powder
1/2 tsp. salt
1/2 tsp. soda
1/2 tsp. nutmeg
1/2 c. butter, softened
2 tbsp. milk
1 tbsp. grated orange rind (opt.)
1 tsp. vanilla extract
1 egg
2 c. whole wheat flour
2 tbsp. sugar
1/2 tsp. cinnamon

Combine . first 10 ingredients together in large bowl, blending well.
Stir . . . . . . flour into creamed mixture.
Shape . . . . into 1-inch balls.
Place . . . . 2 inches apart on cookie sheets, flattening slightly.
Combine . sugar and cinnamon in bowl.
Sprinkle . . over cookies.
Bake . . . . . at 375 degrees for 8 to 10 minutes.

Carole Fisher
Martinsville H. S., Martinsville, Indiana

ZUCCHINI-GRANOLA COOKIES

3/4 c. butter, softened
1 1/2 c. packed brown sugar
1 egg
1 tsp. vanilla extract
Grated rind of 1 orange
3 c. grated zucchini
3 to 3 1/2 c. flour
1 tsp. soda
1 tsp. salt
3 c. granola cereal
1 c. butterscotch chips

Cream . . . butter and sugar together in bowl.
Add . . . . . next 4 ingredients, blending well.
Sift . . . . . . flour, soda and salt together.
Add . . . . . to creamed mixture, blending well.
Stir . . . . . . in cereal and chips.
Drop . . . . by teaspoonfuls onto cookie sheets.
Bake . . . . . at 350 degrees for 12 to 15 minutes.
Yield . . . . 6 dozen.

Barbara Ann Talbot
Natick H. S., Natick, Massachusetts

Candies

APRICOT CANDIES

1 8-oz. package dried apricots, finely
    chopped
2 1/2 c. flaked coconut
3/4 c. sweetened condensed milk
2/3 c. chopped pecans
Pecan meal

Combine . first 4 ingredients in bowl, mixing
            well.
Shape .... into 1-inch balls.
Roll ..... in pecan meal.
Let ...... stand for 2 hours or until firm.
Yield .... 4 dozen candies.

Margaret Hunter
Heritage H. S., Monroeville, Indiana

CARAMELS

1 /2 c. margarine, melted
1 1/8 c. packed brown sugar
Dash of salt
1/2 c. light corn syrup
7 oz. sweetened condensed milk
1/2 tsp. vanilla extract

Blend .... first 4 ingredients in saucepan.
Add ..... condensed milk gradually, stirring
            constantly.
Cook .... over medium heat to firm-ball stage
            or 245 degrees on candy thermom-
            eter, stirring constantly.
Remove .. from heat.
Stir ...... in vanilla.
Pour ..... into buttered 9 x 9-inch pan.
Cut ...... into squares when cooled.
Yield .... 1 1/2 pounds.

Arlene Maisel
Highland Park H. S., Highland Park, New Jersey

CARAMEL APPLES

1 14-oz. can sweetened condensed milk
1 c. sugar
1/2 c. light corn syrup
1/8 tsp. salt
1 tsp. vanilla extract
6 wooden skewers
6 med. apples

Bring .... first 4 ingredients to a boil in heavy
            saucepan over low heat, stirring
            constantly.

Cook .... until 230 degrees on candy ther-
            mometer, stirring constantly.
Remove .. from heat.
Stir ...... in vanilla.
Cool ..... for 5 minutes.
Insert .... skewers in apples.
Dip ...... in syrup until coated.
Place .... on lightly greased baking sheet to
            cool.

Photograph for this recipe on opposite page.

CARAMEL CORN

2 c. packed brown sugar
1 c. butter
1/2 c. light corn syrup
2 tsp. salt
1/4 tsp. cream of tartar
1 tsp. soda
1 c. peanuts
7 1/2 qt. popped corn

Combine . first 5 ingredients in saucepan.
Bring .... to a boil.
Cook .... over medium heat to hard-ball stage
            or 260 degrees on candy
            thermometer.
Remove .. from heat.
Stir ...... in soda and peanuts.
Place .... corn in shallow pan.
Pour ..... sugar mixture over corn, mixing
            well.
Bake ..... at 200 degrees for 1 hour, stirring
            every 15 minutes.
Pour ..... out onto waxed paper, breaking
            into pieces.
Yield .... 7 1/2 quarts.

Linda McAlhaney
Jefferson County H. S., Dandridge, Tennessee

ALMOND CRUNCHIES

1 c. butter
1 1/3 c. sugar
1 tbsp. light corn syrup
1 c. coarsely chopped blanched almonds,
    toasted
4 4 1/2-oz. bars milk chocolate, melted
1 c. finely chopped blanched almonds, toasted

Melt ..... butter in large saucepan.
Add ..... sugar, corn syrup and 3 tablespoons
            water.

Cook . . . . over medium heat to hard-crack stage or 300 degrees on candy thermometer, stirring occasionally.
Stir . . . . . . in coarsely chopped almonds quickly.
Spread . . . in 9 x 13-inch pan; cool thoroughly.
Turn . . . . . onto waxed paper.
Spread . . . top with half the chocolate.
Sprinkle . . with half the finely chopped almonds.
Cover . . . . with waxed paper.
Invert . . . . and repeat with chocolate and almonds.
Chill . . . . . and break into pieces.

Mary Utley
Murfreesboro, Tennessee

JEANIE'S BONBONS

1/4 c. fresh lemon juice
1/4 c. fresh orange juice
1 tbsp. grated orange rind
3 c. finely crushed vanilla wafers
2 tbsp. cocoa
1 c. confectioners' sugar
1 c. finely chopped nuts
Sugar

Combine . all ingredients except sugar in medium bowl.
Blend . . . . well.
Shape . . . . into balls.
Roll . . . . . in sugar.

Jeanie Sharp
Chicago, Illinois

BOURBON BALLS

2 lb. sifted confectioners' sugar
1 c. sweetened condensed milk
1 stick butter
1 7-oz. can flaked coconut
4 c. chopped pecans
Pinch of salt
Bourbon to taste
1 12-oz. package chocolate chips
1 block German's chocolate
1/2 block paraffin

Combine . first 7 ingredients in bowl, mixing well.
Shape . . . . into balls.
Chill . . . . . in refrigerator.

Melt . . . . . chocolate and paraffin in top of double boiler over medium heat.
Dip . . . . . . Bourbon Balls into chocolate mixture.
Store . . . . in refrigerator.

Sarah K. Wilder
Bell County H. S., Pineville, Kentucky

FUDGY CARAMELS

3 sq. unsweetened chocolate, melted
2 c. sugar
1 c. packed brown sugar
1/2 c. butter
1/8 tsp. salt
1 c. corn syrup
1 c. cream
1 tsp. vanilla extract

Combine . first 7 ingredients in saucepan.
Boil . . . . . covered, for 5 minutes.
Cook . . . . uncovered, to firm-ball stage or 240 degrees on candy thermometer, stirring constantly.
Remove . . from heat.
Stir . . . . . . in vanilla.
Pour . . . . . into 6 x 10-inch buttered pan.
Cool . . . . . overnight or until firm.
Cut . . . . . . into 3/4-inch squares.
Yield . . . . 108 squares.

Lois Smith
Corvallis, Oregon

DIPPED CHERRY CANDY

2 lb. confectioners' sugar
1 qt. chopped pecans
1 med. bottle maraschino cherries
1 tsp. vanilla extract
1 sm. can flaked coconut
1 can sweetened condensed milk
1 stick margarine
1 lg. package chocolate chips
1/4 lb. paraffin

Combine . first 7 ingredients in bowl, mixing well.
Chill . . . . . in refrigerator until very firm.
Shape . . . . into balls.
Melt . . . . . chocolate chips and paraffin in top of double boiler over medium heat.
Dip . . . . . . each ball in chocolate mixture.
Place . . . . on waxed paper to cool.

Peggy Haynes
El Reno H. S., El Reno, Oklahoma

CHOCOLATE-BUTTER CRUNCHIES

1 c. margarine
1 c. sugar
1 tbsp. light corn syrup
3/4 c. finely chopped nuts
4 sq. semisweet chocolate, melted

Melt . . . . . margarine in 2-quart saucepan over low heat.
Remove . . from heat.
Add . . . . . sugar, mixing well with wooden spoon.
Bring . . . . to a boil over low heat, stirring constantly.
Add . . . . . 2 tablespoons water and corn syrup, mixing well.
Cook . . . . to 290 degrees on candy thermometer, stirring frequently.
Remove . . from heat.
Add . . . . . nuts quickly.
Spread . . . 1/4 inch thick on lightly greased cookie sheet; cool.
Spread . . . with half the melted chocolate; cool.
Turn . . . . . to other side.
Spread . . . with remaining chocolate; cool.
Break . . . . into pieces.
Store . . . . in tightly covered container.

Wanda Dickens
Rossville, Illinois

CHOCOLATE CLUSTERS

2/3 c. sugar
2/3 c. evaporated milk
1 tbsp. light corn syrup
1 c. semisweet chocolate pieces
1 c. plain natural cereal

Combine . first 3 ingredients in medium saucepan.
Bring . . . . to a boil over medium heat, stirring constantly.
Boil . . . . . for 2 minutes, stirring constantly.
Stir . . . . . . in chocolate pieces until melted.
Fold . . . . . in cereal.
Drop . . . . by teaspoonfuls onto waxed paper.
Chill . . . . until firm.

Mary Jo Eisenburg
Stowe, Vermont

CHOCOLATE SLICES

1/2 c. butter, melted
4 tbsp. cocoa
1 tsp. vanilla extract
1/2 c. sugar
1 egg
2 c. graham cracker crumbs
1/2 c. each shredded coconut, chopped walnuts
2 c. confectioners' sugar
1/4 c. margarine, softened
1/4 c. milk
2 tbsp. custard powder
2 sq. chocolate, melted

Combine . first 5 ingredients in bowl, mixing well.
Mix . . . . . crumbs, coconut and walnuts.
Add . . . . . to cocoa mixture, mixing well.
Press . . . . . into greased 9-inch square pan.
Blend . . . . remaining ingredients except chocolate in bowl until smooth.
Spread . . . over crumb mixture.
Chill . . . . . until firm.
Pour . . . . . chocolate over top.
Chill . . . . until firm.
Cut . . . . . . into slices.

Brenda Oxspring
Butler Middle School, Salt Lake City, Utah

CLUB CRACKER BARS

Club crackers
2/3 c. packed brown sugar
1/3 c. sugar

1/4 c. milk
1/2 c. margarine
1 c. graham cracker crumbs
2/3 c. chocolate chips
2/3 c. butterscotch chips
2/3 c. peanut butter

Line ..... 9 x 13-inch pan with club crackers.
Combine . next 4 ingredients in saucepan, blending well.
Bring .... to a rolling boil.
Remove .. from heat.
Stir ...... in graham cracker crumbs.
Spread ... half the sugar mixture over crackers.
Cover .... with layer of club crackers.
Top ..... with remaining sugar mixture.
Combine . remaining ingredients in saucepan.
Heat ..... until melted and well blended, stirring constantly.
Spread ... over layers.

Rita Poncelet
Irene H. S., Irene, South Dakota

COCONUT DROPS

2 1/3 c. confectioners' sugar
2/3 c. evaporated milk
2 1/3 c. coconut natural cereal
1 c. semisweet chocolate pieces

Combine . confectioners' sugar and 1/3 cup milk in 1 1/2-quart bowl, mixing until smooth.
Stir ...... in cereal, mixing well.
Drop .... by teaspoonfuls onto waxed paper.
Melt ..... chocolate pieces in remaining 1/3 cup milk in saucepan over low heat.
Remove .. from heat.
Top ..... each candy with chocolate.
Chill ..... until firm.

Elsa White
Skywamo, West Virginia

EASY FUDGE

1/4 c. margarine
1 c. sugar
3/4 c. fortified chocolate-flavored syrup
2 1/2 c. sifted confectioners' sugar
1/2 c. chopped nuts

Bring .... first 3 ingredients to a boil in heavy 2-quart saucepan over medium heat, stirring constantly.

Boil ..... over low heat for 5 minutes, stirring occasionally.
Let ...... stand away from heat for 1 minute.
Stir ...... in confectioners' sugar and nuts.
Beat ..... until smooth.
Pour ..... into lightly greased 8 x 8-inch pan.
Yield .... 1 1/2 pounds.

Photograph for this recipe on page 115.

CHOCO-SCOTCH FUDGE

2 c. packed light brown sugar
2 tbsp. cocoa
1/8 tsp. salt
1/2 c. light corn syrup
1/2 c. evaporated milk
1/2 c. milk
2 tbsp. butter
1 tsp. vanilla extract
2 c. chopped pecans

Blend .... first 6 ingredients in saucepan.
Cook .... to soft-ball stage or 240 degrees on candy thermometer, stirring occasionally.
Cool ..... for 10 minutes.
Stir ...... in remaining ingredients.
Beat ..... until gloss disappears completely.
Pour ..... into buttered pan.
Yield .... 30-35 squares.

Nadine Claussen
Widget, New Hampshire

BUTTERSCOTCH

2 c. sugar
2/3 c. dark corn syrup
1/4 c. light cream
1/4 c. margarine

Bring .... first 3 ingredients and 1/4 cup water to a boil in saucepan over medium heat, stirring constantly.
Cook .... until 260 degrees on candy thermometer, stirring occasionally.
Add ..... margarine.
Cook .... until 280 degrees on candy thermometer.
Pour ..... into greased 8-inch square pan.
Cut ...... into squares when almost set.
Break .... apart when cold.
Yield .... 1 1/4 pounds.

Photograph for this recipe on page 115.

QUICK CHOCOLATE FUDGE

1 lb. confectioners' sugar
1/3 c. instant nonfat dry milk powder
1/4 c. margarine
3 oz. unsweetened chocolate
1/2 c. corn syrup
1 tsp. vanilla extract
1/2 c. chopped nuts (opt.)
1 c. miniature marshmallows (opt.)·

Sift . . . . . . sugar and dry milk together.
Melt . . . . . margarine and chocolate in top of 2-quart double boiler over boiling water.
Add . . . . . corn syrup, vanilla and 1 table-spoon water to chocolate mixture.
Stir . . . . . . in dry ingredients gradually, mixing until smooth.
Add . . . . . nuts and marshmallows.
Pour . . . . . into greased 8-inch pan.
Cut . . . . . . cooled candy into squares.

Quick Blonde Fudge

Follow recipe for Quick Chocolate Fudge omitting chocolate and water, using light corn syrup and increasing vanilla to 2 teaspoons.

Quick Brown Sugar Fudge

Follow recipe for Quick Chocolate Fudge omitting chocolate and water, melting 1/2 cup firmly packed brown sugar with margarine and using dark corn syrup.

Quick Peanut Butter Fudge

Follow recipe for Quick Chocolate Fudge omitting chocolate, melting 1/3 cup peanut butter with margarine and using light corn syrup.

Fudge Roll

Prepare 1 recipe each Quick Chocolate Fudge and Quick Blonde Fudge. Pour blonde fudge into greased 9-inch square pan. Pour chocolate fudge into greased 9-inch square pan sprinkled with 2 cups chopped nuts. Let stand until set but not firm. Turn out onto waxed paper. Roll blonde fudge into tight roll. Place on 1 end of chocolate fudge. Roll as for jelly roll. Chill until firm.

Photograph for this recipe on this page.

SHARON'S FUDGE

1 c. chopped nuts
1 c. chocolate chips
1/4 lb. butter, softened
1 tsp. vanilla extract
2 c. sugar
2/3 c. evaporated milk
10 lg. marshmallows

Combine . first 4 ingredients in large bowl.
Bring . . . . sugar, evaporated milk and marsh-mallows to a boil in saucepan over medium heat.
Cook . . . . for 6 minutes, stirring constantly.
Add . . . . . to nut mixture, stirring until glossy and well blended.
Pour . . . . . into buttered 9 x 13-inch pan.
Cool . . . . . and cut into squares.

Sharon Bartschi
Hulett School, Hulett, Wyoming

SOUR CREAM FUDGE

3 c. sugar
1 c. sour cream
1/8 tsp. soda
4 tbsp. dark corn syrup
6 tbsp. cocoa
1/8 tsp. salt
1 tsp. vanilla extract
1 c. chopped nuts

Combine . all ingredients except vanilla and nuts in saucepan.
Cook . . . . to soft-ball stage or 235 degrees on candy thermometer, stirring occasionally.

Set ......aside until cooled to room temperature.
Add .....vanilla, beating until mixture loses its gloss.
Stir ......in nuts, beating until nearly set.
Pour .....into buttered pan.
Cut ......into squares.
Freezes ...well.

Allene Makenna
Charlotte, North Carolina

KENTUCKY COLONELS

1/2 c. butter, softened
3 tbsp. sweetened condensed milk
1/3 c. plus 2 tsp. Bourbon
7 1/2 c. confectioners' sugar
1/2 c. chopped pecans
1 12-oz. package semisweet chocolate chips
2 tbsp. melted paraffin
Pecan halves

Combine .first 4 ingredients in large bowl, mixing well.
Stir ......in chopped pecans and shape into 1-inch balls.
Combine .chocolate chips with paraffin in top of double boiler.
Cook ....over hot water until chocolate is melted, stirring occasionally.
Dip ......candy into chocolate mixture.
Press .....pecan half into each ball.

Carol Stallard
Monroney Jr. H. S., Midwest City, Oklahoma

MARTHA WASHINGTON CANDY

2 boxes confectioners' sugar, sifted
1 stick margarine
1 can sweetened condensed milk
1 tsp. vanilla extract
4 c. pecans, chopped
1/2 lb. semisweet chocolate squares
1 block paraffin

Combine .first 4 ingredients in mixing bowl.
Beat .....until creamy.
Blend ....in pecans.
Roll .....into balls the size of walnuts, using additional confectioners' sugar on hands.

Melt .....chocolate and paraffin in top of double boiler over low heat.
Dip ......balls in chocolate mixture with toothpicks.
Drop ....onto waxed paper.

Claudia Cox
Montgomery, Alabama

AUNT NORMA'S MILLIONAIRES

1 14-oz. package caramels
2 tbsp. butter
3 c. whole pecans
1 6-oz. package chocolate chips
1 oz. paraffin

Melt .....caramels and butter with 2 tablespoons water in saucepan over low heat.
Stir ......in pecans.
Drop ....by spoonfuls into 1-inch mounds onto waxed paper.
Chill .....in refrigerator until firm.
Melt .....chocolate chips and paraffin in saucepan over low heat.
Dip ......caramels into chocolate mixture.
Place ....on waxed paper until cool.
Yield ....48 pieces.

JoAnn R. Sicking
Forestburg H. S., Forestburg, Texas

BRENDA'S PEANUT BUTTER BALLS

1 28-oz. jar peanut butter
2 boxes confectioners' sugar
1 lb. butter, softened
1 block paraffin
1 12-oz. package semisweet chocolate chips

Combine .first 3 ingredients in bowl, mixing well.
Shape ....into balls and chill.
Melt .....paraffin and chocolate chips in saucepan over medium heat, stirring occasionally.
Dip ......balls in chocolate mixture.
Place ....on waxed paper until chocolate is firm.

Brenda Jackson
Thackerville H. S., Thackerville, Oklahoma

CHOCOLATE-PEANUT BUTTER BALLS

1 c. confectioners' sugar
1 c. peanut butter
Vanilla extract to taste
2 tbsp. butter
1/2 c. nuts, ground
1/2 c. chopped dates
1/2 c. chocolate chips
1/4 c. parawax

Combine . sugar, peanut butter, vanilla, 1 tablespoon butter, nuts and dates in saucepan.
Cook .... over low heat until sugar and butter are melted, stirring constantly.
Shape .... into balls.
Melt ..... chocolate chips, 1 tablespoon butter and parawax in top of double boiler.
Dip ...... balls into chocolate.
Place .... on waxed paper to cool.

Ann Fitzhugh
Watseka, Illinois

KRISPIE PEANUT BUTTER BALLS

1 stick margarine, softened
2 c. peanut butter
1 lb. confectioners' sugar
3 c. Rice Krispies
1/2 block paraffin
1 12-oz. package chocolate chips

Cream ... margarine, peanut butter and sugar in large bowl.
Add ..... Rice Krispies, mixing well.
Shape .... into balls.
Melt ..... paraffin and chocolate chips in top of double boiler over hot water.
Place .... toothpick in ball and dip into chocolate mixture.
Cool ..... on waxed paper.
Yield .... 100 balls.

Judy Y. Bennett
East Ridge Jr. H. S., Ridgefield, Connecticut

CHOCOLATE-PEANUT CLUSTERS

1 6-oz. package chocolate chips
2/3 c. sweetened condensed milk
1 tsp. vanilla extract
1 1/2 c. salted Spanish peanuts

Melt ..... chocolate chips in top of double boiler over hot water.
Remove .. from heat.
Add ..... condensed milk, vanilla and peanuts, mixing well.
Drop .... by teaspoonfuls onto waxed paper.
Yield .... 1 1/2 dozen.

Megan Martin
Calumet City, Illinois

PEPPERMINT BARS

3 tbsp. butter
1 6-oz. package chocolate chips
1 c. confectioners' sugar
2 or 3 drops of green food coloring
1/8 tsp. peppermint extract
4 or 5 tsp. milk

Melt ..... 2 tablespoons butter and chocolate chips together in saucepan.
Spread ... in 8-inch square pan.
Chill ..... for 1 hour.
Combine . remaining ingredients with 1 tablespoon softened butter, mixing well.
Frost .... chocolate layer.
Chill ..... until set.
Cut ...... into 1-inch bars.
Yield .... 24 bars.

Karen Olson
North Platte Sr. H. S., North Platte, Nebraska

POMANDERS

1 6-oz. package chocolate chips, melted
Sugar
1/2 c. light corn syrup
2 1/2 c. finely crushed vanilla wafer crumbs
1 c. finely chopped pecans
Orange extract to taste

Combine . melted chocolate chips, 1/2 cup sugar and corn syrup with 1/4 cup water in bowl.
Blend .... in remaining ingredients, mixing well.
Shape .... into 1-inch balls.
Roll ..... in additional sugar.
Store .... in tightly covered container for several days before serving.

Edna Hutchens
Heritage H. S., Maryville, Tennessee

MASHED POTATO CANDY

3/4 c. cold mashed potatoes
4 c. confectioners' sugar
4 c. shredded coconut
1 1/2 tsp. vanilla extract
1/2 tsp. salt
8 sq. baking chocolate, melted

Combine . first 2 ingredients in bowl.
Stir . . . . . . in coconut, vanilla and salt, blending well.
Press . . . . . into 1/2-inch layer in large pan.
Spread . . . melted chocolate over top.
Cut . . . . . . into 32 pieces when cool.

Nicky Peters
Amesville, Georgia

HOMEMADE REESES

1 c. crushed graham crackers
1 box confectioners' sugar
1/2 c. peanut butter
1 c. butter
1 sm. package chocolate chips

Combine . first 2 ingredients in bowl.
Melt . . . . . peanut butter and 3/4 cup butter in small saucepan over medium heat.
Add . . . . . to crumb mixture, mixing well.
Spread . . . in 8 x 8-inch pan.
Melt . . . . . 1/4 cup butter with chocolate chips in saucepan over medium heat, stirring constantly.
Spread . . . over peanut butter layer.
Chill . . . . . until firm.
Cut . . . . . . into 1-inch squares.
Yield . . . . 64 small servings.

Mrs. Jack R. Criswell
Alliance Christian School, Birmingham, Alabama

CHOCOLATE-ALMOND TOFFEE

1 c. packed brown sugar
1 c. sugar
1/3 c. light corn syrup
1/8 tsp. salt
1/3 c. butter
1 6-oz. package semisweet chocolate, melted
1/2 c. toasted almonds, chopped

Combine . sugars, corn syrup, salt and 1/2 cup water in heavy saucepan.
Cook . . . . over medium heat until sugar is dissolved and mixture is boiling.
Cook . . . . to firm-ball stage or 245 degrees on candy thermometer.
Add . . . . . butter.
Cook . . . . to hard-crack stage or 290 degrees on candy thermometer.
Pour . . . . . into lightly oiled 9 x 9-inch pan.
Cool . . . . . until brittle.
Spread . . . with half the melted chocolate.
Sprinkle . . with half the almonds.
Cool . . . . . until chocolate is set.
Loosen . . . and turn onto waxed paper.
Spread . . . other side with remaining chocolate and almonds.
Break . . . . into pieces.

Katie Johnson
Rossville, Georgia

TOFFEE

1/2 c. each butter, margarine
1 c. sugar
1 tbsp. light corn syrup
1 c. chopped nuts
1 12-oz. package chocolate chips
Paraffin

Melt . . . . . butter and margarine in 3-quart heavy saucepan over medium heat.
Add . . . . . sugar, 3 tablespoons water and 1 tablespoon corn syrup.
Cook . . . . to soft-crack stage or 290 degrees on candy thermometer.
Stir . . . . . . in nuts.
Cook . . . . for 3 minutes longer.
Pour . . . . . onto well-greased baking sheet.
Spread . . . thin and cool.
Place . . . . on waxed paper, blotting excess grease with paper towel.
Combine . chocolate chips with small piece of paraffin in top of double boiler.
Melt . . . . . over medium heat.
Frost . . . . candy with chocolate mixture; cool.
Break . . . . into pieces.
Yield . . . . 1 pound.

Mary Louise Hedrick
Doddridge County H. S., West Union, West Virginia

TURTLES

2 1-oz. squares semisweet chocolate
1/3 c. butter
2 eggs, beaten
3/4 c. sugar
1 tsp. vanilla extract
1 c. flour
Confectioners' sugar frosting
Pecan halves

Combine . first 2 ingredients in heavy saucepan.
Melt . . . . . over low heat, stirring constantly; cool.
Add . . . . . eggs, sugar and vanilla, blending well.
Stir . . . . . . in flour, mixing well.
Preheat . . . waffle iron on medium setting.
Drop . . . . batter by teaspoonfuls 2 inches apart on waffle iron.
Close . . . . waffle iron; bake 1 1/2 minutes or until brown.
Cool . . . . . on rack.
Frost . . . . with confectioners' sugar frosting.
Top . . . . . with pecan halves.
Yield . . . . 2 dozen

Emely Sundbeck
Manor H. S., Manor, Texas

TWO-TONE TRUFFLES

1 1/2 c. chopped nuts
1 1/2 c. confectioners' sugar
1 egg white
1 tbsp. rum extract
1 1/2 c. chocolate bits
3/4 c. sweetened condensed milk
1 tbsp. butter

Combine . first 4 ingredients in bowl, mixing well.
Spread . . . in buttered, waxed paper-lined pan.
Place . . . . chocolate bits in saucepan.
Melt . . . . . over low heat.
Stir . . . . . . in condensed milk and butter.
Cook . . . . for 5 minutes or until thick.
Pour . . . . . over nut mixture.
Cut . . . . . . in squares when firm.
Wrap . . . . individually in plastic wrap.

Marilyn Sweeters
El Paso, Texas

CHOCOLATE WHEAT PUFFS

1 sq. unsweetened chocolate
16 lg. fresh marshmallows
3 tbsp. corn syrup
3 c. puffed wheat cereal

Melt . . . . . first 3 ingredients in saucepan over low heat, blending well.
Place . . . . puffed wheat in shallow pan.
Bake . . . . . at 350 degrees for 10 minutes.
Pour . . . . . into large greased bowl.
Pour . . . . . chocolate mixture over cereal.
Stir . . . . . . to coat evenly.
Shape . . . . into small balls.
Chill . . . . . in refrigerator.

Bernice Allen
Lexington, Kentucky

COCONUTTY DATE ROLL

2 c. sugar
1 c. milk
1/4 c. butter
1 c. dates, chopped
1 c. chopped nuts
1 c. shredded coconut

Combine . first 3 ingredients in heavy saucepan.
Cook . . . . to soft-ball stage or 240 degrees on candy thermometer.
Add . . . . . dates, mixing well.
Cook . . . . until very thick, stirring constantly.
Remove . . from heat.
Add . . . . . nuts and coconut, stirring until consistency of soft dough.
Turn . . . . . onto cloth dipped in cold water.
Shape . . . . into two rolls 1 1/2 inches in diameter.
Cut . . . . . . into slices when cool.
Store . . . . wrapped in refrigerator.

Norma Carter
Sarasota, Florida

CREAM CANDY

1 pt. whipping cream
1/2 c. light corn syrup
2 c. sugar
1/2 tsp. vanilla extract
1/2 c. walnuts, chopped

Combine . half the cream, corn syrup and sugar in saucepan.

Cook .... until light brown and creamy, stirring constantly.

Add ..... remaining cream gradually, maintaining boiling point.

Cook .... until firm-ball stage or 240 degrees on candy thermometer.

Remove .. from heat.

Beat ..... until creamy.

Add ..... vanilla and walnuts.

Pour ..... into buttered pan.

Walda Nietfeld
Kansas City, Kansas

DICTATION DROPS

1/2 c. margarine
2 c. sugar
1/2 c. milk
3/4 c. peanut butter
3 c. minute or quick oats

Melt ..... margarine in large saucepan over medium heat.

Add ..... sugar and milk.

Bring .... to a boil.

Cook .... for 2 minutes, stirring constantly.

Remove .. from heat; stir in peanut butter until dissolved.

Add ..... oats, mixing well.

Drop .... by teaspoonfuls onto waxed paper-lined cookie sheet.

Cool ..... in refrigerator until set.

Yield .... 4 dozen.

Betty C. Nutt
Lewis County H. S., Hohenwald, Tennessee

AUNT ESSIE'S DIVINITY

3 c. sugar
1/2 c. light corn syrup
2 egg whites, stiffly beaten
1 tsp. vanilla extract
1 c. chopped pecans

Blend .... sugar and syrup with 1/2 cup water in saucepan.

Cook .... to soft-ball stage or 240 degrees on candy thermometer.

Pour ..... over egg whites gradually, beating constantly until stiff.

Stir ...... in vanilla and pecans.

Spoon ... onto waxed paper.

Yield .... 2 pounds.

Wanda Clark
Crystal Springs H. S.
Crystal Springs, Massachusetts

DIVINE DIVINITY

2 c. sugar
1 tsp. vanilla extract
1/4 tsp. salt
1 7-oz. jar marshmallow creme
Pecans

Bring .... sugar, vanilla, salt and 1/2 cup water to a boil in saucepan over medium heat.

Cook .... to soft-ball stage or 240 degrees on candy thermometer.

Place .... marshmallow creme in bowl.

Pour ..... sugar syrup into bowl, beating until candy loses its gloss.

Drop .... by spoonfuls onto buttered dish.

Top ..... each piece with pecan half.

Yield .... 2-3 dozen pieces.

Mrs. Bobbie Nix
H. M. King H. S., Kingsville, Texas

ELEGANT DIVINITY

2 c. sugar
1/2 c. light corn syrup
1/4 tsp. salt
2 egg whites, stiffly beaten
1 tsp. vanilla extract
3/4 c. chopped candied cherries

Combine . first 3 ingredients and 1/2 cup water in saucepan.

Cook .... over low heat until sugar dissolves, stirring constantly.

Cook .... to firm-ball stage or 248 degrees on candy thermometer; do not stir.

Wipe ..... crystals from sides of pan with damp cloth.

Remove .. from heat.

Pour ..... over egg whites gradually, beating constantly.

Add ..... vanilla, beating until mixture holds shape when dropped from spoon.

Fold ..... in cherries.

Drop .... by spoonfuls onto waxed paper.

Luella Styles
Peaksville, Illinois

JELL-O DIVINITY

3 c. sugar
3/4 c. light corn syrup
2 egg whites
1 pkg. Jell-O
1 c. chopped nuts
1/2 c. coconut (opt.)

Mix ..... sugar, corn syrup and 3/4 cup water in saucepan.
Bring .... to a boil over medium heat.
Stir ...... until sugar dissolves; cover.
Reduce ... heat.
Simmer .. covered, for 3 minutes; uncover.
Cook .... to hard-ball stage or 260 degrees on candy thermometer.
Beat ..... egg whites until foamy.
Add ..... Jell-O, beating until stiff.
Pour ..... hot syrup over egg white mixture.
Beat ..... until it holds shape.
Fold ..... in nuts and coconut.
Drop .... by spoonfuls on buttered dish.

Gloria Butterfield
Raton, New Mexico

PECAN DIVINITY ROLLS

2 1/2 c. sugar
2/3 c. light corn syrup
2 egg whites, stiffly beaten
1/2 tsp. vanilla extract
Caramel Covering
1 qt. coarsely chopped nuts

Combine . sugar, syrup and 1/2 cup water in heavy saucepan.
Cook .... to hard-crack stage or 300 degrees on candy thermometer.
Pour ..... slowly over egg whites, beating constantly.
Add ..... vanilla.
Beat ..... until very stiff and cool enough to handle.
Shape .... into 5 or 6 rolls.
Dip ...... in slightly cooled Caramel Covering.
Coat ..... with nuts.
Chill ..... until firm.

Caramel Covering

1 c. sugar
1/2 c. packed brown sugar
1/2 c. light corn syrup
1/2 c. cream
1 c. milk
1/4 c. butter

Combine . all ingredients in heavy saucepan.
Cook .... to firm-ball stage or 240 degrees on candy thermometer.
Cool ..... slightly before using.

Joy Roberts
Chenyville, Illinois

FRUIT BALLS

1/2 lb. dried apricots
1/2 lb. dried prunes
2 slices candied pineapple
1/4 lb. candied cherries
1 c. nuts
1 c. honey
3/4 c. confectioners' sugar

Force .... fruits and nuts through food grinder twice, using fine cutter.
Add ..... honey to fruit mixture in bowl, mixing well.
Shape .... into balls.
Roll ..... in confectioners' sugar.
Store .... in covered container in cool place.
Yield .... 1 1/2 pounds.

Marilyn Gornto
Perry Jr. H. S., Perry, Georgia

QUICK PENUCHE FUDGE

1/2 c. margarine, melted
1 c. packed brown sugar
1/4 c. milk
1 2/3 to 2 c. confectioners' sugar

Combine . margarine and brown sugar in saucepan.
Cook .... until sugar is dissolved, stirring constantly.
Add ..... milk, blending well.
Cook .... for 1 minute, stirring constantly.
Remove .. from heat and cool.
Stir ...... in enough confectioners' sugar gradually to desired consistency, blending well.
Pour ..... into buttered 8 x 8-inch pan.
Chill ..... until firm.

Diane Norbury
Holton Public Schools, Holton, Michigan

WHITE FUDGE

3 c. sugar
1 c. Milnot
1/3 stick margarine
1 12-oz. package flaked coconut
1 7-oz. jar marshmallow creme
1 c. chopped nuts

Mix ..... first 3 ingredients together in saucepan.
Bring .... to a boil, stirring frequently.
Boil ..... for 5 minutes, stirring constantly.
Remove .. from heat.
Stir ...... in coconut and marshmallow creme until creamy and smooth.
Mix ..... in nuts.
Pour ..... into buttered pan; cool.
Cut ...... into squares.
Yield .... 2 pounds.

Nadine Brown
Chattanooga, Tennessee

MY-OWN MARSHMALLOWS

1 env. unflavored gelatin
1/2 c. sugar
2/3 c. light corn syrup
1 tsp. vanilla extract
1/3 tsp. salt
Confectioners' sugar

Combine . gelatin and 1/3 cup cold water in top of double boiler.
Let ...... stand for 5 minutes.
Cook .... over boiling water until gelatin dissolves.
Add ..... sugar, stirring until completely dissolved.
Combine . syrup, vanilla and salt in large mixer bowl.
Add ..... hot gelatin mixture.
Beat ..... with electric mixer at high speed for 15 minutes or until light and fluffy.
Pour ..... into lightly greased 9-inch square pan.
Cool ..... until set.
Cut ...... into squares.
Roll ..... in confectioners' sugar.
Yield .... 3 dozen.

Bertha Probasco
Los Vegas, Nevada

MEXICAN CANDY

2 1/2 c. sugar
1/4 tsp. salt
1 c. milk, heated
1 1/2 c. pecans
1 tsp. vanilla extract

Cook .... sugar and salt in heavy skillet until sugar lumps and turns light brown.
Stir ...... in milk gradually, mixing well.
Cook .... to soft-ball stage or 234 degrees on candy thermometer, stirring constantly.
Reduce ... heat and stir in pecans.
Cook .... to hard-ball stage or 265 degrees on candy thermometer, stirring constantly.
Remove .. from heat.
Stir ...... in vanilla.
Stir ...... until candy appears creamy.
Drop .... by spoonfuls onto waxed paper.

Daphne Smith
Winnsboro H. S., Winnsboro, Texas

CREAM MINTS

1 egg white
1 tbsp. cream
1 tsp. vanilla extract
3 drops of oil of peppermint
Food coloring
1 box confectioners' sugar
1 tsp. (heaping) soft butter

Combine . first 4 ingredients and desired amount of food coloring in bowl, mixing well.
Add ..... confectioners' sugar in 1 addition, mixing well.
Beat ..... in butter and additional confectioners' sugar if necessary to make firm mixture.
Shape .... into small balls.
Place .... on waxed paper.
Press ..... with fork dipped in confectioners' sugar.
Let ...... stand overnight.
Store .... in tightly covered container with waxed paper between candy layers.
Yield .... 150 mints.

Sue Underwood
Bristol, Virginia

CINNAMON-COFFEE NUTS

2 tsp. instant coffee
1/4 c. sugar
1/4 tsp. cinnamon
Dash of salt
1 1/2 c. pecan halves

Combine . all ingredients in saucepan with 2 tablespoons water.
Bring .... to a boil over medium heat.
Boil ..... for 3 minutes, stirring constantly.
Spread ... on waxed paper using 2 forks to separate pecans.

Vivian Pierson
Paxton, Illinois

CITRUS CANDIED PECANS

2/3 c. orange juice concentrate, thawed
3 c. sugar
2 1/2 to 3 c. pecan halves

Bring .... orange juice and sugar to a boil in large, heavy saucepan over medium heat.
Cook .... to soft-ball stage or 240 degrees on candy thermometer.
Fold ..... nuts in gently.
Spread ... on waxed paper to harden.
Store .... in covered container.
Yield .... 2 1/2-3 cups.

Earleen F. Williams
Williston H. S., Williston, Florida

SEAFOAM CANDY

3 c. sugar
1/2 c. dark corn syrup
1/2 tsp. salt
2 egg whites
1 tsp. vanilla extract
1 c. chopped nuts

Bring .... first 3 ingredients and 2/3 cup water to a boil in saucepan over medium heat, stirring constantly.
Cook .... to firm-ball stage or 248 degrees on candy thermometer. Do not stir.
Beat ..... egg whites until stiff.
Pour ..... syrup over egg whites, beating constantly.
Beat ..... with wooden spoon until very thick.

Fold ..... in vanilla and nuts.
Pour ..... into buttered pan.
Mark .... into squares.
Yield .... 1 3/4 pounds.

Photograph for this recipe on page 115.

ORANGE BALLS

1 6-oz. can orange juice concentrate, thawed
1 box vanilla wafers, finely crushed
1 c. chopped pecans
1 c. flaked coconut
1 box confectioners' sugar

Combine . first 4 ingredients with half the confectioners' sugar in bowl, mixing well.
Shape .... into small balls.
Roll ..... in remaining confectioners' sugar.
Store .... in tightly covered container in refrigerator.

Sister Julie Budai
Providence H. S., San Antonio, Texas

ORANGE DROPS

3 c. sugar
1 1/2 c. milk, scalded
Pinch of salt
1/4 c. butter
Grated rind of 2 oranges
1 c. broken pecans

Caramelize 1 cup sugar in large saucepan.
Add ..... hot milk all at once, stirring vigorously.
Stir ...... in remaining sugar.
Cook .... to firm-ball stage or 246 degrees on candy thermometer.
Remove .. from heat.
Stir ...... in remaining ingredients.
Beat ..... until creamy and slightly cooled.
Drop .... by teaspoonfuls onto waxed paper.

Marilyn Becker
Garden City, Kansas

ORANGE SURPRISE CANDY

3 c. toasted corn natural cereal
Confectioners' sugar
1/4 tsp. salt
2/3 c. evaporated milk, heated
1 tsp. orange extract

Pecan halves
Candied cherries
Dates

Combine	. cereal, 1/2 cup confectioners' sugar and salt in bowl.
Add	. . . . . hot milk gradually, stirring until mixture holds together.
Blend	. . . . in orange extract.
Shape	. . . . into balls around pecan half, cherry or date with buttered hands.
Chill	. . . . . in tightly covered container for 24 hours or longer.
Roll	. . . . . in confectioners' sugar.

Millicent Finecastle
Oxnard, Missouri

SALTED PEANUT CHEWS

1 1/2 c. flour
2/3 c. packed brown sugar
1/2 tsp. baking powder
1/2 tsp. salt
1/2 c. margarine, softened
2 egg yolks
1/4 tsp. soda
3 tsp. vanilla extract
3 c. miniature marshmallows
2/3 c. light corn syrup
1/4 c. butter
2 c. peanut butter chips
2 c. crisp rice cereal
2 c. cocktail peanuts

Combine	. first 7 ingredients with 1 teaspoon vanilla in bowl, mixing well.
Press	. . . . . into 9 x 13-inch baking pan.
Bake	. . . . . at 350 degrees for 12 to 15 minutes or until light brown.
Sprinkle	. . with marshmallows.
Bake	. . . . . for 1 to 2 minutes longer or until marshmallows begin to puff.
Heat	. . . . . next 3 ingredients with 2 teaspoons vanilla in saucepan until smooth.
Stir	. . . . . . in cereal and peanuts.
Spread	. . . over marshmallows.
Chill	. . . . . until firm enough to cut into bars.

Mary Jo Crawford
Caddo-Kiowa AVTC, Ft. Cobb, Oklahoma

PEANUT CRUNCH CANDY

1 c. sugar
1 c. light corn syrup

1 12-oz. jar crunchy peanut butter
6 c. corn flakes

Dissolve	. . sugar with corn syrup in saucepan over medium heat, stirring constantly.
Remove	. . from heat and stir in peanut butter until well blended.
Combine	. with corn flakes in large bowl, mixing well.
Drop	. . . . by spoonfuls onto waxed paper.
Cool	. . . . . and shape into balls.

Jeri O'Quinn
Jones County H. S., Gray, Georgia

PECAN DROPS

2 boxes confectioners' sugar
2 c. chopped pecans
1 can sweetened condensed milk
1 can flaked coconut
1 tsp. vanilla extract
Dash of salt
1 4-oz. block paraffin
1 12-oz. package chocolate chips

Combine	. first 6 ingredients in bowl, mixing well.
Shape	. . . . into balls and chill.
Melt	. . . . . paraffin and chocolate chips in top of double boiler over hot water.
Dip	. . . . . . balls into chocolate mixture.
Cool	. . . . . on waxed paper.

Jerri Williams
Coffee H. S., Douglas, Georgia

POTATO PENNIES

1 med. potato
2 1/2 to 3 1/2 c. confectioners' sugar
Chunk-style peanut butter

Boil	. . . . . potato until done.
Mash	. . . . thoroughly while hot.
Add	. . . . . confectioners' sugar, a small amount at a time, until consistency of dough.
Roll	. . . . . out 1/4-inch thick.
Spread	. . . evenly with peanut butter.
Roll	. . . . . up.
Chill	. . . . . thoroughly.
Slice	. . . . . into 1/4 to 1/2-inch pieces.

Ruby Boyd
Denver, Colorado

BUTTERMILK PRALINES

3 c. sugar
1 tsp. soda
1/8 tsp. salt
1 c. buttermilk
3/4 c. dark corn syrup
2 tbsp. butter, softened
2 c. nuts

Combine . all ingredients except nuts in large saucepan, mixing well.
Cook .... over medium heat to soft-ball stage or 240 degrees on candy thermometer.
Add ..... nuts, beating until candy loses its gloss.
Drop .... by spoonfuls onto waxed paper.
Yield .... 36.

Patricia Stupka
Lamar Consolidated H. S., Rosenberg, Texas

CREAMY PRALINES

1 c. packed brown sugar
1 c. evaporated milk
1/8 tsp. salt
1 c. sugar
1/8 tsp. soda
1/4 c. margarine
2 c. pecans
2 tsp. vanilla extract

Combine . all ingredients except vanilla in large, greased saucepan, mixing well.
Cook .... over medium heat to soft-ball stage or 240 degrees on candy thermometer.
Stir ...... occasionally to prevent sticking.
Remove .. from heat and add vanilla; cool.
Beat ..... by hand until thick.
Drop .... by spoonfuls onto waxed paper.
Cool ..... before removing from paper.
Yield .... 20 pralines.

Dee Dee Guess
Rogers H. S., Rogers, Texas

MICROWAVE SOUTHERN PRALINES

1 1/2 c. packed brown sugar
2/3 c. half and half
1/8 tsp. salt
2 tbsp. margarine, melted
1 1/2 c. pecans

Combine . first 3 ingredients in deep glass dish, mixing well.
Blend .... in margarine.
Microwave on High for 7 to 10 minutes, stirring once.
Stir ...... in pecans.
Cool ..... for 1 minute.
Beat ..... by hand until creamy and thickened.
Drop .... by tablespoonfuls onto waxed paper.

Deborah Jackson
Pine Tree H. S., Longview, Texas

ORANGE PRALINES

3 c. sugar
1 c. cream
2 tbsp. light corn syrup
Rind of 1 orange, finely chopped
2 c. pecans

Combine . first 3 ingredients in saucepan.
Cook .... to soft-ball stage or 240 degrees on candy thermometer.
Remove .. from heat.
Stir ...... in orange rind; cool.
Add ..... pecans, mixing well.
Drop .... onto waxed paper.

Martha Barley
Knoxville, Tennessee

STRAWBERRY CANDY

1 lg. package strawberry gelatin
1 lg. package coconut
1 can sweetened condensed milk
Red sugar
Almond slivers
Green food coloring

Combine . gelatin, coconut and condensed milk in bowl, mixing well.
Chill ..... for 1 hour or longer.
Shape .... into strawberries.
Roll ..... in red sugar.
Add ..... almond slivers tinted with green food coloring for stem.

Patricia L. Walochik
James Madison H. S., Vienna, Virginia

Fruit
Desserts

APPLE BETTY

4 c. sliced tart apples
1/4 c. orange juice
1 c. sugar
3/4 c. flour
1/2 tsp. cinnamon
1/4 tsp. nutmeg
1/2 c. butter

Arrange . . apples in buttered 9-inch pie plate.
Drizzle . . . with orange juice.
Combine . dry ingredients in bowl.
Cut . . . . . . in butter until crumbly.
Sprinkle . . over apples.
Bake . . . . . at 375 degrees for 45 minutes or until tender.
Serve . . . . warm with ice cream.
Yield . . . . 6 servings.

Myrtle Chapman
El Reno H. S., El Reno, Oklahoma

APPLE COCOROON

2 to 4 lg. apples, sliced
Sugar
1 egg, beaten
1/2 tsp. vanilla extract
1/2 c. Bisquick
1 tbsp. melted margarine
1/2 c. coconut

Arrange . . apples in 8-inch pie pan.
Sprinkle . . with 2 tablespoons sugar.
Combine . remaining ingredients with 1/2 cup sugar in bowl.
Beat . . . . . until blended.
Spoon . . . over apples.
Bake . . . . . at 350 degrees for 35 to 40 minutes or until apples are tender.

Marla Hartry
Central Elgin C. I., St. Thomas, Ontario

APPLE CRISP

2 tbsp. sugar
1/2 tsp. cinnamon
4 c. tart apples, pared, sliced
1/2 c. flour
1/8 tsp. salt
1/4 tsp. nutmeg
3 c. packed brown sugar
3 tbsp. butter, softened

Combine . sugar and 1/4 teaspoon cinnamon with apples in greased 8-inch baking dish.
Sprinkle . . with 1/4 cup water.
Mix . . . . . remaining ingredients and 1/4 teaspoon cinnamon in bowl until crumbly.
Spread . . . over apples.
Bake . . . . . at 350 degrees for 40 minutes or until brown and apples are tender.
Yield . . . . 6 servings.

Shelvie L. Miller
Scott H. S., Huntsville, Tennessee

ELAINE'S APPLE CRISP

5 or 6 med. apples, peeled, sliced
1 tbsp. lemon juice
1/4 c. sugar
1/2 tsp. cinnamon
1/4 tsp. nutmeg
1/3 c. flour
1 c. rolled oats
1/2 c. packed brown sugar
1/2 tsp. salt
1/3 c. melted butter

Combine . first 5 ingredients in baking dish, mixing well.
Mix . . . . . remaining ingredients in bowl, blending well.
Spread . . . over apples.
Bake . . . . . at 375 degrees for 30 minutes.
Serve . . . . warm with whipped cream.
Yield . . . . 6 servings.

Elaine Collins
Morgan H. S., McConnelsville, Ohio

RACHEL'S APPLE CRISP

6 apples, sliced
2 tbsp. lemon juice
1/2 c. butter
1/2 tsp. cinnamon
1/2 c. pecans
1 c. sugar
3/4 c. flour

Place . . . . apple slices in baking dish.
Sprinkle . . with lemon juice.
Blend . . . . remaining ingredients in bowl until crumbly.

Press . . . . . over apples.
Bake . . . . . at 375 degrees for 1 hour.
Yield . . . . 4 servings.

Rachel Adams
Cradock H. S., Portsmouth, Virginia

SHIRLEY'S APPLE CRISP

2 20-oz. cans sliced pie apples
3/4 c. oatmeal
3/4 c. packed brown sugar
1/2 c. flour
1/2 c. butter, chilled
1 tsp. cinnamon
1/2 tsp. salt

Place . . . . apples in 9 x 13-inch baking dish.
Combine . remaining ingredients in bowl, mixing until crumbly.
Sprinkle . . over apples.
Bake . . . . . at 350 degrees for 35 to 40 minutes.
Serve . . . . cooled with whipped cream.
Yield . . . . 15 servings.

Shirley Grube
Huron Jr. H. S., Huron, South Dakota

APPLE KUCHEN

1/2 c. butter, softened
1 pkg. yellow cake mix
1/2 c. flaked coconut
1 20-oz. can sliced apples, drained
1/2 c. sugar
1 tsp. cinnamon
1 c. sour cream
1 egg

Cut . . . . . . butter into cake mix in bowl until crumbly.
Mix . . . . . in coconut.
Pat . . . . . . into 9 x 13-inch baking dish.
Bake . . . . . at 350 degrees for 10 minutes.
Arrange . . apple slices over crust.
Sprinkle . . with sugar and cinnamon.
Blend . . . . sour cream and egg in bowl.
Drizzle . . . over apples.
Bake . . . . . at 350 degrees for 25 minutes.
Yield . . . . 12 servings.

Betty Bullock Pitts
Sierra Vista Jr. H. S., Canyon Country, California

APPLE-PECAN COBBLER

4 c. thinly sliced apples
1 1/2 c. sugar
1/2 tsp. cinnamon
3/4 c. pecans
1 c. flour
1 tsp. baking powder
1/4 tsp. salt
1 egg, beaten
1/2 c. evaporated milk
1/3 c. butter, melted

Place . . . . apples in greased 8-inch round baking dish.
Mix . . . . . 1/2 cup sugar, cinnamon and 1/2 cup pecans in bowl.
Sprinkle . . over apples.
Sift . . . . . . 1 cup sugar, flour, baking powder and salt together.
Combine . egg, milk and butter in bowl.
Add . . . . . dry ingredients, mixing until smooth.
Pour . . . . . over apples.
Top . . . . . with remaining pecans.
Bake . . . . . at 325 degrees for 55 minutes.
Yield . . . . 8 servings.

Kimmie Humrichouser
Mapleton H. S., Ashland, Ohio

FIRST FROST APPLE CREAM DESSERT

1 c. whipping cream, chilled
1/4 tsp. vanilla extract
6 tbsp. sugar
1/3 c. fresh orange juice
2 tbsp. lemon juice
6 lg. Delicious apples, peeled, coarsely grated

Whip . . . . first 2 ingredients with 3 tablespoons sugar in bowl until stiff peaks form.
Combine . juices with 3 tablespoons sugar and apples, mixing well.
Chill . . . . . mixtures thoroughly.
Fold . . . . . together.
Serve . . . . in parfait glasses immediately.
Yield . . . . 6 servings.

Della O. Lindsay
Riverside H. S., Boardman, Oregon

MICROWAVE APPLE GOODIE

5 c. apple slices
3/4 c. oatmeal
1/4 c. flour
1 c. packed brown sugar
1/2 tsp. salt (opt.)
1 tsp. cinnamon
1/2 c. butter

Arrange .. apple slices in 3-quart glass baking dish.
Combine . remaining ingredients except butter in bowl, mixing well.
Sprinkle .. over apples.
Dot ..... with butter.
Microwave on High for 15 minutes, stirring every 5 minutes.
Serve .... warm or cold with ice cream.
Yield .... 8-10 servings.

Carolyn VanAmberg
Maurice-Orange City Community School
Orange City, Iowa

MICROWAVE APPLE DELICIOUS

6 med. cooking apples, peeled, sliced
1/4 c. sugar
1/2 tsp. cinnamon
1/4 tsp. cloves
2 tsp. lemon juice
1/2 c. packed brown sugar
3/4 c. sifted flour
1/2 tsp. salt
1/2 c. butter
1/4 c. chopped nuts

Combine . first 5 ingredients in 8-inch baking dish.
Mix ..... remaining ingredients in bowl until crumbly.
Sprinkle .. over apples.
Microwave on High for 12 to 14 minutes or until apples are tender.
Yield .... 6-8 servings.

Relda Smith
Wooster H. S., Wooster, Ohio

MICROWAVE APPLE DESSERT

3 c. sliced apples
1 3-oz. package red gelatin
1 c. flour
3/4 c. sugar
1/2 c. butter, softened

Arrange .. apple slices in buttered 6 x 10-inch glass baking dish.
Sprinkle .. with gelatin.
Combine . flour and sugar in bowl.
Cut ...... in butter until crumbly.
Sprinkle .. over apples and gelatin.
Microwave on Roast for 8 minutes.
Yield .... 4-6 servings.

Clarabel Tepe
Ft. Towson School, Ft. Towson, Oklahoma

APPLE STRUDEL ROLL

6 c. canned sliced apples
3/4 c. raisins
1 tbsp. grated lemon rind
3/4 c. sugar
2 tsp. cinnamon
3/4 c. ground almonds
1/2 box phyllo dough
Melted butter
1 c. fine bread crumbs

Combine . first 6 ingredients in bowl, mixing well.
Layer .... phyllo sheets alternately with butter on foil.
Brown ... bread crumbs in 1/4 cup butter in skillet, stirring constantly.
Sprinkle .. 1/3 cup crumbs over phyllo.
Spread ... half the filling in 3-inch strip along narrow edge of dough.
Roll ..... as for jelly roll, placing on baking sheet.
Brush .... top with butter.
Sprinkle .. with remaining crumbs and additional sugar.
Bake ..... at 400 degrees for 20 to 25 minutes.

Claudia Triolo
Dayton Avenue School, Manorville, New York

AUSTRIAN JELLY TART

2 c. flour
2 tbsp. sugar
2 egg yolks
2 tsp. grated lemon rind
1 c. butter, softened

1 17 1/2-oz. package frozen lemon
   pudding, thawed
1 banana, sliced
2 naval oranges, peeled, sectioned
1 c. strawberries, quartered
1 sm. red apple, thinly sliced
1 c. seedless green grapes
4 peeled apricots, quartered
1 1/2 c. apple jelly

Combine . first 4 ingredients together in bowl.
Cut . . . . . . in butter, with fingers, until soft
           ball forms.
Pat . . . . . . dough evenly on bottom and side
           of 12-inch pizza pan.
Make . . . . fluted rim.
Prick . . . . bottom with fork.
Bake . . . . . at 375 degrees for 15 to 20 minutes
           or until golden brown; cool.
Spread . . . pudding evenly in pastry shell.
Mark . . . . top into 6 wedges with knife.
Fill . . . . . . each wedge with different fruit.
Melt . . . . . jelly in saucepan over low heat, stir-
           ring constantly.
Cool . . . . . to lukewarm.
Spoon . . . evenly over fruit.
Chill . . . . . for several hours.

Photograph for this recipe on page 131.

BLACKBERRY SURPRISE

1/2 c. margarine
1 c. flour
1 c. sugar
1 c. milk
2 tsp. baking powder
1 tsp. cinnamon
1/2 tsp. nutmeg
1/4 tsp. cloves
2 c. blackberries, drained

Melt . . . . . margarine in 8-inch square baking
           dish in 350-degree oven.
Blend . . . . next 7 ingredients together in bowl.
Pour . . . . . batter into melted margarine.
Spoon . . . blackberries into center of batter.
Bake . . . . . at 350 degrees for 1 hour or until
           browned.
Yield . . . . 9 servings.

Barbara P. Hulver
Clarke County H. S., Berryville, Virginia

BLUEBERRY DELIGHT DESSERT

20 graham crackers, crushed
1 stick margarine, melted
1 c. sugar
1 8-oz. package cream cheese, softened
2 eggs
Vanilla extract
1 can blueberry pie filling
1 pt. whipping cream, whipped
6 tbsp. confectioners' sugar
1/8 tsp. salt

Combine . crumbs, margarine and 1/2 cup
           sugar in bowl, mixing well.
Press . . . . . into 9 x 13-inch baking pan.
Beat . . . . . cream cheese in bowl until light,
           adding 1/2 cup sugar gradually.
Stir . . . . . . in eggs and 1 teaspoon vanilla.
Beat . . . . . until smooth.
Pour . . . . . over crumb mixture.
Bake . . . . . at 350 degrees for 20 minutes; cool.
Spread . . . with pie filling.
Blend . . . . whipped cream, confectioners'
           sugar, 1 teaspoon vanilla and salt in
           bowl.
Spread . . . over pie filling.
Chill . . . . . until served.
Yield . . . . 16 servings.

Vickie Marshall
Malabar H. S., Mansfield, Ohio

COMPANY PLEASER

1 can cherries
2 tbsp. flour
1/2 c. sugar
2 c. yellow cake mix
1/4 c. butter

Drain . . . . fruit, reserving liquid.
Place . . . . in greased 1-quart baking dish.
Blend . . . . flour and sugar in bowl.
Add . . . . . reserved juice, mixing well.
Stir . . . . . . into fruit gently.
Bake . . . . . at 350 degrees until bubbly.
Combine . cake mix and butter in bowl until
           crumbly.
Sprinkle . . over fruit.
Bake . . . . . until lightly browned.
Serve . . . . hot with ice cream.
Yield . . . . 6-8 servings.

Mabel Valech
Calaroga Jr. H. S., Hayward, California

MICROWAVE CHERRY COBBLER

1 can cherry pie filling
1 tsp. lemon juice
1/2 c. butter, melted
1 c. flour
1/4 tsp. allspice
1/3 c. packed brown sugar
3/4 tsp. cinnamon
2/3 c. chopped nuts

Combine . pie filling and lemon juice in shallow 1-quart glass casserole.
Combine . remaining ingredients in bowl, mixing until crumbly.
Sprinkle .. over cherries.
Microwave on High for 5 to 6 minutes or until bubbly.

Nancy Roop
Caldwell H. S., Caldwell, Kansas

CHERRY CRISP

1 3/4 c. flour
1 tsp. salt
1/2 tsp. soda
1 c. packed brown sugar
1 c. quick-cooking oatmeal
1/2 c. shortening
1 c. sugar
3/4 c. cherry juice
1 can cherries
1/4 tsp. red food coloring

Sift . . . . . . 1 1/2 cups flour, salt and soda together.
Stir . . . . . . in brown sugar and oatmeal.
Cut . . . . . . in shortening until crumbly.
Press . . . . . half the mixture into bottom of 8 x 12-inch baking pan.
Combine . sugar and 1/4 cup flour in saucepan.
Stir . . . . . . in cherry juice.
Cook . . . . until thick, stirring constantly.
Remove .. from heat.
Add . . . . . cherries and food coloring.
Pour . . . . . over prepared crust when cool.
Cover . . . . with remaining oatmeal mixture, pressing with spoon.
Bake . . . . . at 350 degrees for 25 minutes.
Yield . . . . 8 servings.

Hazel Bailes
Lake Charles, Louisiana

CHERRIES JUBILEE

1 20-oz. can pitted Bing cherries
2 tsp. cornstarch
1/2 c. warm Cognac
Ice cream

Drain . . . . cherries, reserving juice.
Cook . . . . 1 cup juice in saucepan until reduced to 3/4 cup.
Blend . . . . cornstarch and 2 tablespoons cherry juice.
Add . . . . . to hot juice.
Cook . . . . until thick and clear, stirring constantly.
Fold . . . . . in cherries.
Spoon . . . into chafing dish over flame.
Pour . . . . . Cognac over top.
Ignite . . . . Cognac.
Spoon . . . flaming cherries over ice cream.
Yield . . . . 10 servings.

Velma Sansing
Cleveland, Ohio

CRANBERRY AMANDINE DESSERT

1 c. packed brown sugar
1/2 c. butter, softened
1/2 tsp. almond extract
1 1/2 c. bread crumbs
1/2 c. flour
1/2 c. chopped almonds
1 1-lb. can whole cranberry sauce

Cream . . . brown sugar and butter together in bowl.
Add . . . . . remaining ingredients except cranberry sauce, mixing well.
Spread . . . half the mixture in 9 x 13-inch baking dish.
Cover . . . . with cranberry sauce.
Top . . . . . with remaining crumbs.
Bake . . . . . at 350 degrees for 15 to 20 minutes.
Serve . . . . hot or cold.

Sylvia Crandall
Lompoc, California

CRANBERRY CRUNCH

1 c. quick-cooking oats
1/2 c. flour
1 c. packed brown sugar

1/2 c. butter
1 1-lb. can cranberry sauce

Combine . first 3 ingredients in bowl, mixing
well.
Cut . . . . . . in butter until crumbly.
Spread . . . half the mixture in 8 x 8-inch bak-
ing dish.
Cover . . . . with cranberry sauce.
Top . . . . . with remaining crumbs.
Bake . . . . . at 350 degrees for 45 minutes.
Serve . . . . hot with ice cream.

Jimmy Lee Jones
Yatahai, Arizona

MULBERRY COBBLER

1 c. flour
2 tsp. baking powder
1/4 tsp. salt
1/2 c. milk
1/2 tsp. vanilla extract
1 tbsp. butter
1 1/2 c. sugar
1 to 2 c. mulberries

Combine . first 6 ingredients and 1 cup sugar
in bowl, mixing well.
Spread . . . in 7 x 11-inch baking dish.
Top . . . . . with mulberries.
Sprinkle .. with 1/2 cup sugar.
Pour . . . . . 3/4 cup boiling water over batter.
Bake . . . . . at 375 degrees for 25 to 30
minutes.
Serve . . . . warm or cold with ice cream.
Yield . . . . 6 servings.

Sandy Swart
Marysville H. S., Marysville, Kansas

QUICK PEACH COBBLER

Sugar
4 c. sliced peaches
1 stick butter
1 c. milk
1 c. self-rising flour

Sweeten .. peaches to taste.
Melt . . . . . butter in 9 x 12-inch baking dish.
Combine . 1 cup sugar, milk and flour in bowl,
mixing well.
Pour . . . . . over melted butter.
Spoon . . . peaches over batter. Do not stir.

Bake . . . . . at 375 degrees for 40 minutes or
until brown.
Yield . . . . 12 servings.

Karen Thompson
Screven County H. S., Sylvania, Georgia

TAFFY PEACH MERINGUES

1 29-oz. can peach halves, drained
1/3 c. molasses
4 tsp. butter
2 egg whites
1/4 c. sugar
1/2 c. heavy cream

Place . . . . peach halves in shallow baking pan.
Top . . . . . each with 2 teaspoons molasses and
1/4 teaspoon butter.
Bake . . . . . at 450 degrees for 10 minutes.
Beat . . . . . egg whites in bowl until soft peaks
form.
Add . . . . . sugar gradually, beating until stiff.
Pour . . . . . cream around peaches.
Pile . . . . . . meringue on top of each peach half.
Bake . . . . . 5 minutes longer or until meringue
is lightly browned.
Serve . . . . with pan sauce.
Yield . . . . 7-8 servings.

Photograph for this recipe below.

PEACH FLAMBE WITH STRAWBERRY SAUCE

1 10-oz. package frozen strawberries,
  thawed, pureed
1/4 c. currant jelly
1/4 c. frozen orange juice concentrate
1 1-lb. can cling peach halves, drained
1/4 c. slivered blanched almonds (opt.)
3 tbsp. Brandy
1 qt. firm vanilla ice cream

Combine . first 3 ingredients in saucepan.
Cook .... over low heat until jelly melts, stir-
            ring constantly.
Warm .... peaches in strawberry sauce.
Sprinkle .. with almonds.
Pour ..... warm Brandy over peaches.
Ignite .... spooning sauce over peaches as
            Brandy burns.
Spoon ... peach halves into serving dishes.
Top ..... with ice cream and strawberry
            sauce.

Beulah Wilson
Fairbanks, Alaska

STRAWBERRY BONANZA

4 c. sifted flour
2 tbsp. baking powder
2 tsp. salt
Sugar
1 c. shortening
1 1/2 c. milk
2 pt. California strawberries, halved
Orange marmalade
1 pt. sour cream

Mix ..... first 3 ingredients with 1/4 cup
            sugar in large bowl.
Cut ...... in shortening until crumbly.
Stir ...... in milk, blending well.
Knead ... on floured surface 10 times.
Divide ... dough into thirds.
Pat ...... each into 9-inch round cake pan.
Bake ..... at 450 degrees for 12 minutes or
            until browned.
Combine . strawberries and 2/3 cup sugar in
            bowl.
Chill ..... for 30 minutes.
Layer .... warm biscuit layers, marmalade,
            sour cream and strawberries in
            order given until all ingredients are
            used.

Photograph for this recipe on this page.

PEACH FLUFF

1/2 c. butter, melted
1 c. confectioners' sugar
2 eggs, beaten
1 12-oz. box vanilla wafers, crushed
2 c. whipping cream, whipped
2 cans sliced peaches, drained

Blend .... butter, sugar and eggs in double
            boiler.
Cook .... until thick, stirring constantly.
Spread ... 2/3 of the wafer crumbs in 9 x 13-
            inch serving dish.
Pour ..... butter mixture evenly over crumbs.
Spread ... with half the whipped cream.
Arrange .. peaches over whipped cream.
Top ..... with remaining whipped cream.
Sprinkle .. with reserved crumbs.
Chill ..... for 12 hours.
Yield .... 18-24 servings.

Mary Jean Earl
Meritt Hutton Jr. H. S., Thornton, Colorado

GRANOLA PEACHES

1 29-oz. can peach halves, drained
Brown sugar
2/3 c. granola
3 tbsp. margarine, melted
2 tbsp. broken pecans

Place .... peach halves, cut sides up, in un-greased 8-inch square pan.
Sprinkle .. with 2 tablespoons brown sugar.
Broil ..... 5 inches from heat source for 2 to 3 minutes or until lightly browned.
Combine . granola, 1/4 cup packed brown sugar, margarine and pecans in bowl.
Top ..... peaches with granola mixture.
Broil ..... for 1 minute or until mixture is bubbly and browned.
Serve .... with ice cream.

Laura Lewis Henderson
Versailles H. S., Versailles, Missouri

PEACHES AND CREAM KUCHEN

2 c. flour
1 c. sugar
1/2 tsp. salt
1/4 tsp. baking powder
1/2 c. margarine
1 can peach halves, drained
1 tsp. cinnamon
2 egg yolks
1 c. heavy cream

Combine . flour, 2 tablespoons sugar, salt and baking powder in bowl.
Cut ...... in margarine until crumbly.
Press ..... into 8 x 8-inch baking dish.
Arrange .. peach halves, cut side down on crust.
Combine . remaining sugar and cinnamon in small bowl.
Sprinkle .. over peaches.
Bake ..... at 400 degrees for 15 minutes.
Beat ..... egg yolks and cream in bowl until smooth.
Pour ..... over peaches.
Bake ..... for 30 minutes longer or until golden.

Marge French
Alcona H. S., Lincoln, Michigan

MAPLE-GLAZED PEACHES

1/3 c. maple syrup
1 c. sour cream
6 c. sliced fresh peaches
1 tbsp. brown sugar

Blend .... maple syrup and cream in small bowl until smooth.

Chill ..... until serving time.
Arrange .. peaches in serving dishes.
Pour ..... syrup mixture over peaches.
Sprinkle .. with brown sugar.
Yield .... 6 servings.

Lois Cynewski
Portsmouth Jr. H. S., Portsmouth, New Hampshire

PEACH-STUFFED BAKED CANTALOUPE

3 c. sliced peaches
1/2 c. sugar
Several grains of mace
2 cantaloupes, cut in half
Mint sprigs

Combine . peaches, sugar and mace in bowl, mixing well.
Fill ...... cantaloupes with peach mixture, arranging slices attractively.
Bake ..... at 425 degrees for 15 minutes.
Garnish .. with mint.
Serve .... immediately.

Janine Borger
The Dalles, Oregon

PEARS IN WINE SAUCE

2 c. red wine
1 1/2 c. sugar
4 whole cardamom seeds
2 cinnamon sticks
3 tbsp. lemon juice
8 firm pears, peeled

Combine . first 4 ingredients with 1 table-spoon lemon juice and 2 cups water in large skillet.
Cook .... over medium heat until sugar dissolves.
Bring .... to a boil over medium-high heat.
Sprinkle .. pears with remaining 2 tablespoons lemon juice.
Place .... in sugar mixture.
Simmer .. for 8 to 10 minutes until tender, turning once.
Remove .. pears to large bowl.
Boil ..... sauce until reduced to 1 1/2 cups and slightly thickened.
Pour ..... over pears.
Chill ..... covered for several hours.

May Ross
Newport, Ohio

PEARS IN ORANGE SAUCE

6 firm ripe pears
1 tbsp. grated orange rind
1 1/2 c. fresh orange juice
1 tbsp. fresh lemon juice
1/3 c. packed brown sugar
3 to 4 oranges, peeled, chilled

Core . . . . . and peel pears, leaving stem intact.
Place . . . . upright in saucepan.
Mix . . . . . orange rind and juices.
Pour . . . . . over pears.
Cook . . . . covered, over low heat for 15 to 20 minutes or until just tender, basting occasionally.
Remove . . pears carefully to casserole.
Add . . . . . brown sugar to pan juices, mixing well.
Bring . . . . to a boil.
Cook . . . . for 1 minute, stirring constantly.
Pour . . . . . over pears.
Chill . . . . . for several hours, basting occasionally.
Slice . . . . . oranges crosswise and cut into quarters.
Arrange . . orange slices around pears on plate.
Top . . . . . with sauce.

Lucille Timothy
New Haven, Connecticut

GERMAN PLUM CRUMBLE

2 3/4 c. flour
4 1/2 tsp. baking powder
1 c. sugar
1/2 tsp. salt
4 tbsp. margarine
1 egg, beaten
6 tbsp. milk
Blue plums, pitted, cut into halves
2 tbsp. butter
Cream

Sift . . . . . . 2 cups flour, 4 teaspoons baking powder, 1/4 cup sugar and salt together into bowl.
Cut . . . . . . in margarine until crumbly.
Combine . egg and milk.
Add . . . . . to dry ingredients, mixing well.
Pat . . . . . . onto cookie sheet, crimping to make rim.
Arrange . . plums over top.

Combine . remaining 3/4 cup flour, 3/4 cup sugar and 1/2 teaspoon baking powder in bowl, mixing well.
Cut . . . . . . in butter and enough cream to make coarse crumbs.
Spread . . . over plums.
Bake . . . . . at 375 degrees for 1/2 hour.

Elsie Klassen
G. P. Vanier, Donnelly, Alberta, Canada

SPICED PRUNES

2 c. dried prunes
1/2 c. sugar
1/4 tsp. dry mustard
1/8 tsp. cinnamon
1/8 tsp. cloves
1 tbsp. vinegar

Combine . all ingredients with 1 1/2 cups water in casserole, mixing well.
Bake . . . . . covered, at 350 degrees for 1 1/4 hours.
Yield . . . . 8-10 servings.

Samantha Vinson
Terre Haute, Indiana

RASPBERRY-WALNUT DESSERT

1/3 c. confectioners' sugar
1/2 c. butter, softened
1 1/4 c. flour
1 10-oz. package frozen raspberries, thawed
3/4 c. chopped walnuts
2 eggs
1 1/2 c. sugar
1/2 tsp. each salt, baking powder
1 tsp. vanilla extract
2 tbsp. cornstarch
1 tbsp. lemon juice

Combine . first 2 ingredients and 1 cup flour in bowl, blending well.
Press . . . . . into bottom of 9 x 13-inch baking dish.
Bake . . . . . at 350 degrees for 15 minutes.
Drain . . . . raspberries, reserving juice.
Spoon . . . berries over crust.
Sprinkle . . with walnuts.
Beat . . . . . eggs and 1 cup sugar in bowl until light and fluffy.
Add . . . . . salt, baking powder, vanilla and 1/4 cup flour, mixing well.

Pour . . . . . over raspberries.
Bake . . . . . for 30 minutes longer.
Cut . . . . . . into squares when cool.
Combine . reserved raspberry juice with 1/2 cup sugar, cornstarch and 1/2 cup water in saucepan.
Cook . . . . until clear, stirring constantly.
Add . . . . . lemon juice and cool.
Serve . . . . over squares.

Dorothy S. Weirick
Cottonwood H. S., Salt Lake City, Utah

RHUBARB COBBLER

3 c. diced rhubarb
1 3/4 c. sugar
4 tbsp. butter
Flour
3/4 tsp. salt
3 tsp. baking powder
1/4 c. shortening
1 egg, beaten
1/2 c. milk
1 c. light corn syrup
2 tbsp. cinnamon candies

Spread . . . rhubarb in greased 8 x 12-inch baking dish.
Top . . . . . with 1 cup sugar and 3 tablespoons butter.
Sift . . . . . . 3/4 cup sugar, 1 1/2 cups flour, 1/4 teaspoon salt and baking powder into bowl.
Cut . . . . . . in shortening until crumbly.
Beat . . . . . in egg and milk.
Pour . . . . . over rhubarb.
Bake . . . . . at 350 degrees for 30 minutes.
Combine . corn syrup, 2 tablespoons flour, 1/2 teaspoon salt, cinnamon candies and 1 cup water in saucepan.
Cook . . . . for 5 minutes in saucepan.
Stir . . . . . . in 1 tablespoon butter.
Serve . . . . over cobbler.
Yield . . . . 8 servings.

Mary Jean Earl
Meritt Hutton Jr. H. S., Thornton, Colorado

AUNT DELLA'S RHUBARB CRISP

5 c. chopped rhubarb
2 tbsp. Minute tapioca
1 1/2 c. sugar
1 c. flour

1 tsp. baking powder
3/4 tsp. salt
1/3 c. oil

Combine . first 2 ingredients and 1 cup sugar in 8-inch baking dish.
Mix . . . . . 1/2 cup sugar and remaining ingredients in bowl until crumbly.
Spread . . . over rhubarb.
Bake . . . . . at 350 degrees for 30 to 40 minutes or until brown.
Yield . . . . 6 servings.

Grace Harris
Meadowdale H. S., Dayton, Ohio

RHUBARB PUFFS

2 c. diced rhubarb
1 tsp. grated orange rind
Sugar
1/4 c. shortening
1 egg
1 tbsp. orange juice
1 c. flour
1 1/2 tsp. baking powder
1/4 tsp. salt
1/3 c. milk
2 tbsp. cornstarch
4 tbsp. butter
2 tsp. vanilla extract
1 tsp. cinnamon
1 tsp. nutmeg

Combine . rhubarb, orange rind and 6 tablespoons sugar in bowl, mixing well.
Spoon . . . into 6 greased custard cups.
Cream . . . shortening and 1/2 cup sugar in bowl until fluffy.
Beat . . . . . in egg and orange juice.
Add . . . . . sifted flour, baking powder and salt alternately with milk, beating well after each addition.
Pour . . . . . over rhubarb.
Place . . . . tightly covered custard cups in 1-inch water in pan.
Bake . . . . . at 350 degrees for 30 minutes.
Bring . . . . 1 cup sugar, cornstarch and 2 cups water to a boil in saucepan.
Boil . . . . . for 1 minute, stirring constantly.
Blend . . . . in remaining ingredients.
Serve . . . . over unmolded custard.

E. Klassen
Georges P. Vanier School, Donnelly, Alberta, Canada

RHUBARB TORTE

Flour
Sugar
3/4 c. margarine, softened
Salt
4 egg yolks, beaten
1/2 c. milk
4 c. rhubarb
4 egg whites
1/4 tsp. (heaping) cream of tartar
1 tsp. vanilla extract

Blend .... 1 1/2 cups flour, 3 tablespoons sugar, margarine and dash of salt in bowl, mixing well.
Press ..... into 9 x 13-inch baking dish.
Bake ..... at 250 degrees for 20 minutes.
Combine . egg yolks, 2 cups sugar, milk and 3 tablespoons flour in bowl, mixing well.
Fold ..... in rhubarb.
Pour ..... over baked crust.
Bake ..... at 350 degrees for 40 minutes.
Beat ..... egg whites and cream of tartar until stiff peaks form.
Add ..... dash of salt and vanilla.
Beat ..... in 1 cup sugar gradually.
Spread ... over rhubarb mixture, sealing edges.
Bake ..... at 350 degrees for 20 minutes.

Jani Haraldson
Turtle Lake-Mercer H. S., Turtle Lake, North Dakota

SCALLOPED RHUBARB

1 1/4 c. sugar
1/2 c. margarine, melted
3 to 4 drops of red food coloring
2 c. diced rhubarb
3 c. cubed bread

Combine . first 3 ingredients in bowl, mixing well.
Add ..... rhubarb and bread, mixing well.
Place .... in greased 9 x 9-inch baking dish.
Pour ..... 1/4 cup water over mixture.
Bake ..... at 325 degrees for 45 to 50 minutes or until rhubarb is tender.
Yield .... 6 servings.

Nancy Roop
Caldwell H. S., Caldwell, Kansas

STRAWBERRY BLIMPS

2 8-oz. packages cream cheese, softened
1/2 c. sugar
2 egg yolks
2 1-lb. loaves thin-sliced white bread, trimmed
1 c. melted butter
Cinnamon-sugar to taste
1 pt. sour cream
1 pt. strawberry preserves

Beat ..... first 3 ingredients in bowl until smooth.
Roll ..... bread slices flat with rolling pin.
Spread ... with cream cheese mixture.
Roll ..... as for jelly roll.
Dip ...... in butter.
Sprinkle .. with cinnamon-sugar.
Place .... on baking sheet.
Bake ..... at 400 degrees for 8 to 10 minutes.
Serve .... hot, topped with sour cream and preserves.
Yield .... 12-16 servings.

Carolyn Lott
Duck Hill Attendance Center
Duck Hill, Massachusetts

STRAWBERRY FLUFF

1 c. sugar
1 qt. fresh strawberries
3 tbsp. Minute tapioca
1/8 tsp. salt
1 egg white, stiffly beaten

Sprinkle .. 3/4 cup sugar over 1/2 quart strawberries in bowl.
Let ...... stand for 15 minutes.
Crush .... strawberries and sugar into pulp.
Add ..... enough water to measure 2 1/2 cups liquid.
Combine . crushed strawberries, tapioca and salt in double boiler.
Cook .... for 15 minutes or until tapioca is clear, stirring constantly.
Slice ..... remaining strawberries into bowl.
Sprinkle .. with 1/4 cup sugar.
Fold ..... strawberries and egg white into cooled tapioca mixture.
Chill ..... until serving time.
Yield .... 6 servings.

Judy E. Harris
Washington County H. S., Springfield, Kentucky

STRAWBERRY PUFFS

2 egg whites
1/2 tsp. vanilla extract
1/2 c. sugar
4 sponge cake dessert cups
1 pt. strawberry ice cream
1 10-oz. package strawberries, thawed

Beat ..... egg whites in mixer bowl until soft peaks form.
Add ..... vanilla and sugar gradually, beating until stiff.
Spread ... meringue over top and sides of dessert cups on foil-lined baking sheet.
Bake ..... at 450 degrees for 5 minutes.
Top ..... with ice cream and strawberries.
Yield .... 4 servings.

Karen Thompson
Screven County H. S., Sylvania, Georgia

GRANDMOTHER'S OLD-FASHIONED STRAWBERRY SHORTCAKE

1 qt. fresh strawberries
Sugar
1/2 recipe 1-2-3-4 cake
1 box Swan's Down cake flour
1/2 pt. whipping cream

Combine . strawberries and 1/4 cup sugar in bowl, mashing well.
Prepare ... 1-2-3-4 cake using Swan's Down flour directions.
Pour ..... into 9 x 9-inch square pan.
Bake ..... using package directions.
Slice ..... cooled cake into 2 layers.
Beat ..... cream and 2 tablespoons sugar in bowl until stiff.
Place .... cake, cut side up, on plate.
Top ..... with half the strawberries and half the whipped cream.
Repeat ... layers, ending with whipped cream.
Chill ..... for 3 hours or longer.

Marie R. Duggan
Johnson County H. S., Wrightsville, Georgia

STRAWBERRY-CHEESE DESSERT

4 c. sour cream
6 egg yolks
1 8-oz. package cream cheese, softened
1 c. sugar
2 tsp. grated lemon rind
2 pt. strawberries

Heat ..... sour cream in double boiler over hot water.
Combine . next 4 ingredients in large bowl, beating until well mixed.
Stir ...... into sour cream.
Cook .... for 14 minutes or until thick, stirring occasionally.
Remove .. from heat.
Let ...... stand, covered, over hot water for 15 minutes.
Place .... mixture in colander lined with damp cheesecloth over large bowl.
Drain .... for 2 hours.
Fold ..... cheesecloth over cheese.
Wrap .... colander and bowl with plastic wrap.
Chill ..... overnight or longer.
Place .... cheese on serving plate.
Shape .... with spatula.
Top ..... with strawberries.
Serve .... with unsalted crackers.

Ella McDowell
Bakersville, Indiana

CURRIED FRUIT

1 4-oz. can peaches, drained
1 4-oz. can pear halves, drained
1 4-oz. can apricots, drained
1 4-oz. can pineapple chunks, drained
Maraschino cherries, drained
1/2 c. pecan halves, chopped
1/3 c. butter, melted
3/4 c. packed brown sugar
2 tsp. curry powder

Arrange .. fruits in 9 x 13-inch baking dish.
Sprinkle .. with pecans.
Combine . butter, brown sugar and curry in bowl, mixing well.
Pour ..... over fruits.
Let ...... stand for 1 hour.
Bake ..... at 350 degrees for 20 minutes.
Yield .... 18-20 small servings.

Phyllis Dunlap
Dysart-Geneseo Community School, Dysart, Iowa

144 / *Fruit Desserts*

DOUBLE EASY FRUIT DESSERT

1   29-oz. can fruit cocktail, drained
1 c. miniature marshmallows
1 c. sour cream
1 tbsp. lemon juice
1 tbsp. sugar
1/4 tsp. salt
Maraschino cherries

Combine . all ingredients except cherries in large bowl, mixing lightly.
Chill . . . . . for several hours.
Top . . . . . with cherries.

Sonja Ellis
Hattsburg, Georgia

EFFORTLESS FRUIT DESSERT

1   18-oz. can sliced peaches
1   18-oz. can apricot halves
1   18-oz. can pineapple chunks
1   18-oz. can sliced pears
1   10-oz. package strawberries, partially
    thawed
1 pkg. instant vanilla pudding mix
Few drops of almond extract (opt.)

Pour . . . . . juice off canned fruits but do not drain dry.
Place . . . . fruits in large bowl.
Add . . . . . remaining ingredients, mixing well.
Chill . . . . . for 2 hours or longer.
Yield . . . . 2 quarts.

Irene Clements
University of Science and Arts of Oklahoma
Chickasha, Oklahoma

FRUIT DELIGHT

2 lg. bananas, sliced
1 tbsp. lemon juice
1 20-oz. can pineapple chunks
1 16-oz. can fruit cocktail, drained
1 can mandarin oranges, drained
1/2 c. angel flake coconut
1 sm. package instant lemon pudding mix

Combine . bananas and lemon juice in bowl.
Add . . . . . fruit.
Sprinkle . . with coconut and pudding mix, mixing gently.
Yield . . . . 6 servings.

Dorothy Scott
Ponca City H. S., Ponca City, Oklahoma

FRUIT MEDLEY

1 fresh pineapple
1 c. fresh banana slices
1 c. unpeeled fresh apple cubes
1 c. seeded fresh orange cubes
1 c. fresh cantaloupe pieces
Sugar to taste

Cut . . . . . . pineapple in half lengthwise.
Scoop . . . . out centers to form shells.
Cut . . . . . . pineapple pulp into chunks.
Combine . with remaining fruits and sugar in bowl, mixing well.
Spoon . . . into pineapple shells.

Samantha Forbes
Fort Smith, Arkansas

FRUIT-NUT CRISP

1 c. sugar
1 c. flour
1 tsp. soda
1/2 tsp. salt
1 egg
1 No. 2 can fruit cocktail, drained
3/4 c. packed light brown sugar
1/2 c. chopped pecans

Mix . . . . . sugar, flour, soda and salt together in bowl.
Add . . . . . egg, mixing well.
Fold . . . . . in fruit cocktail.
Pour . . . . . into buttered 9-inch square pan.
Sprinkle . . with brown sugar and pecans.
Bake . . . . . at 350 degrees for 30 minutes.

Anne Meeks
Beauregard H. S., Opelika, Alabama

FRUIT PIZZA

1 lg. package refrigerator sugar cookie
    dough, sliced
1 8-oz. package cream cheese, softened
1/3 c. sugar
Fresh fruits
1 6-oz. jar apricot preserves
1/4 c. lemon juice

Place . . . . cookies 1/2 inch apart on pizza pan.
Bake . . . . . using package directions; cool.
Beat . . . . . cream cheese and sugar in bowl until smooth.

Spread ... over cookie crust.
Treat .... fruit to prevent browning.
Arrange .. fruit over cream cheese layer.
Heat ..... preserves and lemon juice in saucepan, mixing well.
Pour ..... over fruit to glaze.
Chill ..... until serving time.
Yield .... 8-10 servings.

Linsae Snider
R. E. Lee H. S., Baytown, Texas

FRUITIE DESSERT

1 20-oz. can apricot pie filling
3 ripe bananas, sliced
1 pkg. frozen strawberries, thawed
1 pkg. frozen peaches, thawed

Combine . all ingredients in large serving bowl, tossing to mix.
Chill ..... until serving time.
Yield .... 8-10 servings.

Vera Sue Flournoy
New Boston Sr. H. S., New Boston, Texas

LO-CAL FRUIT WHIP

1 c. drained fruit
1/2 tsp. lemon juice
Dash of salt
2 egg whites, stiffly beaten

Puree ....first 3 ingredients in blender container.
Fold ..... into egg whites gently.
Spoon ... into sherbet glasses.
Chill ..... until serving time.
Yield .... 4 servings/40 calories each.

Edie Taylor
Ardmore, Alabama

MIXED FRUIT FLUFF

2 c. biscuit mix
Sugar
1/4 c. butter
2 3-oz. packages cream cheese, softened
1 tsp. vanilla extract
2 c. whipping cream, whipped
2 c. miniature marshmallows
4 c. mixed fresh fruit

Combine . biscuit mix and 2 tablespoons sugar in large bowl.
Cut ...... in butter until crumbly.

Press ..... into 9 x 9-inch baking pan.
Bake ..... at 375 degrees for 15 minutes.
Combine . cream cheese, 1 cup sugar and vanilla in bowl, mixing well.
Fold ..... whipped cream and marshmallows into cream cheese mixture.
Spread ... over crust.
Chill ..... for 8 hours or longer.
Serve .... squares topped with fruit.
Yield .... 9 servings.

Bernice Duncan
Gould Public School, Gould, Oklahoma

PLUM FRUITIE

1 29-oz. can purple plums, drained
1 29-oz. can unpeeled whole apricots, drained
1 20-oz. can pineapple spears, drained
2 tbsp. lemon juice
3/4 tsp. nutmeg
1/4 c. honey
1 tbsp. oil

Layer .... fruit in large baking dish.
Sprinkle .. with remaining ingredients.
Bake ..... at 300 degrees until heated through, basting occasionally.
Serve .... hot fruit over ice cream.

Carmen Ginsberg
Hayworth, Kentucky

QUICK FRUIT DESSERT

1 can crushed pineapple
1 can mandarin oranges
1 can fruit cocktail
1/2 c. coconut
2 bananas, sliced
1 tbsp. lemon juice
1 3-oz. package lemon pudding mix
1 angel food cake, sliced
Whipped cream

Combine . canned fruit and coconut in medium bowl.
Add ..... bananas and lemon juice, mixing well.
Stir ...... in pudding mix.
Spoon ... over angel food cake.
Top ..... with whipped cream.
Yield .... 8 servings.

Jeanne M. Lamb
North East H. S., North East, Pennsylvania

CREAM SAUCE FOR FRESH FRUIT

1 egg, beaten
2 tbsp. sugar
2 tbsp. vinegar
1 tbsp. butter
Melon balls
Fresh strawberries

Combine . first 3 ingredients in saucepan.
Cook . . . . over low heat until thickened, stirring constantly.
Add . . . . . butter, mixing well.
Combine . melon balls and strawberries.
Pour . . . . . sauce over top.

Rebecca S. Hughes
J. C. Booth Jr. H. S., Peachtree City, Georgia

BRANDIED FRUIT FONDUE

1/2 c. cream
1 lb. milk chocolate, grated
1 tbsp. instant coffee
2 tbsp. Brandy
1/8 tsp. cinnamon
Banana chunks
Apple slices
Pear slices
Pound cake cubes
Angel food cake cubes

Combine . cream and chocolate in fondue pot.
Cook . . . . over low heat until chocolate melts, stirring constantly.
Stir . . . . . . in instant coffee, Brandy and cinnamon.
Serve . . . . with remaining ingredients for dipping.

Sarah Smith
Albuquerque, New Mexico

COCONUT FRUIT FONDUE

Peaches, sliced
Cherries
Apples, sliced
Lemon juice
1 pkg. coconut-almond frosting mix
1/2 c. instant nonfat dry milk
4 tbsp. margarine
1/4 c. dry white wine

Brush . . . . cut fruits with lemon juice.
Combine . frosting mix and dry milk in saucepan.

Stir . . . . . . in 1/4 cup water.
Add . . . . . margarine.
Cook . . . . until margarine melts, stirring constantly.
Add . . . . . wine and enough water to make of dipping consistency.
Pour . . . . . into fondue pot.
Dip . . . . . . fruits into warm sauce.

Claire Sanders
Daytona Beach, Florida

ZESTY FRUIT FONDUE

1 3-oz. package cream cheese, cubed
3/4 c. grated Cheddar cheese
3/4 c. grated Swiss cheese
1 tbsp. flour
1/2 c. white wine
1/8 tsp. garlic salt
Dash of cayenne pepper
Fresh apple wedges
Fresh pear wedges

Mix . . . . . cheeses with flour in bowl.
Warm . . . . wine in fondue pot until bubbly.
Add . . . . . cheeses gradually, stirring until melted.
Stir . . . . . . in garlic salt and cayenne pepper.
Serve . . . . with fruit for dipping.

Hannah Winslow
Gulf Park, Florida

PEACHY CHOCOLATE FONDUE

1 6-oz. package chocolate bits
1 tbsp. grated orange rind
2 tbsp. butter
1/4 c. orange juice
1 29-oz. can cling peach slices, drained

Combine . first 4 ingredients in fondue pot.
Cook . . . . over low heat until chocolate melts, stirring constantly.
Dip . . . . . . peaches into warm sauce.

Sue Doerner
Winetka, Illinois

BRANDIED STRAWBERRY-ORANGE FONDUE

2 10-oz. packages frozen strawberries, thawed, crushed
1/4 c. cornstarch
2 tbsp. sugar

1/2 c. orange juice
2 3-oz. packages cream cheese, softened
1/4 c. Brandy
Pears, sliced
Peaches, sliced
Pineapple cubes

Place .... strawberries in saucepan.
Blend .... next 3 ingredients in small bowl.
Stir ...... into strawberries.
Cook .... until thick, stirring constantly.
Pour ..... into fondue pot over burner.
Add ..... cream cheese, stirring until melted.
Stir ...... in Brandy gradually.
Dip ...... fruit into warm sauce.
Yield .... 3 cups.

Tammy Naples
Oteka, Kansas

FANTASTIC STRAWBERRY FONDUE

2 tbsp. cornstarch
2 tbsp. sugar
2 10-oz. packages frozen strawberries,
    thawed, crushed
1 4-oz. carton whipped cream cheese,
    softened
1/4 c. Brandy
Pound cake cubes
Marshmallows
Waffles, cubed
Banana chunks
Angel food cake cubes

Blend .... cornstarch and sugar with a small
            amount of water in bowl.
Combine . with strawberries in saucepan,
            blending well.
Cook .... until thick, stirring constantly.
Blend .... in cream cheese and Brandy, stir-
            ring until well mixed.
Pour ..... into fondue pot over low heat.
Dip ...... remaining ingredients into straw-
            berry mixture with fondue forks.

Mary Carson
Selena, Ohio

FRESH TANGERINE BAKED DUMPLINGS

1 3/4 c. sugar
1/2 c. fresh tangerine juice
1 tbsp. fresh lemon juice

3 tbsp. butter
1/4 tsp. cinnamon
2 c. fresh tangerine segments, seeded
1 1/2 c. sifted flour
1 1/2 tsp. baking powder
1/2 tsp. salt
1/2 c. milk
Whipped cream (opt.)

Combine . 1 cup sugar, 1 cup water, juices, 1
            tablespoon butter, cinnamon and
            tangerine segments in saucepan.
Bring .... to a boil over medium heat, stirring
            frequently; reduce heat.
Simmer .. for 8 minutes.
Pour ..... into shallow 2-quart casserole.
Cream ... 2 tablespoons butter in small bowl.
Add ..... 3/4 cup sugar gradually, beating
            until fluffy.
Sift ...... flour, baking powder and salt
            together.
Add ..... to creamed mixture alternately
            with milk, blending until smooth
            after each addition.
Drop .... by tablespoonfuls into sauce.
Bake ..... at 375 degrees for 30 minutes.
Serve .... warm with whipped cream.
Yield .... 6-8 servings.

Photograph for this recipe below.

BLUEBERRY CREPES

2 c. sifted flour
1/2 tsp. salt
8 eggs, beaten
2 2/3 c. milk
1/4 c. melted butter
1 6-oz. can frozen orange juice concentrate
1/2 c. sugar
2 c. blueberries
1/2 c. slivered blanched almonds

Combine . flour and salt in large mixer bowl.
Add . . . . . eggs, milk and butter.
Beat . . . . . with electric mixer at medium speed until smooth.
Pour . . . . . 1/4 cup batter into oiled 6-inch crepe pan.
Cook . . . . quickly on each side.
Stack . . . . crepes on plate separating with paper towels; keep warm.
Combine . orange juice concentrate, sugar, blueberries, almonds and 1/2 cup water in saucepan.
Bring . . . . to a boil.
Simmer . . for 10 minutes.
Dip . . . . . . crepes in sauce 1 at a time with fork and spoon.
Remove . . and fold into quarters.
Serve . . . . with additional sauce over crepes.
Yield . . . . 8 servings.

Eliza Olson
Lord Tweedsmuir School
Surrey, British Columbia, Canada

ELEGANT STRAWBERRY CREPES

3/4 c. milk
3 eggs
1 1/3 c. unsifted all-purpose flour
3 tbsp. butter, melted
1 tbsp. rum or Brandy
4 tbsp. sugar
2 c. sweetened whipped cream
1 pt. fresh strawberries, sliced
1/4 c. orange juice
1 tsp. grated orange rind
2 20-oz. packages frozen sliced strawberries, thawed
1/4 c. warm orange liqueur

Combine . first 5 ingredients with 2 tablespoons sugar and 3/4 cup water in bowl, beating until smooth.

Chill . . . . . for 2 hours.
Pour . . . . . 3 tablespoons batter into hot crepe pan, tilting to cover evenly.
Brown . . . on both sides and stack crepes between waxed paper.
Combine . whipped cream with fresh strawberries in bowl, mixing gently.
Place . . . . 1 spoonful filling in center of each crepe, rolling to enclose filling.
Arrange . . on serving plates.
Combine . orange juice, orange rind and 2 tablespoons sugar with thawed strawberries in chafing dish, mixing well.
Heat . . . . . until bubbly.
Ignite . . . . warm orange liqueur, pouring over strawberry sauce.
Spoon . . . sauce over crepes.
Top . . . . . with additional whipped cream.

Lynette Bassinger
Chicago, Illinois

PEACH DUMPLINGS

Sugar
1 tbsp. cornstarch
Cinnamon
Nutmeg
Cloves
3 c. canned sliced peaches with syrup
1 tsp. lemon juice
1 c. biscuit mix
6 tbsp. milk

Blend . . . . 1/2 cup sugar, cornstarch, 1/2 teaspoon cinnamon and 1/4 teaspoon each nutmeg and cloves in saucepan with peaches and lemon juice.
Cook . . . . over medium heat until thick and clear, stirring constantly.
Combine . biscuit mix, 1 tablespoon sugar, 1/4 teaspoon cinnamon and dash each nutmeg and cloves with milk, stirring until moistened.
Drop . . . . batter by teaspoonfuls into bubbling sauce.
Cook . . . . for 5 minutes.
Cook . . . . tightly covered, for 10 to 12 minutes longer.
Serve . . . . warm with ice cream.
Yield . . . . 6 servings.

Linda Panter
Heppner Sr. H. S., Heppner, Oregon

Refrigerated
Desserts

PARTY APPLE CREAM

1 c. apple juice
1 3-oz. package raspberry gelatin
1 pt. vanilla ice cream, softened
2 c. applesauce

Bring .... apple juice to boiling point over medium heat in saucepan.
Dissolve .. gelatin in hot juice, stirring well.
Pour ..... into 1 1/2-quart bowl.
Blend .... in ice cream.
Fold ..... in 1 1/2 cups applesauce.
Chill ..... until thickened.
Spoon ... into serving bowls.
Garnish .. with remaining applesauce.

Brenda Brandt
Logan Middle School, La Crosse, Wisconsin

APRICOT SUPREME

1 lg. package waffle cream wafers
12 graham crackers
1/2 c. margarine, softened
1 c. confectioners' sugar
2 eggs, separated
2 c. dried apricots, cooked
1/2 pt. whipping cream, whipped

Crush .... wafers and graham crackers; mix well.
Spread ... half the crumbs in greased 8 x 13-inch pan.
Cream ... margarine and sugar in mixer bowl.
Add ..... egg yolks, beating well.
Beat ..... egg whites in small bowl until stiff.
Fold ..... into creamed mixture.
Spread ... over crumbs in pan.
Spoon ... apricots over creamed mixture.
Top ..... with whipped cream.
Sprinkle .. with remaining crumbs.
Chill ..... for several hours.
Yield .... 10-12 servings.

Correne Williford
Los Angeles, California

APRICOT SMOOTHY

1 20-oz. can apricots
1 pkg. lemon gelatin
1 pt. vanilla ice cream

Drain .... apricots, reserving juice.
Add ..... enough water to juice to measure 1 1/4 cups liquid.

Bring .... to a boil in saucepan.
Dissolve .. gelatin in apricot juice.
Add ..... ice cream, stirring until melted.
Chill ..... until thickened.
Puree .... apricots.
Fold ..... pureed apricots into thickened gelatin.
Spoon ... into dessert dishes.
Chill ..... until set.
Garnish .. with whipped cream.

Denise Lawford
Hannibal, Missouri

KATIE'S BANANA SPLIT CAKE

1 stick margarine, melted
3 c. graham cracker crumbs
1 lb. confectioners' sugar
2 sticks margarine, softened
2 eggs
5 bananas, sliced
1 lg. can pineapple chunks, drained
1 13-oz. carton Cool Whip
1 jar maraschino cherries, sliced
1/2 c. chopped nuts
1 can chocolate syrup (opt.)

Combine . first 2 ingredients in bowl, blending well.
Press ..... into jelly roll pan.
Bake ..... at 350 degrees for 10 minutes.
Cream ... confectioners' sugar, softened margarine and eggs in bowl until fluffy.
Spread ... over cooled crust.
Arrange .. bananas and pineapple over creamed layer.
Top ..... with Cool Whip.
Garnish .. with cherries and nuts.
Drizzle ... chocolate syrup over top.
Chill ..... for several hours.

Katie Johnston
Mohave Middle School
Scottsdale, Arizona

BANANA DAIQUIRI SOUFFLE

2 env. unflavored gelatin
1 c. sugar
1/8 tsp. salt
6 eggs, separated
1 tsp. grated lime rind
1/4 c. lime juice
1/4 c. rum
2 tbsp. banana liqueur (opt.)

4 med. bananas, diced
1 1/2 c. heavy cream, whipped
1 banana, sliced

Combine . gelatin, 1/2 cup sugar and salt in saucepan.
Blend .... in beaten egg yolks and 1 1/4 cups water.
Cook .... over low heat for 5 minutes or until thickened, stirring constantly.
Remove .. from heat.
Stir ...... in rind, juice, rum and liqueur.
Chill ..... until partially set, stirring occasionally.
Add ..... 1/2 cup sugar gradually to softly beaten egg whites, beating until stiff.
Fold ..... into gelatin mixture with diced bananas and 2/3 of the whipped cream.
Pour ..... into 1 1/2-quart souffle dish with 3-inch collar.
Chill ..... for 4 hours or until set.
Garnish .. with remaining whipped cream and sliced banana.
Yield .... 8-10 servings.

Photograph for this recipe on page 1.

BANANA SPLIT LAYER CAKE

3 c. graham cracker crumbs
1 1/2 sticks butter, melted
2 sticks butter, softened
2 c. confectioners' sugar
2 eggs
1 tsp. vanilla extract
6 bananas, sliced
1 20-oz. can crushed pineapple, drained
3 env. Dream Whip
1/2 c. crushed nuts
12 maraschino cherries

Combine . graham cracker crumbs and melted butter in bowl, mixing well.
Press ..... into bottom of 11 x 17-inch pan.
Cream ... softened butter with next 3 ingredients in bowl until smooth.
Spread ... over crust.
Arrange .. bananas over confectioners' sugar layer.
Spread ... pineapple over bananas.
Prepare ... Dream Whip using package directions.

Spread ... over pineapple.
Top ..... with nuts and cherries.
Chill ..... until serving time.

Candy L. Shafer
Maplewood H. S., Cortland, Ohio

ICEBOX BANANA PUDDING

3 c. cold milk
2 3-oz. packages instant vanilla pudding mix
1 can sweetened condensed milk
1 4 1/2-oz. carton Cool Whip
1 lg. package vanilla wafers
4 to 6 bananas, sliced

Combine . milk and pudding mix in large bowl.
Beat ..... for 2 minutes.
Stir ...... in sweetened condensed milk.
Fold ..... in Cool Whip.
Layer .... wafers, bananas and pudding mixture in 9 x 13-inch serving dish.
Chill ..... until serving time.

Betty Carman
Northwest H. S., Justin, Texas

BANANA SURPRISE

1 box white cake mix
1 sm. box strawberry gelatin
4 bananas, sliced
2 sm. packages vanilla instant pudding mix
1 9-oz. carton Cool Whip

Prepare ... cake mix using package directions.
Pour ..... into greased 13 x 19-inch baking pan.
Bake ..... using package directions.
Chill ..... in refrigerator.
Prepare ... gelatin using package directions; cool.
Punch .... holes in cake with fork.
Pour ..... gelatin over surface.
Chill ..... until firm.
Arrange .. bananas over top.
Prepare ... pudding mix using package directions.
Spread ... over bananas.
Top ..... with Cool Whip.
Yield .... 18 servings.

Johnnie T. Broome
Pierce County H. S., Blackshear, Georgia

COMPANY BANANA PUDDING

3 pkg. vanilla instant pudding mix
5 c. cold milk
1 8-oz. carton sour cream
1 9-oz. carton Cool Whip
Vanilla wafers
4 to 5 bananas, sliced

Prepare ... pudding mix according to package directions, using 5 cups milk.
Stir ...... in sour cream and Cool Whip.
Layer .... pudding mixture with vanilla wafers and bananas in large serving dish.
Chill ..... until serving time.
Yield .... 12-15 servings.

Susan Campbell
Independence School, Charlotte, North Carolina

BLUEBERRY-BANANA LOAF

2 c. graham cracker crumbs
1 c. confectioners' sugar
1 stick margarine, melted
1 8-oz. package cream cheese, softened
2 eggs
1 c. sugar
1 tsp. vanilla extract
3 bananas, sliced
1 can blueberry pie filling
2 c. Cool Whip

Combine . first 3 ingredients in bowl mixing well.
Press ..... into 9 x 13-inch baking pan.
Beat ..... cream cheese, eggs, sugar and vanilla together until well mixed.
Pour ..... over crumb mixture.
Bake ..... at 350 degrees for 20 minutes; cool.
Layer .... last 3 ingredients on cake in order given.
Chill ..... until serving time.

Betsy Mowery
White Oak Middle School, White Oak, Texas

BLUEBERRY-BUTTERSCOTCH RUSSE

1 pkg. butterscotch pudding and pie filling mix
2 c. milk
2 tsp. angostura aromatic bitters
2 tsp. grated orange rind
2 c. fresh blueberries

1 c. heavy cream, whipped
Ladyfingers

Prepare ... pudding according to package directions, using 2 cups milk.
Cook .... until mixture bubbles and thickens, stirring constantly.
Cool ..... covered, to room temperature.
Fold ..... in next 4 ingredients.
Line ..... sherbet glasses with ladyfingers.
Spoon ... blueberry mixture into center.
Garnish .. with additional blueberries.
Chill ..... until serving time.
Yield .... 6 servings.

Photograph for this recipe below.

BLUEBERRY PUDDING SUPREME

1/2 angel food cake, cut into bite-sized pieces
2 boxes French vanilla instant pudding mix
3 c. milk
1 8-oz. carton sour cream
1 can blueberry pie filling

Place .... cake in large glass serving dish.
Prepare ... pudding mix according to package directions, using 3 cups milk.
Blend .... in sour cream.
Pour ..... over cake.
Stir ...... in pie filling.
Chill ..... until serving time.
Yield .... 10 servings.

Lona T. Smith
Saint Joseph's Academy, Baton Rouge, Louisiana

BLUEBERRY TART

1 c. margarine
2 c. flour
1/2 c. packed brown sugar
1 c. chopped pecans
8 oz. cream cheese, softened
1 c. confectioners' sugar
1 tsp. vanilla extract
1 lg. carton frozen whipped topping, thawed
1 can blueberry pie filling

Cut . . . . . . margarine into flour in large bowl until crumbly.
Add . . . . . brown sugar and pecans, mixing well.
Press . . . . . into bottom of 9 x 13-inch glass baking dish.
Bake . . . . . at 350 degrees for 10 to 12 minutes.
Beat . . . . . cream cheese, confectioners' sugar and vanilla in large bowl until smooth.
Fold . . . . . in whipped topping.
Pour . . . . . into cooled crust.
Spread . . . with pie filling.
Chill . . . . . for 12 hours.
Yield . . . . 10-12 servings.

Mary Ann Hoffman
Clear Lake H. S. Annex, Houston, Texas

BLUEBERRY TORTE

12 graham crackers, crushed
1 c. sugar
1/2 c. margarine, melted
8 oz. cream cheese, softened
2 eggs
2 cans blueberry pie filling

Combine . graham cracker crumbs, 1/2 cup sugar and margarine in bowl, mixing well.
Press . . . . . into 9 x 13-inch baking pan.
Beat . . . . . cream cheese, eggs and 1/2 cup sugar in bowl until smooth.
Spread . . . over crust.
Bake . . . . . at 350 degrees for 15 minutes.
Spread . . . pie filling over top of cooled crust.
Chill . . . . . overnight.
Serve . . . . with whipped cream.
Yield . . . . 15-18 servings.

Doris L. Oitzman
Victor Valley Sr. H. S., Victorville, California

BLUEBERRY REFRIGERATOR DESSERT

1 pkg. vanilla cream cookies, crushed
1/2 c. butter, softened
1 c. confectioners' sugar
2 egg yolks
2 egg whites, stiffly beaten
1 can blueberry pie filling
1 c. chopped walnuts
1 c. whipped cream

Press . . . . . 2/3 of the cookie crumbs into greased 9 x 13-inch serving dish.
Cream . . . butter, confectioners' sugar and egg yolks together in large bowl.
Fold . . . . . in egg whites.
Drop . . . . by teaspoonfuls over crumbs.
Spread . . . pie filling over top.
Sprinkle . . with walnuts.
Top . . . . . with whipped cream.
Sprinkle . . with remaining crumbs.
Chill . . . . . for 12 hours.

Marcy McPhee
Millcreek Jr. H. S., Bountiful, Utah

BUTTERSCOTCH SUPREME

1 stick margarine, softened
1 c. cake flour
1 1/2 c. chopped nuts
1 8-oz. package cream cheese, softened
1 c. confectioners' sugar
1 1/2 c. Cool Whip
2 pkg. instant butterscotch pudding mix
3 c. milk

Cream . . . margarine and flour together in bowl.
Mix . . . . . in 1 cup nuts.
Press . . . . . into 9 x 13-inch baking dish.
Bake . . . . . at 350 degrees for 15 minutes.
Blend . . . . cream cheese and confectioners' sugar together in bowl.
Fold . . . . . in 1 cup Cool Whip.
Spread . . . over cooled crust.
Beat . . . . . pudding mix with milk in bowl until thick.
Spread . . . over cream cheese layer.
Top . . . . . with remaining Cool Whip.
Sprinkle . . with remaining nuts.
Chill . . . . . in refrigerator.

Mrs. Carolyn L. Kelly
Bainbridge H. S., Bainbridge, Georgia

COCONUT-BUTTERSCOTCH DESSERT

1 c. flour
1/2 c. butter
1/2 c. chopped walnuts
1 8-oz. package cream cheese, softened
1 c. confectioners' sugar
2 c. Cool Whip
1 pkg. instant coconut cream pudding mix
1 pkg. instant butterscotch pudding mix
3 c. milk
1/2 c. toasted coconut

Blend .... flour and butter together in bowl.
Pat ...... into bottom of 9 x 13-inch baking pan.
Sprinkle .. with walnuts.
Bake ..... at 350 degrees for 15 to 20 minutes.
Blend .... cream cheese, confectioners' sugar and 1 cup Cool Whip in bowl.
Spread ... over cooled crust.
Beat ..... pudding mixes with milk in bowl for 2 minutes.
Spread ... over cream cheese layer.
Top ..... with remaining Cool Whip.
Sprinkle .. with coconut.
Chill ..... in refrigerator.
Yield .... 15 servings.

Joan Jacobsen
Boyden-Hull Community H. S., Hull, Iowa

BUTTERSCOTCH ICEBOX DESSERT

1 c. flour
1 stick margarine, softened
Chopped nuts
1 8-oz. package cream cheese, softened
1 c. confectioners' sugar
1 lg. container Cool Whip
1 lg. package instant butterscotch pudding mix
3 c. milk

Combine . first 2 ingredients with 1 cup nuts in bowl, mixing well.
Press ..... into 9 x 13-inch baking dish.
Bake ..... at 350 degrees for 20 minutes.
Mix ..... cream cheese, confectioners' sugar and 1/2 of the Cool Whip in large bowl.
Spread ... over cooled crust.

Prepare ... pudding mix according to package directions using 3 cups milk.
Spread ... over cream cheese layer.
Cover .... with remaining Cool Whip.
Sprinkle .. with chopped nuts.
Chill ..... until serving time.
Yield .... 16 servings.

Sue Lawson
Haworth H. S., Haworth, Oklahoma

CANTALOUPE TREAT

1 20-oz. can crushed pineapple
1 pkg. lime gelatin
1 pt. vanilla ice cream
3 cantaloupes, cut in half

Drain .... pineapple, reserving juice.
Add ..... enough water to juice to measure 1 1/4 cups liquid.
Bring .... to a boil in large saucepan.
Add ..... gelatin, stirring until dissolved.
Blend .... ice cream into gelatin mixture until smooth.
Chill ..... until partially set.
Fold ..... in 1 cup pineapple.
Spoon .... gelatin mixture into cantaloupe cavities.
Chill ..... for 3 hours or until firm.
Cut ...... into wedges just before serving.
Yield .... 10-12 servings.

Deloras Love
Winter Haven, Florida

CARAMEL CRUNCH ANGEL CAKE

2/3 c. sugar
1 10-in. angel food cake
1 lg. container Cool Whip
1/2 c. slivered almonds

Melt ..... sugar in heavy saucepan over medium heat, stirring constantly.
Cook .... until caramel colored.
Spread ... thinly on greased cookie sheet.
Cool ..... until hard.
Crush .... with mallet.
Cut ...... cake into 2 layers.
Spread ... Cool Whip over bottom layer.
Sprinkle .. with half the caramel sugar.
Top ..... with remaining layer.
Frost .... with remaining Cool Whip.
Sprinkle .. with remaining caramel sugar and almonds.

Chill . . . . . until serving time.
Yield . . . . 12-16 servings.

Ella Jo Adams
Allen H. S., Allen, Texas

MAVIE'S CARAMEL MALLOW

1 1/2 c. crushed graham crackers
1/4 c. melted butter
1 tbsp. sugar
16 caramels
1/2 c. milk
24 lg. marshmallows
1 c. whipping cream, whipped
1/4 c. chopped pecans

Combine . cracker crumbs, butter and sugar in mixing bowl.
Reserve . . 1/4 cup for topping.
Press . . . . . remaining crumb mixture into 8 x 12-inch pan.
Melt . . . . . caramels in milk in double boiler.
Add . . . . . marshmallows, mixing well.
Heat . . . . . until melted; chill.
Fold . . . . . in whipped cream and pecans.
Pour . . . . . into crust.
Sprinkle . . with reserved crumbs.
Chill . . . . . for 6 hours or overnight.
Yield . . . . 12 servings.

Mavie Smith
Sacramento, California

FRESH CHERRY PARFAIT

2 c. fresh sweet cherries, halved
Sugar
1/4 c. fresh lemon juice
1 env. unflavored gelatin
3 eggs, separated
1/4 tsp. salt

Combine . 1 cup cherries, 1/4 cup sugar, lemon juice and 2 tablespoons water in saucepan. Cover.
Simmer . . over low heat for 5 minutes.
Drain . . . . reserving 3/4 cup juice and cherries.
Chill . . . . . in refrigerator.
Soften . . . gelatin in 1/4 cup cold water.
Combine . egg yolks and 1/3 cup sugar in top of double boiler.
Stir . . . . . . in salt and chilled cherry juice.
Cook . . . . over hot water until mixture coats metal spoon, stirring constantly.

Remove . . from heat.
Add . . . . . gelatin, mixing well.
Chill . . . . . until partially set.
Fold . . . . . in chilled cherries.
Beat . . . . . egg whites in bowl until soft peaks form.
Add . . . . . 1/4 cup sugar gradually, beating until stiff.
Fold . . . . . into gelatin mixture.
Chill . . . . . until firm.
Alternate . layers of gelatin mixture and remaining 1 cup cherries in parfait glasses, beginning and ending with gelatin mixture.
Garnish . . with whipped cream.
Yield . . . . 6 servings.

Photograph for this recipe below.

CHERRY DELIGHT

1 5-oz. package instant vanilla pudding mix
2 1/2 c. whipping cream, whipped
1 sm. box graham crackers
1 lg. can cherry pie filling

Prepare . . . pudding using package directions.
Fold . . . . . in half the whipped cream.
Arrange . . layer of crackers in bottom of 9 x 13-inch pan.
Pour . . . . . in half the pudding mixture.
Repeat . . . layers ending with crackers.
Spread . . . pie filling over top.
Spoon . . . remaining whipped cream over pie filling.
Yield . . . . 12-16 servings.

Edith B. Carroll
Northwest Intermediate School, Salt Lake City, Utah

CHERRIES IN THE SNOW

1 lg. container Cool Whip
1 angel food cake, cubed
1 can cherry pie filling

Combine . Cool Whip and cake cubes in large bowl, mixing well.
Spread ... in 9 x 13-inch pan.
Top ..... with pie filling.
Chill .... until serving time.
Yield .... 20 squares.

Janet Grant
Chandler H. S., Chandler, Arizona

CHERRIES-ON-A-CLOUD

3 egg whites
1/4 tsp. cream of tartar
1 1/4 c. sugar
1 3-oz. package cream cheese, softened
1/2 tsp. vanilla extract
1 c. whipping cream, whipped
1 c. miniature marshmallows
1 tsp. lemon juice
1 21-oz. can cherry pie filling

Beat ..... egg whites and cream of tartar in large mixer bowl until soft peaks form.
Add ..... 3/4 cup sugar gradually, beating until stiff.
Shape .... meringue into 9-inch circles on foil-lined baking sheet, building up sides.
Bake ..... at 275 degrees for 1 1/2 hours.
Turn ..... off oven, leaving meringue in oven with door closed for 1 hour.
Combine . cream cheese, 1/2 cup sugar and vanilla in mixer bowl, beating until smooth.
Fold ..... whipped cream and marshmallows into cream cheese mixture.
Spoon ... into meringue shells.
Chill ..... for 12 hours or longer.
Stir ...... lemon juice into pie filling.
Spoon ... over cream cheese filling.
Cut ...... into wedges to serve.
Yield .... 8 servings.

Marlys Hauck-Fenner
Freeman Jr.-Sr. H. S., Freeman, South Dakota

CHERRY-RICE MOLD

1 16-oz. can pitted sweet cherries
3 c. cooked rice
3 c. milk
2 tbsp. grated orange rind
2/3 c. sugar
1 tbsp. unflavored gelatin
1 tsp. vanilla extract
1 tsp. butter flavoring (opt.)
2 egg whites, stiffly beaten
1 tbsp. cornstarch

Drain .... cherries, reserving juice.
Combine . next 4 ingredients in saucepan.
Cook .... over medium heat for 20 to 25 minutes or until thick and creamy, stirring occasionally.
Soften ... gelatin in 2 tablespoons cold water in small bowl.
Stir ...... into rice mixture.
Add ..... vanilla, butter flavoring and cherries, mixing well.
Chill ..... until partially set.
Fold ..... in stiffly beaten egg whites.
Turn ..... into 2-quart mold.
Chill ..... until set.
Unmold .. onto serving plate.
Blend .... reserved cherry juice with cornstarch in small saucepan.
Cook .... until slightly thickened, stirring constantly.
Spoon ... cooled sauce over Cherry-Rice Mold.
Yield .... 10-12 servings.

Ruby Boyd
Denver, Colorado

AMERICANIZED FRENCH MOUSSE

4 eggs, separated
1 12-oz. package chocolate chips, melted
1 tsp. vanilla extract
1 tbsp. sugar
1 c. heavy cream, whipped
1 lg. angel food cake, sliced thin
Chopped nuts

Beat ..... egg yolks with 1 tablespoon water in bowl.
Combine . with chocolate chips in double boiler, stirring vigorously.

Beat . . . . . egg whites in large bowl until stiff peaks form.
Pour . . . . . chocolate mixture over egg whites.
Fold . . . . . vanilla and sugar into whipped cream.
Combine . whipped cream and chocolate mixtures.
Place . . . . layer of angel food cake in 9 x 13-inch dish.
Pour . . . . . layer of chocolate mousse over cake.
Sprinkle . . with nuts.
Layer . . . . remainder of cake and mousse.
Sprinkle . . with nuts.
Chill . . . . . until serving time.

Gladys Fletcher
Heritage H. S., Maryville, Tennessee

BARBARA'S BEST PUDDING

1/4 c. confectioners' sugar
1 c. flour
1/8 tsp. salt
1/2 c. butter, softened
1/2 c. chopped pecans
1 8-oz. package cream cheese, softened
1/2 tsp. Creme de Menthe
1 lg. container Cool Whip
1 lg. box chocolate instant pudding mix
1 lg. box vanilla instant pudding mix

Combine . first 5 ingredients in bowl, mixing well.
Press . . . . . into 7 x 11-inch baking dish.
Bake . . . . . at 350 degrees for 25 minutes.
Blend . . . . cream cheese, Creme de Menthe and half the Cool Whip together in bowl.
Spread . . . over cooled crust.
Prepare . . . chocolate pudding using package directions.
Spread . . . over cream cheese layer.
Prepare . . . vanilla pudding using package directions.
Spread . . . over chocolate layer.
Top . . . . . with remaining Cool Whip.
Sprinkle . . with chocolate shavings.
Chill . . . . . until serving time.
Yield . . . . 12-15 servings.

Mrs. Barbara Tongate
Brownwood Jr. H. S., Brownwood, Texas

CHOCOLATE ANGEL FOOD CAKE DESSERT

1/2 chocolate angel food cake
1 c. sugar
2 c. milk
4 egg yolks, beaten
1 pt. whipping cream, whipped
4 egg whites, stiffly beaten
Vanilla extract to taste

Tear . . . . . cake into pieces.
Place . . . . in glass serving dish.
Blend . . . . sugar, milk and egg yolks in saucepan.
Cook . . . . over medium heat until mixture coats metal spoon, stirring constantly.
Fold . . . . . in whipped cream, egg whites and vanilla.
Pour . . . . . over cake pieces.
Chill . . . . . until firm.

JoAnn Bauer
Hurst Jr. H. S., Hurst, Texas

CHOCOLATE DELIGHT

1 c. flour
1 c. finely chopped nuts
1 stick margarine, melted
11 oz. cream cheese, softened
1 c. confectioners' sugar
1 lg. container Cool Whip
2 pkg. chocolate instant pudding mix
3 c. milk

Combine . first 3 ingredients in bowl, mixing well.
Press . . . . . into 9 x 13-inch baking dish.
Bake . . . . . at 300 degrees for 15 minutes.
Blend . . . . cream cheese, confectioners' sugar and 1 cup whipped topping in bowl.
Spread . . . over cooled crust.
Mix . . . . . instant pudding mix with milk in bowl until thickened.
Spread . . . over cream cheese layer.
Top . . . . . with remaining whipped topping.
Chill . . . . . overnight.
Yield . . . . 4-6 servings.

Thelma Lee
Seneca Sr. H. S., Seneca, South Carolina

BARBARA'S CHOCOLATE ECLAIR CAKE

Graham crackers
2 sm. boxes vanilla instant pudding mix
3 1/2 c. milk
1 8-oz. carton Cool Whip
2 sq. unsweetened chocolate
3 tbsp. margarine
1 1/2 to 2 c. confectioners' sugar
1 tsp. vanilla extract
3 tbsp. milk
3 tbsp. cornstarch

Line ..... bottom and sides of 9 x 13-inch pan with graham crackers.
Combine . pudding mix and milk in large bowl, mixing well.
Fold ..... in Cool Whip.
Pour ..... 1/2 of the mixture over graham crackers.
Top ..... with layer of graham crackers.
Pour ..... remaining Cool Whip mixture on second layer.
Top ..... with graham crackers.
Melt ..... chocolate and margarine in top of double boiler.
Add ..... remaining ingredients, stirring until well blended.
Pour ..... over top of cake.
Chill ..... for several hours before serving.

Barbara Gaylor
Home Economics Education Unit, Michigan Dept. of
Education, Vocational-Technical Education Service
Lansing, Michigan

CALIFORNIA CHOCOLATE ECLAIR CAKE

Butter
1 box graham crackers
1 lg. box French vanilla instant pudding mix
Milk
9 oz. Cool Whip
2 sq. unsweetened chocolate
2 tsp. light corn syrup
1 tbsp. vanilla extract
1 1/2 c. confectioners' sugar

Line ..... buttered 9 x 13-inch pan with graham crackers.
Prepare ... pudding according to package directions, using 3 1/4 cups milk.

Blend .... in Cool Whip.
Spread ... half the pudding mix over crackers.
Repeat ... layers, ending with graham crackers.
Melt ..... 3 tablespoons butter and chocolate together in saucepan.
Add ..... remaining ingredients and 3 tablespoons milk, mixing well.
Spread ... over crackers.
Chill ..... overnight.

Jennifer Hemstreet
Santa Maria H. S., Santa Maria, California

JOANNE'S CHOCOLATE ECLAIR CAKE

2 pkg. French vanilla pudding mix
1 c. heavy cream
Milk
8 oz. Cool Whip
1 box graham crackers
2 pkg. liquid chocolate
3 tbsp. butter, softened
3 tbsp. vanilla extract
2 tbsp. light corn syrup
1 1/2 c. sifted confectioners' sugar

Combine . pudding mix, cream and 2 cups milk in bowl, beating until smooth.
Fold ..... in Cool Whip.
Place .... layer of graham crackers on bottom of 9 x 13-inch pan.
Pour ..... half the pudding over crackers.
Repeat ... layers, ending with crackers.
Combine . remaining ingredients and 3 tablespoons milk in bowl, beating until smooth.
Spread ... over crackers.
Chill ..... for 1 to 2 hours.

Joanne M. Wooley
F. D. Roosevelt H. S., Hyde Park, New York

EASY ECLAIR CAKE

1 box graham crackers
2 sm. packages French vanilla instant pudding mix
3 1/2 c. milk
1 8-oz. carton Cool Whip

Line ..... bottom of buttered 9 x 13-inch dish with graham crackers.
Mix ..... pudding mix with milk in bowl.

Beat ..... in Cool Whip.
Alternate . layers of pudding mixture and graham crackers, ending with crackers.
Chill ..... for 2 hours or longer.
Frost .... with additional Cool Whip.
Yield .... 12 servings.

Barbara P. Witten
Richlands Middle School, Richlands, Virginia

CHOCOLATE ICEBOX DESSERT

2 sq. bitter chocolate
Sugar
1 c. evaporated milk
4 eggs, separated
2 tbsp. butter
1 tsp. vanilla extract
1 c. walnuts
48 chocolate wafers, crushed

Melt ..... chocolate in double boiler.
Add ..... 1 cup sugar, evaporated milk, egg yolks and 1/4 cup water, mixing well.
Cook .... until thick and smooth.
Add ..... butter, mixing well.
Stir ...... vanilla and walnuts into slightly cooled chocolate mixture.
Cool ..... completely.
Beat ..... egg whites and 2 tablespoons sugar in bowl until stiff.
Fold ..... into chocolate mixture.
Place .... half the crumbs in 9 x 13-inch dish lined with waxed paper.
Pour ..... chocolate mixture over top.
Top ..... with remaining crumbs.
Garnish .. with whipped cream.

Carolyn F. Chipman
Alta H. S., Sandy, Utah

CHOCOLATE-MINT DREAM

2 c. milk
1 sq. unsweetened chocolate
1 tbsp. unflavored gelatin
Sugar
1/4 tsp. salt
1/2 tsp. vanilla extract
8 marshmallows, cut into sm. pieces
1 egg white, stiffly beaten
1 drop of oil of peppermint
Green food coloring

Scald .... milk and chocolate in double boiler.
Beat ..... until smooth.
Soften ... gelatin in 2 tablespoons cold water in small bowl.
Add ..... 3 tablespoons sugar, salt and gelatin to chocolate mixture, stirring until gelatin dissolves.
Add ..... vanilla.
Pour ..... into mold.
Chill ..... until firm.
Boil ..... 1/2 cup sugar and 1/4 cup water in saucepan for 5 minutes.
Add ..... marshmallows, stirring until melted.
Add ..... to egg white gradually, beating constantly.
Stir ...... in oil of peppermint and desired amount of food coloring.
Serve .... with molded gelatin.

Ester Morgan
Detroit, Michigan

CHOCOLATE MOUSSE

4 egg yolks
3/4 c. sugar
1/4 c. rum
6 oz. chocolate chips, melted
1/4 c. coffee
3/4 c. butter, softened
Grated orange rind (opt.)
1 c. whipping cream, whipped

Combine . egg yolks and sugar in top of double boiler.
Beat ..... until light and fluffy.
Add ..... rum.
Cook .... until hot but not boiling, beating constantly.
Fill ...... bottom of double boiler with cold water.
Beat ..... mixture until consistency of mayonnaise.
Add ..... chocolate, coffee and butter.
Beat ..... until well blended.
Blend .... orange rind into whipped cream.
Fold ..... whipped cream mixture into chocolate mixture.
Pour ..... into 1 1/2-quart mold.
Chill ..... covered, overnight.

Relda Epperson Blythe
Olive Vista Jr. H. S., Sylmar, California

CHOCOLATE-PEANUT SOUFFLE

8 tbsp. sugar
1 env. unflavored gelatin
1/4 tsp. salt
4 sq. semisweet chocolate, melted
1 c. milk
5 eggs, separated
1/4 c. rum
1 tsp. vanilla extract
1/4 c. coarsely chopped peanuts
2 c. heavy cream

Stir . . . . . . 6 tablespoons sugar, gelatin and salt into chocolate in saucepan.
Add . . . . . milk gradually, stirring until smooth.
Beat . . . . . egg yolks slightly.
Add . . . . . to chocolate mixture.
Cook . . . . over low heat until mixture boils, stirring constantly.
Remove . . from heat.
Stir . . . . . . in rum, vanilla and 1/4 cup peanuts.
Chill . . . . . until slightly thickened, stirring occasionally.
Beat . . . . . egg whites until soft peaks form.
Whip . . . . 1 cup heavy cream.
Fold . . . . . egg whites and whipped cream into chocolate mixture.
Attach . . . 2-inch foil collar around top of 3-cup souffle dish.
Pour . . . . . in chocolate mixture.
Chill . . . . . until firm.
Whip . . . . 1 cup cream and 2 tablespoons sugar together in bowl.
Decorate . souffle with whipped cream.
Garnish . . with finely chopped peanuts.
Yield . . . . 6-8 servings.

Photograph for this recipe above.

COOL AND CREAMY CHOCOLATE

2 c. confectioners' sugar
4 tbsp. cocoa
1/4 tsp. salt
3/4 c. butter, softened
2 eggs, separated
1 c. chopped nuts
1 1/2 tsp. vanilla extract
1 3/4 c. vanilla wafer crumbs

Sift . . . . . . first 3 ingredients together.
Cream . . . butter in bowl.
Add . . . . . sifted dry ingredients and egg yolks, mixing well.
Stir . . . . . . in nuts and vanilla.
Fold . . . . . in stiffly beaten egg whites.
Line . . . . . 7 x 9-inch pan with waxed paper.
Spread . . . 2/3 of the crumbs in bottom of pan.
Pour . . . . . in chocolate mixture.
Sprinkle . . with remaining crumbs.
Chill . . . . . for 12 hours.
Cut . . . . . . into squares.

Alice Nash
Longmont, Colorado

REFRIGERATOR CHOCOLATE CAKE

3/4 c. chopped walnuts
1 stick margarine, softened
1 c. flour
1 8-oz. package cream cheese, softened
1 lg. carton Cool Whip
1 c. confectioners' sugar
2 1/2 c. milk
1 3-oz. package vanilla instant pudding mix
1 3-oz. package chocolate instant pudding mix
1 Hershey bar, grated

Combine . first 3 ingredients in mixing bowl, blending well.
Press . . . . . into bottom of 9 x 12-inch baking pan.
Bake . . . . . at 350 degrees for 20 minutes or until light brown.
Beat . . . . . cream cheese, 1 cup Cool Whip and confectioners' sugar in mixer bowl until light and fluffy.
Spread . . . on cooled crust.
Combine . milk and pudding mixes in 1-quart jar.

Shake . . . . until smooth.
Spread . . . on cream cheese layer.
Top . . . . . with remaining Cool Whip.
Sprinkle . . grated Hershey bar over top.
Chill . . . . . until serving time.
Yield . . . . 15 servings.

Denise Potter
Alta H. S., Sandy, Utah

PEPPERMINT CHOCOLATE CUPS

1 1/2 c. semisweet chocolate chips
2 tbsp. shortening
1 env. unflavored gelatin
1/2 c. sugar
1/8 tsp. salt
2 eggs, separated
1 1/4 c. milk
1/2 tsp. peppermint extract
3 to 4 drops of red food coloring
1 c. heavy cream, whipped
1 sq. semisweet chocolate, melted

Melt . . . . . first 2 ingredients in double boiler over hot water, blending well.
Coat . . . . . insides of paper-lined muffin cups evenly with chocolate mixture.
Combine . gelatin, 1/4 cup sugar and salt in saucepan.
Beat . . . . . egg yolks and milk together in bowl.
Stir . . . . . . into gelatin mixture.
Cook . . . . over low heat for 5 minutes until slightly thickened, stirring constantly.
Remove . . from heat.
Stir . . . . . . in flavoring and food coloring.
Chill . . . . . until partially set, stirring occasionally.
Add . . . . . 1/4 cup sugar gradually to softly beaten egg whites, beating until stiff.
Fold . . . . . stiffly beaten egg whites and whipped cream into gelatin mixture.
Fill . . . . . . peeled chocolate cups.
Spread . . . melted chocolate into 6-inch square on foil-covered cookie sheet.
Chill . . . . . until firm.
Cut . . . . . . into desired shapes, placing on filled chocolate cups.

Photograph for this recipe on page 1.

RIBBON PIE

1 c. flour
2 tsp. brown sugar
1/2 c. butter, melted
1/2 c. chopped nuts
1 lg. carton Cool Whip
1 c. confectioners' sugar
1 8-oz. package cream cheese, softened
2 pkg. chocolate instant pudding mix
3 c. milk

Combine . first 4 ingredients in bowl, mixing well.
Press . . . . . into 9 x 13-inch baking pan.
Bake . . . . . at 350 degrees for 15 minutes.
Beat . . . . . half the Cool Whip, confectioners' sugar and cream cheese in large bowl until well blended.
Spread . . . over cooled crust.
Combine . pudding mix and milk in bowl, mixing well.
Spread . . . over cream cheese layer.
Top . . . . . with remaining Cool Whip.
Chill . . . . . for several hours.
Yield . . . . 15 servings.

Joyce Mann
Harmony Grove H. S., Camden, Arkansas

COFFEE DATER

1 lb. marshmallows
1 c. hot strong coffee
1 c. chopped dates
1/2 c. chopped pecans
1 sm. bottle of maraschino cherries, drained, sliced
2 c. whipped cream
1 c. graham cracker crumbs

Melt . . . . . marshmallows and coffee in double boiler; cool.
Add . . . . . dates, pecans and cherries, mixing well.
Fold . . . . . in whipped cream.
Sprinkle . . half the cracker crumbs in greased pan.
Spread . . . date mixture over crumbs.
Sprinkle . . with remaining crumbs.
Chill . . . . . overnight or until set.
Yield . . . . 12-15 servings.

Edythe Metz
Colorado Springs, Colorado

COFFEE MALLOW

1 c. hot coffee
24 marshmallows
1 c. whipped cream
1 c. chopped nuts
18 graham crackers, crushed

Pour ..... coffee over marshmallows in large saucepan.
Cook .... over low heat until marshmallows melt, stirring constantly.
Chill ..... until thickened.
Fold ..... in whipped cream and nuts.
Spread ... half the crumbs in 8 x 8-inch pan.
Pour ..... marshmallow mixture over crumbs.
Top ..... with remaining crumbs.
Chill ..... until firm.
Yield .... 6 servings.

Stevie Welch
El Paso, Texas

CRUNCHY CRANBERRIES

2 c. sugar
2 1/2 tbsp. unflavored gelatin
4 c. cranberries, ground
1 med. orange with rind, chopped
1 c. chopped celery
1 c. chopped nuts
1 c. yogurt, whipped

Cook .... sugar and 1 cup water in saucepan to make thin syrup.
Soften ... gelatin in 1/2 cup cold water.
Add ..... to syrup, stirring until dissolved.
Add ..... remaining ingredients except yogurt, mixing well.
Pour ..... into mold.
Chill .... until firm.
Serve .... with yogurt.
Yield .... 16 servings.

Jerri Dickson
Norman, Oklahoma

DAIQUIRI DESSERT

1 env. unflavored gelatin
1/2 c. lime juice
3 eggs, separated
1/2 tsp. salt
1 1/3 c. sugar
1 tbsp. grated lime rind
3 drops of green food coloring
1/3 c. light rum

Combine . gelatin, lime juice, egg yolks, salt, 2/3 cup sugar and 1/2 cup cold water in double boiler pan.
Cook .... over simmering water until mixture coats spoon.
Add ..... lime rind and food coloring to slightly cooled custard.
Cool ..... to room temperature.
Stir ...... in rum.
Chill .... until partially set.
Beat ..... egg whites in bowl until soft peaks form.
Add ..... remaining 2/3 cup sugar by tablespoonfuls, beating until stiff.
Fold ..... in gelatin mixture.
Spoon ... into dessert dishes.
Chill ..... until firm.

Tessie Derberville
Salem, North Carolina

EASY-DOES-IT DESSERT

1 pkg. strawberry gelatin
1 c. vanilla wafer crumbs
1 pkg. vanilla pudding and pie filling mix
2 c. sliced bananas

Prepare ... gelatin using package directions.
Chill ..... until partially set.
Spread ... half the wafer crumbs in 8-inch square pan.
Prepare ... pudding and pie filling mix using package directions.
Pour ..... hot mixture over crumbs.
Arrange .. half the bananas over pudding.
Top ..... with remaining crumbs; cool.
Spoon ... gelatin over top.
Press ..... remaining bananas into gelatin to cover.
Chill ..... until firm.

Carolyn VanAmberg
Maurice-Orange City Community School
Orange City, Iowa

DIET FRUIT TREAT

1 16-oz. can dietetic fruit salad
1 env. unflavored gelatin
Juice of 1 lemon
1 10-oz. can low-calorie ginger ale

2 oranges, sectioned
1 banana, diced

Drain .... fruit salad, reserving juice.
Soften ... gelatin in reserved juice in saucepan.
Heat ..... until dissolved; cool.
Add ..... lemon juice and ginger ale, blending well.
Chill ..... until thickened.
Combine . all fruits in large bowl, mixing gently.
Fold ..... in gelatin mixture.
Spoon ... into mold.
Chill ..... until firm.
Yield .... 6 servings.

Emma Owens
Ames, Iowa

FOUR-FOLD DELIGHT

1 1/2 sticks margarine, melted
1 c. chopped pecans
1 1/2 c. flour
8 oz. cream cheese, softened
1 c. confectioners' sugar
3 tsp. vanilla extract
1 lg. carton Cool Whip
2 sm. packages instant pudding mix

Combine . first 3 ingredients in bowl, mixing well.
Press ..... into 9 x 13-inch baking dish.
Bake ..... at 350 degrees for 30 minutes.
Beat ..... cream cheese with confectioners' sugar, vanilla and half the Cool Whip in bowl.
Spread ... over cooled crust.
Prepare ... instant pudding using package directions.
Spread ... over cream cheese layer.
Top ..... with remaining Cool Whip.
Chill ..... in refrigerator.

Peggy White
Califf Middle School, Gray, Georgia

LOW-CAL GRASSHOPPER SANDWICHES

1 1/2 c. low-calorie whipped topping
1 oz. Creme de Menthe
1 oz. white Creme de Cacao
Unfrosted chocolate wafers

Mix ..... toppi
          Creme
Spread ... small
Repeat ... until a
Chill ..... in refr

HAZELNUT DREAM

1/2 c. peeled hazelnuts, grated
1 c. milk
2 egg yolks, beaten
1/4 c. sugar
1 tsp. vanilla extract
1/2 env. unflavored gelatin
1/2 c. heavy cream, whipped

Combine . hazelnuts with milk, egg yolks, sugar and vanilla in double boiler.
Cook .... over medium heat until thickened, stirring constantly.
Remove .. from heat.
Soften ... gelatin in 1/4 cup cold water.
Stir ...... into hazelnut mixture.
Chill ..... until thickened.
Fold ..... in whipped cream.
Pour ..... into serving dishes.
Chill ..... until firm.
Garnish .. with additional whipped cream.

Geneva Barnhill
Bloomington, Illinois

LEMON-COCONUT SQUARES

3 tbsp. margarine
1 can shredded coconut
1 3-oz. package lemon gelatin
1 pt. vanilla ice cream
2 tbsp. lemon juice
1 tsp. grated lemon rind

Spread ... margarine over 8-inch square pan.
Press ..... coconut into margarine.
Bake ..... at 350 degrees until lightly browned.
Dissolve .. gelatin in 1 cup boiling water.
Stir ...... in ice cream until melted.
Add ..... lemon juice and rind.
Pour ..... into coconut crust.
Chill ..... until firm.
Cut ...... into squares.

Jonelle Fulton
Woodbridge, New Jersey

DESSERT

separated
tsp. cream of tartar
ugar
6 tbsp. lemon juice
1 9-oz. carton whipped topping

Beat . . . . . egg whites and cream of tartar in large bowl until soft peaks form.
Add . . . . . 1 1/2 teaspoons sugar gradually, beating until stiff.
Spread . . . in 9 x 13-inch baking pan.
Bake . . . . . at 275 degrees for 1 hour.
Combine . egg yolks, lemon juice, 1 tablespoon water and 3/4 cup sugar in top of double boiler.
Cook . . . . over medium heat until thick, stirring constantly.
Slice . . . . . top from meringue layer.
Alternate . layers of whipped topping and lemon mixture over meringue crust.
Top . . . . . with meringue top.
Chill . . . . . for several hours.

Marilyn Kay Clark
Fremont Jr. H. S., Fremont, Nevada

LEMON-HONEY FLUFF

1 pkg. lemon gelatin
1/3 c. honey
1/8 tsp. salt
3 tbsp. lemon juice
Grated rind of 1 lemon
1 14 1/2-oz. can evaporated milk, chilled
2 1/2 c. vanilla wafer crumbs

Dissolve . . gelatin in 1 1/4 cups boiling water.
Stir . . . . . . in remaining ingredients except evaporated milk and crumbs.
Chill . . . . . evaporated milk until partially set.
Beat . . . . . chilled evaporated milk until stiff.
Fold . . . . . in gelatin mixture.
Spread . . . half the crumbs in 10 x 12-inch pan.
Pour . . . . . in lemon mixture.
Top . . . . . with remaining crumbs.
Chill . . . . . for 3 hours.

Leslie Blaik
Stevens Point, Wisconsin

LEMON LUSH

2 c. flour
2 sticks butter, melted

1 1/2 c. nuts
1 8-oz. package cream cheese
1 c. confectioners' sugar
1 9-oz. carton Cool Whip
3 sm. packages lemon instant pudding mix
4 1/2 c. milk

Combine . first 2 ingredients with 1 cup nuts in bowl, mixing well.
Press . . . . . into 9 x 13-inch baking dish.
Bake . . . . . at 375 degrees for 20 minutes.
Combine . cream cheese, confectioners' sugar and half the Cool Whip in bowl, beating well.
Spread . . . over cooled crust.
Mix . . . . . pudding mix and milk in bowl.
Let . . . . . . stand for 2 minutes.
Spread . . . over cream cheese layer.
Top . . . . . with remaining Cool Whip.
Chill . . . . . for several hours.
Sprinkle . . with remaining nuts.

Russie Davis
Dawson Springs H. S., Dawson Springs, Kentucky

LOW-CALORIE LEMON MOUSSE

1 tbsp. unflavored gelatin
1/2 c. fresh lemon juice
1/2 c. sugar
4 eggs, beaten
2 tsp. grated lemon rind
1/2 c. heavy cream, whipped

Soften . . . gelatin in lemon juice in small saucepan for 5 minutes.
Cook· . . . . over low heat until gelatin dissolves, stirring constantly.
Beat . . . . . sugar into eggs gradually with electric mixer on high speed until tripled in volume.
Beat . . . . . in gelatin mixture and lemon rind.
Fold . . . . . in whipped cream gently.
Spoon . . . mousse into dessert glasses.
Chill . . . . . for several hours before serving.
Yield . . . . 8 servings/150 calories each.

Teresa L. Wellman
Keene H. S., Keene, New Hampshire

LIME DELIGHT

2 c. chocolate wafer crumbs
1/2 c. butter, melted
1 3-oz. box lime gelatin

1 c. sugar
1/4 c. lime juice
2 tsp. lemon juice
1 14 1/2-oz. can evaporated milk, chilled,
    whipped
1 sq. semisweet chocolate, shaved (opt.)

Combine . first 2 ingredients in bowl, mixing
            well.
Press . . . . . into 7 x 11-inch serving dish.
Dissolve . . gelatin in 1 3/4 cups boiling water
            in bowl.
Chill . . . . . until partially set.
Whip . . . . gelatin until fluffy.
Mix . . . . . in sugar and juices.
Fold . . . . . in whipped evaporated milk.
Pour . . . . . over crumb crust.
Top . . . . . with chocolate shavings.
Chill . . . . . until serving time.

Jean Fink
Ellet H. S., Akron, Ohio

MINT DAZZLER

 2 c. crushed vanilla wafers
Butter
1 1/2 c. confectioners' sugar
3 eggs
3 sq. baking chocolate, melted
3 1/2 c. colored miniature marshmallows
1 c. whipping cream, whipped
1/4 c. crushed pillow mints

Combine . wafer crumbs and 6 tablespoons
            melted butter in bowl, mixing well.
Press . . . . . over bottom of 9 x 13-inch baking
            dish.
Cream . . . 1/2 cup softened butter in bowl.
Add . . . . . confectioners' sugar gradually, mix-
            ing well.
Beat . . . . . in eggs 1 at a time, beating well
            after each addition.
Add . . . . . melted chocolate.
Beat . . . . . until light and fluffy.
Spoon . . . over prepared crust.
Chill . . . . . in refrigerator.
Fold . . . . . marshmallows into whipped cream.
Spread . . . over chocolate layer.
Sprinkle . . mints over top.
Chill . . . . . for 3 hours or longer.
Yield . . . . 18-24 servings.

Doris M. Swinehart
Necedah Area H. S., Necedah, Wisconsin

NUTTY MOUSSE

2 env. unflavored gelatin
2 1/4 c. milk
6 eggs, separated
1 c. sugar
2 tbsp. Cognac (opt.)
1 tsp. vanilla extract
1 1/2 c. ground toasted filberts
1 c. heavy cream, whipped

Soften . . . gelatin in 1/3 cup cold water.
Dissolve . . gelatin in hot milk in heavy
            saucepan.
Beat . . . . . egg yolks and sugar in large bowl
            until light and fluffy.
Stir . . . . . . into hot milk gradually, stirring
            constantly.
Cook . . . . until mixture thickens. Do not boil.
Remove . . from heat.
Stir . . . . . . in Cognac, vanilla and filberts.
Chill . . . . . until partially set.
Beat . . . . . egg whites until stiff but not dry.
Fold . . . . . into filbert mixture with whipped
            cream.
Pour . . . . . into 5-cup souffle dish with 4-inch
            waxed paper collar.
Chill . . . . . until set; remove collar.
Garnish . . sides of mousse with toasted
            chopped filberts.
Yield . . . . 8 servings.

Marcia Bailey
Comstock, Nevada

INSTANT ORANGE FLUFF

1 pt. small curd creamed cottage cheese
1 6-oz. box orange gelatin
1 14-oz. can mandarin oranges, drained
1 7-oz. can crushed pineapple, drained
1 16-oz. carton Cool Whip, thawed

Beat . . . . . cottage cheese in large mixer bowl
            until smooth.
Sprinkle . . gelatin over cheese.
Beat . . . . . until gelatin is dissolved.
Cut . . . . . . orange sections in half.
Add . . . . . both fruits to cottage cheese
            mixture.
Fold . . . . . in Cool Whip.
Chill . . . . . covered, for 4 hours.
Yield . . . . 10-12 servings.

F. Tymosko
Derby H. S., Derby, Connecticut

ORANGE FLUFF FOR TWO

2 tbsp. quick-cooking tapioca
4 tbsp. sugar
1/4 tsp. salt
1 egg, separated
1 c. orange juice

Combine . tapioca, 2 tablespoons sugar and salt in 1 1/2-quart saucepan.
Blend .... in egg yolk and juice; let stand 5 minutes.
Bring .... to a boil over medium heat, stirring often.
Remove .. from heat; set aside.
Beat ..... egg white until soft peaks form.
Add ..... 2 tablespoons sugar gradually, beating until stiff.
Fold ..... orange mixture into egg white.
Spoon ... into sherbet glasses; chill.

Marilyn Jean Mancewicz
Ottawa Hills H. S., Grand Rapids, Michigan

ORANGE-RICE RING

1 11-oz. can mandarin oranges
Milk
3 c. cooked rice
1/2 tsp. salt
1/3 c. sugar
Grated rind and juice of 1 orange
1 tsp. vanilla extract
Whipped cream

Drain .... oranges reserving juice.
Add ..... enough milk to reserved juice to measure 3 cups liquid.
Combine . with rice, salt and sugar in saucepan.
Cook .... over medium heat for 30 minutes or until thick and creamy, stirring occasionally.
Stir ...... in orange rind, fresh orange juice and vanilla.
Spoon ... into 6-cup ring mold.
Chill ..... until firm.
Unmold .. onto serving plate.
Spoon ... whipped cream into center of ring.
Arrange .. orange segments around mold.
Garnish .. with additional orange segments, banana slices and chocolate pieces.
Yield .... 8 servings.

Janie Bly
Winwood, Arkansas

LAYERED PEACH DESSERT

1 lg. can sliced peaches
1 pkg. butter pecan cake mix
1/2 c. butter, melted
1 can coconut
1 c. chopped pecans (opt.)

Layer .... first 3 ingredients in 9 x 13-inch baking dish.
Sprinkle .. with coconut and pecans.
Bake ..... at 350 degrees for 1 hour.
Chill ..... thoroughly before serving.

Debra Nelson
Donnybrook H. S., Donnybrook, North Dakota

FOUR-LAYER DESSERT

1 sm. package yellow cake mix
1 pkg. French vanilla instant pudding mix
1 8-oz. package cream cheese, softened
1 can peach pie filling
1 lg. carton Cool Whip

Prepare ... cake mix using package directions.
Pour ..... into 9 x 13-inch baking pan.
Bake ..... at 350 degrees until cake tests done.
Prepare ... pudding mix using package directions.
Blend .... with cream cheese.
Spread ... over cake.
Spoon ... pie filling over cream cheese layer.
Top ..... with Cool Whip.
Chill ..... for several hours.
Yield .... 15 servings.

Joyce Sonnanstine
Wadsworth Sr. H. S., Wadsworth, Ohio

PEANUT BUTTER DESSERT CAKE

1 c. flour
1 stick margarine, softened
Finely chopped peanuts
1 8-oz. package cream cheese, softened
1/2 c. peanut butter
1 c. confectioners' sugar
1 16-oz. container Cool Whip
1 pkg. vanilla instant pudding mix
1 pkg. chocolate instant pudding mix
2 1/2 c. cold milk
Chocolate syrup

Combine . first 2 ingredients and 1 cup pea-
nuts in bowl, mixing well.
Press . . . . . into greased 9 x 13-inch pan.
Bake . . . . . at 350 degrees for 20 minutes or
until golden brown.
Combine . cream cheese and peanut butter in
bowl, beating until creamy.
Fold . . . . . sugar and 1 cup Cool Whip into
cream cheese mixture.
Spread . . . over cooled crust.
Chill . . . . . until partially set.
Combine . pudding mixes and milk in bowl,
blending until thick.
Spread . . . over peanut butter layer.
Chill . . . . . until set.
Spread . . . remaining Cool Whip over pudding
layer.
Sprinkle . . with additional peanuts.
Swirl . . . . chocolate syrup over top.
Chill . . . . . until serving time.
Yield . . . . 24 servings.

Lana Giehl
Groveport Freshman School, Groveport, Ohio

PEPPERMINT ICEBOX PUDDING

2 med. boxes vanilla wafers
1 pt. whipping cream, whipped
2 c. miniature marshmallows
3/4 c. nuts
5 sticks peppermint candy, crushed

Alternate . layers of vanilla wafers, whipped
cream, marshmallows, nuts and
peppermint in shallow serving bowl
until all ingredients are used, ending
with peppermint.
Chill . . . . . for several hours.
Yield . . . . 10 servings.

Norma R. Settles
Washington County H. S., Springfield, Kentucky

PINEAPPLE BUTTERFLY MOUSSE

1 env. unflavored gelatin
1 13 1/4-oz. can crushed pineapple
1/2 c. sugar
2 eggs, separated
1 c. sour cream
1 tsp. vanilla extract
1/2 tsp. grated lemon rind
1 tbsp. lemon juice

1/2 tsp. salt
32 vanilla wafers
Currant jelly

Sprinkle . . gelatin over pineapple in saucepan.
Let . . . . . . stand for 5 minutes.
Add . . . . . 1/4 cup sugar and beaten egg yolks.
Cook . . . . over low heat until thick, stirring
constantly; cool.
Stir . . . . . . in sour cream, vanilla, lemon rind
and lemon juice.
Chill . . . . . until slightly thickened.
Beat . . . . . egg whites with salt until soft peaks
form.
Add . . . . . 1/4 cup sugar gradually, beating
until stiff.
Fold . . . . . into thickened gelatin.
Make . . . . sandwiches of vanilla wafers with
currant jelly filling.
Spoon . . . a small amount of mousse into serv-
ing dishes.
Top . . . . . with vanilla wafer sandwiches.
Cover . . . . with additional mousse.
Cut . . . . . . remaining wafer sandwiches into
halves.
Arrange . . 2 halves, cut side down, butterfly
fashion in each dish.
Garnish . . with additional pineapple.
Chill . . . . . for several hours.

Photograph for this recipe below.

LOW-CAL PINEAPPLE SNOWBALLS

2 env. plain gelatin
1 c. crushed pineapple
1 c. sugar
1/2 tsp. salt
1 tbsp. lemon juice
3 pkg. whipped topping mix
1 9-in. angel food cake

Soften ... gelatin in 1/4 cup cold water in large bowl.
Add ..... 1 cup boiling water, pineapple and next 3 ingredients, stirring well.
Chill ..... until partially set.
Prepare ... 2 packages topping mix using package directions.
Fold ..... into gelatin mixture.
Break .... cake into bite-sized pieces.
Fold ..... into gelatin mixture, coating well.
Spoon ... into 12 muffin cups.
Chill ..... overnight.
Remove .. from muffin cups.
Prepare ... remaining package topping mix using package directions.
Frost .... desserts.
Yield .... 12 servings/89 calories each.

Nola Kay Scott
Revere H. S., Richfield, Ohio

PINEAPPLE DELIGHT

1 1/2 c. graham cracker crumbs
1 c. butter, melted
1 1/2 c. confectioners' sugar
2 eggs
1 lg. can crushed pineapple, drained
Whipped cream

Mix ..... cracker crumbs with 1/2 cup butter in bowl until blended.
Press ..... into 8 x 8-inch serving dish.
Chill ..... in refrigerator until firm.
Cream ... 1/2 cup butter with confectioners' sugar in mixer bowl.
Beat ..... eggs into mixture until smooth.
Spread ... on crust.
Spread ... pineapple over creamed layer.
Chill ..... until serving time.
Cut ...... into squares and garnish with whipped cream.
Yield .... 8 servings.

Brenda Oxspring
Butler Middle School, Salt Lake City, Utah

PINEAPPLE ICEBOX PUDDING

3/4 lb. vanilla wafers, crushed
1 lb. marshmallows
2 c. milk
1 16-oz. can crushed pineapple, drained
1 tsp. salt
1 oz. chopped almonds
1 oz. maraschino cherries, chopped
1 c. whipping cream, whipped

Spread ... wafer crumbs in bottom of 9 x 13-inch glass dish, reserving enough for garnish.
Combine . marshmallows and milk in saucepan.
Heat ..... until marshmallows melt.
Chill ..... in refrigerator.
Stir ...... in next 4 ingredients.
Fold ..... in whipped cream.
Pour ..... over crumbs.
Garnish .. with reserved crumbs.
Chill ..... overnight.
Yield .... 10-12 servings.

Ann Morgan
Seabreeze Sr. H. S., Daytona Beach, Florida

PINEAPPLE REFRIGERATOR DESSERT

1/2 lb. butter, softened
3/4 lb. confectioners' sugar
4 egg yolks
4 egg whites
1/8 tsp. cream of tartar
1 c. nuts, chopped
1 1-lb. can crushed pineapple
1 sm. jar candied cherries
2 doz. ladyfingers, split
1 pt. whipping cream, whipped

Cream ... butter and confectioners' sugar in large bowl.
Add ..... egg yolks 1 at a time, beating well after each addition.
Beat ..... egg whites with cream of tartar in mixing bowl until stiff peaks form.
Fold ..... into creamed mixture.
Combine . nuts, pineapple and cherries in bowl, mixing well.
Layer .... half the ladyfingers, creamed mixture and fruit mixture in serving dish.

Repeat ... layers.
Spread ... whipped cream over top.
Chill ..... for 24 hours.
Yield .... 8-10 servings.

Mrs. Grace Edwards
Robert E. Lee H. S., Baytown, Texas

PINEAPPLE-ORANGE BREEZE

2 eggs, separated
1 c. milk, scalded
1 pkg. orange gelatin
Vanilla wafer crumbs
Brown sugar
Butter
1 sm. can crushed pineapple, drained
1/4 c. sugar
1/2 c. cream, whipped

Combine . egg yolks and milk in saucepan, beating well.
Cook .... until thick, stirring constantly.
Dissolve .. gelatin in 1 cup boiling water in small bowl; cool.
Pour ..... into egg mixture, mixing well.
Chill ..... until partially set.
Spread ... 1/4-inch layer of crumbs in loaf pan.
Cover .... with thin layer of brown sugar and butter.
Add ..... pineapple.
Beat ..... egg whites until soft peaks form.
Add ..... sugar gradually, beating until stiff.
Fold ..... in whipped cream.
Fold ..... into gelatin mixture.
Spread ... over pineapple.
Chill ..... until firm.
Sprinkle .. with wafer crumbs before serving.
Yield .... 8 servings.

Marilee Erickson
Brentwood, Tennessee

WANDA'S DESSERT

1 14-oz. can sweetened condensed milk
1 12-oz. container Cool Whip
1 20-oz. can crushed pineapple, drained
1 can cherry pie filling
1 6-oz. package chopped walnuts

Mix ..... sweetened condensed milk and Cool Whip in large bowl until well blended.

Add ..... remaining ingredients, mixing well.
Chill ..... until serving time.
Yield .... 16 servings.

Mary R. Cerrone
Kempsville Jr. H. S., Virginia Beach, Virginia

WIKI WIKI WALK AWAY

1 8-oz. package cream cheese, softened
1 c. milk
1 8-oz. can crushed pineapple
1 3-oz. package vanilla instant pudding mix
1 sm. container whipped topping
8 ice cream cones (opt.)

Combine . first 2 ingredients in mixer bowl.
Beat ..... with electric mixer until smooth.
Add ..... pineapple and pudding mix.
Beat ..... for 1 minute longer.
Fold ..... in whipped topping.
Serve .... in ice cream cones.

Rena S. Humerickhouse
Pierre Moran Jr. H. S., Elkhart, Indiana

OREO-PISTACHIO DESSERT

25 Oreos, crushed
1/4 c. melted margarine
1/4 c. chopped pecans, toasted
1 8-oz. package cream cheese, softened
1 lg. container whipped topping
1 c. confectioners' sugar
1 3-oz. package pistachio instant pudding mix
1 c. milk

Combine . first 2 ingredients in bowl, mixing well.
Press ..... into 9 x 13-inch pan.
Sprinkle .. with pecans.
Blend .... cream cheese, 1/3 of the whipped topping and confectioners' sugar in bowl until smooth.
Spread ... over crust.
Mix ..... pudding mix, milk and half the remaining whipped topping in bowl until thickened.
Spread ... over cream cheese layer.
Top ..... with remaining whipped topping.
Chill ..... for several hours.
Garnish .. with grated sweet chocolate.

Connie Page
Adrian H. S., Adrian, Georgia

PISTACHIO NUT TORTE

1 stick margarine, softened
1 c. flour
Confectioners' sugar
1/4 c. chopped nuts
8 oz. cream cheese, softened
1 lg. container Cool Whip
2 pkg. instant pistachio pudding mix
2 1/2 c. milk

Combine . margarine, flour, 2 tablespoons con-
fectioners' sugar and nuts in bowl,
beating well.
Press . . . . . into 9 x 13-inch baking dish.
Bake . . . . . at 325 degrees for 15 to 20
minutes.
Mix . . . . . cream cheese, 2/3 cup confec-
tioners' sugar and 1/2 of the Cool
Whip in bowl, blending well.
Spread . . . evenly over cooled crust.
Prepare . . . pudding mixes according to pack-
age directions using 2 1/2 cups
milk.
Spread . . . thickened pudding mixture over
cream cheese layer.
Top . . . . . with remaining Cool Whip.
Sprinkle . . with additional nuts, if desired.
Chill . . . . . overnight.
Yield . . . . 24 squares.

Mrs. Kay Keen
Lake Wales Jr. H. S., Lake Wales, Florida

PISTACHIO DREAM

1 stick margarine, softened
1 c. flour
2 tbsp. sugar
1/2 c. chopped pecans
1 8-oz. package cream cheese, softened
2/3 c. confectioners' sugar
1 6-oz. cartons Cool Whip
2 boxes instant pistachio pudding mix
2 1/2 c. milk

Combine . first 3 ingredients and 1/4 cup
pecans in bowl, mixing well.
Press . . . . . into 9 x 13-inch baking pan.
Bake . . . . . at 350 degrees for 15 minutes.
Mix . . . . . cream cheese, confectioners' sugar
and half the Cool Whip in bowl,
blending well.
Spread . . . over cooled crust; refrigerate.

Combine . pudding mix and milk in large
bowl.
Pour . . . . . over cream cheese layer.
Mix . . . . . remaining Cool Whip and 1/4 cup
pecans in bowl.
Spread . . . over entire mixture.
Chill . . . . . for 2 hours or longer.

Waneta Richards
Greeley West H. S., Greeley, Colorado

PUMPKIN DESSERT

2 c. graham cracker crumbs
2/3 c. sugar
1/3 c. margarine, softened
1 lb. marshmallows
1/3 c. milk
1 1-lb. can solid-pack pumpkin
1/4 tsp. salt
3/4 tsp. cinnamon
2 c. whipped cream

Combine . graham cracker crumbs, 1/3 cup
sugar and margarine in bowl, mix-
ing well.
Press . . . . . into 9 x 13-inch pan.
Melt . . . . . marshmallows in milk in saucepan.
Mix . . . . . pumpkin, 1/3 cup sugar, salt and
cinnamon in bowl.
Blend . . . . in marshmallow mixture.
Fold . . . . . whipped cream into cooled pump-
kin mixture.
Pour . . . . . into prepared pan.
Chill . . . . . until serving time.
Yield . . . . 12-15 servings.

Marilyn Jean Mancewicz
Ottawa Hills H. S., Grand Rapids, Michigan

RAINBOW MOUSSE

1 pkg. black cherry gelatin
1 c. grape juice
1 pkg. strawberry gelatin
1 pkg. lime gelatin
1 pkg. raspberry gelatin
1/4 c. sugar
2 c. whipped cream
1/2 c. drained crushed pineapple
1 can shredded coconut

Dissolve . . black cherry gelatin in 1 cup boiling
water.
Stir . . . . . . in 1/2 cup grape juice.
Pour . . . . . into 8-inch square pan.

Chill . . . . . until firm.
Prepare . . . strawberry and lime gelatins separately according to package directions using 1 cup boiling water and 1/2 cup cold water for each.
Pour . . . . . each into 8-inch square pan.
Chill . . . . . until firm.
Dissolve . . raspberry gelatin and sugar in 1 cup boiling water.
Add . . . . . remaining grape juice.
Chill . . . . . until thickened.
Fold . . . . . in whipped cream and pineapple.
Cut . . . . . . congealed gelatins into 1/2-inch cubes.
Fold . . . . . into whipped cream-pineapple mixture.
Pour . . . . . into tube pan.
Chill . . . . . for 8 hours or longer.
Unmold . . and sprinkle with coconut.

Clarissa Dolan
Wildcat, Arkansas

RASPBERRY ANGEL DELIGHT

1 3-oz. package raspberry gelatin
1 10-oz. package frozen raspberries
2 c. whipped cream
1 lg. angel food cake, cubed

Dissolve . . gelatin in 1 1/4 cups boiling water in large bowl.
Add . . . . . raspberries, stirring until thawed.
Chill . . . . . until partially set.
Whip . . . . until fluffy.
Fold . . . . . in 1 cup whipped cream.
Place . . . . 1/2 of the cake in serving dish.
Alternate . layers of gelatin mixture and remaining cake until all ingredients are used.
Frost . . . . with remaining whipped cream.
Yield . . . . 10-12 servings.

Kathryn Jensen
Box Elder H. S., Brigham City, Utah

RASPBERRY DANISH DESSERT

2 c. graham cracker crumbs
1/4 c. melted butter
1 tbsp. flour
Sugar
1 6-oz. package lemon gelatin
2 env. Dream Whip
1 c. milk

1 lb. cream cheese, softened
2 tsp. vanilla extract
1 pkg. raspberry junket
1 10-oz. package frozen raspberries, partially thawed

Combine . first 3 ingredients with 2 tablespoons sugar in bowl, mixing well.
Press . . . . . into 9 x 13-inch dish.
Chill . . . . . in freezer for 45 minutes.
Dissolve . . gelatin in 2 cups boiling water in bowl.
Chill . . . . . until partially set.
Whip . . . . Dream Whip with 1 cup milk.
Blend . . . . in cream cheese, vanilla and 1 cup sugar.
Fold . . . . . in gelatin.
Pour . . . . . over prepared crust.
Chill . . . . . until set.
Combine . junket with 1 cup cold water in saucepan.
Boil . . . . . for 1 minute.
Add . . . . . raspberries.
Spread . . . over gelatin layer.
Chill . . . . . until serving time.

Joanne Parry Dankey
Washington Sr. H. S., Sioux Falls, South Dakota

RASPBERRY DESSERT

1 recipe graham cracker crust
1 8-oz. package cream cheese, softened
1 c. confectioners' sugar
1 pkg. Dream Whip
1 sm. package raspberry Jell-O
1 10-oz. package frozen raspberries

Pat . . . . . . graham cracker crust into 9 x 12-inch dish.
Mix . . . . . cream cheese and sugar with 3 tablespoons water in bowl.
Pour . . . . . over crust.
Prepare . . . Dream Whip using package directions.
Spread . . . half the Dream Whip over cream cheese layer.
Dissolve . . Jell-O in 1 cup boiling water.
Add . . . . . raspberries, stirring to thaw.
Chill . . . . . until partially set.
Pour . . . . . over Dream Whip.
Top . . . . . with remaining Dream Whip.

Shirley Miller
Coopersville Public Schools, Coopersville, Michigan

SNOW PUDDING WITH RASPBERRY SAUCE

3 tbsp. unflavored gelatin
1 1/4 c. sugar
Salt
4 egg yolks
4 c. milk
1 tsp. vanilla extract
1 tsp. grated lemon rind
4 egg whites
2   10-oz. packages frozen raspberries, thawed
1/4 c. cornstarch
2 tbsp. lemon juice

Combine . gelatin, 1/4 cup sugar and 1/8 tea-spoon salt in 2-quart saucepan.
Beat . . . . . egg yolks and 1 cup milk together in bowl.
Add . . . . . to gelatin, mixing well.
Cook . . . . over low heat until gelatin dissolves, stirring constantly.
Stir . . . . . . in remaining 3 cups milk, vanilla and rind.
Chill . . . . . until partially set.
Beat . . . . . egg whites until soft peaks form.
Add . . . . . 1/2 cup sugar gradually, beating until stiff.
Fold . . . . . into custard.
Pour . . . . . into 7-cup mold.
Chill . . . . . until firm.
Drain . . . . raspberries, reserving syrup.
Add . . . . . enough water to reserved syrup to measure 2 cups liquid.
Combine . remaining 1/2 cup sugar, cornstarch and 1/4 teaspoon salt in 1-quart saucepan.
Stir . . . . . . in raspberry liquid gradually.
Cook . . . . over medium heat until thick, stir-ring constantly.
Boil . . . . . for 2 minutes.
Add . . . . . lemon juice; cool.
Fold . . . . . in raspberries.
Unmold . . snow pudding onto serving platter.
Serve . . . with raspberry sauce.

Photograph for this recipe on page 149.

RICE DESSERT

2 c. milk
1/3 c. sugar

1 env. unflavored gelatin
1/4 tsp. salt
1/4 c. rice
1/4 c. chopped blanched almonds
1 tsp. vanilla extract
1/2 tsp. lemon extract
1 c. heavy cream, whipped

Place . . . . first 3 ingredients in top of double boiler.
Bring . . . . to boiling point over low heat, stir-ring occasionally.
Stir . . . . . . in salt and rice.
Cook . . . . covered, over boiling water for 1 hour or until rice is soft.
Stir . . . . . . in almonds and extracts.
Cool . . . . . to room temperature.
Fold . . . . . whipped cream into rice mixture.
Chill . . . . . until serving time.

Virginia E. Grafe
Bertrand Community School, Bertrand, Nevada

SHERRY'S DESSERT

1 1/2 sticks margarine
1 1/2 c. flour
1 c. chopped pecans
1 1/2 c. confectioners' sugar
16 oz. cream cheese, softened
Cool Whip
3 pkg. instant pudding mix
4 1/2 c. milk

Combine . first 3 ingredients in bowl mixing well.
Press . . . . . into 12 x 18-inch baking pan.
Bake . . . . . at 350 degrees for 15 to 20 minutes.
Cream . . . sugar, cream cheese and 1 1/2 cups Cool Whip in bowl until smooth.
Spread . . . over cooled crust.
Beat . . . . . instant pudding mix with milk in bowl for 2 minutes.
Spread . . . over cream cheese mixture.
Top . . . . . with additional Cool Whip.
Chill . . . . . for several hours.
Yield . . . . 20 servings.

Angeline Boehnke
Flatonia H. S., Flatonia, Texas

BERRIES ON THE SQUARE

9 whole graham crackers
1 sm. package vanilla instant pudding mix

2 c. cold milk
1 4-oz. container frozen whipped topping, thawed
1 c. finely chopped strawberries, sweetened to taste
9 whole strawberries

Arrange .. half the graham crackers in bottom of 9-inch square serving dish.
Prepare ... pudding mix with milk using package directions.
Fold ..... in whipped topping.
Pour ..... half the pudding mixture over graham crackers.
Top ..... with chopped strawberries.
Arrange .. remaining graham crackers on strawberry layer.
Spread ... remaining pudding mixture on graham crackers.
Garnish .. with whole strawberries.
Chill ..... until serving time.
Serve .... cut into squares.
Yield .... 9 squares.

Charla P. Vaught
Wagoner H. S., Wagoner, Oklahoma

STRAWBERRY ANGEL SURPRISE

1 3-oz. package strawberry gelatin
20 drops of red food coloring
1 10-in. angel food cake
3 c. heavy cream, whipped
1 1/2 c. fresh strawberries
1/2 tsp. vanilla extract
1 1/2 c. sliced fresh strawberries
1/4 c. confectioners' sugar

Dissolve .. gelatin in 1 cup boiling water in bowl.
Stir ...... in food coloring.
Chill ..... until partially set.
Slice ..... 1-inch layers from top and bottom of cake.
Scoop .... out center layer to 1 inch from edges and bottom.
Place .... bottom layer on serving dish.
Cover .... with shell layer.
Fold ..... thickened gelatin into half the whipped cream.
Blend .... in 1 1/2 cups strawberries and vanilla.
Fill ...... shell layer with mixture.
Top ..... with remaining layer.

Combine . sliced strawberries and confectioners' sugar in bowl.
Let ...... stand for 30 minutes.
Fold ..... into remaining whipped cream.
Frost .... top and sides of cake.

Elizabeth Richards
Russell County H. S., Russell Springs, Kentucky

STRAWBERRY-BANANA DELIGHT

1 6-oz. package strawberry-banana gelatin
1 10-oz. package frozen strawberries, thawed
2 lg. bananas, sliced
4 c. cubed angel food cake
1 sm. package vanilla instant pudding mix
Cool Whip

Dissolve .. gelatin in 2 cups boiling water in 9 x 13-inch baking dish.
Add ..... strawberries, bananas and cake pieces, mixing well.
Chill ..... until firm.
Prepare ... pudding mix using package directions.
Spread ... over gelatin mixture.
Top ..... with Cool Whip.
Yield .... 12 servings.

Joan E. Lowery
Meyersdale Area H. S., Meyersdale, Pennsylvania

STRAWBERRY CREAM SQUARES

2 3-oz. packages strawberry gelatin
2 10-oz. packages frozen strawberries
1 13 1/2-oz. can crushed pineapple
2 lg. bananas, finely diced
1 c. sour cream

Dissolve .. gelatin in 2 cups boiling water in bowl.
Add ..... strawberries, stirring to thaw.
Fold ..... in pineapple and bananas.
Pour ..... half the mixture into 8 x 8-inch dish.
Chill ..... until firm.
Spread ... sour cream over top.
Pour ..... remaining gelatin mixture over sour cream.
Chill ..... until firm.
Top ..... with additional sour cream and fresh strawberry halves.

Lorene L. Arent
Wausa Public Schools, Wausa, Nebraska

STRAWBERRY DELIGHT

1/2 pkg. white cake mix
1 egg
1 pt. whipping cream
1 1/2 c. confectioners' sugar
5 tsp. vanilla extract
1 8-oz. package cream cheese, softened
3 10-oz. packages frozen strawberries, thawed
1 4 3/4-oz. package strawberry Danish dessert

Prepare . . . cake mix according to package directions, using half the water and 1 egg.
Pour . . . . . into prepared 9 x 13-inch baking pan.
Bake . . . . . for 10 minutes, using package directions; do not overbake.
Combine . 4 tablespoons whipping cream and next 3 ingredients in bowl.
Beat . . . . . until smooth.
Whip . . . . remaining cream in bowl until very thick.
Fold . . . . . into cream cheese mixture.
Spread . . . on cooled cake.
Drain . . . . strawberries, reserving juice.
Combine . juice with enough water to measure 1 3/4 cups liquid.
Combine . with Danish Dessert in saucepan.
Cook . . . . until thickened, stirring constantly.
Remove . . from heat; add strawberries.
Cool . . . . . to room temperature.
Spread . . . on top of cake.
Chill . . . . . covered, for 24 hours or longer.

Vera Robinson
Granite Park Jr. H. S., Salt Lake City, Utah

STRAWBERRY DESSERT

1 1-lb. box vanilla creme cookies, crushed
1/4 lb. butter, softened
2 eggs
2 c. confectioners' sugar
2 qt. sliced strawberries
1/2 pt. whipping cream, whipped

Place . . . . crushed cookies in bottom of 9 x 13-inch pan, reserving enough crumbs for garnish.
Mix . . . . . butter, eggs and confectioners' sugar in bowl, beating well.

Pour . . . . . over crumb mixture.
Add . . . . . layer of strawberries.
Top . . . . . with whipped cream.
Garnish . . with remaining crumbs.
Chill . . . . . until served.
Yield . . . . 15 servings.

Barbara Fitch
West Bend H. S., West Bend, Iowa

MAKE-AHEAD STRAWBERRY SHORTCAKE

1 loaf angel food cake, sliced
1 lg. package instant vanilla pudding mix
1/2 c. milk
1 pt. vanilla ice cream, softened
1 lg. package strawberry gelatin
2 pt. frozen strawberries, thawed
Whipped cream (opt.)

Line . . . . . 9 x 13-inch dish with cake slices.
Combine . pudding mix and milk in large bowl.
Add . . . . . ice cream, beating well.
Pour . . . . . over cake slices.
Dissolve . . gelatin in 1/2 cup boiling water in large bowl.
Stir . . . . . . in strawberries.
Chill . . . . until partially set.
Spoon . . . over pudding mixture.
Chill . . . . . until firm.
Garnish . . with whipped cream.
Yield . . . . 12 servings.

Connie Y. Crouch
Palatka H. S., Palatka, Florida

TWINKIE CAKE

10 Twinkies, sliced in half
1 lg. package instant vanilla pudding mix
4 to 5 lg. bananas, sliced
1 med. package frozen strawberries, thawed
1 lg. container Cool Whip

Place . . . . Twinkies in bottom of 9 x 13-inch dish.
Prepare . . . pudding mix using package directions.
Spread . . . over Twinkies.
Layer . . . . bananas and strawberries over top.
Top . . . . . with Cool Whip.
Chill . . . . . until serving time.

Winn Williams
Lake Hamilton H. S., Pearcy, Arkansas

Frozen
Desserts

DELPHINE'S BAKED ALASKA

1 baked 9-in. brownie cake layer
1 qt. chocolate chip ice cream, softened
6 egg whites
3/4 c. sugar

Place .... brownie layer on foil-covered cookie sheet.
Chill ..... in freezer.
Line ..... 1 1/2-quart mixing bowl with foil.
Press ..... ice cream into bowl.
Place .... foil over bowl and press to flatten top.
Freeze ... until firm.
Beat ..... egg whites in bowl with electric mixer until soft peaks form.
Add ..... sugar gradually, beating until stiff.
Remove .. foil covering from ice cream.
Invert .... ice cream onto brownie layer; remove foil.
Cover .... ice cream and cake quickly with meringue.
Return ... to freezer.
Preheat ... oven to 500 degrees 15 minutes before serving time.
Bake ..... Alaska for 4 to 5 minutes or until delicately browned.
Transfer .. to chilled plate.
Serve .... immediately.
Yield .... 8 servings.

Mrs. Delphine Senn
Hayfield Secondary School, Alexandria, Virginia

ICE CREAM SANDWICH BAKED ALASKAS

6 egg whites
1/2 tsp. cream of tartar
1/4 tsp. salt
1 tsp. vanilla extract
3/4 c. sugar
6 ice cream sandwiches

Beat ..... egg whites in bowl until soft peaks form.
Add ..... next 4 ingredients gradually, beating until stiff and sugar is dissolved.
Cut ...... ice cream sandwiches in half.
Stack .... 2 halves together on cookie sheet.
Cover .... completely with meringue, making sure all holes are sealed.

Bake ..... at 350 degrees until browned.
Serve .... immediately.
Yield .... 6 servings.

Phyllis D. Smith
Taylor County H. S., Butler, Georgia

INDIVIDUAL BAKED ALASKAS

6 individual sponge dessert shells
1 9-oz. can crushed pineapple, drained
1 qt. strawberry ice cream
6 egg whites
3/4 c. sugar

Place .... shells on baking sheet.
Spoon ... 1 tablespoon pineapple and 1 scoop ice cream into each shell.
Freeze ... until firm.
Beat ..... egg whites in bowl until soft peaks form.
Add ..... sugar gradually, beating until stiff.
Cover .... shells completely with meringue.
Bake ..... at 500 degrees for 4 minutes.
Serve .... immediately.
Yield .... 6 servings.

Mrs. Evelyn Piper
Devils Lake Central School
Devils Lake, North Dakota

OPEL'S ORANGE BAKED ALASKAS

3 lg. oranges, halved
3 egg whites
1/4 tsp. cream of tartar
6 tbsp. sugar
1/2 tsp. lemon extract
6 scoops vanilla ice cream

Cut ...... thin slice from bottom of each orange half.
Remove .. fruit and membrane from orange shells.
Place .... fruit in bottom of shells.
Chill ..... in refrigerator.
Beat ..... egg whites and cream of tartar in bowl until foamy.
Add ..... sugar and lemon extract gradually, beating until stiff.
Place .... orange cups on baking sheet.
Fill ...... each with 1 scoop ice cream.
Cover .... ice cream completely with meringue.

Bake . . . . . in preheated 500-degree oven for 3 minutes or until light brown.

Serve . . . . immediately.

Opel Askew
Frederick Douglass H. S., Atlanta, Georgia

ELEGANT RAINBOW ALASKA

1 17-oz. package pound cake mix
1 pt. strawberry ice cream, softened
1 pt. vanilla ice cream, softened
1 1/2 pt. pistachio ice cream, softened
5 egg whites
1/4 tsp. cream of tartar
1/2 tsp. vanilla extract
2/3 c. sugar
Flaked coconut

Prepare . . . 1/2 of the cake mix using package directions.

Pour . . . . . into 8-inch round layer cake pan.

Bake . . . . . using package directions.

Line . . . . . deep 1 1/2-quart bowl wlth foil allowing 1 inch to extend over edge.

Spread . . . strawberry ice cream evenly in bottom of bowl.

Freeze . . . until firm.

Repeat . . . process with vanilla and pistachio ice creams.

Top . . . . . with foil.

Freeze . . . until firm.

Place . . . . cake on cookie sheet.

Remove . . ice cream from freezer while preparing meringue.

Beat . . . . . egg whites with cream of tartar and vanilla in bowl until soft peaks form.

Add . . . . . sugar gradually, beating until stiff.

Remove . . foil from top of ice cream.

Invert . . . . onto cake.

Ice . . . . . . side and top with meringue.

Sprinkle . . with flaked coconut.

Bake . . . . . in preheated 500-degree oven for 3 minutes or until light brown.

Photograph for this recipe on this page.

FROZEN APPLE SOUFFLE

4 egg yolks
1 c. sugar
1 env. unflavored gelatin
1/8 tsp. salt
1 c. light cream
2 c. canned applesauce
2 c. heavy cream, whipped
1 tsp. vanilla extract
Stemmed cherries (opt.)
Walnuts (opt.)

Beat . . . . . egg yolks in top of double boiler over hot water until light.

Beat . . . . . in sugar, gelatin and salt gradually.

Heat . . . . . cream and applesauce in saucepan.

Add . . . . . to egg mixture slowly, stirring constantly.

Cook . . . . until thick and smooth.

Empty . . . water from bottom of double boiler and fill with ice cubes.

Cool . . . . . cooked mixture over ice, stirring often.

Combine . whipped cream, vanilla and cooled apple custard.

Chill . . . . . until thick.

Fasten . . . 3-inch band of foil around top of 1-quart souffle dish.

Spoon . . . apple mixture into prepared dish.

Freeze . . . overnight.

Garnish . . with cherries and nuts.

Yield . . . . 6-8 servings.

Photograph for this recipe on page 175.

CHOCOLATE PEPPERMINT FREEZE

15 graham crackers, crushed
1/4 c. sugar
3/4 c. margarine
2 1/2 sq. unsweetened chocolate
3 eggs
1 c. confectioners' sugar
1/2 gal. peppermint ice cream, softened
1 lg. container Cool Whip
1/2 lg. chocolate bar, shredded

Combine . first 2 ingredients and 1/4 cup melted margarine in bowl, mixing well.
Press . . . . . into 9 x 13-inch baking dish.
Bake . . . . . at 350 degrees for 10 minutes.
Melt . . . . . 1/2 cup margarine and unsweetened chocolate in saucepan over low heat.
Combine . eggs and confectioners' sugar in bowl.
Add . . . . . chocolate mixture, beating until thickened.
Pour . . . . . over cooled crust.
Freeze . . . until firm.
Spread . . . ice cream into layer over chocolate mixture.
Frost . . . . with Cool Whip.
Sprinkle . . shredded chocolate over top.
Freeze . . . until firm.

Betty Stomm
DeKalb H. S., Waterloo, Indiana

CHOCOLATE SUNDAE CRUNCH

1 c. flour
1/4 c. packed brown sugar
1/2 c. margarine, softened
1/2 c. chopped walnuts
1 pkg. vanilla instant pudding mix
1 c. milk
2 c. vanilla ice cream, softened
1/2 c. chocolate chips
1/2 c. miniature marshmallows
3 tbsp. evaporated milk

Combine . first 4 ingredients in bowl, mixing well.
Press . . . . . into 9 x 9-inch pan.
Bake . . . . . at 350 degrees for 25 minutes.
Cool . . . . . and crumble.

Beat . . . . . pudding mix and milk in bowl with electric mixer on low speed for 2 minutes.
Add . . . . . ice cream, beating until smooth.
Remove . . 1/2 cup crumbs, spreading remaining crumbs evenly.
Pour . . . . . pudding mixture over crumbs.
Melt . . . . . chocolate chips and marshmallows with evaporated milk in saucepan over low heat.
Drizzle . . . over pudding mixture.
Top . . . . . with reserved crumbs.
Freeze . . . until firm.
Soften . . . in refrigerator for 1 hour before serving.

Bonnie Mielke
Holgate Jr. H. S., Aberdeen, South Dakota

FROZEN CHOCOLATE CRUNCHY

24 Oreo cookies, crushed
1/2 c. melted margarine
1/2 gal. vanilla ice cream, softened
1 1/2 sq. semisweet chocolate
2/3 c. sugar
1/8 tsp. salt
1 tsp. vanilla extract
2/3 c. evaporated milk
Pecans

Combine . cookie crumbs and 1/4 cup melted margarine in bowl, mixing well.
Press . . . . . into rectangular serving dish.
Freeze . . . until firm.
Spread . . . ice cream over cookie crust and return to freezer.
Melt . . . . . 1/4 cup margarine with chocolate in saucepan over medium heat.
Add . . . . . remaining ingredients except pecans to saucepan.
Cook . . . . for 4 to 5 minutes until thickened, stirring constantly.
Pour . . . . . cooled sauce over ice cream.
Sprinkle . . with pecans.
Freeze . . . covered, until served.
Yield . . . . 15-20 squares.

Pam Byce
Greene County H. S., Greensboro, Georgia

FROZEN CHOCOLATE TORTE

3 egg whites
1/2 tsp. cream of tartar

3/4 c. sugar
3/4 c. chopped pecans
2 c. whipping cream
3/4 c. chocolate syrup
1 tsp. vanilla extract
1 chocolate bar, shaved

Beat ..... egg whites in bowl until soft peaks form.
Add ..... next 2 ingredients gradually, beating until stiff.
Fold ..... in pecans.
Spread ... into two 8-inch circles on foil-lined baking sheet.
Bake ..... at 275 degrees for 45 minutes.
Turn ..... off oven, leaving meringues for 45 minutes longer.
Whip .... cream until very stiff.
Fold ..... in syrup and vanilla.
Place .... 1 meringue on serving plate.
Spread ... with half the whipped cream.
Add ..... remaining meringue.
Top ..... with remaining whipped cream.
Sprinkle .. shaved chocolate on top.
Freeze ... until serving time.

Karen G. Smith
Groton Dunstable Regional Secondary School
Groton, Massachusetts

FROZEN FUDGE SUNDAE

1/2 c. butter
2 sq. unsweetened chocolate
1 tsp. vanilla extract
1/2 c. chopped pecans
2 c. confectioners' sugar
3 egg yolks, well beaten
3 egg whites, stiffly beaten
1 sm. box vanilla wafers, crumbled
1/2 gal. vanilla ice cream, softened

Melt ..... butter and chocolate in saucepan over low heat.
Add ..... next 3 ingredients, mixing well.
Fold ..... in egg yolks and egg whites.
Spread ... half the cookie crumbs in bottom of 9 x 13-inch serving dish.
Add ..... chocolate mixture.
Spread ... ice cream over chocolate.
Sprinkle .. reserved crumbs on top.
Freeze ... until serving time.

Sandra J. Holter
Pitts Middle School, Pueblo, Colorado

DONNA'S ICE CREAM DESSERT

1/2 c. packed brown sugar
1 c. chopped nuts
2 c. flour
1/2 c. quick-cooking oats
1 c. melted margarine
1 lg. jar chocolate topping
1/2 gal. ice cream, softened

Combine . first 5 ingredients in bowl, mixing well.
Pour ..... into baking dish.
Bake ..... at 400 degrees for 15 minutes.
Crumble .. while hot.
Spread ... 1/2 of the crumbs in 9 x 13-inch serving dish.
Pour ..... 1/2 of the topping over crumbs.
Spread ... ice cream on top.
Sprinkle .. with remaining crumbs.
Drizzle ... with reserved topping.
Freeze ... until serving time.
Yield .... 12 servings.

Donna Syverson
Mobridge Jr.-Sr. H. S., Mobridge, South Dakota

CRANBERRY CREAM FREEZE

2/3 c. graham cracker crumbs
Sugar
4 tbsp. butter, melted
1 8-oz. package cream cheese, softened
1 pt. vanilla ice cream, softened
1 16-oz. can whole cranberry sauce

Combine . graham cracker crumbs, 2 tablespoons sugar and butter in bowl, mixing well.
Press ..... into bottom of 8-inch springform pan.
Beat ..... cream cheese with 1/4 cup sugar in bowl until fluffy.
Add ..... ice cream by tablespoonfuls, beating to blend quickly.
Pour ..... over crust.
Stir ...... cranberry sauce.
Drop .... by spoonfuls over ice cream mixture.
Freeze ... covered, for 4 hours or until firm.
Yield .... 8 servings.

Mrs. Magdalene R. Robinson
Greenville H. S., Greenville, Alabama

CREAM FROZEN DESSERT

1 1/2 c. sugar
1 c. sour cream
2 tbsp. lemon juice
2 9-oz. cartons Cool Whip
1 1/2 c. chopped pecans
1/2 c. chopped maraschino cherries
2 mashed bananas
1 lg. can pineapple, drained

Cream ... sugar and sour cream in bowl until sugar is dissolved.
Add ..... remaining ingredients, mixing well.
Pour ..... into serving dish.
Freeze ... until firm.
Thaw .... partially before serving.

Elsie J. LaFever
Eahly H. S., Eahly, Oklahoma

FRENCH PUDDING FREEZE

1/4 lb. butter, softened
1 c. confectioners' sugar
2 eggs
1/2 lb. vanilla wafers, crushed
1/2 c. chopped walnuts
1/2 c. maraschino cherries
1/4 tsp. vanilla extract
1 c. whipping cream, whipped

Cream ... butter and confectioners' sugar in large bowl.
Add ..... eggs 1 at a time, beating well after each addition.
Cover .... bottom of 9 x 9-inch pan with 3/4 of the wafer crumbs.
Pour ..... creamed mixture over crumbs.
Chill ..... until firm.
Fold ..... nuts, cherries and vanilla into whipped cream.
Spread ... over butter mixture.
Top ..... with remaining crumbs.
Freeze ... until firm.
Yield .... 12 servings.

Marilyn Meade
LeMars Community School, LeMars, Iowa

TROPICAL FRUIT FREEZE

1 egg, separated
1/2 c. sugar
2 tbsp. orange juice

1/2 tsp. grated orange rind
Several grains of salt
1/2 c. evaporated skimmed milk, partially frozen
2 tbsp. lemon juice

Mix ..... egg yolk, sugar, orange juice, rind and salt in 1-quart bowl.
Place .... milk and egg white into cold mixer bowl.
Beat ..... with electric mixer at high speed until fluffy.
Add ..... lemon juice, beating until stiff.
Beat ..... in sugar mixture gradually at low speed.
Pour ..... into a 5 1/2-cup ring mold.
Freeze ... until firm.
Unmold .. on serving plate.
Garnish ..with mandarin oranges and coconut.
Yield .... 4-6 servings.

Photograph for this recipe on opposite page.

FROZEN CHEESECAKE

18 to 20 graham crackers, crushed
1/4 c. margarine, melted
1 c. sugar
3 egg yolks
1 lg. package cream cheese, softened
Pinch of salt
1/2 pt. whipping cream, whipped
3 egg whites, stiffly beaten

Combine . crumbs and margarine in bowl, mixing well.
Press ..... into bottom of serving dish.
Cream ... sugar, egg yolks, cream cheese and salt in bowl.
Fold ..... whipped cream and egg whites into cheese mixture.
Pour ..... over crust.
Freeze ... until firm.
Yield .... 8-10 servings.

Carla J. Sutton
Center Grove H. S., Greenwood, Indiana

FROZEN FRUIT CUPS

1 30-oz. can apricots
1 17-oz. can crushed pineapple
6 sliced bananas
2 tbsp. lemon juice

12 oz. orange juice concentrate
Ginger ale, chilled

Drain . . . . apricots, reserving juice.
Chop . . . . into bite-sized pieces.
Combine . apricots, apricot juice and next 4
ingredients in large bowl.
Spoon . . . into paper-lined muffin cups.
Freeze . . . until firm.
Place . . . . in serving dishes, removing paper
liners.
Pour . . . . . ginger ale over top.
Yield . . . . 30 fruit cups.

Kriste Speaker
Washington Sr. H. S., Sioux Falls, South Dakota

FROZEN FRUIT DESSERT

1 lg. can pineapple tidbits, drained
1 med. jar maraschino cherries,
drained, chopped
1 sm. package almonds, chopped
1 can white cherries, drained, chopped
1 lg. package miniature marshmallows
4 tbsp. pineapple juice
4 tbsp. sugar
4 egg yolks
1 pt. whipping cream, whipped
4 egg whites, stiffly beaten

Combine . first 5 ingredients in bowl, mixing
well.
Combine . pineapple juice, sugar and egg yolks
in saucepan.
Cook . . . . over medium heat until thick, stir-
ring constantly.
Stir . . . . . . into fruit mixture.
Fold . . . . . in whipped cream and egg whites.
Pour . . . . . into serving dish.
Freeze . . . until firm.
Yield . . . . 24 servings.

Mrs. Mary Jane Smith
Pleasant View Jr. H. S., Richmond, Indiana

ICE CREAM CAKE

1 10-oz. package frozen strawberries,
thawed
1 angel food cake, cubed
1 3-oz. package strawberry gelatin
Vanilla ice cream, softened
1 can blueberries, drained

1 3-oz. package lime gelatin
1 can mandarin oranges, drained
1 3-oz. package orange gelatin

Spread . . . strawberries in bundt pan.
Alternate . layers of cake with remaining ingredients in following order: cake,
strawberry gelatin, ice cream, blueberries, cake, lime gelatin, ice
cream, oranges, cake, orange gelatin, ice cream.
Freeze . . . until firm.
Unmold . . onto serving platter.

Jane Pesterfield
Heritage H. S., Maryville, Tennessee

ICE CREAM SANDWICH DESSERT

1 stick butter, softened
1 c. packed brown sugar
1 c. coconut
Nuts to taste
2 1/2 c. Rice Krispies
1 qt. ice cream, softened

Combine . first 5 ingredients in bowl, mixing
well.
Press . . . . . half the mixture into 9 x 9-inch
dish.
Spoon . . . ice cream evenly over top.
Top . . . . . with remaining coconut mixture.
Freeze . . . until firm.
Cut . . . . . . into squares.

Doris Bradley
Kelso H. S., Kelso, Washington

ISLAND COCONUT TREATS

3/4 c. evaporated milk
1/3 c. sugar
1/2 c. light corn syrup
1 egg, well beaten
1/2 c. lime juice
2 tsp. grated lime rind
1/2 c. shredded coconut

Chill . . . . . evaporated milk in freezer tray until ice crystals form around edges.
Add . . . . . sugar and corn syrup gradually to beaten egg in bowl, beating well.
Pour . . . . . milk into chilled bowl.
Beat . . . . . rapidly until thickened and soft peaks form.
Add . . . . . lime juice, rind and egg mixture, mixing well.
Fold . . . . . in coconut.
Pour . . . . . into freezer tray.
Freeze . . . for about 3 1/2 hours or until firm.
Garnish . . with toasted coconut.
Yield . . . . 4-6 servings.

Hassie Hunter Rodgers
Goshen H. S., Goshen, Alabama

FROZEN LEMON DESSERT

3/4 c. crushed vanilla wafers
3 egg whites
1/2 c. sugar
Grated rind and juice of 1 lemon
1 c. cream, whipped
3 egg yolks, well beaten

Line . . . . . 9 x 9-inch serving dish with wafer crumbs.
Beat . . . . . egg whites in bowl until soft peaks form.
Add . . . . sugar gradually, beating until stiff.
Stir . . . . . . lemon rind and juice into whipped cream.
Fold . . . . . egg yolks into egg white mixture.
Fold . . . . . egg mixture into whipped cream.
Pour . . . . . into crumb-lined pan.
Freeze . . . overnight.
Garnish . . with sugar cube soaked in lemon extract.
Flame . . . . sugar cube.
Yield . . . . 9 servings.

Shirley J. Kanne
Central Middle School, Eden Prairie, Minnesota

FROSTY LEMON COOLER

1 1/3 c. crushed vanilla wafers
3 tbsp. margarine, melted
3 egg yolks
1 1/2 tsp. grated lemon rind
1/2 c. lemon juice
1 c. sugar
Dash of salt
3 egg whites
1 c. nonfat dry milk powder

Combine . cookie crumbs with margarine in bowl, mixing well.
Sprinkle . . 3/4 of the crumbs in 9 x 13-inch baking dish.
Combine . next 5 ingredients in bowl, mixing well.
Beat . . . . . egg whites, milk powder and 1 cup water in bowl at high speed of electric mixer for 5 minutes until stiff peaks form.
Add . . . . . egg yolk mixture, beating at low speed just until blended.
Pour . . . . . over crumbs in pan.
Top . . . . . with reserved crumbs.
Freeze . . . until serving time.
Dip . . . . . . bottom of pan into warm water for 10 seconds.
Cut . . . . . . into squares.
Yield . . . . 16 servings.

Kristie Harker
Lakeridge Jr. H. S., Orem, Utah

LEMON FREEZE

1/2 c. margarine, melted
1 1/2 c. graham cracker crumbs
1/4 c. confectioners' sugar
1 3-oz. package Jell-O pudding and pie filling mix
1 can sweetened condensed milk
1/2 c. lemon juice
1 lg. carton Cool Whip

Combine . first 3 ingredients in bowl, mixing well.
Reserve . . 1/4 cup of crumbs.
Press . . . . . remaining crumbs into 8 x 12-inch baking dish.
Bake . . . . . at 375 degrees for 5 minutes.
Prepare . . . Jell-O pie filling using package directions.

Combine . p ie filling, condensed milk and lemon juice in bowl, mixing well.
Spread . . . over cooled crust.
Cover . . . . with Cool Whip.
Top . . . . . with reserved crumbs.
Freeze . . . covered until firm.

Barbara Langley
Ocmulgee Academy, Lumber City, Georgia

LUCKY FROZEN LEMON CAKE

2 3-oz. packages ladyfingers
2 14-oz. cans sweetened condensed milk
2 tsp. grated lemon rind
14 tbsp. lemon juice
8 eggs, separated
1/4 tsp. cream of tartar
Confectioners' sugar
1 thin slice lemon

Cover . . . . bottom of lightly greased 9 x 3-inch springform pan with ladyfingers, cutting to fit.
Arrange . . ladyfingers around side of pan, cutting to fit even with top.
Combine . next 3 ingredients and egg yolks in large bowl, mixing well.
Beat . . . . . egg whites with cream of tartar until stiff peaks form.
Fold . . . . . into lemon mixture.
Pour . . . . . into prepared pan.
Bake . . . . . at 375 degrees for 25 minutes or until lightly browned.
Remove . . from pan and dust with confectioners' sugar.
Freeze . . . until firm.
Thaw . . . . for 15 minutes before serving.
Garnish . . with confectioners' sugar and twisted lemon slice.

Laurie Anderson
El Camino H. S., South San Francisco, California

MINT DESSERT

24 to 30 Oreo cookies, crushed
1/3 c. butter, softened
1/2 gal. mint bonbon ice cream, softened
1 jar Kraft fudge topping
1 9-oz. carton Cool Whip
Nuts

Combine . cookie crumbs and butter in bowl, mixing well.

Press . . . . . into 9 x 13-inch serving dish.
Spread . . . ice cream over crumbs.
Freeze . . . until firm.
Add . . . . . fudge topping to ice cream layer.
Freeze . . . until firm.
Add . . . . . Cool Whip.
Sprinkle . . with nuts.
Freeze . . . overnight.
Yield . . . . 24 servings.

Lynne Hatle
Vermillion Public Schools, Vermillion, South Dakota

OREO-ICE CREAM DESSERT

1 8-oz. container Cool Whip, softened
1/2 gal. vanilla ice cream, softened
1 15-oz. package Oreo cookies, crushed

Combine . Cool Whip and ice cream in large bowl, mixing well.
Fold . . . . . in cookie crumbs.
Pour . . . . . into serving dish.
Freeze . . . until firm.
Yield . . . . sixteen 1/2-cup servings.

Carole S. Curts
South Whitley Middle School
South Whitley, Indiana

PEARS DIJON

8 firm pears with stems, peeled
Lemon juice
2 c. sugar
4 sticks cinnamon
1 qt. raspberry ice
Crystallized violets

Brush . . . . pears with lemon juice.
Combine . sugar and cinnamon sticks with 4 cups water in large saucepan.
Boil . . . . . for 5 minutes.
Add . . . . . pears carefully.
Reduce . . . heat to low.
Simmer . . until tender but not soft.
Cool . . . . . pears in syrup.
Chill . . . . . in refrigerator.
Pack . . . . . raspberry ice into ring mold.
Freeze . . . for several hours or until firm.
Unmold . . on serving plate.
Arrange . . pears around ring.
Garnish . . with crystallized violets.

Mary Ann Gray
Webster County H. S., Dixon, Kentucky

PINK LADY

1 can cherry pie filling
1 can crushed pineapple
1 can sweetened condensed milk
1 c. crushed nuts (opt.)
1 8-oz. carton whipped topping
1 tsp. vanilla extract

Combine . first 4 ingredients in bowl, mixing
       well.
Fold . . . . . in remaining ingredients.
Press . . . . . into serving dish.
Freeze . . . overnight.
Slice . . . . . before serving.
Yield . . . . 6-8 servings.

Alice R. Carroll
West Hopkins H. S., Nebo, Kentucky

PUMPKIN PARFAIT

1 1/2 c. graham cracker crumbs
1/4 c. sugar
1/4 c. melted butter
1 1/2 c. pumpkin
1/2 c. packed brown sugar
1/2 tsp. salt
1 tsp. cinnamon
1/4 tsp. ginger
1/8 tsp. cloves
1 qt. vanilla ice cream, softened

Combine . first 3 ingredients in bowl, mixing
       well.
Press . . . . . in 9-inch square pan.
Combine . next 6 ingredients in bowl.
Fold . . . . . into softened ice cream.
Pour . . . . . over crumb mixture.
Freeze . . . covered, until firm.
Yield . . . . 9 servings.

Jan Thomas
Indian Valley South H. S., Gnadenhatten, Ohio

RAINBOW DELIGHT

1 pt. heavy cream
3 tbsp. sugar
18 macaroons, crushed
1 c. chopped nuts
1 pt. each lime, orange, raspberry sherbets

Whip . . . . cream in bowl until soft peaks
       form.
Add . . . . . sugar gradually, beating until stiff.
Fold . . . . . in macaroons and nuts.

Spread . . . half the mixture in bottom of
       greased serving dish.
Add . . . . . scoops of sherbet.
Cover . . . . with remaining cream mixture.
Freeze . . . covered, until served.
Yield . . . . 15 servings.

Catherine Scarsella
Girard H. S., Girard, Ohio

FROSTY RASPBERRY SQUARES

1 c. flour
1/2 c. packed brown sugar
1/2 c. chopped walnuts
1/2 c. butter, melted
2 egg whites
2/3 c. sugar
2 c. frozen raspberries
2 tbsp. lemon juice
1 c. whipping cream, whipped

Combine . first 4 ingredients in bowl, mixing
       well.
Press . . . . . into jelly roll pan.
Bake . . . . . at 350 degrees for 20 minutes, stir-
       ring occasionally.
Sprinkle . . 2/3 of the nut mixture into 9 x
       13-inch baking pan.
Combine . egg whites, sugar, raspberries and
       lemon juice in large mixing bowl.
Beat . . . . . with electric mixer on high speed
       for 10 minutes or until stiff.
Fold . . . . . in whipped cream.
Spoon . . . over nut mixture in pan.
Top . . . . . with reserved mixture.
Freeze . . . for 6 hours or longer.
Yield . . . . 12-15 servings.

Thyra K. Davis
Auburn Middle School, Auburn, Kansas

RIBBON CAKE

1 pt. strawberry ice cream, softened
1 lg. angel food cake, sliced into thirds
1 pt. mint ice cream, softened
1 tbsp. sugar
1 tsp. vanilla extract
1 pt. whipping cream, whipped
3 1/2 oz. shredded coconut

Spread . . . strawberry ice cream over first cake
       layer.
Top . . . . . with second layer.

Spread ... with mint ice cream.
Place .... remaining cake layer on top.
Freeze ... until firm.
Blend .... sugar and vanilla into whipped cream.
Frost .... cake with whipped cream.
Sprinkle .. with coconut.
Freeze ... covered, until firm.

Velma H. Ransom
Mexia H. S., Mexia, Texas

STRAWBERRY ICE CREAM CAKE

2 c. halved strawberries
1 qt. vanilla ice cream, softened
4 eggs
2 c. sugar
2 tsp. vanilla extract
2 c. sifted cake flour
2 tsp. baking powder
1/2 tsp. salt
1 c. milk
2 tbsp. butter
1/3 c. confectioners' sugar
1 pt. heavy cream, whipped

Fold ..... strawberries into ice cream in bowl.
Pack ..... firmly into 9-inch layer cake pan.

Freeze ... until firm.
Beat ..... eggs in large mixing bowl until light and fluffy.
Add ..... sugar and vanilla gradually, mixing well.
Sift ...... dry ingredients together.
Beat ..... into eggs.
Bring .... milk and butter to boiling point in saucepan over medium heat, stirring constantly.
Stir ...... quickly into batter, beating slightly.
Pour ..... into 2 greased 9-inch round layer cake pans.
Bake ..... at 350 degrees for 30 minutes.
Remove .. from pans to cool.
Loosen ... ice cream from layer pan.
Invert .... onto cake.
Top ..... with remaining layer.
Add ..... confectioners' sugar to whipped cream, stirring well.
Frost .... cake with sweetened whipped cream.
Freeze ... until firm.
Thaw .... for 30 minutes before serving.
Yield .... 8-10 servings.

Photograph for this recipe below.

STRAWBERRY DELIGHT

1 c. flour
1/4 c. packed brown sugar
1/2 c. chopped pecans
1/2 c. melted margarine
2 egg whites
1   10-oz. package frozen strawberries,
*   thawed*
1 c. sugar
2 tsp. lemon juice
1/2 pt. cream, whipped

Combine . first 4 ingredients in bowl, mixing
well.
Press . . . . . into 9 x 9-inch baking dish.
Bake . . . . . at 350 degrees for 20 minutes, stir-
ring often.
Combine . egg whites, strawberries, sugar and
lemon juice in bowl.
Beat . . . . . with electric mixer on high speed
for 20 minutes or until light and
fluffy.
Fold . . . . . whipped cream into strawberry
mixture.
Remove . . 1/3 of the crumbs.
Spread . . . remaining crumbs over dish.
Pour . . . . . strawberry mixture over crumbs.
Sprinkle . . with reserved crumbs.
Freeze . . . until serving time.
Yield . . . . 8 servings.

Betty P. Lee
Springfield Central Jr. H. S., Springfield, Georgia

STRAWBERRY-PINEAPPLE FREEZE

12 oz. vanilla wafers, crushed
1 c. chopped nuts
4 eggs, beaten
1 box confectioners' sugar
1 stick margarine
3 c. whipping cream, whipped
1 sm. can crushed pineapple
1 lg. package frozen strawberries, thawed

Combine . cookie crumbs and nuts in bowl,
mixing well.
Press . . . . . half the mixture into serving dish.
Combine . eggs, confectioners' sugar and mar-
garine in top of double boiler.
Cook . . . . over hot water for 30 minutes, stir-
ring constantly.
Pour . . . . . hot mixture over crumbs.

Cool . . . . . in refrigerator.
Spread . . . half the whipped cream over cooled
sugar mixture.
Top . . . . . with pineapple and strawberries.
Cover . . . . with remaining whipped cream.
Sprinkle . . with remaining crumbs, pressing in
gently.
Freeze . . . until serving time.
Yield . . . . 10-12 servings.

Joy Kay Hillhouse
Caldwell School, Columbus, Mississippi

TUTTI-FRUTTI TORTONI

1   17-oz. can fruit cocktail, drained
1 pt. vanilla ice cream, softened
1/2 c. macaroons, crumbled
1/3 c. chopped pecans, toasted
1/3 c. peach Brandy

Combine . all ingredients in bowl, mixing well.
Spoon . . . into 12 muffin cups lined with
paper liners.
Cover . . . . with plastic wrap.
Freeze . . . for 3 hours or longer.
Yield . . . . 12 servings.

Carole Lamartina
Thibodaux H. S., Thibodaux, Louisiana

FROZEN YOGURT

1 10-oz. package frozen strawberries, thawed
2 tsp. unflavored gelatin
2 c. yogurt
3/4 c. sugar
1 tsp. vanilla extract
2 egg whites, stiffly beaten

Combine . first 5 ingredients in large bowl,
stirring well.
Fold . . . . . egg whites gently into fruit
mixture.
Freeze . . . until firm.
Thaw . . . . for 15 to 30 minutes before serving.
Garnish . . with fresh fruit.
Yield . . . . 6-8 servings.

Sharon L. Bouldin
Westerville South H. S., Westerville, Ohio

RASPBERRY FROZEN YOGURT

1 env. unflavored gelatin
2 c. sugar

6 c. plain yogurt
2 10-oz. packages frozen raspberries, thawed

Soften ... gelatin in 1/2 cup cold water in saucepan.
Cook .... over low heat until dissolved, stirring constantly.
Combine . sugar, 1 cup yogurt and raspberries with gelatin, mixing well.
Stir ..... in remaining yogurt.
Chill ..... overnight in refrigerator.
Pour ..... into freezer container.
Freeze ... according to freezer instructions.
Yield .... 2 1/2 quarts.

Karen Rackow
Algoma H. S., Algoma, Wisconsin

BUTTER BRICKLE ICE CREAM

4 eggs
2 c. sugar
2 sm. boxes instant butter pecan pudding mix
1 9-oz. carton Cool Whip, softened
1/2 c. butter brickle chips (opt.)
1 tsp. vanilla extract
Milk

Beat ..... eggs in large mixing bowl.
Add ..... sugar gradually, mixing well.
Pour ..... in pudding mix, beating well.
Stir ...... in Cool Whip, butter brickle chips and vanilla.
Pour ..... into 1-gallon freezer container.
Add ..... milk to fill-line, stirring well.
Freeze ... according to freezer directions.
Yield .... 1 gallon.

Sandy Swart
Marysville H. S., Marysville, Kansas

BUTTER PECAN ICE CREAM

2 c. chopped pecans
3 tbsp. butter, melted
3 cans evaporated milk
3 sm. packages vanilla instant pudding mix
2 1/2 c. sugar
1 tsp. vanilla extract
2 qt. milk

Saute .... pecans in butter in skillet for 5 minutes or until toasted.
Combine . remaining ingredients in bowl, mixing well.

Pour ..... into 1 1/2 to 2-gallon ice cream freezer container.
Freeze ... for 10 minutes using freezer directions.
Add ..... pecans to ice cream mixture.
Freeze ... for 1 hour longer.
Yield .... 1 1/2 gallons.

Gail M. Skelton
Biggersville H. S., Corinth, Mississippi

CHOCOLATE ICE CREAM

1/2 gal. chocolate milk
2 cans sweetened condensed milk
1 lg. container Cool Whip
1/2 to 3/4 c. chocolate syrup

Combine . all ingredients in bowl, mixing well.
Pour ..... into ice cream freezer container.
Freeze ... following freezer directions.
Yield .... 1 gallon.

Cissy Worley
Booneville H. S., Booneville, Mississippi

PISTACHIO ICE CREAM

2 eggs, beaten
1 1/2 to 2 c. sugar
1 3-oz. box pistachio instant pudding mix
1 qt. milk
4 c. half and half
1 tbsp. almond extract (opt.)

Combine . all ingredients in large mixer bowl.
Beat ..... until sugar and pudding mix dissolve.
Pour ..... into ice cream freezer container.
Freeze ... using freezer directions.

Ann Litten Bost
Fred T. Foard H. S., Newton, North Carolina

EASY STRAWBERRY ICE CREAM

2 cans sweetened condensed milk
2 pkg. frozen strawberries, thawed
10 c. milk

Combine . condensed milk, strawberries and milk in ice cream freezer container.
Freeze ... using freezer directions.
Yield .... 1 gallon.

Elceone Roberts
Santa Fe H. S., Santa Fe, Texas

OLD-FASHIONED FREEZER STRAWBERRY ICE CREAM

4 or 5 eggs, beaten
1 tbsp. vanilla extract
1/2 to 3/4 c. sugar
1 can sweetened condensed milk
1 1/2 pkg. fresh strawberries, mashed
Red food coloring (opt.)
1 lg. container Cool Whip
1 to 1 1/2 gal. milk

Combine . eggs, vanilla, sugar and condensed milk in bowl, mixing well.
Pour . . . . . into ice cream freezer container.
Add . . . . . strawberries and food coloring.
Fold . . . . . in Cool Whip.
Add . . . . . milk to fill-line on freezer container.
Freeze . . . following freezer directions.
Let . . . . . . stand for 1 hour before serving.

Ruthe Hoel
Larry C. Kennedy School, Phoenix, Arizona

STRAWBERRY ICE CREAM

2 cans strawberry soda
2 cans sweetened condensed milk
2 qt. strawberries
2 c. sugar
Milk

Combine . all ingredients except milk in bowl, mixing until sugar is dissolved.
Pour . . . . . into ice cream freezer container.
Add . . . . . enough milk to bring to fill-line.
Freeze . . . using freezer instructions.
Yield . . . . 2 gallons

Hazel Rogers
Van Buren H. S., Van Buren, Arkansas

FRENCH VANILLA ICE CREAM

2 qt. milk
1 c. heavy cream
1 can sweetened condensed milk
1 1/4 c. sugar
6 eggs
2 tsp. vanilla extract

Combine . all ingredients in bowl, mixing until sugar is dissolved.
Pour . . . . . into 4-quart freezer container.
Freeze . . . according to freezer instructions.

Add . . . . . fruit for fruit-flavored ice cream.
Yield . . . . 3-4 quarts.

Debra A. Patterson
Commodore Perry H. S., Hadley, Pennsylvania

HOMEMADE ICE CREAM

4 c. milk
4 eggs, beaten
1 1/2 c. sugar
2 tbsp. flour
1/2 tsp. salt
4 c. light cream
4 tsp. vanilla extract

Scald . . . . milk in top of double boiler over medium heat.
Stir . . . . . . in eggs, sugar, flour and salt.
Cook . . . . over hot water for about 15 minutes or until custard coats spoon, stirring constantly.
Stir . . . . . . in cream and vanilla.
Freeze . . . following freezer directions.
Yield . . . . 1 gallon.

Dolly Rose Holley
Daingerfield Lone Star H. S., Daingerfield, Texas

JANE'S HOMEMADE ICE CREAM

3 eggs
2 c. sugar
2 13-oz. cans Milnot
2 tbsp. vanilla extract
Milk

Beat . . . . . eggs in bowl, adding sugar gradually.
Add . . . . . Milnot and vanilla, mixing well.
Pour . . . . . into 1-gallon freezer container.
Add . . . . . milk to fill-line.
Freeze . . . using freezer directions.
Yield . . . . sixteen 1-cup servings.

Jane Woods
Wood Memorial H. S., Oakland City, Indiana

KIWI SHERBET

2 c. sugar
3 c. pureed kiwi fruit
Juice of 3 lemons

Combine . sugar and 2 cups water in saucepan.
Bring . . . . to a boil over medium heat.
Simmer . . for 10 minutes.
Cool . . . . . to room temperature.

Puree .... kiwi fruit with lemon juice.
Force .... through sieve, discarding seeds.
Fold ..... into syrup.
Pour ..... into ice cream freezer container.
Freeze ... following freezer directions.
Yield .... 8 servings.

Teresa L. Wellman
Keene H. S., Keene, New Hampshire

MOM'S FRUIT SHERBET

1 1/2 c. sugar
1 c. orange juice
1 c. crushed pineapple
1/4 c. lemon juice
2 c. milk

Combine . first 4 ingredients in large bowl.
Let ...... stand 5 minutes.
Add ..... milk slowly, stirring constantly.
Pour ..... into freezer trays.
Freeze ... for 1 1/2 hours, stirring every 30 minutes.
Freeze ... until firm.

Sally M. Roe
Fremd H. S., Palatine, Illinois

CREAMY COCONUT PIE

3 1/3 c. flaked coconut
1/4 c. butter, softened
1 3-oz. package cream cheese, softened
1 tbsp. sugar
1/2 c. milk
1 8-oz. container frozen whipped
  topping, softened

Combine . 2 cups coconut with butter in bowl, mixing well.
Press ..... into greased 9-inch pie plate.
Bake ..... at 325 degrees for 20 minutes or until lightly browned.
Combine . remaining ingredients except whipped topping in blender container.
Process ... at medium speed for 30 seconds.
Fold ..... into whipped topping in bowl.
Spoon ... into cooled crust.
Freeze ... for 4 hours or until firm.
Let ...... stand at room temperature for 5 minutes before serving.
Yield .... 6-8 servings.

Sally A. Goode
Norwayne H. S., Creston, Ohio

FROZEN LEMON PIE

1 1/2 c. vanilla wafers, finely crushed
2 tbsp. melted butter
3 egg yolks, beaten
1/4 c. lemon juice
1 tsp. grated lemon rind
1 c. sugar
1/2 pt. whipping cream, whipped
3 egg whites

Combine . vanilla wafers and butter in bowl, blending well.
Press ..... over bottom and side of 9-inch pie pan, reserving 1/4 cup for topping.
Combine . next 3 ingredients and 3/4 cup sugar in top of double boiler.
Cook .... until thick, stirring constantly.
Chill ..... until cooled.
Fold ..... in whipped cream.
Beat ..... egg whites until soft peaks form.
Add ..... 1/4 cup sugar gradually, beating until stiff.
Fold ..... egg white mixture into lemon mixture.
Pour ..... into crust.
Sprinkle .. with 1/4 cup crumbs.
Freeze ... until firm.

Mary A. McDermott
Terra Nova H. S., Pacifica, California

MACADAMIA NUT ICE CREAM PIE

2 c. graham cracker crumbs
2 tbsp. sugar
1/4 c. melted butter
1 qt. vanilla ice cream
1/2 c. light corn syrup
1/3 c. creamy peanut butter
2/3 c. macadamia nuts

Combine . first 3 ingredients in bowl, mixing well.
Press ..... into 9-inch pie pan.
Bake ..... at 350 degrees until brown.
Spoon ... half the ice cream into cooled crust.
Combine . corn syrup and peanut butter in bowl, mixing well.
Pour ..... half the mixture over ice cream.
Sprinkle .. with half the macadamia nuts.
Repeat ... layers.
Freeze ... for 5 hours.

Murna Hansemann
Streamwood H. S., Streamwood, Illinois

CREAMY PEANUT BUTTER PIE

4 oz. cream cheese, softened
6 oz. creamy peanut butter
1/2 box confectioners' sugar
3/4 c. milk
8 oz. Cool Whip
2 graham cracker pie crusts

Combine . first 4 ingredients in bowl, mixing well.
Blend .... in Cool Whip.
Pour ..... into pie crusts.
Freeze ... until firm.
Slice ..... with wet knife.

Margaret W. Lyles
Westminster H. S., Toccoa, Georgia

JUDY'S PEANUT BUTTER PIE

8 oz. cream cheese, softened
1 1/2 c. sugar
3/4 c. milk
18 oz. chunky peanut butter
12 oz. Cool Whip
2 graham cracker pie crusts

Combine . first 5 ingredients in large bowl in order given, beating well.
Pour ..... into crusts.
Freeze ... until firm.

Judy Swinny
Crittenden County H. S., Marion, Kentucky

PEANUT BUTTER-ICE CREAM PIE

12 chocolate cookies, finely crushed
1/4 c. melted butter
3/4 c. sifted confectioners' sugar
1 8-oz. package cream cheese, softened
2/3 c. chunky peanut butter
2 c. packed vanilla ice cream, softened

Combine . cookie crumbs and butter in bowl, mixing well.
Press ..... over bottom and side of pie pan.
Chill ..... in freezer.
Cream ... sugar and cream cheese in bowl until fluffy.
Add ..... peanut butter, beating until smooth.
Beat ..... in ice cream with electric mixer on low speed until creamy.
Pour ..... into prepared crust.

Garnish .. with chopped peanuts and chocolate curls.
Freeze ... until firm.
Yield .... 8-10 servings.

Helen Boren
Ponca City H. S., Ponca City, Oklahoma

CHUNKY PEANUT BUTTER-ICE CREAM PIE

1 1/2 c. graham cracker crumbs
1/4 c. sugar
1/2 c. butter, melted
1 qt. vanilla ice cream
1/2 c. chunk-style peanut butter
1/2 c. whipping cream, whipped

Combine . first 3 ingredients in bowl.
Reserve .. several tablespoons crumbs for garnish.
Press ..... remaining crumbs into 9-inch pie pan.
Chill ..... until firm.
Stir ...... ice cream in bowl until just softened.
Fold ..... in peanut butter.
Blend .... in whipped cream.
Pour ..... into prepared crust.
Sprinkle .. with reserved crumbs.
Freeze ... until firm.

Sharon S. Reints
Alta Community School, Alta, Iowa

FROZEN RIBBON PIE

1 pt. vanilla ice cream
1 pt. sherbet
1 graham cracker pie shell

Beat ..... ice cream in bowl with electric mixer until of whipped cream consistency.
Spread ... in pie shell.
Freeze ... until firm.
Beat ..... sherbet in bowl with electric mixer until of whipped cream consistency.
Spread ... over ice cream layer.
Freeze ... until firm.
Yield .... 8 servings.

Mrs. Roseann Campbell
Warren Harding H. S., Bridgeport, Connecticut

Pies
and Pastries

APPLE PIE WITH CINNAMON

2 1/2 c. sifted flour
3 tbsp. sugar
1/2 tsp. salt
1/4 tsp. lemon peel
6 tbsp. butter
1 egg
4 or 5 apples, peeled, sliced
1 tbsp. lemon juice
2 tsp. cinnamon
1/2 c. heavy cream
1 egg yolk

Combine . flour, 2 tablespoons sugar, salt and lemon rind in bowl.
Cut . . . . . . in butter until crumbly.
Add . . . . . egg and enough cold water to make firm dough, mixing thoroughly.
Chill . . . . . in refrigerator.
Combine . apples, lemon juice, 1 tablespoon sugar and cinnamon in bowl.
Roll . . . . . out dough on floured surface.
Fit . . . . . . dough into buttered 9-inch pie plate.
Prick . . . . with fork.
Arrange . . apples in circular pattern in crust.
Bake . . . . . at 375 degrees for 20 minutes.
Blend . . . . cream and egg yolk together until smooth.
Spread . . . over pie.
Bake . . . . . for 10 minutes longer or until set.

Priscilla Erat Goldner
Norwalk H. S., Norwalk, Connecticut

CHEESE CRUMBLE APPLE PIE

2 c. Cheddar cheese, shredded
1 pkg. pie crust mix
3 lb. apples, peeled, sliced
1 tbsp. flour
Freshly grated nutmeg
1/2 c. sugar
1/2 c. packed brown sugar
3/4 tsp. cinnamon
3 tbsp. butter

Mix . . . . . 1 cup Cheddar cheese with 1/2 package pie crust mix in bowl.
Blend . . . . in 2 to 2 1/2 tablespoons water.
Roll . . . . . dough on floured surface to fit 9-inch pie plate.
Place . . . . in pie plate, making 3/4-inch rim to hold in juices.

Arrange . . apples in pastry.
Sprinkle . . flour over apples.
Dust . . . . . with nutmeg.
Mix . . . . . remaining pie crust mix with sugars and cinnamon.
Cut . . . . . . in butter until crumbly.
Sprinkle . . half the crumb mixture over apples.
Sprinkle . . remaining 1 cup cheese over crumb mixture.
Top . . . . . with remaining crumb mixture.
Bake . . . . . at 375 degrees for 40 minutes or until apples are tender.

Photograph for this recipe on opposite page.

MOCK APPLE PIE

1 1/2 c. sugar
2 tbsp. butter
2 tsp. cream of tartar
1 tsp. cinnamon
1/2 tsp. nutmeg
15 saltine crackers, broken
Raisins (opt.)
1 recipe 2-crust pie pastry

Combine . first 5 ingredients with 1 1/2 cups water in saucepan.
Bring . . . . to a boil.
Pour . . . . . over crackers and raisins in bowl.
Line . . . . . pie plate with half the pastry.
Turn . . . . . cracker mixture into pie pastry.
Cover . . . . with remaining pastry, sealing and fluting edges.
Make . . . . several slits in top crust.
Bake . . . . . at 350 degrees for 30 minutes or until brown.

Sue Farris
Altus-Denning H. S., Altus, Arkansas

SOUR CREAM-APPLE PIE

Flour
Sugar
1/2 tsp. salt
1 egg
1 c. sour cream
1 tsp. vanilla extract
1/4 tsp. nutmeg
2 c. peeled diced apples
1   9-in. unbaked pie shell
1 1/4 tsp. cinnamon
1/2 c. butter, softened

Sift . . . . . . 2 tablespoons flour, 3/4 cup sugar and salt together into large bowl.
Add . . . . . egg, sour cream, vanilla and nutmeg, beating until smooth.
Stir . . . . . . in apples.
Pour . . . . . into pie shell.
Bake . . . . . at 400 degrees for 15 minutes.
Reduce . . . temperature to 350 degrees.
Bake . . . . . for 30 minutes longer.
Combine . 1/3 cup flour, 1/3 cup sugar and cinnamon in bowl, mixing well.
Cut . . . . . . in butter until crumbly.
Sprinkle . . over pie.
Bake . . . . . for 10 minutes longer.

Dolores Hastings
Edmond Mid H. S., Edmond, Oklahoma

YOGURT-APPLE PIE

2 c. flour, sifted
1/2 tsp. salt
1/4 tsp. baking powder
Sugar
1/2 c. butter
3 1/2 lb. apples, peeled, thinly sliced
Cinnamon
1 egg
1 c. yogurt

Sift . . . . . . first 3 ingredients and 2 tablespoons sugar together into bowl.
Cut . . . . . . in butter until crumbly.
Press . . . . . into 9-inch pie plate.
Arrange . . apples over crust.
Sprinkle . . with 1/2 cup sugar and 1 teaspoon cinnamon.
Bake . . . . . at 425 degrees for 15 minutes.
Beat . . . . . egg and yogurt together until smooth.
Spoon . . . over apples.
Bake . . . . . for 30 minutes longer.
Sprinkle . . hot pie with additional cinnamon and sugar.
Serve . . . . warm.

Barsha Elzey
Terra Linda H. S., San Rafael, California

AVOCADO PIE

1 avocado, peeled, chopped
2/3 c. lemon juice
1 can sweetened condensed milk
1 graham cracker pie crust
Whipped cream

Place . . . . avocado in blender container.
Process . . . until smooth.
Add . . . . . lemon juice and sweetened condensed milk, blending well.
Pour . . . . . into pie crust.
Chill . . . . until set.
Top . . . . . with whipped cream.

Stephanie Peindl
Marana H. S., Marana, Arizona

CARAMELIZED BANANA PIE

1 can sweetened condensed milk
Vanilla wafers
2 lg. bananas, sliced
2 tbsp. lemon juice
1 sm. carton Cool Whip
Maraschino cherries

Place . . . . condensed milk can in heavy saucepan in water to cover.
Boil . . . . . for 3 hours.
Chill . . . . . in refrigerator.
Line . . . . . bottom and side of 10-inch pie plate with vanilla wafers.
Open . . . . condensed milk can and remove caramelized milk by scraping side of can carefully with knife.
Slice . . . . . caramelized milk into thin slices, arranging over wafers.
Arrange . . bananas over milk slices.
Drizzle . . . with lemon juice.
Top . . . . . with Cool Whip and cherries.
Chill . . . . . until serving time.

Sue Dennis
Huntsville H. S., Huntsville, Arkansas

LEMON-CRUSTED BLUEBERRY PIE

2 c. sifted flour
Salt
Fresh grated lemon rind
2/3 c. shortening
Fresh lemon juice
4 c. fresh blueberries
3/4 to 1 c. sugar
3 tbsp. flour
1 tbsp. butter

Combine . sifted flour, 1 teaspoon salt and 1/2 teaspoon lemon rind in bowl.
Cut . . . . . . in shortening until crumbly.
Sprinkle . . with 1 tablespoon lemon juice and enough cold water to make dough.
Line . . . . . 9-inch pie plate with half the pastry.
Combine . blueberries, sugar, 3 tablespoons flour, 1/2 teaspoon lemon rind and dash of salt in bowl, mixing well.
Pour . . . . . into pastry.
Drizzle . . . with 1 to 2 teaspoons lemon juice.
Dot . . . . . with butter.
Cover . . . . with remaining pastry, sealing and fluting edges.
Make . . . . several slits in top crust.
Bake . . . . . at 400 degrees for 30 to 35 minutes or until brown.

Judy Touby
Scottsdale H. S., Scottsdale, Arizona

FRESH BLUEBERRY PIE

1. baked pie shell
4 c. fresh blueberries
1 c. sugar
3 tbsp. cornstarch
1/4 tsp. salt
1 tsp. butter

Fill . . . . . . pie shell with 2 cups blueberries.
Combine . remaining blueberries with sugar, cornstarch, salt and 1/4 cup water in saucepan.
Cook . . . . until well blended and thickened.
Stir . . . . . . in butter; cool.
Pour . . . . . over blueberries in pie shell.
Chill . . . . . until serving time.
Top . . . . . with whipped cream.

Frances V. Hamlet
Alton Park Jr. H. S., Chattanooga, Tennessee

BANANA-BERRY PIE

1 8-oz. package cream cheese, softened
1 can sweetened condensed milk
1/3 c. lemon juice
3 med. bananas, mashed
1 butter cookie pie crust
1 can blueberry pie filling

Beat . . . . . cream cheese in bowl until light and fluffy.
Add . . . . . condensed milk, lemon juice and bananas, beating well.
Pour . . . . . into crust.
Chill . . . . until firm.
Top . . . . . with pie filling.
Chill . . . . until serving time.

Linda W. Skelton
Walterboro H. S., Walterboro, South Carolina

BLUEBERRY TORTE PIE

14 graham crackers, crushed
1/3 c. butter, melted
1/4 c. sugar
3 egg yolks, beaten
1/2 c. confectioners' sugar
8 oz. cream cheese, softened
3 egg whites, stiffly beaten
1 tsp. vanilla extract
1 can blueberry pie filling

Combine . first 3 ingredients in bowl, mixing well.
Press . . . . . into 9-inch pie plate.
Beat . . . . . next 3 ingredients in bowl until smooth.
Fold . . . . . in stiffly beaten egg whites and vanilla.
Spread . . . in crust.
Bake . . . . . at 300 degrees for 30 minutes.
Spoon . . . pie filling over cooled pie.
Chill . . . . . for 2 hours or longer.
Serve . . . . with whipped cream.

Diane Gibbs
New Bloomfield R III H. S.
New Bloomfield, Missouri

CARAMEL PIE

2/3 stick margarine
1 c. packed brown sugar
2 tbsp. (heaping) cornstarch

2 c. milk
2 egg yolks, beaten
1   9-in. baked pie shell
1 recipe meringue

Combine . margarine and brown sugar in saucepan.
Boil ..... over low heat for 1 minute, stirring constantly.
Blend .... cornstarch with milk in bowl.
Add ..... egg yolks, mixing well.
Stir ...... into brown sugar mixture.
Boil ..... until thickened, stirring constantly.
Pour ..... into pie shell.
Top ..... with meringue.
Bake ..... at 400 degrees for 8 minutes or until brown.

Darla J. Hillier
Westerville South H. S., Westerville, Ohio

BLACK FOREST PIE

2 tsp. cornstarch
1   21-oz. can cherry pie filling
1/2 tsp. grated orange rind
2 c. miniature marshmallows
1/2 c. milk
1/2 tsp. vanilla extract
1 c. whipping cream, whipped
1 chocolate-flavored pie crust
Fudge sauce

Combine . cornstarch with 3 tablespoons water in saucepan, mixing well.
Stir ...... in cherry pie filling.
Cook .... until thick, stirring constantly.
Remove .. from heat; cool.
Add ..... orange rind.
Combine . marshmallows and milk in saucepan.
Cook .... over low heat until melted.
Add ..... vanilla.
Fold ..... into whipped cream.
Spoon ... into crust, shaping depression in center.
Fill ...... center with cherry mixture.
Spoon ... additional whipped cream around edge.
Drizzle ... fudge sauce over whipped cream.
Chill ..... until serving time.

Barbara Porter
Horizon H. S., Scottsdale, Arizona

CANDY-APPLE CHIFFON PIE

1/2 lb. vanilla caramels
1 tbsp. butter
1 baked 9-in. pie shell
4 tsp. unflavored gelatin
2 c. canned applesauce
1/4 tsp. salt
2 tbsp. sugar
1 egg, beaten
2 tbsp. lemon juice
1 c. whipping cream, whipped
Whole walnuts (opt.)

Combine . half the caramels, 2 tablespoons hot water and butter in top of double boiler.
Cook .... over hot water until smooth, stirring constantly.
Pour ..... into pie shell, spreading immediately to cover bottom.
Soften ... gelatin in 1/4 cup cold water.
Place .... remaining caramels and 6 tablespoons hot water in double boiler pan.
Cook .... until smooth, stirring constantly.
Add ..... applesauce and gelatin to caramels.
Mix ..... until well blended.
Stir ...... in salt, sugar and egg.
Cook .... for 5 minutes or until smooth and well blended.
Cool ..... until slightly thickened.
Blend .... lemon juice into whipped cream.
Whip .... applesauce mixture until fluffy.
Fold ..... in whipped cream.
Spoon ... into pie shell.
Chill ..... until firm.
Garnish .. with walnuts.

Photograph for this recipe above.

CHERRY-PECAN PIE

1 sm. can evaporated milk
1 can sweetened condensed milk
1 c. chopped pecans
1 can sour pie cherries, drained
Pinch of salt
Juice of 3 lemons
2 graham cracker pie crusts

Blend .... evaporated milk and condensed milk in bowl.
Stir ...... in pecans, cherries and salt.
Fold ..... in lemon juice.
Pour ..... into pie crusts.
Chill ..... until set.

Linda Owens
Mt. Vernon H. S., Mt. Vernon, Texas

SUNRISE CHERRY PIE

1 8 1/4-oz. can crushed pineapple
1 8-oz. package cream cheese, softened
1/2 tsp. vanilla extract
1 can cherry pie filling
1/4 c. confectioners' sugar
1 c. whipping cream
1 graham cracker crust

Drain .... pineapple reserving 2 tablespoons syrup.
Blend .... cream cheese, vanilla and reserved syrup in bowl until smooth.
Stir ...... in 1/4 cup pineapple and 1/2 cup pie filling.
Add ..... sugar to whipping cream gradually, beating until soft peaks form.
Fold ..... in cream cheese mixture.
Pour ..... into crust.
Top ..... with pie filling mounded in center and pineapple around edge.

Elaine Young
Pasadena H. S., Pasadena, Texas

CHERRY-CHEESE PIE

1 8-oz. package cream cheese, softened
1 can sweetened condensed milk
1/3 c. lemon juice
1 tsp. vanilla extract
1 graham cracker pie crust
1 can cherry pie filling, chilled

Beat ..... cream cheese in bowl until light and fluffy.

Blend .... in condensed milk, lemon juice and vanilla.
Pour ..... into crust.
Top ..... with pie filling.

Mary Beth Talerico
Maplewood Area Joint Vocational School
Ravenna, Ohio

CHESS PIE

2 c. sugar
2 tbsp. cornmeal
1 tbsp. vinegar
1/2 c. melted margarine
1 tbsp. milk
1 tsp. vanilla extract
4 eggs, beaten
1 unbaked pie shell

Combine . first 4 ingredients in bowl, mixing well.
Stir ...... in milk, vanilla and eggs.
Pour ..... into pie shell.
Bake ..... at 325 degrees for 1 hour.

Julia A. Arnelt
Madison County Technical Center, Huntsville, Alabama

GAIL'S LEMON CHESS PIE

2 c. sugar
4 eggs
1 tbsp. flour
1 tbsp. cornmeal
1/4 c. milk
1/4 c. melted butter
1/4 c. lemon juice
3 tsp. grated lemon rind
1 unbaked pie shell

Beat ..... sugar, eggs, flour and cornmeal in bowl until blended.
Add ..... remaining ingredients except pie shell, mixing well.
Pour ..... into pie shell.
Bake ..... at 400 degrees for 10 minutes.
Reduce ... temperature to 300 degrees.
Bake ..... for 30 minutes longer.

Gail M. Skelton
Biggersville H. S., Corinth, Mississippi

LEMON CHESS PIE

1 1/2 tbsp. flour
1 1/2 c. sugar

3 eggs
1/2 c. butter, melted
4 tbsp. lemon juice
1/2 c. buttermilk
1 tsp. vanilla extract
1 9-in. unbaked pie shell

Combine . flour and sugar in large bowl.
Add . . . . . eggs and butter.
Beat . . . . . with electric mixer until blended.
Stir . . . . . . in lemon juice, buttermilk and vanilla.
Pour . . . . . into pastry shell.
Bake . . . . . at 325 degrees for 45 minutes or until top is light golden brown.
Cool . . . . . on wire rack.
Chill . . . . . until serving time.

Susanna Franklin
Afton H. S., Afton, Oklahoma

CARIBBEAN FUDGE PIE

1/4 c. butter, softened
3/4 c. packed brown sugar
3 eggs
1 12-oz. package semisweet chocolate chips, melted
2 tsp. instant coffee
1 tsp. rum extract
1/4 c. flour
Pecans, chopped
1 unbaked 9-in. pie shell

Cream . . . butter and sugar together in bowl.
Add . . . . . eggs 1 at a time, beating well after each addition.
Blend . . . . in next 3 ingredients.
Stir . . . . . . in flour and 1 cup pecans.
Pour . . . . . into pie shell.
Sprinkle . . with additional pecans.
Bake . . . . . at 375 degrees for 25 minutes; cool.
Top . . . . . with whipped cream.

Katherine A. Winchester
Winter Park H. S., Winter Park, Florida

CHOCOLATE-MARSHMALLOW PIE

20 lg. marshmallows
3/4 c. milk
2 tbsp. cocoa
Pinch of salt
1 tsp. vanilla extract
1 tbsp. rum

1 c. whipping cream, whipped
1 baked pie shell

Combine . first 4 ingredients in top of double boiler.
Cook . . . . over medium heat until marshmallows melt; cool.
Add . . . . . vanilla and rum.
Fold . . . . . in whipped cream.
Pour . . . . . into pie shell.
Chill . . . . . until set.
Garnish . . with whipped cream and pecans.

Broxie C. Stuckey
Gordo H. S., Gordo, Alabama

CHOCOLATE SILK PIE

3 1/2 tbsp. cocoa
1 1/2 c. sugar
2 eggs, beaten
1 sm. can evaporated milk
1 tsp. vanilla extract
1 8-in. unbaked pie shell

Mix . . . . . cocoa and sugar.
Combine . eggs, evaporated milk and vanilla in bowl, beating well.
Add . . . . . cocoa mixture, beating until dissolved.
Pour . . . . . into pie shell.
Bake . . . . . at 350 degrees for 35 minutes.
Top . . . . . with whipped cream.

Wyvonnie Campbell
East Forsyth Sr. H. S., Kernersville, North Carolina

ANN'S EASY CHOCOLATE PIE

1/2 c. margarine, softened
1 tsp. vanilla extract
2 eggs
1/2 c. sugar
1 sq. chocolate, melted
1 c. pecans, chopped
1 graham cracker crust
1 8-oz. carton Cool Whip

Combine . first 5 ingredients in small bowl.
Beat . . . . . with electric mixer on medium speed for 20 minutes.
Stir . . . . . . in pecans.
Pour . . . . . into pie crust.
Chill . . . . . for 6 hours or longer.
Top . . . . . with Cool Whip.

Ann Hardin Ford
Joyce Kilmer Intermediate School, Vienna, Virginia

FRENCH SILK CHOCOLATE PIE

1/2 c. margarine, softened
3/4 c. sugar
1 sq. baking chocolate, melted
1 tsp. vanilla extract
2 eggs
1 baked pie shell

Cream . . . margarine and sugar in bowl until fluffy.
Blend . . . . in chocolate and vanilla.
Add . . . . . eggs 1 at a time, beating with electric mixer at high speed for 5 minutes after each addition.
Pour . . . . . into pie shell.
Chill . . . . . for 2 hours or longer.
Serve . . . . with whipped cream.

Sally S. Harms
Wheatland-Chili H. S., Scottsville, New York

CHOCO-NUT CHIFFON PIE

1 c. corn flake crumbs
2 tbsp. finely chopped nuts
1/3 c. butter, melted
Sugar
1 env. unflavored gelatin
1/8 tsp. salt
1 1/2 c. milk
1 c. chocolate chips
1 tsp. vanilla extract
1 c. whipping cream, whipped

Combine . first 3 ingredients with 2 tablespoons sugar in bowl, mixing well.
Press . . . . . into 9-inch pie pan; chill.
Mix . . . . . gelatin, salt and 1/2 cup sugar in saucepan.
Add . . . . . milk and chocolate chips.
Cook . . . . until chocolate chips melt, stirring constantly.
Beat . . . . . until smooth.
Stir . . . . . . in vanilla; chill.
Fold . . . . . whipped cream into chocolate mixture.
Pour . . . . . into pie shell.
Chill . . . . . until firm.

Kathy Ferguson
Moore H. S., Moore, Oklahoma

DELUXE CHOCOLATE PIE

1/3 c. smooth peanut butter
1/4 c. brown sugar
1/8 tsp. salt
1/4 c. margarine, melted
1 c. corn flake crumbs
1 3-oz. package instant chocolate pudding mix
1 1/2 c. milk
1 pt. vanilla ice cream, softened
1 pkg. Dream Whip
1 tsp. vanilla extract

Combine . first 4 ingredients in bowl, blending well.
Stir . . . . . . in crumbs, mixing well.
Press . . . . . into 8-inch pie pan; chill.
Prepare . . . pudding mix according to package directions using 1 cup milk.
Blend . . . . in ice cream.
Pour . . . . . into pie crust.
Prepare . . . Dream Whip with 1/2 cup milk using package directions.
Fold . . . . . in vanilla.
Spread . . . over pie.
Chill . . . . . until serving time.

Karlene Gullberg
Cahokia H. S., Cahokia, Illinois

FUDGE PIE

1/2 c. butter, softened
1 c. sugar, sifted
2 eggs, separated
1/3 c. sifted flour
1/2 c. cocoa
1 tsp. vanilla extract
1/8 tsp. salt
1 unbaked 9-in. pie crust

Cream . . . butter and sugar together in bowl.
Stir . . . . . . in egg yolks.
Blend . . . . in flour, cocoa and vanilla.
Beat . . . . . egg whites and salt until stiff.
Fold . . . . . into chocolate mixture.
Pour . . . . . into pie crust.
Bake . . . . . at 325 degrees for 30 minutes.

Judy Newcomb
Lake Hamilton Jr. H. S., Pearcy, Arkansas

FUDGE PIE

1 stick butter, softened
1 c. sugar
3 tbsp. cocoa
1/4 c. flour

Pinch of salt
1/4 c. milk
2 eggs
1 c. chopped pecans (opt.)
1 tsp. vanilla extract
1 unbaked pie shell

Cream ... butter and sugar together in bowl.
Stir ...... in remaining ingredients except pie shell, mixing well.
Pour ..... into pie shell.
Bake ..... at 350 degrees for 20 minutes.
Top ..... with whipped cream.

Lynne Otwell
Beauregard H. S., Opelika, Alabama

GERMAN CHOCOLATE PIE

1/4 c. butter
3/4 c. sugar
2 oz. German's chocolate
1/3 c. evaporated milk
3 eggs
1 tsp. vanilla extract
1 c. flaked coconut
1/3 c. chopped pecans
1 unbaked 8-in. pie shell

Melt ..... first 3 ingredients in saucepan over low heat, stirring constantly; cool.
Add ..... milk, eggs and vanilla, beating well.
Sprinkle .. coconut and pecans in pie shell.
Cover .... with chocolate mixture.
Bake ..... at 375 degrees on lower oven rack for 45 minutes.

Gloria Lloyd
Taylorsville H. S., Salt Lake City, Utah

HEATH ANGEL PIE

1/2 lb. marshmallows
1/2 c. milk
2 tbsp. (heaping) cocoa
3/4 c. crushed Heath bars, chilled
3/4 lg. container Cool Whip
1 graham cracker pie crust

Melt ..... first 3 ingredients in saucepan over low heat, mixing well.
Cool ..... completely.
Fold ..... in crushed Heath bars and Cool Whip.

Spoon ... into pie crust.
Chill ..... in refrigerator.

Judy Lorenz
Coopersville Area Public Schools
Coopersville, Michigan

HERSHEY BAR PIE

1 8-oz. Hershey bar with almonds
1 tsp. instant coffee (opt.)
1 13 1/2-oz. carton Cool Whip
1 chocolate crumb pie crust

Peel ..... a few chocolate curls from edge of candy bar, reserving for decoration.
Melt ..... candy bar with 1 tablespoon water in saucepan over low heat.
Blend .... in instant coffee.
Beat ..... chocolate mixture and Cool Whip together until well blended.
Pour ..... into pie shell.
Top ..... with chocolate curls.
Freeze ... until firm.

Marcy Helser
East H. S., Cheyenne, Wyoming

MICROWAVE GRASSHOPPER PIE

1 1/2 c. chocolate cookie crumbs
3 tbsp. butter, melted
3 c. miniature marshmallows
1/2 c. milk
2 to 3 tbsp. Creme de Cacao
2 to 3 tbsp. Creme de Menthe
1 c. whipping cream, whipped

Blend .... cookie crumbs with butter in bowl.
Press ..... into bottom and side of glass pie plate.
Microwave on High for 2 minutes.
Combine . marshmallows and milk in large glass bowl.
Microwave on High for 2 minutes or until marshmallows puff.
Blend .... melted marshmallows with Creme de Cacao and Creme de Menthe.
Cool ..... for 30 minutes or until thickened but not set.
Fold ..... in whipped cream.
Pour ..... into crust.
Chill ..... for 4 hours or longer.

Betty Stephenson
Independent Living Class, Brighton Sr. H. S.
Brighton, Colorado

TOLLHOUSE COOKIE PIE

2 eggs
1/2 c. flour
1/2 c. sugar
1/2 c. packed brown sugar
1 c. melted butter
1 6-oz. package semisweet chocolate chips
1 c. chopped walnuts
1 unbaked 9-in. pie shell

Beat . . . . . eggs in bowl until foamy.
Add . . . . . flour, sugars and butter gradually, beating constantly.
Stir . . . . . . in chocolate chips and walnuts.
Pour . . . . . into pie shell.
Bake . . . . . at 325 degrees for 1 hour.
Garnish . . with whipped cream.

Tamara Bowyer
Virginia Beach Schools, Virginia Beach, Virginia

WHITE CHRISTMAS PIE

1 c. sugar
1/4 c. flour
1 tbsp. unflavored gelatin
1/2 tsp. salt
1 1/4 c. milk
3 egg whites
1/4 tsp. cream of tartar
1/4 tsp. vanilla extract
2 drops of almond extract
1 c. flaked coconut
1 c. whipping cream, whipped
1 baked 9-in. pie crust

Blend . . . . 1/2 cup sugar, flour, gelatin and salt together in saucepan.
Stir . . . . . . in milk.
Cook . . . over medium heat until mixture boils.
Boil . . . . . for 1 minute; cool.
Beat . . . . . egg whites with cream of tartar until soft peaks from.
Add . . . . . 1/2 cup sugar gradually, beating until stiff.
Fold . . . . . in flavorings, coconut and whipped cream.
Blend . . . . in gelatin mixture.
Spoon . . . into pie crust; chill.
Top . . . . . with whipped cream.

Phyllis K. Sams
Muskogee H. S., Muskogee, Oklahoma

COCONUT CREAM PIE

1/3 c. flour
Sugar
1/4 tsp. salt
2 c. milk, scalded
3 egg yolks, slightly beaten
2 tbsp. butter
1 1/2 c. coconut
1/2 tsp. vanilla extract
1 baked 9-in. pie shell
2 tbsp. cornstarch
3 egg whites, stiffly beaten

Combine . flour, 2/3 cup sugar and salt in saucepan.
Add . . . . . milk gradually, blending well.
Bring . . . . to a boil over medium heat, stirring constantly.
Cook . . . . for 2 minutes, stirring constantly.
Stir . . . . . . a small amount of hot mixture into egg yolks; stir egg yolks into hot mixture.
Cook . . . . for 1 minute, stirring constantly.
Stir . . . . . . in butter, 1 cup coconut and vanilla; cool slightly.
Pour . . . . . into pie shell.
Blend . . . . cornstarch, 1/2 cup sugar and 1/2 cup water in saucepan.
Cook . . . . until clear, stirring constantly.
Add . . . . . 2 tablespoons sugar to stiffly beaten egg whites gradually, beating constantly.
Fold . . . . . in cornstarch mixture.
Spread . . . over filling, sealing well to crust.
Sprinkle . . with 1/2 cup coconut.
Bake . . . . . at 375 degrees for 12 to 15 minutes or until brown.

Dorothy G. Rothermel
Pasadena H. S., Pasadena, Texas

MARTHA'S CREAM PIE

7 tbsp. shortening
Milk
Flour
1/2 tsp. salt
1 tbsp. cornstarch
Sugar
3 egg yolks, beaten
1 tbsp. butter
1/2 tsp. vanilla extract
3 egg whites, stiffly beaten

Beat . . . . . shortening, 2 teaspoons milk and 3 tablespoons boiling water in bowl until light and fluffy.

Stir . . . . . . in 1 1/4 cups flour and salt with fork until dough leaves side of bowl.

Roll . . . . . out on floured surface.

Fit . . . . . . into pie plate, pricking with fork.

Bake . . . . . at 450 degrees for 14 minutes.

Combine . 1/4 cup flour with cornstarch, 2/3 cup sugar and 2 cups milk in saucepan, blending well.

Cook . . . . over low heat until thick, stirring constantly.

Stir . . . . . . a small amount of hot mixture into egg yolks; stir egg yolks into hot mixture.

Cook . . . . until thick, stirring constantly.

Stir . . . . . . in butter and vanilla.

Pour . . . . . into pie shell.

Add . . . . . 6 tablespoons sugar gradually to stiffly beaten egg whites, beating constantly.

Cover . . . . filling with meringue.

Bake . . . . . at 375 degrees for 10 minutes or until brown.

Martha Pearce
Muskogee H. S., Muskogee, Oklahoma

DREAM PIE

1 lg. can tart cherries
1/4 c. flour
1/2 c. sugar
1 tsp. vanilla extract
1 sm. package orange gelatin
1 to 2 tsp. red food coloring
8 to 10 bananas, sliced
1 lg. can crushed pineapple, drained
1 c. chopped pecans
2 baked pie shells

Drain . . . . cherries, reserving juice.

Combine . cherry juice with flour and sugar in saucepan.

Cook . . . . until thick, stirring constantly.

Stir . . . . . . in vanilla, gelatin and food coloring.

Cool . . . . . until very thick.

Place . . . . bananas, cherries, pineapple and pecans in bowl.

Pour . . . . . cooled sauce over fruit, mixing well.

Spoon . . . into pie shells.

Chill . . . . . until serving time.

Debbie Jacoway
Central Jr. H. S., Oklahoma City, Oklahoma

EGG CUSTARD PIE

1/4 lb. butter, softened
1 1/2 c. sugar
4 tbsp. cornstarch
4 eggs
2 1/2 c. milk
1 tsp. vanilla extract
1 tsp. nutmeg
2 unbaked 9-in. pie shells

Cream . . . butter, sugar and cornstarch together in bowl.

Add . . . . . eggs 1 at a time, beating well after each addition.

Stir . . . . . . in milk, vanilla and nutmeg, mixing thoroughly.

Pour . . . . . into pie shells.

Bake . . . . . at 425 degrees for 15 minutes.

Reduce . . . temperature to 325 degrees.

Bake . . . . . for 20 minutes longer.

Mrs. William Cooke
Bainbridge H. S., Bainbridge, Georgia

FRUIT COCKTAIL PARFAIT PIE

1 1/4 c. graham cracker crumbs
1/2 c. melted margarine
1 1-lb. can fruit cocktail
1 3-oz. package lemon gelatin
1 pt. vanilla ice cream, softened
1/2 c. chopped nuts (opt.)

Combine . first 2 ingredients in bowl, mixing well.

Press . . . . . firmly into greased 9-inch pie pan.

Drain . . . . fruit cocktail, reserving juice.

Add . . . . . enough water to measure 1 cup liquid.

Heat . . . . . to boiling point in saucepan.

Add . . . . . gelatin, stirring to dissolve.

Stir . . . . . . in 1/2 cup cold water and ice cream, stirring until thickened.

Fold . . . . . in fruit cocktail and nuts.

Pour . . . . . into crust.

Chill . . . . . for 45 minutes or until firm.

Julia Wilson
Woodlan H. S., Woodburn, Indiana

JAPANESE PIE

1 stick margarine, melted
1 c. sugar
3 eggs
1 tsp. vinegar
1/2 c. raisins
1/2 c. chopped pecans
1/2 c. coconut
1 unbaked pie shell

Combine . first 7 ingredients in bowl, beating well.
Pour ..... into pie shell.
Bake ..... at 325 degrees until firm.

Mary H. McMillin
Ripley H. S., Ripley, Mississippi

KOOL-AID PIE

1 lg. can evaporated milk, chilled
2/3 c. sugar
1 pkg. unsweetened lemon-lime Kool-Aid
1 graham cracker pie crust
Decorator sprinkles

Beat ..... milk in chilled mixer bowl with electric mixer at high speed until thick.
Add ..... sugar and Kool-Aid, mixing well.
Pour ..... into pie crust.
Top ..... with sprinkles.
Freeze ... until firm.
Thaw .... for 30 minutes before serving.

Katy Smith
Morristown-Hamblen West H. S.
Morristown, Tennessee

BEST-EVER LEMON PIE

Sugar
7 tbsp. cornstarch
3 eggs, separated
1/3 c. lemon juice
3 tbsp. butter
1 1/2 tsp. lemon extract
2 tsp. vinegar
1 9-in. baked pie shell
Pinch of salt
1 tsp. vanilla extract

Combine . 1 1/4 cups sugar and 6 tablespoons cornstarch in double boiler.
Add ..... 2 cups water, stirring well.
Beat ..... egg yolks and lemon juice together.

Stir ...... into sugar mixture.
Cook .... over boiling water for 25 minutes or until thick.
Add ..... next 3 ingredients, mixing well.
Pour ..... into pie shell.
Blend .... 1 tablespoon cornstarch with 2 tablespoons cold water in saucepan.
Add ..... 1/2 cup boiling water.
Cook .... until thick and clear, stirring constantly.
Let ...... stand until completely cool.
Beat ..... egg whites until foamy.
Add ..... 6 tablespoons sugar, beating until stiff.
Mix ..... in salt and vanilla.
Beat ..... in cold cornstarch mixture gradually.
Spread ... over pie filling.
Bake ..... at 350 degrees for 10 minutes.

Kay Caskey
Manogue H. S., Reno, Nevada

EASY LEMON CUSTARD PIE

3/4 c. sugar
1/3 c. lemon juice
1 tsp. grated lemon rind
1/4 tsp. salt
3 eggs
1 unbaked 8-in. pie shell, chilled
Nutmeg

Combine . first 5 ingredients and 3/4 cup water in mixing bowl.
Beat ..... with electric mixer on medium speed for 7 to 8 minutes.
Place .... pie shell on oven rack.
Fill ...... with egg mixture.
Bake ..... at 425 degrees for 20 minutes.
Reduce ... temperature to 250 degrees.
Bake ..... for 10 minutes longer.
Sprinkle .. with nutmeg.
Cool ..... before serving.

Mavis Holley
Palatka H. S., Palatka, Florida

LEMON ICEBOX PIE

3 eggs, separated
Juice of 2 lemons
1 can sweetened condensed milk
1 graham cracker pie crust
1/4 c. sugar

Beat . . . . . egg yolks lightly in bowl.
Add . . . . . lemon juice, mixing well.
Blend . . . . in condensed milk.
Pour . . . . . into crust.
Beat . . . . . egg whites in bowl until soft peaks form.
Add . . . . . sugar gradually, beating until stiff.
Spread . . . over filling, sealing edge.
Bake . . . . . at 325 degrees until meringue is light brown.
Chill . . . . . until serving time.

Betty Lewis
Princess Anne Jr. H. S., Virginia Beach, Virginia

LEMON PIE

1 can sweetened condensed milk
1/2 c. lemon juice
1 8-oz. container whipped topping
1 graham cracker pie shell

Combine . milk and lemon juice in bowl, mixing well.
Fold . . . . . in whipped topping, blending thoroughly.
Pour . . . . . into pie shell.
Chill . . . . . for several hours before serving.

Lillian Spencer
Ft. Pierce Central H. S., Ft. Pierce, Florida

LEMONADE PIE

1 6-oz. can frozen lemonade concentrate, thawed
1 1/2 pt. whipping cream, whipped
1 can sweetened condensed milk
3 to 5 drops of yellow food coloring
1 8-in. baked pie shell

Combine . first 3 ingredients in bowl, mixing well.
Tint . . . . . with food coloring.
Pour . . . . . into prepared pie shell.
Chill . . . . . until firm.

Paula Swanson
St. Joseph's H. S., Santa Maria, California

LEMON PIE A LA MODE

1/2 c. butter, melted
2 tsp. grated lemon rind
1/3 c. lemon juice
1/2 tsp. salt
1 1/2 c. sugar

2 eggs
3 eggs, separated
1 qt. vanilla ice cream, softened
1 10-in. baked pie shell

Combine . butter, lemon rind, lemon juice, salt and 1 cup sugar in double boiler pan.
Beat . . . . . eggs and egg yolks in bowl.
Stir . . . . . . into lemon mixture.
Cook . . . . until thick and smooth, stirring constantly.
Chill . . . . . in refrigerator.
Spoon . . . half the ice cream into pie shell.
Spread . . . half the lemon mixture on top.
Freeze . . . until firm.
Repeat . . . layers with remaining ice cream and filling.
Beat . . . . . egg whites in bowl until soft peaks form.
Add . . . . . 1/2 cup sugar gradually, beating until stiff.
Spread . . . over pie, sealing tightly to crust.
Bake . . . . . at 475 degrees for 3 minutes or until lightly browned.
Freeze . . . until serving time.

Edith G. Gray
Cottonwood H. S., Salt Lake City, Utah

LUSCIOUS LEMON PIE

1 c. sugar
3 tbsp. cornstarch
1 tbsp. lemon rind
1/4 c. butter
1/4 c. lemon juice
1 c. milk
3 egg yolks, slightly beaten
1 c. sour cream
1 9-in. baked pie shell

Combine . first 7 ingredients in heavy saucepan.
Cook . . . . over medium heat until smooth and thick, stirring constantly.
Cover . . . . to prevent film and cool.
Fold . . . . . in sour cream.
Pour . . . . . into pie shell.
Chill . . . . . for 2 hours or longer.

Naomi Mayes
Warren East H. S., Bowling Green, Kentucky

KEY LIME PIE

1 sm. can frozen limeade
1 can sweetened condensed milk
1 med. container Cool Whip
Dash of green food coloring
1 graham cracker pie crust

Combine . first 4 ingredients in bowl, mixing well.
Pour . . . . . into pie crust.
Chill . . . . . until firm.

Linda Tuttle
Milwee Middle School, Longwood, Florida

SUMMERTIME LIME PIES

1 lg. package lime gelatin
1 c. sugar
1 8-oz. package cream cheese, softened
3 c. whipping cream, whipped
1 tsp. vanilla extract
4 9-in. graham cracker pie crusts

Prepare . . . gelatin using package directions.
Chill . . . . . until partially set.
Mix . . . . . sugar and cream cheese in bowl.
Fold . . . . . in whipped cream and vanilla.
Add . . . . . gelatin gradually, beating well.
Pour . . . . . into pie crusts.
Chill . . . . . for 12 hours.
Yield . . . . 4 pies.

Karen Robinson
Alta H. S., Sandy, Utah

LUSCIOUS HAWAIIAN PIES

1 c. sugar
1/4 c. flour
1 lg. can crushed pineapple
1 sm. box orange gelatin
1 can sour cherries, drained
1 c. chopped pecans
6 bananas, diced
2 lg. baked pie shells

Combine . sugar and flour in saucepan.
Add . . . . . pineapple and gelatin, mixing well.
Cook . . . . until thick, stirring constantly.
Stir . . . . . . remaining ingredients except pie shells into cooled pineapple mixture.

Spoon . . . into pie shells.
Chill . . . . . until serving time.

Nancy A. Marrow
Salisbury H. S., Salisbury, North Carolina

MICROWAVE HONEY CREAM PIE

1 c. rolled oats
1/3 c. finely chopped nuts
2 tbsp. brown sugar
3 to 4 tbsp. butter, melted
1/2 tsp. cinnamon
4 1/2 tsp. unflavored gelatin
3 c. lemon yogurt
1/4 c. honey
1 1/2 c. heavy cream, whipped

Combine . first 5 ingredients in bowl, mixing well.
Press . . . . . into bottom and side of oiled 9-inch pie plate.
Microwave on High for 3 to 4 minutes; cool.
Soften . . . gelatin in 1/2 cup water in glass bowl.
Microwave on High for 1 to 2 minutes or until dissolved.
Blend . . . . yogurt and honey in bowl.
Blend . . . . in gelatin gradually.
Chill . . . . . until slightly thickened.
Fold . . . . . in whipped cream.
Chill . . . . . until slightly thickened.
Pour . . . . . into pie shell.
Chill . . . . . until firm.

Mary Lukan
Boron H. S., Boron, California

MICROWAVE MELBA CHEESECAKE PIE

1/2 c. butter, melted
1 1/4 c. graham cracker crumbs
Sugar
1 16-oz. can sliced peaches, drained
1 8-oz. package cream cheese, softened
1/2 c. sour cream
1 egg
1/2 tsp. almond extract
1/3 c. raspberry jam

Combine . butter, crumbs and 2 tablespoons sugar in bowl, mixing well.
Press . . . . . over bottom and side of pie plate.

Microwave on High for 1 1/2 to 2 minutes or until hot.

Arrange .. peaches over crust.

Combine . 1/3 cup sugar and remaining ingredients except jam in bowl, mixing well.

Pour ..... over peaches.

Microwave on High for 3 1/2 to 4 1/2 minutes or until edges are set, rotating once.

Spread ... jam over cooled pie.

Chill ..... in refrigerator.

Marilyn Jean Mancewicz
Ottawa Hills H. S., Grand Rapids, Michigan

PEACH MELBA PIE

3/4 c. corn flake crumbs
1/2 c. toasted blanched almonds, finely chopped
2 tbsp. packed light brown sugar
1/4 c. butter, melted
1 qt. vanilla ice cream, softened
1 16-oz. can peach slices, drained, chilled
Toasted whole blanched almonds
1/2 c. currant jelly
1 c. seedless red raspberry preserves

Combine . first 4 ingredients in bowl, mixing well.

Press ..... onto bottom and side of 9-inch pie plate.

Bake ..... at 375 degrees for 8 minutes.

Cool ..... completely on wire rack.

Spoon ... ice cream into crust, pressing until smooth.

Freeze ... covered, until firm.

Soften ... in refrigerator for 30 minutes before serving.

Arrange .. peach slices on pie.

Garnish .. with whole almonds.

Melt ..... jelly in saucepan over low heat.

Stir ...... in raspberry preserves.

Serve .... with pie.

Photograph for this recipe on page 191.

FRENCH PEACH PIE

1 deep-dish unbaked shell
2 eggs
1 tbsp. lemon juice
1/3 c. sugar

2 pt. frozen peaches
1 c. finely crushed vanilla wafers
1/2 c. chopped toasted almonds
1/4 c. butter, melted

Bake ..... pie shell at 450 degrees for 5 minutes.

Beat ..... eggs and lemon juice together in bowl.

Stir ...... in sugar, mixing well.

Fold ..... in peaches.

Pour ..... into pie shell.

Combine . remaining ingredients in bowl, mixing well.

Sprinkle .. over peach mixture.

Bake ..... at 375 degrees for 20 minutes.

Top ..... with cheese or ice cream.

Pamela Truhett
Woodland H. S., Woodland, Mississippi

PEAR CHESS PIE

1 recipe pie crust pastry
1/2 c. butter, softened
3/4 c. sugar
3/4 c. packed brown sugar
1/4 tsp. salt
3 eggs
2 tbsp. flour
1 tsp. vanilla extract
1/2 c. sour cream
1/2 c. chopped pecans
1 29-oz. can pear halves, drained

Line ..... 9-inch pie pan with pastry, making high edge.

Flute .... edge and prick with fork.

Bake ..... at 425 degrees for 5 minutes.

Cream ... next 4 ingredients in bowl.

Add ..... eggs 1 at a time, beating well after each addition.

Stir ...... in flour, vanilla, sour cream and pecans.

Chop .... pears, reserving 2 for garnish.

Fold ..... into batter.

Pour ..... into pie shell.

Slice ..... reserved pears, arranging over filling.

Bake ..... at 325 degrees for 50 to 60 minutes or until brown.

Cool ..... completely before serving.

Mrs. Pearl V. Reed
Justin F. Kimball H. S., Dallas, Texas

PEANUT BUTTER CHIFFON PIE

1 env. unflavored gelatin
3 eggs, separated
1/2 c. sugar
1/2 tsp. salt
1/2 c. smooth peanut butter
1/2 tsp. vanilla extract
1 unbaked 9-in. graham cracker crust
1/2 c. heavy cream, whipped (opt.)

Soften ... gelatin in 1/4 cup cold water.
Combine . egg yolks, 1/4 cup sugar, 1/4 cup water and salt in top of double boiler, blending well.
Add ..... gelatin.
Beat ..... over boiling water with rotary beater for 5 minutes or until thick and fluffy; cool.
Beat ..... peanut butter and 1/2 cup water in bowl until smooth.
Add ..... vanilla and egg yolk mixture, blending well.
Chill ..... for 10 to 15 minutes or until syrupy.
Beat ..... egg whites until soft peaks form.
Add ..... 1/4 cup sugar gradually, beating until stiff.
Fold ..... into peanut butter mixture.
Pour ..... into pie crust.
Chill ..... until firm.
Top ..... with whipped cream to serve.

Johanna Beun
Waynedale H. S., Apple Creek, Ohio

CYNTHIA'S PEANUT BUTTER PIE

6 oz. cream cheese, softened
3/4 c. sifted confectioners' sugar
1/2 c. peanut butter
2 tbsp. milk
2 c. whipped topping
1 9-in. graham cracker pie crust
Chopped peanuts

Beat ..... cream cheese and sugar in bowl with electric mixer until light and fluffy.
Add ..... peanut butter and milk, beating until smooth.
Fold ..... in whipped topping.
Pour ..... into crust.

Chill ..... for 5 to 6 hours.
Sprinkle .. peanuts on top.

Cynthia Kolberg
Fairfield Jr.-Sr. H. S., Goshen, Indiana

BETTY'S PEANUT BUTTER PIE

1/4 c. peanut butter
3 oz. cream cheese, softened
1 c. confectioners' sugar
9 to 13 oz. Cool Whip
1 graham cracker pie crust

Cream ... peanut butter and cream cheese in bowl.
Add ..... confectioners' sugar, mixing well.
Beat ..... in Cool Whip with electric mixer on low speed.
Pour ..... into crust.
Chill ..... for 2 hours or until firm.

Betty Jeanne Callaway Schuchmann
Hughes-Quinn Jr. H. S., East Saint Louis, Illinois

PEANUT BUTTER PIE

1/2 c. cornstarch
1/4 tsp. salt
2/3 c. sugar
2 c. milk, scalded
3 egg yolks, beaten
2 tbsp. margarine
1/4 tsp. vanilla extract
1 c. confectioners' sugar
1/2 c. peanut butter
1 9-in. pie shell, baked
1 recipe meringue

Combine . first 4 ingredients in double boiler pan, mixing well.
Stir ...... a small amount of hot mixture into egg yolks; stir egg yolks into hot mixture.
Cook .... until thickened, stirring frequently.
Add ..... margarine and vanilla.
Combine . confectioners' sugar and peanut butter in bowl until crumbly.
Spread ... in pie shell, reserving 1/4 for topping.
Pour ..... cooked mixture over top.
Top ..... with meringue, sealing edge.
Sprinkle .. with remaining peanut butter mix.
Bake ..... at 350 degrees until golden brown.

Beverly Brooks
Houston H. S., Houston, Mississippi

PEANUT BUTTER CREAM PIE

1/3 c. sugar
1/3 c. packed brown sugar
1/4 c. cornstarch
1/2 tsp. salt
3 c. milk
4 egg yolks, slightly beaten
1/4 c. creamy peanut butter
1 tbsp. butter
1 tbsp. vanilla extract
1 9-in. pie shell, baked
1 sm. carton Cool Whip

Combine . first 4 ingredients in saucepan.
Mix ..... milk and egg yolks in bowl.
Stir ...... into sugar mixture gradually, mix-
ing well.
Cook .... over medium heat until thickened,
stirring constantly.
Boil ..... for 1 minute, stirring constantly.
Remove .. from heat.
Blend .... in peanut butter, butter and vanilla.
Pour ..... into pie shell.
Press ..... plastic wrap over top.
Chill ..... for 2 hours.
Top ..... with Cool Whip.

Mary Anne Power
Sidney H. S., Sidney, Texas

CARAMEL PECAN PIE

1 c. corn syrup
1 pkg. Jell-O caramel instant pudding mix
3/4 c. evaporated milk
1 egg, slightly beaten
1 c. chopped pecans
1 8-in. unbaked pie shell

Combine . syrup and pudding mix in bowl.
Add ..... milk and egg gradually, blending
well.
Stir ...... in pecans.
Pour ..... into pie shell.
Bake ..... at 375 degrees for 45 minutes or
until set.

Mrs. Mary Jo Lyle
Gatewood School, Eatonton, Georgia

PECAN PIE

3 eggs, slightly beaten
1/2 c. melted butter

1 c. dark corn syrup
1/2 c. sugar
1 tsp. vanilla extract
1/8 tsp. salt
1 1/2 c. pecan halves
1 unbaked pie crust

Combine . eggs and butter in bowl.
Stir ...... in next 5 ingredients, mixing well.
Pour ..... into pie crust.
Bake ..... at 350 degrees for 50 minutes.

Debbie Bradley
Clinton Jr. H. S., Clinton, Tennessee

HEAVENLY PECAN PIE

3 egg whites
1 c. sugar
1 tsp. baking powder
1 c. chopped pecans
1 tsp. vanilla extract
24 Ritz crackers, finely crushed

Combine . first 3 ingredients in bowl.
Beat ..... until stiff peaks form.
Fold ..... in pecans, vanilla and crackers.
Pour ..... into buttered pie plate.
Bake ..... at 325 degrees for 20 to 25
minutes.
Top ..... cooled pie with whipped topping or
ice cream.

Margaret S. Campbell
Chumuckla H. S., Milton, Florida

KENTUCKY PIE

1 c. sugar
1/2 c. flour
2 eggs, slightly beaten
1 stick butter, melted
1 c. pecans, broken
1 6-oz. package semisweet chocolate bits
1 tsp. vanilla extract
1 unbaked pie shell

Combine . first 3 ingredients in bowl, mixing
well.
Add ..... cooled butter, pecans, chocolate
chips and vanilla, blending well.
Pour ..... into pie shell.
Bake ..... at 325 degrees for 1 hour.

Mrs. Nancy Weis
Glasgow H. S., Glasgow, Kentucky

MOCK PECAN PIE

3 eggs, beaten
1 c. packed brown sugar
2/3 c. sugar
2 tbsp. melted margarine
1/2 tsp. vanilla extract
2/3 c. quick-cooking oats
2/3 c. coconut
1 9-in. unbaked pie shell

Combine . first 5 ingredients in bowl, mixing
well.
Stir . . . . . . in oats and coconut.
Pour . . . . . into pie shell.
Bake . . . . . at 350 degrees for 30 to 35 minutes
or until pie tests done.

Alicia G. Russell
New Franklin H. S., New Franklin, Missouri

NELLIE'S PECAN PIES

1 box brown sugar
1 stick margarine, melted
4 eggs
1 tsp. vanilla extract
2 tbsp. corn syrup
4 tbsp. milk
Pinch of salt
1 c. pecans
2 unbaked pie shells

Combine . first 7 ingredients in bowl, mixing
well.
Stir . . . . . . in pecans.
Pour . . . . . into pie shells.
Bake . . . . . at 350 degrees for 45 minutes.

Mrs. Maurice Eugene Eskridge
Bessemer City Jr. H. S.
Bessemer City, North Carolina

SOUTHERN PECAN PIE

3 eggs
2/3 c. sugar
Dash of salt
1 c. dark corn syrup
1/3 c. butter, melted
1 c. pecan halves
1 9-in. unbaked pie shell

Combine . first 5 ingredients in bowl, beating
well.
Stir . . . . . . in pecans.
Pour . . . . . into pie shell.

Bake . . . . . at 350 degrees for 50 minutes or
until pie tests done.
Cool . . . . . before serving.

Dorothy Tipping
Yantis H. S., Yantis, Texas

SHOOFLY PIE

1 1/2 c. flour
1/2 c. sugar
1/8 tsp. salt
1/2 tsp. cinnamon
1/4 tsp. ginger
1/4 tsp. nutmeg
1/4 c. margarine, softened
1 unbaked 8-in. pie shell
1/2 c. molasses
1/2 tsp. soda

Combine . first 6 ingredients in bowl, mixing
well.
Cut . . . . . . in margarine until crumbly.
Spread . . . 1 1/3 cups crumb mixture in pie
shell.
Combine . molasses, soda and 3/4 cup boiling
water in bowl, mixing well.
Pour . . . . . over crumb mixture.
Sprinkle . . remaining crumbs over top.
Bake . . . . . at 375 degrees for 30 to 40 minutes
or until lightly brown.

Vivian C. Pike
Bunker Hill H. S., Claremont, North Carolina

PENNSYLVANIA DUTCH
SHOOFLY PIE

1 c. flour
2/3 c. packed brown sugar
1 tbsp. shortening
1 egg
1 c. dark corn syrup
1 tsp. soda
1 9-in. unbaked pie shell

Combine . flour, brown sugar and shortening
in bowl, mixing until crumbly.
Reserve . . 1/2 cup of mixture for topping.
Beat . . . . . egg and corn syrup into flour
mixture.
Dissolve . . soda in 3/4 cup hot water.
Beat . . . . . into syrup mixture.
Pour . . . . . into pie shell.
Sprinkle . . with reserved topping.
Bake . . . . . at 400 degrees for 25 minutes.

Reduce . . . temperature to 350 degrees.
Bake . . . . . for 25 minutes longer.

Connie M. Amendola
Johnsonburg Area Jr.-Sr. H. S.
Johnsonburg, Pennsylvania

COCONUT-PINEAPPLE PIE

1/4 c. butter, softened
1 3/4 c. sugar
1 tbsp. cornmeal
1 tsp. flour
4 lg. eggs
1 8 1/4-oz. can crushed pineapple
1 3 1/4-oz. can flaked coconut
1 10-in. unbaked pie shell

Combine . first 4 ingredients in bowl, mixing
            well.
Add . . . . . eggs 1 at a time, beating well after
            each addition.
Stir . . . . . . in pineapple and coconut.
Spoon . . . into pie shell.
Bake . . . . . at 425 degrees for 10 minutes.
Reduce . . . temperature to 325 degrees.
Bake . . . . . for 30 to 40 minutes longer or until
            pie tests done.

Oleta Hayden
Milford ISD, Milford, Texas

FROSTY PINEAPPLE PIE

1 1/4 c. crushed pineapple
1 pkg. lemon gelatin
3/4 to 1 c. sugar
1 c. evaporated milk, partially frozen
1 tbsp. lemon juice
1 baked pie shell

Bring . . . . crushed pineapple to a boil in
            saucepan over medium heat.
Stir . . . . . . in gelatin until dissolved.
Add . . . . . sugar to taste.
Chill . . . . . until partially set.
Whip . . . . evaporated milk with lemon juice in
            bowl until stiff.
Beat . . . . . in chilled gelatin mixture.
Pour . . . . . into pie crust.
Chill . . . . . until serving time.

Patricia L. Walochik
James Madison H. S., Vienna, Virginia

GRANNY'S SPECIAL PIE

1 8-oz. can crushed pineapple
3 oz. cream cheese, softened

Sugar
1 3-oz. package lemon pudding and
   pie filling mix
2 eggs, separated
1 10-in. baked pie shell

Drain . . . . pineapple, reserving juice.
Add . . . . . enough water to pineapple juice to
            measure 2 cups liquid.
Combine . 1/4 cup juice mixture and cream
            cheese in bowl, mixing until
            smooth.
Stir . . . . . . in pineapple.
Mix . . . . . 1/2 cup sugar, pudding mix and 1/4
            cup juice mixture in 2 1/2-quart
            saucepan.
Beat . . . . . egg yolks and 1/4 cup juice mixture
            in bowl.
Add . . . . . to pudding mixture, mixing well.
Stir . . . . . . in remaining juice mixture.
Cook . . . . until thick, stirring constantly.
Beat . . . . . egg whites in bowl until soft peaks
            form.
Add . . . . . 2 tablespoons sugar gradually, beat-
            ing until stiff.
Pour . . . . . hot mixture over egg whites, mixing
            well.
Fold . . . . . in pineapple mixture.
Chill . . . . . until thick.
Pour . . . . . into pie shell.

Jan Nell Reed
Rhodes Jr. H. S., Mesa, Arizona

MILLIONAIRE PIE

1 can sweetened condensed milk
3 tbsp. lemon juice
1 sm. can crushed pineapple, drained
1 1/2 oz. Cool Whip
1 c. pecans
1 graham cracker pie crust
2 chopped red cherries
2 chopped green cherries

Combine . condensed milk and lemon juice in
            bowl, mixing well.
Add . . . . . next 3 ingredients.
Pour . . . . . into crust.
Garnish . . with cherries.
Chill . . . . . until serving time.

Carol Harding
Florence H. S., Florence, Texas

BRENDA'S MILLIONAIRE PIES

1 8-oz. package cream cheese, softened
1 pkg. Dream Whip
1 1/2 c. confectioners' sugar
1 stick butter, softened
1/2 tsp. vanilla extract
2 8-in. baked pie shells
Sugar to taste
1 c. whipping cream, whipped
1 sm. can crushed pineapple, drained
1/2 c. chopped pecans

Combine . first 4 ingredients in bowl, beating
           until creamy.
Add . . . . . vanilla, beating well.
Spoon . . . into 2 pie shells.
Sweeten . . whipped cream to taste.
Fold . . . . . in pineapple and pecans.
Spread . . . over cream cheese mixture.
Chill . . . . . until serving time.

Brenda Simmons
Dayton H. S., Dayton, Texas

MOTHER'S PINEAPPLE PIE

Flour
1 tsp. salt
2/3 c. shortening
2 c. crushed pineapple
1/2 c. sugar

Combine . 2 cups flour and salt in bowl.
Cut . . . . . . in shortening until crumbly.
Add . . . . . 1/3 cup ice water, mixing until
           dough clings together.
Roll . . . . . out on floured surface into 2 crusts.
Place . . . . 1 crust in pie pan.
Combine . pineapple, sugar and 2 tablespoons
           flour in bowl.
Pour . . . . . into crust.
Top . . . . . with remaining pastry.
Bake . . . . . at 450 degrees for 15 minutes.
Reduce . . . temperature to 350 degrees.
Bake . . . . . for 30 minutes longer.

Syble K. Ditzler
Holdenville H. S., Holdenville, Oklahoma

PINEAPPLE CREAM PIE

1/3 c. lemon juice
1 can sweetened condensed milk
1 9-oz. carton Cool Whip

1 lg. can crushed pineapple, drained
1 graham cracker pie crust

Combine . first 2 ingredients in bowl, mixing
           well.
Fold . . . . . in Cool Whip and pineapple.
Pour . . . . . into crust.
Chill . . . . . until set.

Joan Kinzer
Highland H. S., Craigmont, Idaho

PINEAPPLE-OATMEAL PIE

2/3 c. sugar
1 c. packed brown sugar
3 eggs, beaten
2 tbsp. melted butter
1 tsp. vanilla extract
2/3 c. oatmeal
2/3 c. coconut
1 c. raisins
1 8 1/4-oz. can crushed pineapple
1 9-in. unbaked pie shell

Add . . . . . sugars to eggs, beating well.
Blend . . . . in butter and vanilla.
Stir . . . . . . next 4 ingredients into egg mixture.
Pour . . . . . into pie shell.
Bake . . . . . at 350 degrees for 50 minutes.
Cool . . . . . on wire rack.

Diane E. Mills
Pavilion Central School, Pavilion, New York

PINEAPPLE-SOUR CREAM PIE

1 c. sugar
1/4 c. flour
1/2 tsp. salt
1 20-oz. can crushed pineapple, drained
1 c. sour cream
2 egg yolks, slightly beaten
1 9-in. baked pie shell
2 egg whites
1/2 tsp. vanilla extract
1/4 tsp. cream of tartar

Combine . 3/4 cup sugar, flour and salt in
           saucepan.
Stir . . . . . . in next 3 ingredients.
Bring . . . . to a boil, stirring constantly.
Cook . . . . for 2 minutes longer.
Stir . . . . . . a small amount of hot mixture into
           egg yolks; stir egg yolks into hot
           mixture.

Cook .... for 2 minutes, stirring constantly.
Cool ..... to room temperature.
Spoon ... into pie shell.
Beat ..... egg whites, vanilla and cream of tartar in bowl until soft peaks form.
Add ..... 1/4 cup sugar gradually, beating until stiff.
Spread ... over pie, covering completely.
Bake ..... at 350 degrees for 12 to 15 minutes.

Phyllis J. Miller
Buena H. S., Ventura, California

GOLDEN NUGGET PIE

1 env. unflavored gelatin
1 c. sugar
2 egg yolks
1 tsp. pumpkin pie spice
1/2 tsp. salt
3/4 c. evaporated milk
1 1-lb. can pumpkin
1 1/2 tsp. grated orange rind
2 egg whites
Pecan pie crust shell, baked, cooled

Soften ... gelatin in 1/4 cup water in 2-quart saucepan.
Stir ...... in 1/2 cup sugar and next 3 ingredients until smooth.
Add ..... evaporated milk.
Cook .... over low heat until thick, stirring constantly.
Remove .. from heat.
Stir ...... in pumpkin and rind.
Chill .... until thick but not firm.
Beat ..... egg whites until soft peaks form.
Add ..... 1/2 cup sugar gradually, beating until stiff.
Fold ..... in pumpkin mixture.
Spoon ... into pie shell.
Garnish .. with chopped pecans.
Chill ..... for 2 to 3 hours or until firm.

Photograph for this recipe on this page.

HOLIDAY PIES

3/4 c. sugar
1 tsp. vanilla extract
1 can pumpkin pie filling
1 1/4 c. chopped walnuts
1 c. whipping cream, whipped
2 8-in. baked pie shells

Combine . first 3 ingredients and 1 cup walnuts in bowl, mixing well.
Fold ..... in whipped cream.
Pour ..... into pie shells.
Freeze ... for 4 hours.
Sprinkle .. with 1/4 cup walnuts.
Thaw .... for 30 minutes before serving.

Gail L. Ferrin
Woods Cross H. S., Woods Cross, Utah

NEW ENGLAND PUMPKIN PIE

1 tbsp. cornstarch
1/2 tsp. each cinnamon, ginger, nutmeg
1/2 tsp. (scant) salt
1 16-oz. can pumpkin
1 1/2 tbsp. butter, melted
1 1/2 c. evaporated milk
1 c. sugar
2 tbsp. molasses
2 eggs, beaten
1 9-in. unbaked pie shell

Sift ...... cornstarch with spices and salt into bowl.
Add ..... pumpkin, butter, evaporated milk, sugar, molasses and eggs, mixing well.
Pour ..... into pie shell.
Bake ..... at 450 degrees for 15 minutes.
Reduce ... temperature to 350 degrees.
Bake ..... for 50 minutes longer or until pie tests done.

Anne V. McClerkin
Adams City H. S., Commerce City, Colorado

PUMPKIN PIE

1 1/2 c. flour
1/2 c. oil
1 1/2 tsp. salt
1 16-oz. can pumpkin
2 eggs, beaten
2 tsp. pumpkin pie spice
1 can sweetened condensed milk
1 box vanilla instant pudding mix
2 tbsp. butter
1/2 c. packed brown sugar
1/3 c. chopped pecans

Place .... flour in pie pan.
Bring .... oil, 1 teaspoon salt and 1/4 cup water to boil in saucepan.
Pour ..... over flour, mixing well.
Pat ...... over bottom and side of pan.
Combine . next 5 ingredients and 1/2 teaspoon salt in large bowl, mixing well.
Pour ..... over crust.
Bake ..... at 425 degrees for 15 minutes.
Reduce ... temperature to 350 degrees.
Bake ..... for 45 minutes longer.
Combine . butter, brown sugar and pecans in bowl.
Spread ... over pie.
Broil ..... for 1 minute.

Judy Sandlin
Del Crest Jr. H. S., Del City, Oklahoma

MAXINE'S RHUBARB PIE

2 c. chopped rhubarb
1 unbaked pie shell
1 c. sugar
1/3 c. flour
1/2 pt. whipping cream, whipped

Spread ... rhubarb in pie shell.
Fold ..... sugar and flour into whipped cream.
Pour ..... over rhubarb.
Bake ..... at 425 degrees for 10 minutes.
Reduce ... temperature to 350 degrees.
Bake ..... for 30 to 40 minutes longer.

Lucy Calhoun
Kelso H. S., Kelso, Washington

RASPBERRY-RHUBARB PIES

3 tbsp. flour
1 1/4 c. sugar
2 unbaked pie shells
2 c. raspberries
2 c. chopped rhubarb

Mix ..... flour and sugar in bowl.
Sprinkle .. 3 tablespoons of sugar mixture in 1 pie shell.
Combine . raspberries and rhubarb in bowl, mixing well.
Alternate . layers of fruit mixture and sugar mixture in pie shell until all ingredients are used.
Top ..... with second pie shell, sealing edges well.
Bake ..... at 425 degrees for 10 minutes.
Reduce ... temperature to 375 degrees.
Bake ..... for 40 to 50 minutes longer or until brown.

Kathleen Niemi
Chippewa Intermediate School, Port Huron, Michigan

RHUBARB CUSTARD PIE

3 c. chopped rhubarb
1 unbaked pie shell
1 1/2 c. sugar
3 tbsp. flour
1/2 tsp. nutmeg
1/4 tsp. salt
1 tbsp. butter, softened
2 eggs, beaten

Spread ... rhubarb in pie shell.
Combine . remaining ingredients in bowl, beating well.
Pour ..... over rhubarb.
Bake ..... at 450 degrees for 10 minutes.
Reduce ... temperature to 350 degrees.
Bake ..... for 30 minutes longer or until knife inserted halfway to center comes out clean.

Elnora Snyder
Loudonville H. S., Loudonville, Ohio

BETTY'S STRAWBERRY PIE

1 c. sugar
6 tbsp. cornstarch
2 tbsp. strawberry gelatin
3 drops of lemon juice
4 or 5 drops of red food coloring
1 qt. strawberries
1 9-in. baked pie shell
Whipping cream, whipped (opt.)

Combine . first 5 ingredients with 2 cups water in saucepan, mixing well.
Cook .... until thick and clear, stirring constantly.
Cool ..... to room temperature.
Fold ..... in strawberries.
Pour ..... into pie shell.
Chill ..... for 2 hours or longer.
Top ..... with whipped cream.

Betty Jones
Cedarville H. S., Cedarville, Michigan

CRISPY PINK PIE

1 30-oz. can pear halves, drained
1 9-in. unbaked pastry shell
1 20-oz. can strawberry pie filling
1 tbsp. lemon juice
3/4 c. flour
1/2 c. sugar
1 tsp. cinnamon
1/3 c. butter

Cut ...... pear halves in half lengthwise.
Arrange .. in pastry shell.
Combine . pie filling and lemon juice in bowl.
Spoon ... over pears.
Mix ..... flour, sugar and cinnamon in bowl.
Cut ...... in butter until crumbly.
Sprinkle .. over fruit.
Bake ..... at 425 degrees for 30 minutes or until lightly browned.

Photograph for this recipe on this page.

FRESH STRAWBERRY PIE

1 c. sugar
3 1/2 tbsp. cornstarch
Pinch of salt
2 tbsp. lemon juice
Red food coloring
1 1/2 pt. sliced strawberries
1 baked pie shell
Whipped cream (opt.)

Blend .... 2 tablespoons water with sugar and cornstarch in saucepan.
Stir ...... in 1 cup boiling water gradually.
Cook .... until thick and clear, stirring constantly.
Add ..... salt, lemon juice and food coloring; cool.

Fold ..... in strawberries.
Spoon ... into pie shell.
Chill ..... for 2 hours or longer.
Top ..... with whipped cream.

Beverly Plyler
Glenwood H. S., Glenwood, Arkansas

QUICK STRAWBERRY PIES

2 env. unflavored gelatin
3/4 c. cold milk
1 3-oz. package strawberry gelatin
1 16-oz. package frozen strawberries, thawed
1 pkg. Dream Whip
1 3/4 c. crushed ice
2 graham cracker crusts

Dissolve .. gelatin in 1/2 cup boiling water.
Add ..... to 1/4 cup cold milk, strawberry gelatin and strawberries in blender container.
Process ... for 30 seconds.
Add ..... 1/2 cup milk and Dream Whip.
Process ... for 30 seconds.
Add ..... crushed ice gradually, blending constantly.
Pour ..... into crusts.
Chill ..... until set.

Wanda Lilly
Iberia R-V School, Iberia, Missouri

STRAWBERRY DESSERT PIES

1 can sweetened condensed milk
1 lg. carton Cool Whip
1 6-oz. can frozen pink lemonade, thawed
2 c. sliced fresh strawberries
2 graham cracker crusts

Blend .... first 3 ingredients in bowl until smooth.
Fold ..... in strawberries.
Spoon ... into crusts.
Chill ..... for 2 hours or longer.

Ramona Warwick
Castlewood H. S., Castlewood, South Dakota

STRAWBERRY-MARSHMALLOW PIES

1/2 c. milk
1/2 lb. marshmallows
1 pkg. frozen strawberries, thawed, drained
1 c. whipping cream, whipped
1 10-oz. box vanilla wafers, crushed
1 tbsp. melted butter

Combine . milk and marshmallows in saucepan.
Heat ..... until marshmallows melt.
Fold ..... cooled marshmallow mixture and strawberries into whipped cream.
Combine . wafer crumbs and butter, mixing well.
Press ..... into two 8-inch pie pans, reserving a small amount for topping.
Pour ..... strawberry mixture into pie shell.
Top ..... with reserved wafer crumbs.
Chill ..... for 4 hours or longer.

Fleda Lambert
Duncanville H. S., Duncanville, Texas

CREAM PUFFS WITH CREAMY APRICOT FILLING

1 16-oz. can apricot halves, drained, pureed
2/3 c. sugar
1/4 tsp. ground cinnamon
1 c. sour cream
1/2 c. butter
1 c. flour
4 eggs
1 c. confectioners' sugar
2 to 3 tbsp. milk

Bring .... pureed apricots and sugar to a boil in medium saucepan.
Simmer .. for 15 minutes or until very thick.
Cool ..... to room temperature.
Stir ...... in cinnamon and sour cream.
Chill ..... until serving time.
Bring .... butter and 1 cup water to full boil in large saucepan.
Stir ...... in flour.
Cook .... over low heat for 1/2 minute or until mixture forms ball, stirring vigorously.
Remove .. from heat.
Beat ..... in eggs in 1 addition, beating until smooth.
Drop .... by 1/4 cupfuls 3 inches apart on baking sheet.
Bake ..... at 400 degrees for 35 to 40 minutes or until puffed and golden brown.
Cut ...... off top 1/3 of each cooled puff.
Remove .. excess soft dough.
Spoon ... 1 1/2 tablespoons chilled apricot filling into each puff.
Replace .. tops.
Combine . confectioners' sugar and enough milk in bowl to make glaze.
Drizzle ... over cream puffs.
Yield .... 1 dozen.

Photograph for this recipe on page 4.

CREAMY SWEET POTATO PIES

3 1/2 c. cooked mashed sweet potatoes
1/2 c. butter, softened
2 c. sugar
4 eggs
1/2 tsp. each nutmeg, salt
1 13-oz. can evaporated milk
2 tsp. lemon extract
2 9-in. unbaked pie shells

Combine . first 3 ingredients in bowl, mixing well.
Add ..... eggs 1 at a time, beating well after each addition.
Stir ...... in nutmeg, salt, evaporated milk and lemon flavoring.
Pour ..... into pie shells.
Place .... on cookie sheet.
Bake ..... at 425 degrees for 20 minutes.

Reduce ... temperature to 325 degrees.
Bake ..... for 30 to 45 minutes longer or until pie tests done.

Lucille H. Wiggins
I. C. Norcom H. S., Portsmouth, Virginia

FRIED PEACH PIES

1 1-lb. can sliced peaches, drained
3 tbsp. honey
2 tsp. butter
1 tsp. shredded lemon rind
1 tsp. lemon juice
1/4 tsp. cinnamon
1 pkg. refrigerator biscuits, separated
Oil for deep frying
Confectioners' sugar

Combine . first 6 ingredients in saucepan.
Cook .... over medium heat for 15 minutes until thick and glossy, stirring frequently.
Roll ..... out biscuits into 5-inch ovals.
Spoon ... rounded tablespoon peach mixture lengthwise down dough.
Fold ..... dough over.
Seal ..... edges with fork.
Fry ...... in deep fat at 375 degrees for 1 minute, turning once.
Sprinkle .. with confectioners' sugar.

Clarazina H. Lovett
Seabreeze Jr. H. S., Daytona Beach, Florida

APRICOT CREAM TARTS

1 16-oz. can apricot halves, drained
1 3 1/4-oz. package vanilla pudding and pie filling mix
1 c. light cream
3/4 tsp. grated lemon rind
1/2 c. sugar
10 baked tart shells
Fruits for garnish
1/2 c. apricot preserves, strained, warmed
1/2 c. heavy cream, whipped, sweetened

Puree .... apricots in electric blender.
Blend .... apricot puree, pudding mix, cream, lemon rind and sugar in medium saucepan.
Bring .... to a boil, stirring constantly.
Remove .. from heat.

Spoon ... into tart shells.
Chill ..... until serving time.
Garnish .. half the tarts with fruits.
Brush .... with preserves.
Garnish .. remaining tarts with whipped cream.
Yield .... 10 tarts.

Photograph for this recipe on page 4.

CALIFORNIA WALNUT MAPLE TARTS

1/2 c. butter
3/4 c. packed light brown sugar
1/2 c. maple syrup
3 eggs
1/4 c. heavy cream
1 1/4 c. chopped California walnuts
1/2 tsp. vanilla extract
8 unbaked tart shells
Whipped cream
8 California walnut halves

Combine . first 3 ingredients in saucepan.
Heat ..... to boiling point.
Beat ..... eggs lightly in large bowl.
Stir ...... in cream, walnuts and vanilla.
Mix ..... in hot mixture gradually.
Pour ..... into tart shells.
Bake ..... at 375 degrees for 20 minutes or until custard tests done.
Garnish .. cooled tarts with whipped cream.
Top ..... with walnut halves.
Yield .... 8 tarts.

Photograph for this recipe below.

CHERRY TARTS

24 vanilla wafers
2 8-oz. packages cream cheese, softened
2 eggs
1 c. sugar
1 tsp. vanilla extract
1 can cherry pie filling

Place .... 1 vanilla wafer in bottom of each of 24 cupcake paper-lined muffin cups.
Beat ..... remaining ingredients except pie filling in bowl until smooth.
Spoon ... over wafers.
Bake ..... at 350 degrees for 10 minutes.
Top ..... cooled tarts with pie filling.

Linda Cherry
Griggsville H. S., Griggsville, Illinois

CURRANT TARTS

3 or 4 eggs
1/2 c. melted butter
1 lb. brown sugar
2 tbsp. milk
1 box currants
1 c. chopped walnuts
1 tsp. vanilla extract
24 unbaked tart shells

Combine . first 7 ingredients in bowl, mixing well.
Fill ...... tart shells in ungreased muffin cups 1/2 full with currant mixture.
Bake ..... at 375 degrees for 20 minutes or until golden brown.

Janet M. Burns
Newaygo H. S., Newaygo, Michigan

PINEAPPLE SURPRISE TARTS

1 pkg. lemon gelatin
2 c. miniature marshmallows
1 can crushed pineapple
1/2 c. sugar
1 c. walnuts, chopped
1 c. heavy cream, whipped
6 baked tart shells

Dissolve .. gelatin in 1 1/2 cups hot water.
Add ..... marshmallows, stirring to dissolve.
Stir ...... next 3 ingredients into cooled marshmallow mixture, mixing until sugar dissolves.

Chill ..... until thick.
Fold ..... in whipped cream.
Pour ..... into tart shells.
Chill ..... until firm.

Dorothy Moore
Central Jr. H. S., Sand Springs, Oklahoma

GOODIES

1 c. margarine, softened
1 c. cream-style cottage cheese
2 c. sifted flour
1 c. finely ground pecans
Corn syrup
3 doz. pecan halves

Combine . margarine and cottage cheese in bowl, blending well.
Mix ..... in flour.
Shape .... into ball.
Chill ..... for 1 hour or longer.
Divide ... dough into thirds.
Roll ..... out 1/8-inch thick on floured cloth.
Cut ...... into 3-inch squares.
Mix ..... ground pecans with 1/2 cup corn syrup in bowl.
Place .... 1 teaspoon on each dough square.
Fold ..... in corners, overlapping in center.
Dip ...... pecan halves into corn syrup.
Press ..... into center of each pastry.
Place .... on ungreased cookie sheet.
Bake ..... at 350 degrees for 25 minutes.
Yield .... 3 dozen.

Photograph for this recipe below.

SOUTHERN TASSIES

1 3-oz. package cream cheese, softened
1 stick butter, softened
1 c. flour
1/2 c. chopped pecans
1 egg
1 c. packed brown sugar
1 tsp. vanilla extract

Combine . first 3 ingredients in bowl, mixing well.
Shape .... into 24 balls.
Press ..... into bottom and side of small muffin cups.
Place .... several pecans in each shell.
Mix ..... remaining ingredients in bowl, blending well.
Place .... 1 teaspoon egg mixture in each shell.
Bake ..... at 325 degrees for 35 minutes.
Yield .... 2 dozen.

Mary Jo Jackson
Central H. S., Switz City, Indiana

GREEK DATE-STUFFED PASTRIES

Sugar
1 stick cinnamon
1/2 lb. unsalted butter, softened
2 egg yolks
1 c. oil
1 c. orange juice
1 oz. rum
1/4 tsp. salt
2 tsp. baking powder
1/3 tsp. soda
7 1/2 c. sifted flour
Dates, pitted
Walnut halves
1 1/2 c. ground walnuts
1/2 tsp. cinnamon

Combine . 4 cups sugar, cinnamon stick and 3 cups water in saucepan.
Boil ..... for 10 minutes; set aside to cool.
Cream ... butter and 1 cup sugar together in bowl.
Add ..... next 8 ingredients, mixing thoroughly.
Stuff .... dates with walnut halves.
Roll ..... out dough on floured surface 1/4 inch thick.

Cut ...... into rectangles.
Cover .... each date with dough, sealing edges.
Place .... on baking sheet.
Bake ..... at 375 degrees for about 45 minutes or until golden brown.
Combine . ground walnuts, cinnamon and 2 teaspoons sugar on waxed paper.
Dip ...... hot pastries in cold syrup.
Remove .. with slotted spoon.
Roll ..... in walnut mixture to coat.

Constance Lebel
Mascenic Regional School
New Ipswich, New Hampshire

FLAKY PASTRY

2 c. flour
1 tsp. salt
2/3 c. shortening
2 tbsp. butter
1 tbsp. vinegar

Sift ...... flour and salt into bowl.
Cut ...... in shortening and butter until crumbly.
Mix ..... vinegar with 5 tablespoons cold water.
Add ..... to flour mixture.
Stir ...... with fork until dough clings together.
Divide ... in half.
Roll ..... each half out on floured surface.

Karen A. Ogg
Keene H. S., Keene, New Hampshire

SURE-FIRE PASTRY

1 1/2 c. sifted flour
1/2 tsp. salt
1/2 c. shortening

Sift ...... flour and salt together into bowl.
Reserve .. 1/4 cup mixture.
Cut ...... shortening into remaining flour until crumbly.
Combine . reserved flour and 3 tablespoons water to make smooth paste.
Stir ...... paste into shortening mixture.
Shape .... into ball.
Roll ..... out on floured surface.

Darla Lane
Boyd H. S., Boyd, Texas

Count-Your-Calories Chart

Almonds, shelled, 1/4 cup 213	Cauliflower: cooked, 1/2 cup 13
Apples: 1 med. 70	fresh, 1/2 lb. 60
chopped, 1/2 cup 30	Celery, chopped, 1/2 cup 8
Apple juice, 1 cup .117	Cereals: bran flakes, 1/2 cup 53
Applesauce: sweetened 1/2 cup 115	corn flakes, 1/2 cup 50
unsweetened, 1/2 cup 50	oatmeal, cooked, 1/2 cup 65
Apricots: fresh, 3 55	Cheese: American, 1 oz. 105
canned, 1/2 cup .110	Cheddar: 1 oz. 113
dried, 10 halves .100	shredded, 1 cup 452
Apricot nectar, 1 cup 140	Cottage: creamed, 1/2 cup 130
Asparagus: fresh, 6 spears 19	uncreamed, 1/2 cup 85
canned, 1/2 cup 18	Cream, 1 oz. 107
Avocado, 1 med. 265	Mozzarella, 1 oz. 80
Bacon, 2 sl. crisp-cooked, drained 90	shredded, 1 cup 320
Banana, 1 med. 100	Parmesan, 1 oz. 110
Beans: baked, 1/2 cup 160	Velveeta, 1 oz. 84
dry, 1/2 cup 350	Cherries: canned, sour in water, 1/2 cup 53
green, 1/2 cup 20	fresh, sweet, 1/2 cup 40
lima, 1/2 cup 95	Chicken, meat only, 4 oz. serving:
soy, 1/2 cup 95	boned, chopped 1/2 cup 170
Bean sprouts, 1/2 cup 18	broiled 155
Beef, cooked, 3 oz. serving:	canned, boned .230
roast, rib 375	roast, dark meat 210
roast, heel of round 165	roast, light meat 207
steak, sirloin 330	Chili peppers: green, fresh, 1/2 lb. 62
Beer, 12 oz. 150	red, fresh, 1/2 lb. 108
Beets, cooked, 1/2 cup 40	Chili powder with seasonings, 1 tbsp. 51
Biscuit, from mix, 1 90	Chocolate, baking, 1 oz. 143
Bologna, all meat, 3 oz. 235	Cocoa mix, 1-oz. package 115
Bread: roll, 1 85	Cocoa powder, baking, 1/3 cup 120
white, 1 slice 65	Coconut, dried, shredded, 1/4 cup 166
whole wheat, 1 slice 65	Coffee 0
Bread crumbs, dry, 1 cup 390	Corn: canned, cream-style, 1/2 cup 100
Broccoli, cooked, 1/2 cup 20	canned, whole kernel, 1/2 cup 85
Butter: 1/2 cup 800	Cornbread, mix, prepared, 1 x 4-in. piece 125
1 tbsp. 100	Corn chips, 1 oz. 130
Buttermilk, 1 cup 90	Cornmeal, 1/2 cup .264
Cabbage: cooked, 1/2 cup 15	Cornstarch, 1 tbsp. 29
fresh, shredded, 1/2 cup 10	Crab, fresh, meat only, 3 oz. 80
Cake: angel food, 1/12 pkg. prepared 140	canned, 3 oz. 85
devil's food, 1/12 pkg. prepared 195	Crackers: graham, 2 1/2-in. square 28
yellow, 1/12 pkg. prepared 200	Ritz, each 17
Candy: caramel, 1 oz. 115	saltine, 2-in. square 13
chocolate, sweet, 1 oz. 145	Cracker crumbs, 1/2 cup 281
hard candy, 1 oz. 110	Cranberries: fresh, 1/2 lb. 100
Marshmallows, 1 oz. 90	juice, cocktail, 1 cup 163
Cantaloupe, 1/2 med. 60	sauce, 1/2 cup 190
Carrots, cooked, 1/2 cup 23	Cream: half-and-half, 1 tbsp. 20
fresh, 1 med. 20	heavy, 1 tbsp. 55
Catsup, 1 tbsp. 18	light, 1 tbsp. 30

Creamer, imitation powdered, 1 tsp. 10
Cucumber, 1 med. 30
Dates, dried, chopped, 1/2 cup 244
Eggs: 1 whole, large 80
    1 white 17
    1 yolk 59
Eggplant, cooked, 1/2 cup 19
Fish sticks, 5 200
Flour: rye, 1 cup 286
    white: 1 cup 420
       1 tbsp. 28
    whole wheat, 1 cup 400
Fruit cocktail, canned, 1/2 cup 98
Garlic, 1 clove 2
Gelatin, unflavored, 1 env. 25
Grapes: fresh, 1/2 cup 35-50
    juice, 1 cup 170
Grapefruit: fresh, 1/2 med. 60
    juice, unsweetened, 1 cup 100
Ground beef, patty, lean 185
    regular 245
Haddock, fried, 3 oz. 140
Ham, 3 oz. servings:
    boiled 200
    fresh, roast 320
    country-style 335
    cured, lean 160
Honey, 1 tbsp. 65
Ice cream, 1/2 cup .135
Ice milk, 1/2 cup 96
Jams and preserves, 1 tbsp. 54
Jellies, 1 tbsp. 55
Jell-O, 1/2 cup 80
Lamb, 3 oz. serving, leg roast 185
    1 1/2 oz., rib chop 175
Lemon juice, 1 tbsp. 4
Lemonade, sweetened, 1 cup 110
Lentils, cooked, 1/2 cup 168
Lettuce, 1 head 40
Liver, 2 oz. serving: beef, fried 130
    chicken, simmered 88
Lobster, 2 oz. 55
Macaroni, cooked, 1/2 cup 90
Mango, 1 fresh 134
Margarine: 1/2 cup .800
    1 tbsp. 100
Mayonnaise: 1 tbsp. 100
Milk: whole, 1 cup .160
    skim, 1 cup 89
    condensed, 1 cup 982
    evaporated, 1 cup 345
    dry nonfat, 1 cup 251
Muffin, plain 120

Mushrooms: canned, 1/2 cup 20
    fresh, 1 lb. 123
Mustard: prepared, brown, 1 tbsp. 13
    prepared, yellow, 1 tbsp. 10
Nectarine, 1 fresh 30
Noodles: egg, cooked, 1/2 cup 100
    fried, chow mein, 2 oz. 275
Oil, cooking, salad, 1 tbsp. 120
Okra, cooked, 8 pods 25
Olives: green, 3 lg. 15
    ripe, 2 lg. 15
Onion: chopped, 1/2 cup 32
    dehydrated flakes, 1 tbsp. 17
    green, 6 20
    whole, 1 40
Orange: 1 whole 65
    juice, 1 cup 115
Oysters, meat only, 1/2 cup 80
Pancakes, 4-in. diameter, 1 60
Peaches: fresh, 1 med. 35
    canned, 1/2 cup .100
    dried, 1/2 cup 210
Peanuts, shelled, roasted, 1 cup 420
Peanut butter, 1 tbsp. 100
Pears: fresh, 1 med. 100
    canned, 1/2 cup 97
    dried, 1/2 cup 214
Peas: black-eyed, 1/2 cup 70
    green, canned, 1/2 cup 83
    green, frozen, 1/2 cup 69
Pecans, chopped, 1/2 cup 400
Peppers: sweet green, 1 med. 14
    sweet red, 1 med. 19
Perch, white, 4 oz. 50
Pickles: dill, 1 lg. 15
    sweet, 1 average 30
Pie crust, mix, 1 crust 626
Pie, 8-in. frozen, 1/6 serving
    apple 234
    cherry 300
    peach 280
Pimento, canned, 1 avg. 10
Pineapple: fresh, diced, 1/2 cup 36
    canned, 1/2 cup 90
    juice, 1 cup 135
Plums: fresh, 1 med. 30
    canned, 3 101
Popcorn, plain, popped, 1 cup 54
Pork, cooked, lean:
    Boston butt, roasted, 4 oz. 280
    chop, broiled, 3.5 oz. 260
    loin, roasted, 4 oz. 290
Potato chips, 1 oz. .322

Potatoes, white:
  baked, 1 sm. with skin 93
  boiled, 1 sm. 70
  French-fried, 10 pieces 155
  hashed brown, 1/2 cup 225
  mashed, with milk and butter, 1/2 cup 90
Potatoes, sweet:
  baked, 1 avg. 155
  candied, 1 avg. 295
  canned, 1/2 cup .110
Prune: 1 lg. 19
  dried, cooked, 1/2 cup 137
  juice, 1 cup 197
Puddings and pie fillings, prepared:
  banana, 1/2 cup .165
  butterscotch, 1/2 cup 190
  chocolate, 1/2 cup 190
  lemon, 1/2 cup .125
Puddings, instant, prepared:
  banana, 1/2 cup .175
  butterscotch, 1/2 cup 175
  chocolate, 1/2 cup 200
  lemon, 1/2 cup .180
Pumpkin, canned, 1/2 cup 38
Raisins, dried, 1/2 cup 231
Rice: cooked, white, 1/2 cup 90
  cooked, brown, 1/2 cup 100
  precooked, 1/2 cup 105
Salad dressings, commercial:
  blue cheese, 1 tbsp. 75
  Fresh, 1 tbsp. 70
  Italian, 1 tbsp. 83
  mayonnaise, 1 tbsp. 100
  mayonnaise-type, 1 tbsp. 65
  Russian, 1 tbsp. 75
  Thousand Island, 1 tbsp. 80
Salami, cooked, 2 oz. 180
Salmon: canned, 4 oz. 180
  steak, 4 oz. 220
Sardines, canned, 3 oz. 175
Sauces: barbecue, 1 tbsp. 17
  hot pepper, 1 tbsp. 3
  soy, 1 tbsp. 9
  white, med. 1/2 cup 215
  Worcestershire, 1 tbsp. 15
Sauerkraut, 1/2 cup 21
Sausage, cooked, 2 oz. 260
Sherbet, 1/2 cup 130
Shrimp: cooked, 3 oz. 50
  canned, 4 oz. 130
Soft drinks, 1 cup .100
Soup, 1 can, condensed:
  chicken with rice 116

cream of celery 215
cream of chicken 235
cream of mushroom 331
tomato 220
vegetable-beef 198
Sour cream, 1/2 cup 240
Spaghetti, cooked, 1/2 cup 80
Spinach: fresh, 1/2 lb. 60
  cooked, 1/2 cup 20
Squash: summer, cooked, 1/2 cup 15
  winter, cooked, 1/2 cup 65
Strawberries, fresh, 1/2 cup 23
Sugar: brown, packed, 1/2 cup 410
  confectioners', sifted, 1/2 cup 240
  granulated: 1/2 cup 385
    1 tbsp. 48
Syrups: chocolate, 1 tbsp. 50
  corn, 1 tbsp. 58
  maple, 1 tbsp. 50
Taco shell, 1 shell 50
Tea, 1 cup 0
Tomatoes: fresh, 1 med. 40
  canned, 1/2 cup 25
  juice, 1 cup 45
  paste, 6-oz. can .150
  sauce, 8-oz. can 34
Toppings: caramel, 1 tbsp. 70
  chocolate fudge, 1 tbsp. 65
  Cool Whip, 1 tbsp. 14
  Dream Whip, prepared, 1 tbsp. 8
  Strawberry, 1 tbsp. 60
Tortilla, corn, 1 65
Tuna: canned in oil, drained, 4 oz. 230
  canned in water, 4 oz. 144
Turkey: dark meat, roasted, 4 oz. 230
  light meat, roasted, 4 oz. 200
Veal: cutlet, broiled, 3 oz. 185
  roast, 3 oz. 230
Vegetable juice cocktail, 1 cup 43
Vinegar, 1 tbsp. 2
Waffles, 1 130
Walnuts, chopped, 1/2 cup 410
Water chestnuts, sliced, 1/2 cup 25
Watermelon, fresh, cubed, 1/2 cup 26
Wheat germ, 1 tbsp. 29
Wine: dessert, 1/2 cup 140
  table, 1/2 cup 85
Yeast: compressed, 1 oz. 24
  dry, 1 oz. 80
Yogurt: plain, w/whole milk, 1 cup 153
  plain, w/skim milk, 1 cup 123
  with fruit, 1 cup .260

Candy Testing Chart

PRODUCT	TEST IN COLD WATER*	DEGREES F. ON CANDY THERMOMETER			
		SEA LEVEL	2000 FEET	5000 FEET	7500 FEET
FUDGE, PANOCHA, FONDANT	SOFT BALL (can be picked up but flattens)	234° - 240° F.	230° - 236° F.	224° - 230° F.	219° - 225° F.
CARAMELS	FIRM BALL (holds shape unless pressed)	242° - 248° F.	238° - 244° F.	232° - 238° F.	227° - 233° F.
DIVINITY, TAFFY AND CARAMEL CORN	HARD BALL (holds shape though pliable)	250° - 268° F.	246° - 264° F.	240° - 258° F.	235° - 253° F.
BUTTERSCOTCH, ENGLISH TOFFEE	SOFT CRACK (separates into hard threads but not brittle)	270° - 290° F.	266° - 286° F.	260° - 280° F.	255° - 275° F.
BRITTLES	HARD CRACK (separates into hard and brittle threads)	300° - 310° F.	296° - 306° F.	290° - 300° F.	285° - 295° F.

* Drop about 1/2 teaspoon of boiling syrup into one cup water, and test firmness of mass with fingers.

Metric Conversion Chart

VOLUME

1 tsp.	=	4.9 cc
1 tbsp.	=	14.7 cc
1/3 c.	=	28.9 cc
1/8 c.	=	29.5 cc
1/4 c.	=	59.1 cc
1/2 c.	=	118.3 cc
3/4 c.	=	177.5 cc
1 c.	=	236.7 cc
2 c.	=	473.4 cc
1 fl. oz.	=	29.5 cc
4 oz.	=	118.3 cc
8 oz.	=	236.7 cc

1 pt.	=	473.4 cc
1 qt.	=	.946 liters
1 gal.	=	3.7 liters

CONVERSION FACTORS:

Liters	X	1.056	=	Liquid quarts
Quarts	X	0.946	=	Liters
Liters	X	0.264	=	Gallons
Gallons	X	3.785	=	Liters
Fluid ounces	X	29.563	=	Cubic centimeters
Cubic centimeters	X	0.034	=	Fluid ounces
Cups	X	236.575	=	Cubic centimeters
Tablespoons	X	14.797	=	Cubic centimeters
Teaspoons	X	4.932	=	Cubic centimeters
Bushels	X	0.352	=	Hectoliters
Hectoliters	X	2.837	=	Bushels

WEIGHT

1 dry oz.	=	28.3 Grams
1 lb.	=	.454 Kilograms

CONVERSION FACTORS:

Ounces (Avoir.)	X	28.349	=	Grams
Grams	X	0.035	=	Ounces
Pounds	X	0.454	=	Kilograms
Kilograms	X	2.205	=	Pounds

Equivalent Chart

WHEN RECIPE CALLS FOR:		YOU NEED:
DAIRY	1 c. freshly grated cheese	1/4 lb.
	1 c. cottage cheese or sour cream	1 8-oz. carton
	2/3 c. evaporated milk	1 sm. can
	1 2/3 c. evaporated milk	1 tall can
	1 c. whipped cream	1/2 c. heavy cream
SWEET	1 c. semisweet chocolate pieces	1 6-oz. package
	2 c. granulated sugar	1 lb.
	4 c. sifted confectioners' sugar	1 lb.
	2 1/4 c. packed brown sugar	1 lb.
NUTS	1 c. chopped nuts	4 oz. shelled
		1 lb. unshelled
FRUIT	4 c. sliced or chopped apples	4 medium
	2 c. pitted cherries	4 c. unpitted
	3 to 4 tbsp. lemon juice plus 1 tsp. grated peel	1 lemon
	1/3 c. orange juice plus 2 tsp. grated peel	1 orange
	1 c. mashed banana	3 medium
	4 c. cranberries	1 lb.
	3 c. shredded coconut	1/2 lb.
	4 c. sliced peaches	8 medium
	1 c. pitted dates or candied fruit	1 8-oz. package
	2 c. pitted prunes	1 12-oz. package
	3 c. raisins	1 15-oz. package

COMMON EQUIVALENTS

1 tbsp. = 3 tsp.	4 qt. = 1 gal.
2 tbsp. = 1 oz.	6 1/2 to 8-oz. can = 1 c.
4 tbsp. = 1/4 c.	10 1/2 to 12-oz. can = 1 1/4 c.
5 tbsp. + 1 tsp. = 1/3 c.	14 to 16-oz. can (No. 300) = 1 3/4 c.
8 tbsp. = 1/2 c.	16 to 17-oz. can (No. 303) = 2 c.
12 tbsp. = 3/4 c.	1-lb. 4-oz. can or 1-pt. 2-oz. can (No. 2) = 2 1/2 c.
16 tbsp. = 1 c.	1-lb. 13-oz. can (No. 2 1/2) = 3 1/2 c.
1 c. = 8 oz. or 1/2 pt.	3-lb. 3-oz. can or 46-oz. can or 1-qt. 14-oz. can = 5 3/4 c.
4 c. = 1 qt.	6 1/2 lb. or 7-lb. 5-oz. can (No. 10) = 12 to 13 c.

Substitutions Chart

	INSTEAD OF:	USE:
BAKING	1 tsp. baking powder	1/4 tsp. soda plus 1/2 tsp. cream of tartar
	1 c. sifted all-purpose flour	1 c. plus 2 tbsp. sifted cake flour
	1 c. sifted cake flour	1 c. minus 2 tbsp. sifted all-purpose flour
	1 tsp. cornstarch (for thickening)	2 tbsp. flour or 1 tbsp. tapioca
SWEET	1 1-oz. square chocolate	3 to 4 tbsp. cocoa plus 1 tsp. shortening
	1 2/3 oz. semisweet chocolate	1 oz. unsweetened chocolate plus 4 tsp. sugar
	1 c. granulated sugar	1 c. packed brown sugar or 1 c. corn syrup, molasses, honey minus 1/4 c. liquid
	1 c. honey	1 to 1 1/4 c. sugar plus 1/4 c. liquid or 1 c. molasses or corn syrup
DAIRY	1 c. sweet milk	1 c. sour milk or buttermilk plus 1/2 tsp. soda
	1 c. sour milk	1 c. sweet milk plus 1 tbsp. vinegar or lemon juice or 1 c. buttermilk
	1 c. buttermilk	1 c. sour milk or 1 c. yogurt
	1 c. light cream	7/8 c. skim milk plus 3 tbsp. butter
	1 c. heavy cream	3/4 c. skim milk plus 1/3 c. butter
	1 c. sour cream	7/8 c. sour milk plus 3 tbsp. butter

Index

COLOR PHOTOGRAPH RECIPES

PHOTOGRAPHY CREDITS

Cover: Florida Department of Citrus; Knox Gelatine, Inc.; Sunkist Growers, Inc.; Wear-Ever Aluminum, Inc.; Hershey Foods Corporation; J. M. Smucker Company; M & M Mars; Ocean Spray Cranberries, Inc.; The Quaker Oats Company; California Apricot Advisory Board; Diamond Walnut Kitchen; American Dairy Association; Processed Apples Institute; Ruth Lundgren, Ltd.; California Raisin Advisory Board; California Plum Commodity Committee; California Peach Advisory Board; General Electric Company; National Cherry Growers and Industries Foundation; The Banana Bunch; National Dairy Council; Dried Fig Advisory Board; Wheat Flour Institute; M & M Plain Chocolate Candies; National Peanut Council; Best Foods, A Unit of CPC North America; Advisory Council for Jams, Jellies and Preserves; Grandma's West Indies Molasses; California Strawberry Advisory Board; United Fresh Fruit and Vegetable; Planters Cocktail Peanuts; Pineapple Growers Association; C and H Sugar Company; National Biscuit Company; Pet Evaporated Milk; and Pie Filling Institute.